The End of the Roman Republic, 146 to 44 BC

The Edinburgh History of Ancient Rome
General Editor: J. S. Richardson

Visit The Edinburgh History of Ancient Rome website at
www.euppublishing.com/series/ehar

The End of the Roman Republic, 146 to 44 BC

Conquest and Crisis

Catherine Steel

EDINBURGH
University Press

For Alice

© Catherine Steel, 2013

Edinburgh University Press Ltd
22 George Square, Edinburgh EH8 9LF

www.euppublishing.com

Typeset in Sabon
by Norman Tilley Graphics Ltd

A CIP record for this book is available from the
British Library

ISBN 978 0 7486 1944 3 (hardback)
ISBN 978 0 7486 1945 0 (paperback)
ISBN 978 0 7486 2902 2 (webready PDF)
ISBN 978 0 7486 7854 9 (epub)
ISBN 978 0 7486 7855 6 (Amazon ebook)

Published with the support of the Edinburgh University
Scholarly Publishing Initiatives Fund.

Contents

Illustrations

Series editor's preface

Rome, the city and its empire, stands at the centre of the history of Europe, of the Mediterranean and of lands which we now call the Middle East. Its influence through the ages which followed its transformation into the Byzantine empire down to modern times can be seen across the world. This series is designed to present for students and all who are interested in the history of western civilisation the changing shape of the entity that was Rome, through its earliest years, the development and extension of the Republic, the shift into the Augustan empire, the development of the imperial state which grew from that, and the differing patterns of that state which emerged in east and west in the fourth to sixth centuries. It covers not only the political and military history of that shifting and complex society but also the contributions of the economic and social history of the Roman world to that change and growth and the intellectual contexts of these developments. The team of contributors, all scholars at the forefront of research in archaeology and history in the English-speaking world, present in the eight volumes of the series an accessible and challenging account of Rome across a millennium and a half of its expansion and transformation. Each book stands on its own as a picture of the period it covers and together the series aims to answer the fundamental question: what was Rome, and how did a small city in central Italy become one of the most powerful and significant entities in the history of the world?

John Richardson, General Editor

Author's preface

This book began with John Richardson's invitation to write the third volume of the Edinburgh History of Ancient Rome; I am extremely grateful to him for the invitation, for his painstaking editorial work, and his help and guidance. Carol Macdonald and her colleagues at Edinburgh University Press have been patient and supportive throughout. Richard Bapty in Glasgow University Library and Colin Annis at the ICS Library have helped at various stages, and Elizabeth Moignard and Donal Bateson provided invaluable assistance with the illustrations. Many of the ideas here were first tried out on my students in Glasgow; one could not wish for a more lively or responsive audience. The book is dedicated to Alice Jenkins, without whom it, and so much else, would be infinitely poorer.

Abbreviations

CAH   *The Cambridge Ancient History*, 2nd edn, Cambridge: Cambridge University Press 1961–2006

FGrH   *Die Fragmente der griechischen Historiker*, ed. F. Jacoby, Berlin: Weidmann 1923–

ILS   *Inscriptiones Latinae Selectae*, ed. H. Dessau, Berlin: Weidmann 1892–1916

MRR   T. R. S. Broughton, *The Magistrates of the Roman Republic*, 3 vols, New York/Atlanta: Scholars Press 1951–86.

ORF⁴   *Oratorum Romanorum Fragmenta*, ed. H. Malcovati, 4th edn, Milan: Paravia 1976–9

SIG   *Sylloge Inscriptonum Graecarum*, ed. W. Dittenberger, 3rd edn, Leipzig: Hirzel 1915–24

Abbreviations of ancient authors and works follow the *Oxford Classical Dictionary* (4th edn, eds S. Hornblower and A. Spawforth, Oxford: Oxford University Press 2012); those of journals, *L'Année Philologique*.

Map 1 Italy in the second and first centuries BC

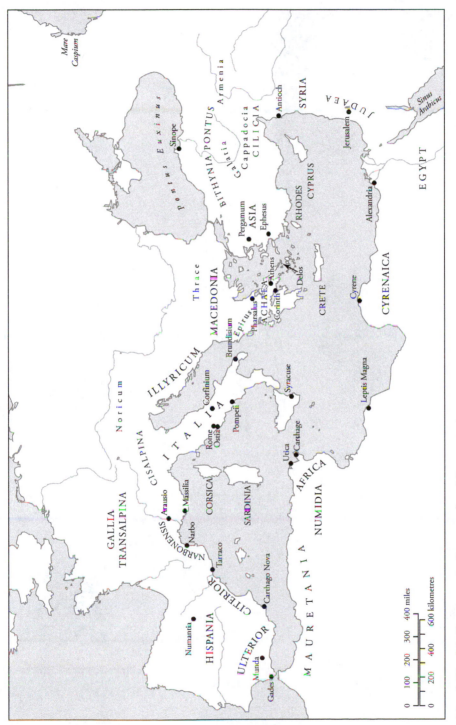

Map 2 The Mediterranean in the second and first centuries BC

Introduction

The period of Roman history which this volume covers is defined by two moments of violence. In 146 BC, the violence was external, official and prolonged, with the destruction of the cities of Carthage and Corinth at the end of military campaigns. In 44 BC, it was internal, even intimate, and sudden, as the consul and dictator Caesar was killed at a meeting of the Senate by a group of senators. Despite the differences in kind between these events, both dates derive their significance from a focus on political history; and a major concern of this book is to trace the processes of political change at Rome through which autocracy emerged. To that end, a sketch of the organisation of Roman politics in the middle of the second century is an essential preliminary to the narrative and analysis which follows.

Rome was a city-state in which power was distributed between different groups. Adult male citizens, forming the people, *populus*, were in control, through voting, of major issues. But many decisions were in practice entrusted to the Senate, an assembly of around three hundred men drawn from the governing class; and substantial executive power was at the disposal of annually elected magistrates. Roman political life was constructed as a continuous dialogue between the citizen body as a whole, a small number of individual citizens to whom the people entrusted power – citizens whose role in the *res publica* was sustained by an ideology of distinction – and the Senate, the collective body of those distinguished individuals.

Res publica, res populi: 'the state is the people's property'.[1] The extensive power of the Roman people rested on a number of bases. Only the Roman people, voting in a properly constituted assembly, could pass laws and make the decision to go to the war.[2] Secondly,

1. Cic. *Rep.* 1.39; for a discussion of this work, see below, pp. 245–7.
2. K. Sandberg, *Magistrates and Assemblies: A Study of Legislative Practice in Republican Rome*, Rome: Institutum Romanum Finlandiae 2001.

assemblies of the Roman people elected magistrates. Thirdly, capital charges were heard and judged by the people.[3] Fourthly, the Roman army was still, in 146, a citizen militia. Individuals either were or were not Roman citizens, but the relationship between citizenship and political participation was mediated through the institution of the census, which took place every five years under the direction of two elected censors, who had already held senior magistracies. The census classified citizens in terms of their wealth, age and geographical location, which in turn determined the units in which adult male citizens voted. As the results of voting were determined by the aggregation of units rather than by individual votes, the composition of voting units was of course vitally important; and, despite a great deal of uncertainty of detail, Roman voting units were constructed in a way which privileged the wealthy, the elderly and the extra-urban over the poor, the young and the growing population of Rome itself.[4] Assemblies themselves could only be summoned by magistrates, who determined their agendas.

The hereditary division of the citizen body into patricians and plebeians had long since ceased to be a driving motor of political action, but the distinction continued to have consequences.[5] Members of the dozen or so surviving patrician families were disproportionately influential within the ruling elite. Conversely, the institution of the tribunate of the plebs retained its extensive capacity to challenge measures detrimental to the interests of the plebs. The ten annually elected tribunes possessed physical inviolability, *sacrosanctitas*, deriving from the notional willingness of the plebeians as a whole to take immediate vengeance on anyone who harmed a tribune. More significantly for political practice, tribunes' obligation to protect individual plebeians was supplemented by their

3. In practice, this power appears frequently to have been delegated to a magistrate; and there was also the possibility of creating ad hoc boards of inquiry (such as that formed to investigate the Bacchanalian conspiracy in 186). The formal transfer of judicial authority from the people to specially constituted standing courts began in 149, with the *lex Calpurnia*, which established a standing court to deal with extortion. See A. Lintott, *The Constitution of the Roman Republic*, Oxford: Oxford University Press, 1999, 149–58.
4. On the census, G. Pieri, *L'histoire du cens jusqu'à la fin de la République romaine*, Paris: Sirey 1968; A. Astin, 'Censorships in the late Republic', *Historia* 34, 1985, 175–90; on voting, E. S. Staveley, *Greek and Roman Voting and Elections*, London: Thames and Hudson 1972, 121–216; it is unclear how nimble the census was in recording changes of abode.
5. C. J. Smith *The Roman Clan: The Gens from Ancient Ideology to Modern Anthropology*, Cambridge: Cambridge University Press 2006, 251–80.

ability to propose legislation and to interpose their veto on the actions of magistrates and Senate. Importantly, too, tribunes could exercise this power individually, raising the possibility of conflict between tribunes.[6] The plebs had, by 146 BC, long been indistinguishable in practice from the mass of ordinary citizens. Thus powers formed during the 'Struggle of the Orders' to defend plebeians from patrician abuse had been transferred to managing the relationship between the citizen body as a whole and those whom it elected to public office. That many members of the governing class were themselves now of plebeian birth and thus eligible to stand for this office is one of a number of factors which complicate any assessment of the power of people in the Roman *res publica*.

The role of the Senate is intriguingly difficult to articulate: it was in theory an advisory body, but a variety of factors contributed to the importance and range of its deliberations. Crucially, its decisions – based on majority voting of individual members – had the force of law provided they were not vetoed by a tribune of the plebs. Such *senatus consulta* were used in a variety of areas, particularly those related to foreign policy, and diplomacy short of war and peace was regularly handled by the Senate without reference to the people. The oversight of religious practice was also in the purview of the Senate, acting on the advice of the relevant group of experts. It could be described as the organism which protected the *res publica* through mediation with external threats, whether these were foreign powers or the gods.

Membership of the Senate was determined by the censors during the five-yearly census, though their choice of senators operated within quite prescriptive limits. Those who had held at least the aedileship or praetorship were always included. Beyond that, the censors seem to have had the capacity to enrol anyone they chose, with criteria apparently including membership of distinguished families and tenure of priesthoods.[7] The popular will, as

---

6. L. Thommen, *Das Volktribunat der späten römischen Republik*, Stuttgart: Steiner 1989.

7. M. Bonnefond-Coudry, *Le Sénat de la République romaine: de la guerre d'Hannibale à Auguste: pratiques délibératives et prises de décisions*, Rome École Française de Rome 1989; F. X. Ryan, *Rank and Participation in the Republican Senate*, Stuttgart: Steiner 1998; Lintott, *Consitution*, 70. These senators may have included men from politically active families who had chosen not to seek office, but the majority will have been chosen pre-emptively – that is, they were men who would in time hold the relevant offices. Senatorial membership also seems in practice to have been confined to those who met the

expressed in elections, shaped the Senate but only through the mediation of the censors – whom they had of course also elected. The censors' starting point in reviewing senatorial membership was the previous censors' list, with the expectation that those who appeared previously would continue to be included. Hence the interest in occasions when the censors omitted the names of existing members, expelling them: the justification for expulsion was overwhelmingly in moral terms, thus establishing a criterion of moral worth for membership of the Senate in addition to popular choice. Expulsions were, however, uncommon and thus turnover in membership was primarily triggered by death: although attendance at meetings was, in theory at least, a duty of senators, we do not know of any senators retiring or being retired on grounds of age or infirmity. This norm of life-long membership was an important element in the Senate's practical effectiveness. Another important institution was the position of *princeps senatus*, the senator placed by the censors at the head of the list of members. The *princeps senatus* was invariably a patrician and ideally one who had held the censorship; once chosen, he held the position until death.[8] Since the *princeps senatus* was asked to speak first during senatorial debates, the holder had substantial opportunity to direct policy.

Members of the Senate were drawn from the wider group of men who met the equestrian property qualification, which originally defined those whose military obligation was in the cavalry but by our period defined the wealthiest section of society. The sons of senators who were unable or chose not to pursue a political career and enter the Senate would remain equestrians. In the mid-second century, the distinction between senators and everyone else who met the equestrian property qualification was simply the presence or absence of political activity; over the next century, the equestrians developed a political identity and interests separate from the Senate, which were central to many aspects of the unfolding political crisis.

The third element in the Roman *res publica* was annually elected magistrates, holding office for a year. These offices had by the middle of the second century BC evolved into a standard sequence, the *cursus honorum*, beginning with the quaestorship, which was primarily concerned with financial administration, through the

equestrian property qualification. Tribunes of the plebs were regularly enrolled following the passage of a *lex Atinia* (Gell. *NA*. 14.8), but its date is unclear.
8. J. Suolahti '*Princeps senatus*', Arctos 7, 1972, 207–18, with a list of holders; M. Bonnefond-Coudry, 'Le *princeps senatus*', MEFRA 105, 1993, 103–34.

praetorship to the consulship.[9] These last two positions involved
imperium, state-sanctioned coercive power, which enabled their
holders to command armies, and the activity of the consuls and the
majority of the six praetors was usually military.[10] The *imperium*-
holding magistracies wielded enormous executive power and, particularly outside Rome, their power seemed genuinely regal.[11] In
such contexts, too, the impression their power made was enhanced
because they were operating in the absence of their colleagues.
But their position was constrained by the principle of collegiality,
by the limited duration of their office, and by the impossibility of
immediate re-election. Whilst the extension of command through
prorogation was possible, it required the authorisation of the
Senate, which also identified the tasks to be entrusted to the year's
magistrates. Given the limited number of positions, even the most
successful politician would spend the majority of his public career as
a *priuatus*, a private individual.

A public career depended on electoral success, and elections were
competitive.[12] For individuals, the possibility of failure was always
present. But there was an astonishingly high level of continuity in
office-holding from one generation to another. That is, although

9. There were in addition a number of poorly attested junior positions (Lintott, *Constitution*, 137–44) and the aedileship, which was a Rome-based position concerned above
all with the organisation of religious festivals; it was held between quaestorship and
praetorship, but since there were fewer aediles than praetors it was not a compulsory
part of the *cursus honorum*. Minimum ages for each office appear to have been in force.
10. T. C. Brennan, *The Praetorship in the Roman Republic*, New York: Oxford University Press 2000; F. Pina Polo, *The Consul at Rome*, Cambridge: Cambridge University
Press 2011. Two of the praetors, the *praetor urbanus* and the *praetor peregrinus*, were
legal positions. Praetorian and consular responsibilities were allocated by lot, though the
lot did not always operate randomly.
11. E. Rawson, 'Caesar's heritage: Hellenistic kings and their Roman equals', *JRS* 65,
1975, 148–59; the nature of Roman *imperium* is brilliantly encapsulated in the
encounter described by Polybius (29.27.1–10) between Popillius Laenas (cos. 172) and
Antiochus IV in 168, shortly before the start of the period covered in this volume.
12. A. Yakobson, *Elections and Electioneering in Rome: A Study in the Political System
of the Late Republic*, Stuttgart: Steiner 1999. Livy provides the most detailed accounts
of electoral competitions, but his account is not available for this period. Elections generated a particular form of anecdote concerning *repulsae*, defeats: Val. Max. 7.5; T. R. S.
Broughton, *Candidates Defeated in Roman Elections: Some Ancient Roman 'Also-
Rans'*, Philadelphia: American Philological Association 1991; C. Konrad 'Notes on
Roman also-rans', in J. Linderski, ed., *Imperium sine Fine: T. Robert S. Broughton and
the Roman Republic*, Stuttgart: Steiner 1996, 104–43; G. Farney, 'Some more Roman
Republican "also-rans"', *Historia* 53, 2004, 246–50. The consulship and censorship
generated the most intense competition; election to the praetorship was by this period
much more straightforward, given the number of positions available in relation to possible candidates (i.e. those who had held the quaestorship and were of the right age).

membership of the Senate was not hereditary, the tools by which membership could be acquired to a very large extent *were*.[13] We can as a result talk with confidence of a senatorial class, whose political dominance was secured from generation to generation through a combination of economic and ideological factors. One way of controlling the composition of an elected ruling class is by controlling who can stand for office, and it appears that at Rome this was achieved by making eligibility for office depend on meeting a (high) minimum property qualification. Thus the electorate made their choice among candidates who offered a relatively homogenous economic and social profile. In addition, the possession of politically active ancestors appears to have been a positive factor in acquiring votes.

For the contemporary observer Polybius, this dispersal of power among different groups and individuals gave Rome a mixed constitution, with democratic, oligarchic and monarchical elements, which as a result possessed an enviable stability that was vital to understanding its extraordinary military success.[14] In practice, however, the system proved far from stable, not least because there was no government to co-ordinate the management of affairs, and no good way to give the ambitious lasting power. The consequences of its instabilities were far-reaching.

Polybius, a historian of contemporary events, is a rarity among the ancient sources from which the history of this period is constructed. A major problem – perhaps the major difficulty – in the study of the late Republic lies precisely in the frustrating quality of the surviving sources. It is an extraordinary fact that the earliest extensive narrative of the late Republic dates from more than two centuries later.[15] Appian, and the slightly later Cassius Dio, are inescapable in the task, but their distance, chronologically and intellectually, from what

13. The seminal work of Hopkins and Burton (K. Hopkins and G. Burton, 'Political succession in the late Republic (249–50 BC)', in K. Hopkins, *Death and Renewal: Sociological Studies in Roman History 2*, Cambridge: Cambridge University Press 1983, 31–119) should be understood within a research context which emphasised family connections; their findings do not undermine the claim that membership of the political elite was closely linked to ancestry. Moreover, the reasons for the failure of families are not well documented, and chance – that is, the accidents of mortality and gender distribution – may have dominated.
14. Polyb. 6.1–18; B. McGing, *Polybius' Histories*, Oxford: Oxford University Press 2010, 169–202. For an account of the Roman constitution, Lintott, *Constitution*.
15. That is, Appian's account (on which see K. Brodersen, 'Appian und sein Werk', *ANRW* 2.34.1, 1993, 339–63).

they describe cannot be ignored. Livy's lost account is preserved only in book-by-book summaries, which omit much explanatory and contextual material; Sallust's *Histories* exist only in fragments; Velleius is brief.[16] Establishing what might have happened is a large part of studying the history of this period, and confusion and misrepresentation in the ancient sources have had a lasting effect on modern interpretations. This is particularly relevant to the Social War (where the changing nature of Roman citizenship has obscured the origins of the conflict) and to Sulla, where a misleading narrative of continuity was accepted and upheld by the survivors of his brutal regime; but it is certainly not confined to those episodes.[17]

In contrast to these gaps stands Cicero, whose extraordinary written output appears to illuminate the final decades of Republican government with a lucid insider perspective. This is, unfortunately, far from the case: Cicero's writings were always for someone, and between his alert understanding of what his audience wanted (whether it be jury, affronted correspondent or close friend) and his own powerful desires for the *res publica* and his own place within it, it is easy to be misled. Entire books can and have been written on the interpretation of Cicero; this one will probably say too much. But how to read Cicero remains a central problem for any historian of the period.

The book is structured in three parts, each of which offers a narrative of events followed by interpretation of developments in foreign and domestic affairs. The first is arguably the only one to deal with the Roman Republic: it closes with the outbreak of war between Rome and its Italian allies, which destroyed the state Polybius had described and replaced it with something rather different.[18] The second covers this war, its continuation in civil war, the victory of Sulla's side and the initial attempts to make his constitutional reforms work. The final period takes the year 70, which in various ways marked what seemed to be a fresh start, as its starting point: it ends with a pleasingly exact date, the death of Caesar on 15 March 44. That end date is only one of many possibilities; as this book will

16. His surviving monographs on Jugurtha and Catiline are themselves distant from the events they analyse (in the case of the former, over half a century).
17. A good example of the problem of sources is A. Greenidge and A. Clay, *Sources for Roman History 133-70 B.C.*, 2nd edn, rev. Gray, E., Oxford: Oxford University Press 1960; a textbook for Oxford students of ancient history, it attempted to overcome ancient deficiencies through modern scholarship to create a coherent narrative.
18. H. Flower, *Roman Republics*, Princeton: Princeton University Press 2010: 117–34.

attempt to show, the process of political change was lengthy, often obscure to its participants, and full of unintended consequences. We should resist the temptation to make its outlines too neat.

CHAPTER 1

The crises of the later second century BC

The year 146 BC was a bad one for ancient cities. Carthage was captured by forces under the command of Scipio Aemilianus and the city destroyed. In Greece, Lucius Mummius defeated the Achaean league at the isthmus of Corinth and proceeded, on the instructions of the Senate, to destroy the city of Corinth. By the end of the year the inhabitants of Rome had watched three triumphal processions; those of Scipio and Mummius, as well as that of Mummius' predecessor in Greece, Q. Caecilius Metellus. Anecdotes clustered around both campaigns and their endings and 146 BC was subsequently identified as a turning point in Roman history, and more specifically in the history of Rome's decline from virtue and freedom to enslavement under a single autocrat.[1]

The immediate impact of this year's events on Romans' perceptions of their city and its success was surely as strong as their subsequent resonance in Roman historiography. But, whilst the ends of Carthage and of Corinth make 146 an attractive date to use in periodising Roman history, both these campaigns can be seen as codas to the extraordinary half-century or so between 220 and 167 BC, Polybius' 'period of not quite fifty-three years' during which the Romans conquered 'practically the whole known world'.[2] Moreover, neat breaks of this kind seldom fit with all relevant events. In Spain, the Romans were already embroiled in a destructive and bitter conflict, which would last until 134, absorb most of the Republic's military resources and attention while it lasted, and contribute to major domestic disturbances. At home, contentious tribunician

1. R. Ridley, 'To be taken with a pinch of salt: the destruction of Carthage', *CPh* 80, 1986, 140–6; N. Purcell 'On the sacking of Carthage and Corinth', in D. Innes, H. Hine and C. Pelling, eds, *Ethics and Rhetoric: Classical Essays for Donald Russell on his Seventy-Fifth Birthday*, Oxford: Oxford University Press 1995, 133–48; E. O'Gorman, 'Cato the Elder and the destruction of Carthage', *Helios* 31, 2004, 99–125; for Roman responses to the two captures, see below, Chapter 3.
2. Polyb. 1.1.1; for prior events, N. Rosenstein, *Rome and the Mediterranean 290 to 146 BC: The Imperial Republic*, Edinburgh: Edinburgh University Press 2012, 229–39.

legislation was already beginning to challenge the consensus of the period after the war with Hannibal, and to indicate issues which would recur with greater intensity over the next decades. The extraordinary successes of 146 marked in fact the start of a half-century marked by imperial stagnation and domestic conflict.

The wars in Spain

Roman military involvement in Spain began with the second Punic war, and the area had been the site of frequent conflicts in the early part of the second century to the extent that the need for a permanent presence led to an increase in the number of praetors.[3] From a planning perspective it was divided into two areas, 'Nearer' (*Citerior*) and 'Further' (*Ulterior*), though the north and west of the peninsula remained outside Roman control. Subsequent to the command of Ti. Sempronius Gracchus between 180 and 178, fighting seems to have become less intense, with a reduction both in manpower devoted to the area and in the frequency of triumphs.[4] This period of relative calm came to an end in the mid-150s, as the Senate responded strongly to what it perceived as threats.[5] In Further Spain, Appian dates the start of renewed fighting to 155; this campaign culminated in the slaughter of a large number of Lusitanians, who had surrendered on terms, by the consul Ser. Sulpicius Galba in 150.[6] In Nearer Spain, Rome responded in 153 to what it perceived as defiance by the town of Segeda by sending out one of the consuls, Fulvius Nobilior; and his successors in 152 and 151 were consular as well.[7] The outbreak of the war against Carthage then displaced Roman attention on Spain, until the campaigning of the praetor C. Vetilius in Further Spain, probably in 147. The Lusitanians escaped from Roman encirclement by following the advice of a man called Viriathus, a survivor of Galba's massacre.

3. J. S. Richardson, *Hispaniae: Spain and the Development of Roman Imperialism*, Cambridge: Cambridge University Press 1986, 62–125; on the praetorship, T. C. Brennan, *The Praetorship in the Roman Republic*, New York: Oxford University Press 2000, 154–81.
4. Richardson, *Hispaniae*, 104–9.
5. Rosenstein, *Rome*, 226–9.
6. App. *Hisp.* 56–60. Galba was prosecuted, apparently for breach of *fides*, 'good faith', by one of the tribunes of 150 (Cic. *Brut.* 80, 89); Cato spoke against him, in one of his last speeches, but Galba was nonetheless acquitted.
7. On the interpretation of these campaigns as the result of the Senate's searching for military campaigns for the consuls, see Richardson, *Hispaniae*, 132–7.

Virathus was chosen by the Lusitanians as their leader, and ambushed and defeated the Roman force: Vetilius was killed, and Vetilius' successor Plautius was twice defeated the following year, losing four legions.[8] Moreover, the war seems to have spread to other Spanish province as well, with a defeat of the praetor Claudius Unimanus recorded, probably in 146 BC.

The Romans thus found themselves engaged in both Spanish provinces in wars which resisted swift or satisfactory conclusions and which were, moreover, deeply unpopular with those who were asked to fight.[9] With the end of fighting in Africa and Greece, it was possible to devote renewed resources to fighting Viriathus but without decisive results. One of the consuls of 145, Q. Fabius Maximus Aemilianus, was sent to Further Spain, and during the two years of his command there he had some success, though not overwhelming victory, against Viriathus. Meanwhile, in Nearer Spain, after the defeat of C. Nigidius, who was probably in command in 145, the praetor Laelius is recorded by Cicero as having 'broken and diminished him [sc.Viriathus] and contained his fierceness so as to leave an easy war for his successors'.[10] In 143, Nearer Spain was allocated to the consul Q. Caecilius Metellus Macedonicus, one of the victors of the recent Greek campaign, who captured Contrebia and besieged the town of Numantia; but in Further Spain, Aemilianus' successor Quintus Pompeius was defeated by Viriathus and his replacement was one of the consuls of 142, Q. Fabius Maximus Servilianus. In 142, therefore, for the first time since the Romans had established two Spanish tasks (*prouinciae*), both were commanded by men who had held the consulship, a clear indication of the gravity of the situation as well as of the lack of competing military crises elsewhere. By 140, both commanders decided to negotiate. Servilianus' agreement with Viriathus, ratified by the Roman people, recognised Viriathus as a friend of the Roman people and granted his followers the land that they occupied.[11] Pompeius (Macedonicus' successor in Nearer Spain) arranged with the Numantines that they should surrender unconditionally, claiming that no other outcome would publicly satisfy the Romans, but guaranteed to them that the terms would in practice merely be the handing over of hostages and a sum of silver.

Neither agreement proved to be durable. In Further Spain,

8. App. *Hisp.* 61–4.
9. Polyb. 35.4.1–14.
10. Cic. *Off.* 2.40; cf. *Brut.* 84.
11. App. *Hisp.* 69.

Servilianus' successor Q. Servilius Caepio tried to persuade the Senate to allow him to ignore the treaty and renew the war against Viriathus. According to Appian, he was at first given permission to do so secretly, and then authorised to breach the treaty openly.[12] He concluded the war by bribing some of Viriathus' close associates to murder him as he slept; Viriathus' successor as commander, Tantalus, was defeated by Caepio and surrendered to him. Caepio's successor in Further Spain, Decimus Junius Brutus (cos. 138), earned a triumph with further campaigns in north-western Spain.[13] This was the first triumph from either Spanish province since 152, but thereafter Roman enthusiasm for military activity in Further Spain seems to have evaporated.[14]

In Nearer Spain, meanwhile, it became apparent, once Pompeius' successor M. Popillius Laenas had arrived, that the Numantines had not, in fact, surrendered unconditionally. Pompeius now attempted to deny that any negotiations had taken place, but this was contradicted by members of his entourage as well as the Numantines, and Popillius sent them all back to Rome to sort the matter out whilst himself resuming the conflict.[15] He was replaced in 137 by C. Hostilius Mancinus, who was surrounded and trapped by the Numantines and forced to surrender. Despite the Romans' desperate position, they did manage to negotiate a treaty, which Appian describes as 'on equal terms';[16] the negotiator was Mancinus' quaestor Ti. Sempronius Gracchus, who apparently depended for his success on the reputation of his father.[17]

---

12. App. *Hisp.* 70.
13. Brutus also founded in 138 the city of Valentia for his veterans: S. Keay, 'Innovation and adaptation: the contribution of Rome to urbanism in Iberia', in B. Cunliffe and S. Keay, eds, *Social Complexity and the Development of Towns in Iberia: From the Copper Age to the Second Century AD*, Oxford: Oxford University Press 1995, 291–337; A. Ribera i Lacomba, 'The Roman foundation of Valencia and the town in the 2nd–1st c. B.C.', in L. Abad Casal, S. Keay and S. Ramallo Asensio, eds, *Early Roman Towns in Hispania Tarraconensis*, Portsmouth: Journal of Roman Archaeology 2006, 75–89.
14. The next documented campaign is that of Q. Servilius Caepio, who was praetor in Further Spain in 109 and triumphed in 107; he was subsequently involved in the disastrous campaign against the Cimbri (below, pp. 29–31).
15. The Senate decided, having heard from both sides, that the war should be continued (App. *Hisp.* 79). The issue appears to have been the Roman decision that the war in Nearer Spain could only be brought to an end if their opponents surrendered unconditionally: Richardson, *Hispaniae*, 140–9. Popillius was subsequently tried for extortion (*de repetundis*) and acquitted.
16. App. *Hisp.* 80.
17. D. Stockton, *The Gracchi*, Oxford: Oxford University Press 1979, 29–30. For his father's career and popularity in Spain, Richardson, *Hispaniae*, 101–3.

The Romans were fortunate to secure terms as favourable as these, but in Rome the reaction was one of horror. The Senate refused to ratify the treaty, deciding instead to replace Mancinus immediately with the other consul of 137, M. Aemilius Lepidus Porcina. Once Mancinus had returned to Rome in 136, the consul Philus investigated the affair and the Senate concluded by voting to repudiate the treaty and return Mancinus to the Numantines.[18] In Spain, meanwhile, Lepidus ignored his instructions from the Senate and attacked the Vaccaei, perhaps attempting to co-ordinate his actions with those of Brutus in Further Spain. It was, of course, not at all unusual for generals in the field to exceed their instructions; but on this occasion the Senate sent out an embassy to order him to desist, a striking indication of the panic which the Spanish situation had created. Lepidus ignored this embassy and after he suffered a defeat when besieging Pallantia, the Senate stripped him of his *imperium* and, when he returned to Rome as a private citizen, fined him as well. His successor, L. Furius Philus, attempted to hand over Mancinus to the Numantines (they refused to take him) and neither Philus nor his successor, Q. Calpurnius Piso (consul in 135) seem to have achieved much more in this campaign.

The extraordinary reactions of the Senate to the unfolding situation in Spain demonstrated the extent of the crisis. It is difficult to find any good precedent either for the surrender of Mancinus, or for the removal of *imperium* from Lepidus.[19] Repeated consular failure led to the election of Scipio Aemilianus as consul for 134 and then assigned Nearer Spain as his province. The Spanish problems were intensified by a slave revolt which had broken out in Sicily at some

---

18. Ö. Wikander, 'Caius Hostilius Mancinus and the *Foedus Numantinum*', *ORom* 11, 1976, 85–104; N. Rosenstein, '"Imperatores victi": the case of C. Hostilius Mancinus', *Cl Ant* 5, 1986, 230–52; Cic. *Rep.* 3.14; *Off.* 3.109 with A. Dyck, *A Commentary on Cicero, De Officiis*, Ann Arbor: University of Michigan Press 1996. The return of Mancinus was intended to defuse the breach of *fides*, and consequent risk to the peace with the gods (*pax deorum*), involved in repudiating the treaty; although the idea was not unprecedented, there were no recent examples of its actually happening, and the ceremony was notably archaicising (E. Rawson, 'Scipio, Laelius, Furius and the ancestral religion', *JRS* 63, 1973, 161–74, at 166–8). Mancinus – whom Philus, in *De republica*, describes as an excellent man (*uir optimus*), characterised by decency (*pudor*), uprightness (*probitas*) and *fides* – agreed to his return. A striking aspect of the case is that Mancinus was able – after his status as a citizen was clarified – to resume his political career, including a second tenure of the praetorship; and (Plin. *HN*. 34.18) he commemorated himself with a statue 'with the appearance he had when surrendered to the enemy'.
19. Richardson, *Hispaniae*, 151–2.

point during the earlier part of the 130s or at the very end of the 140s. The sources are scanty, but agree that a number of praetors were defeated before the other consul of 134, C. Fulvius Flaccus, was assigned this province (the first time a consul had commanded an army in Sicily since the second war against Carthage).[20]

The sources on Scipio's campaign against Numantia are much more extensive than those available for the earlier stages of this phase of Roman activity in Spain. Scipio himself was a compelling figure for historians, because of his role as the destroyer of Carthage, and subsequently Numantia, and because of his sudden and mysterious death in 129.[21] In addition, he offered to later writers the model of a man who held magistracies in violation of normal patterns of office-holding, yet remained in harmony with senatorial government, thus providing a contrast with later figures such as Pompeius and Caesar who similarly held exceptional commands and by means of them challenged the whole Republican system.[22] The sack of Numantia itself was the culmination of a long and at times desperate war, which offered historians scenes of extreme pathos as well as valour; and those gathered in his army included many who would be prominent over the next forty years. Jugurtha, subsequently to be Rome's opponent towards the end of the century, was present with elephants and auxiliary forces, sent by his uncle Micipsa, ruler of Numidia; the experience was, for Sallust, crucial for Jugurtha's development of an understanding of the Romans' military tactics as well as their social *mores*.[23] Present too were Marius and Gaius Gracchus; the satirist Lucilius; and, among the military tribunes, two men who would subsequently write history, Sempronius Asellio and Rutilius Rufus. It is not possible to trace a later public career for Asellio; Rutilius Rufus reached the consulship

20. The fragmentary narrative of Diodorus Siculus (34/35.2) is the main ancient source; K. Bradley, *Slavery and Rebellion in the Roman World, 140 B.C.–70 B.C.*, London: Batsford 1989, 46–65; T. Urbainczyk, *Slave Revolts in Antiquity*, Stocksfield: Acumen 2008, 10–14. The Sicilian slave revolt was not brought under control until 132. Rupilius followed his victory by reorganising the entire province, his *lex Rupilia* remaining the basis for the government of the island for the rest of the Republican period; and, as further indication of the importance of his success, he may have been awarded a triumph, despite the fact that victories over slaves were usually ineligible for such an honour.
21. A. E. Astin, *Scipio Aemilianus*, Oxford: Oxford University Press 1967; L. Beness, 'Scipio Aemilianus and the crisis of 129 B.C.', *Historia* 54, 2005, 37–48; T. Stevenson, 'Readings of Scipio's dictatorship in Cicero's *De re publica* (6.12)', *CQ* 55, 2005, 140–52.
22. See below, pp. 239–44.
23. Sall. *Iug.* 7–10.

in 105, was exiled on extortion charges in the mid-90s, and probably wrote his history whilst in exile.[24]

Much information and detail about this campaign is available, therefore, in both historical narratives and biography and in anecdotes preserved in other genres. It is clear that Scipio had enormous forces at his disposal; and that, once he had established firm control over the surrounding areas, his strategy was to avoid battle and starve the inhabitants of Numantia into surrender.[25] When they did surrender, he sold the inhabitants into slavery and destroyed the city: this was done without senatorial authorisation. Subsequently, the Senate sent out the usual commission of ten to resolve outstanding issues from the campaign.[26]

The tribunate of Tiberius Gracchus

When Aemilianus and his army returned to Italy in 132, he might well have expected an enthusiastic welcome, the celebration of a second triumph, and the resumption of a position of leadership within the res publica bolstered by his success in solving a long-standing military problem. He did triumph; but in a Rome now preoccupied with the consequences of domestic catastrophe. Towards the end of the previous year, the chief pontiff and ex-consul Scipio Nasica had led a lynch mob of senators in killing a tribune of the plebs, Mancinus' quaestor Tiberius Gracchus.

Tiberius' death arose directly from the actions he had taken as tribune, which in turn responded to a range of problems, and attempted solutions, over the previous decade and beyond.[27] One was the recruiting of troops for the Spanish war, which culminated in 138 when the consuls were imprisoned by the tribunes because they were conducting the levy too vigorously.[28] Another concerned the redistribution of economic resources. Gaius Laelius put forward a proposal about land-ownership at some point in the years before Tiberius' tribunate, which he withdrew in the face of senatorial opposition; and in 138, the tribune Curiatius – when he was not

24. F. Pina Polo, 'Über die sogenannte *cohors amicorum* des Scipio Aemilianus', in M. Peachin, ed., *Aspects of Friendship in the Graeco-Roman World*, Portsmouth: Journal of Roman Archaeology 2001, 89–98.
25. M. Dobson, *The Army of the Roman Republic: The Second Century B.C., Polybius and the Camps at Numantia, Spain*, Oxford: Oxbow 2008.
26. App. *Hisp.* 99.
27. L. R. Taylor, 'Forerunners of the Gracchi', *JRS* 52, 1962, 19–27.
28. Cic. *Leg.* 3.20; Livy, *Epit.* 55; something similar had also happened in 151.

imprisoning consuls – was urging them to do something about the high price of grain.[29] Moreover, processes as well as issues came under scrutiny, particularly the powers and operation of tribunes of the plebs. In 143 the Senate did not vote the consul Appius Claudius Pulcher a triumph following his campaigns in northern Italy, but Pulcher proceeded to hold one anyway. One of the tribunes attempted to stop his triumph by pulling Appius from the chariot he was riding in; Appius resisted this by interposing his daughter, who was a Vestal Virgin, between him and the tribune, who retreated.[30] Three years later, another tribune appears to have tried to stop the consul Caepio from leaving Rome for his province of Further Spain; Caepio ignored the veto.[31] These episodes demonstrated that it was possible to circumvent or ignore a tribunician veto without provoking any immediate consequences. Once that had happened, the process of vetoing ceased to be an unquestioned fact in political life and became a manoeuvre which could potentially be challenged. The importance of popular participation had been emphasised by C. Licinius Crassus, who in 145 was the first politician to position himself on the speaker's platform so as to address the people as a whole in the forum.[32] Moreover, the secret ballot had been introducted for voting in elections by a tribunician law in 139.[33] Popular authority was being asserted during these years alongside grievances, particularly about material conditions, which were not receiving satisfactory responses.

Tiberius Gracchus launched his tribunate – and, we should assume, had stood on this platform – with a proposal to regulate the use of public land, *ager publicus*, in Italy in favour of small peasant farmers. *Ager publicus* was territory which the Roman state had retained after its conquest of Italy; it was scattered across the penin-

29. P. Garnsey, *Famine and Food Supply in the Graeco-Roman World: Responses to Risk and Crisis*, Cambridge: Cambridge University Press 1988, 195–6. A sumptuary law in 143 may also point to tensions around over- and under-consumption.
30. Val. Max. 5.4.6.
31. Livy, *Epit.* 54.
32. Cic. *Amic.* 96; R. Morstein-Marx, *Mass Oratory and Political Power in the Late Roman Republic*, Cambridge: Cambridge University Press 2004, 42–51. Previously, speakers faced the much smaller space, and audience, in the area between the platform and the Senate house.
33. This was the first of a series of secret ballot laws; see below, pp. 52–3. In 145 C. Licinius Crassus had put forward a law which would have filled vacancies in the priestly colleges by popular vote rather than co-option, though the opposition to this, led by Laelius, was successful; such a law was eventually passed in 104.

sula, and was, in theory, rented out by the state to private tenants.[34] Tiberius' law restricted the amount which any individual could use, and provided for the distribution of the excess in small parcels to Roman citizens, for rent. The limit on maximum possession was the same as the one set in a Licinian-Sextian law, allegedly passed in the early fourth century. The historicity of this earlier legislation does not matter in this context; what is important is that Tiberius wished his measure to appear not as an innovation but rather as a return to ancestral practice. At the same time, he considered his measure to be a response to contemporary problems: Plutarch records a pamphlet by Tiberius' brother Gaius, which claimed that Tiberius was alerted to the problem through his observation of the absence of free labour in Etruria.[35] He wished, that is, to use state resources to support free peasants rather than wealthy proprietors.

Tiberius' agrarian law was, unsurprisingly, deeply unpopular with the wealthy, including many members of the Senate, who were major beneficiaries of the existing pattern of tenancy. His opponents attempted to prevent its passage by arranging for another of the tribunes that year, M. Octavius, to veto it. Tiberius' response was novel: he asked the people to depose Octavius from his office as tribune, on the grounds that his veto did not represent the popular will and therefore, since the purpose of the office of tribune was to represent the popular will, Octavius could not be a real tribune.[36] Following the success of this manoeuvre and the deposition of Octavius from the tribunate, the agrarian law was passed. It was to be implemented by a commission of three, which consisted of Tiberius, his younger brother Gaius (who was at this point absent from Rome at the siege of Numantia) and his father-in-law Ap. Claudius Pulcher. The choice of commissioners is noteworthy: by choosing close allies to implement his law, Tiberius either did not

---

34. S. Roselaar, *Public Land in the Roman Republic: A Social and Economic History of Ager Publicus in Italy, 396–89 B.C.*, Oxford: Oxford University Press 2010.

35. Plut. *Ti. Gracch.* 8.7; K. Adshead, 'Further inspiration for Tiberius Gracchus?', *Antichthon* 15, 1981, 119–28.

36. App. *B Civ.* 12; Plut. *Ti. Gracch.* 10–12; A. Erskine, *The Hellenistic Stoa: Political Thought and Action*, London: Duckworth 1990, 171–80; C. Steel, 'Tribunician sacrosanctity and oratorial performance in the late Republic', in D. Berry and A. Erskine, eds, *Form and Function in Roman Oratory*, Cambridge: Cambridge University Press 2010, 37–50; H. Flower, 'Beyond the *contio*: political communication in the tribunate of Tiberius Gracchus', in C. Steel and H. van der Blom, eds, *Community and Communication: Oratory and Politics in Republican Rome*, Oxford: Oxford University Press, forthcoming, 85–100.

wish to explore any compromise with opponents of his law, or regarded such a compromise as impossible. Nonetheless, Appius, an former consul, censor and *princeps senatus*, brought considerable seniority to the enterprise.[37]

The Senate could not prevent the passage of the agrarian law but it could ensure that the commissioners were starved of funding to carry out their task. At this point, domestic and foreign affairs intersected. News arrived of the bequest to Rome of the kingdom of Pergamum by its late monarch Attalus.[38] Tiberius put another law to the people, which arranged for the revenues from Pergamum to be dedicated to financing his agrarian law.[39] By so doing, Tiberius solved his immediate financial problem; but he also set up a direct challenge to the convention that foreign policy was the purview of the Senate. Nonetheless, the act of Tiberius which provoked crisis was neither his deposition of Octavius nor his subjection of foreign policy matters to popular determination. It was his attempt to be re-elected as tribune for the following year. Scipio Aemilianus provided a very recent example of laws regulating office-holding being set aside in the face of emergency. Tiberius presumably regarded re-election as a necessary device to ensure that his reforms were implemented. He must have hoped that a demonstration that he was the people's choice, through the fact of being elected again, would override the convention which prevented continuous office-holding, just as he had earlier wielded popular votes to override conventions about tribunician vetoes and foreign policy decisions.[40] But he appears to have misjudged. As the people assembled on the Capitol to vote in the tribunician elections, the Senate met in the temple of Fides.[41] Scipio Nasica urged the presiding consul, Scaevola, to take steps to resist Gracchus. When Scaevola refused, Nasica called on everyone present who wished to preserve the state to follow him, and he led a crowd of senators to the electoral assembly. In the

37. He was also the man who celebrated a triumph in defiance of tribunician veto in 143; a useful reminder of the inescapably tangled relationship between ideology and personal ambition in Roman politics.
38. See below, p. 72.
39. Stockton, *Gracchi*, 67–9.
40. There are intriguing links between Tiberius' actions and trends in contemporary Hellenistic philosophy: Erskine, *Stoa*, 150–80.
41. J. Linderski, 'The Pontiff and the Tribune: the death of Tiberius Gracchus', *Athenaeum* 90, 2002, 339–66; A. Clark, *Divine Qualities: Cult and Community in Republican Rome*, Oxford: Oxford University Press 2007, 167–71.

ensuing fracas, Tiberius and some hundreds of his followers were killed, and their bodies thrown into the Tiber.

It was Tiberius' violent death in office, rather than his legislative programme, that turned his tribunate into a transitional point. The administration of the land law continued even after his death, with P. Licinius Crassus as the third commissioner, despite the continuing resentment of those dispossessed.[42] But Gracchus' death, murdered by a posse led by the chief priest (*pontifex maximus*) in opposition to the judgement of the consul posed a huge challenge to the legitimacy and unity of the ruling class. Flower has documented the extraordinary range of apotropaic gestures which the Senate undertook in the aftermath of the lynching; and Scipio Nasica himself left Rome on an embassy to Asia Minor. He was the first *pontifex maximus* to leave the city; at this moment of crisis, the normal management of state religion yielded to exceptional measures designed to enable the resumption of civic life.[43]

There was no immediate repetition of the violence of 133. Nonetheless, the issues which had arisen continued to reverberate. Adherents of Tiberius were prosecuted, and it is likely that some of those convicted were executed. In 131 one of the tribunes, C. Papirius Carbo, put forward a proposal to make re-election to the tribunate possible. That proposal failed, with Scipio Aemilianus, who had returned from Spain the previous year, identified in the sources as its major opponent; but Carbo was successful with a law which extended the secret ballot to legislative assemblies.[44] The land commissioners continued their work, though their effectiveness may have been reduced by the rapid turnover among members: Appius Claudius died in or before 129 and Crassus presumably gave up his place when he went to Asia as consul in 131. Their replacements were M. Fulvius Flaccus and Carbo himself. More seriously, the activities of the commissioners stirred up resentment among Rome's Italian allies. According to Appian, they appealed in 129 to Scipio Aemilianus for help in the face of injustice from the commissioners.[45] Unfortunately, Appian gives no further details, either on the identity of those complaining or on the nature of their complaints; but it is

42. Crassus was the brother of Mucius Scaevola, adopted into the Licinii; he succeeded Nasica as *pontifex maximus* and his daughter married Gaius Gracchus.
43. H. Flower, *The Art of Forgetting: Disgrace and Oblivion in Roman Political Culture*, Chapel Hill: University of North Carolina Press 2006, 69–76.
44. Cic. *Amic.* 95; *Leg.* 3.35.
45. App. *B Civ.* 1.19.

probable that disputes were arising over what counted as public land as opposed to land which belonged to allied communities. It is easy to see how the commission's enthusiasm for identifying as much public land as possible for redistribution could lead to decisions over boundary lines unfavourable to non-Romans.

Aemilianus secured a review of the commissioners' activities, to be led by one of the consuls of 129, C. Sempronius Tuditanus. Tuditanus, however, soon departed for campaign in Illyria; Appian plausibly ascribes reluctance to deal with the problem of the land commissioners as a motive for his going.[46] But the relationship between Rome and the other communities in the Italian peninsula remained on the political agenda. Three years later, one of the tribunes put forward a law physically expelling non-Romans from Rome.[47] In 125, the commissioner Fulvius Flaccus was consul and put forward legislation extending the Roman citizenship, which he subsequently withdrew in the face of opposition within the Senate.[48] In the same year the Latin community of Fregellae, little more than 50 miles down the *via Latina* from Rome, revolted and was destroyed by one of the praetors, L. Opimius.[49]

Rome and the eastern Mediterranean, 146–122

In comparison with the material which documents Rome's activities in Spain, the evidence for its dealings with the eastern Mediterranean, in the years immediately after the sack of Corinth and Mummius' subsequent settlement in Greece, is very scanty.[50] Nonetheless, it seems as though military activity was confined to Macedonia, where the Romans faced an insurrection in the late

46. Aemilianus himself died suddenly early in 129.
47. Cic. *Off.* 3.47.
48. Who might have benefited from Flaccus' measure is much debated: Appian (*B Civ.* 1.21) thought it was the Italians, which seems implausible at this date: H. Mouritsen, *Italian Unification: A Study in Ancient and Modern Historiography*, London: Institute of Classical Studies 1998, 109–13, and see below. A renegotiation of the relationship with those of Latin status, though unprovable, provides a good context for events at Fregellae.
49. P. Conole, 'Allied disaffection and the revolt of Fregellae', *Antichthon* 15, 1981, 129–40; Mouritsen, *Unification*, 118–19.
50. E. S. Gruen, *The Hellenistic World and the Coming of Rome*, Berkeley: University of California Press 1984, 578–92; R. M. Kallet-Marx, *Hegemony to Empire: The Development of the Roman Imperium in the East from 148 to 62 B.C.*, Berkeley: University of California Press 1995, 97–9.

140s; two praetors are attested there before 133, the latter of which, M. Cosconius, campaigned successfully against some Thracian tribes. Elsewhere, Roman activity was diplomatic, and is attested only patchily. The best-documented episode is an embassy of Scipio Aemilianus, Metellus Calvus and Spurius Mummius to a wide area of the eastern Mediterranean; the presence of Scipio has ensured wide anecdotal coverage but its geopolitical significance is less clear. The prolonged and often unsuccessful war in Spain precluded any serious activity in the eastern Mediterranean, and the Romans appear to have been happy to acquiesce in the power of Pergamum as the dominant non-Roman force in the region.

The situation changed abruptly in 133. In the midst of the debates over Ti. Gracchus' agrarian law, news arrived in Rome that the king of Pergamum, Attalus III, had died and left his kingdom to Rome. Rome's eventual reaction to this surprising news was to bring about substantial change in its dealings with the eastern Mediterranean, and the trigger for these changes was the tribunate of Ti. Gracchus. In 133, domestic politics and external affairs interacted with immediate and abrupt effect upon one another. Attalus' bequest was unexpected; he was in his thirties at the time of his death, and he may well never have intended his will in favour of Rome to come into force. Other examples of such testamentary devices among the Hellenistic monarchies seem to have been designed to remove the incentive for assassination, and Attalus may well have intended likewise.[51] After his death, Aristonicus, who claimed to be an illegitimate son of Eumenes II, seized the kingdom; he quickly gathered considerable support and may well have expected the Romans not to intervene. It was, after all, nearly sixty years since there had been a Roman army in Asia Minor. Nonetheless, the news came at precisely the point when the Romans were largely free from other overseas crises. The war in Spain had just come to an end, and the slave revolt in Sicily was finally being suppressed. Whatever the Senate's view of the popular acceptance of the bequest at the prompting of Tiberius Gracchus, it put in place the mechanisms to incorporate this new possession. It got rid of Scipio Nasica in the aftermath of Tiberius Gracchus' death by sending him there as a legate; and it allocated Asia as a province to Crassus, one of the consuls of 131.

Aristonicus made the process of accepting the bequest unexpect-

---

51. D. Braund, 'Royal wills and Rome', *PBSR* 51, 1983, 16–57; A. N. Sherwin-White, *Roman Foreign Policy in the East, 168 B.C. to A.D. 1*, London: Duckworth 1984, 80–4.

edly difficult. Crassus was killed in battle; his successor, Perperna, defeated Aristonicus, who was taken to Rome and there executed, but Perperna himself was unable to triumph, since he died at Pergamum while on his return to Rome. It was his successor in Asia, M'. Aquillius, who undertook the organisation of Pergamum in collaboration with a senatorial commission of ten men. They allocated some territory to Rome's allies in the region, but seem to have envisaged that from then onwards a Roman magistrate and some military forces would also be present in Pergamum. It is not clear whether they also arranged for regular collection of taxes; this may have been an innovation that Gaius Gracchus introduced.[52]

Once Asia was peaceful, Rome's external interests appear to have turned further west, though the sources are extremely sparse for the earlier part of the 120s. It was a campaign in Illyria which took Tuditanus away from the intractable problems of the land commission, and Fulvius Flaccus campaigned in Liguria during his consulship and then in Gaul, bringing assistance to the Massilians. The war in Gaul was continued over three years by C. Sextius Calvinus before being concluded by Cn. Domitius Ahenobarbus and Q. Fabius Maximus, both of whom celebrated triumphs. Domitius also saw to the construction of the *via Domitia*, linking Rome with Spain by land. Routes to Spain had been strengthened too by the conquest of the Balearic isles by Metellus, consul in 123, and by the foundation of cities populated by Roman settlers from Spain – evidence for the size of Roman communities there by this time.[53]

The tribunates of Gaius Gracchus

In 123 Tiberius Gracchus' younger brother Gaius held the tribunate and embarked on a legislative programme which, though clearly in some ways a development of his brother's activities, offered an enormously ambitious overhaul of the Roman state. The sources on the younger Gracchus are comparatively extensive and it is possible to construct his career before 123 in unusual detail. He was with Aemilianus' army at Numantia, a land commissioner from 133 onwards, and held the quaestorship in 126. As quaestor he was allocated to Sardinia, where the consul L. Aurelius Orestes was suppressing a revolt; his office was extended by the Senate into 125

52. Gruen, *Hellenistic World*, 592–608.
53. Strabo 3.5.1.

and then 124. Gracchus ignored the second extension of his
term and returned to Rome, where he successfully defended his early
departure to the censors. He also supported Carbo's unsuccessful
attempt to permit re-election to the tribunate, and opposed Pennus'
law expelling non-Romans from Rome. Nonetheless, the chronology
of some of his actions as tribune can be difficult to ascertain.[54]

One of his laws dealt with land: this seems to have enabled the
resumption of activity by Tiberius' commissioners, of whom Gaius
was still one, though it is not clear in what ways it modified Tiberius'
legislation. In practice, the bulk of Gaius' agrarian activity involved
the foundation of citizen colonies, rather than the allocation of land
to individual settlers: these were established at Capua and Tarentum
and, most strikingly, the site of Carthage was resettled with a new
name, Junonia. Gaius also successfully put forward a law which
regulated the supply of wheat, permitting every male citizen to buy
a certain quantity each month at a fixed price, which was probably
comparable to the open market price after a good harvest.[55] It thus
protected citizens from profiteering at times of scarcity and gave
them direct access to the benefits of imperial power, as manifest in
revenue, whilst limiting the capacity of the rich to win political
support through handouts. At the same time, the measure acknowledged that land grants could benefit only a proportion of the urban
poor.[56] The corn law was very popular, and its repeal and reinstate-
ment became a barometer of popular power for the rest of the
Republican period. It is a matter for debate whether Gaius was
motivated primarily by a desire to widen his support base, or to
share the benefits of empire more widely. Another element of
Gracchus' programme which also appears to lead directly from his
brother's tribunate is a measure proposing that magistrates who had
been deposed from their office by the people should not hold office
a second time, and another enacting that capital courts could be set
up only by the people. The latter was clearly designed to prevent the
establishment of the kind of judicial inquiry which had been directed
at Tiberius' followers after his death, and its force was retroactive.[57]

54. Stockton, *Gracchi*, 226–39. Gracchus' repeated tenure of the tribunate compounds
the difficulty.
55. G. Rickman, *The Corn Supply of Ancient Rome*, Oxford: Oxford University Press
1980, 156–61.
56. Access to subsidised grain was only possible for those physically present in Rome.
57. Popillius Laenas, cos. 132, was tried and went into exile: M. Alexander, *Trials in the
Late Roman Republic 149 BC to 50 BC*, Toronto: University of Toronto Press 1990, 14.
Velleius, probably erroneously, adds his colleague Rupilius (2.7.4).

Tiberius had intervened on an ad hoc basis in foreign policy matters; Gaius established measures whereby foreign policy decisions were exposed to regular public scrutiny. The *lex Sempronia de prouinciis consularibus* established that the Senate must decide the tasks with which the consuls would be entrusted before the consular elections: the people therefore had the opportunity to factor this information into their choice. His law on the Asian tax revenues set up the system of contracting out tax collection; from now on, the right to collect these taxes was sold to the highest bidder, thus protecting the treasury from lower than expected yields. And he introduced a new law on provincial extortion. This differed from earlier *repetundae* laws in the composition of the jury, since it barred senators and their close male relatives from serving; it also imposed higher penalties on those convicted. The latter two measures greatly increased the political clout of the *equites* (equestrians); but Gaius may not have intended this result. In the case of the *repetundae* courts, his aim was surely to improve the chances of a fair trial, since by definition only members of the Senate could find themselves charged with provincial extortion. At the same time, he needed jurors whose wealth might insulate them from bribery (and he also passed a law which made judicial bribery a capital offence).[58]

Although we cannot establish the dates of Gaius' legislation with certainty, it seems reasonable to assume that the majority of these laws were promulgated early in his first tribunate. Plutarch records his popularity, and for Plutarch this explains his re-election to the tribunate at the elections for 122; he may well be right to ascribe Gaius' re-election to a surge of popular enthusiasm, since it is difficult to see how it could have provoked so little opposition unless it was presented to the Senate as a fait accompli. One piece of legislation which does seem to belong to the second tribunate rather than the first is a proposal to grant Roman citizenship to the Latins; at any rate, Cicero records a speech delivered against it by C. Fannius, whom he identifies as consul, which dates it to 122.[59] A quotation

---

58. This law seems to have been aimed only at senators; it may therefore have been passed before the *repetundae* law (i.e. at a time when only senators could be jurors) and even to have been Gracchus' initial solution to the problem of *repetundae*; A. Lintott, *Judicial Reform and Land Reform in the Roman Republic*, Cambridge: Cambridge University Press 1992: 10–33; M. Crawford, *Roman Statutes*, 2 vols, London: Institute of Classical Studies 1996, 39–112. Other measures included a variety of infrastructure projects and some improvements to the conditions of military service: *MRR* 1.513–14.
59. Cic. *Brut.* 99. H. Mouritsen, 'The Gracchi, the Latins, and the Italian allies', in L. de Ligt and S. Northwood, eds, *People, Land and Politics: Demographic Develop-*

from this speech survives, which shows Fannius provoking fears among his urban audience of a loss of their privileges: 'if you give the citizenship to the Latins, Quirites, do you think that you will still have space at public meetings as you do now, or to participate in games and festivals? Surely you see that they will take over everything?'[60] Given that the law did not pass, it seems as though Fannius' tactics struck a chord, and the proposal may have been an important factor in explaining why Gracchus' support should have evaporated during 122. But Gaius' opponents had also developed different means of countering his measures from the blunt approach that had been used against Tiberius. Among his colleagues in the tribunate for 122 was M. Livius Drusus, who competed for popularity with him by proposing a much more extensive colonisation programme. Moreover, Appian and Plutarch both record Gaius' going to Africa this year to supervise the foundation of Junonia. Why he should have done so is unclear; his absence from Rome was contrary to the convention which prevented tribunes of the people from being absent from Rome for more than twenty-four hours and it gave Drusus the opportunity to further his own position.

Gaius did not hold office in 121 and one of the tribunes of the year, Minucius Rufus, attempted to repeal some or all of his laws, including the foundation of Junonia.[61] The desire to protect his reforms was presumably among the reasons which led Gaius to seek a third tribunate, and towards the end of the year, during the campaigning, Gaius and Flaccus attended a public meeting (contio) that Minucius was holding. A brawl broke out, during which an associate of the consul Opimius was killed. Opimius – the man who had destroyed Fregellae – called a meeting of the Senate, which summoned Gaius and Flaccus to explain themselves; they attempted to negotiate, but Opimius persuaded the Senate to instruct him to defend the res publica.[62] Gaius and Flaccus took refuge on the Aventine hill with their supporters, and were attacked by Opimius, who had a detachment of Cretan archers at his disposal. The presence of armed forces to hand suggests that he had planned the

ments and the Transformation of Roman Italy, 300 BC–AD 14, Leiden: Brill 2008, 471–83.
60. Iulius Victor 6.4.
61. Plut. C. Gracch. 13; Stockton, Gracchi, 195–6.
62. This was the first use of the so-called senatus consultum ultimum: A. Drummond, Law, Politics and Power: The Execution of the Catilinarian Conspirators, Stuttgart: Steiner 1995, 81–95; Lintott, Constitution, 89–93.

possibility of using force; he was also accompanied by at least some members of the Senate, since the *princeps senatus*, P. Lentulus, is recorded as having been wounded there.[63] Flaccus died on the Aventine, and Gaius ordered one of his slaves to kill him to avoid being captured. Their bodies were thrown into the Tiber, and subsequently Opimius had 3,000 of their supporters executed.

The similarities between the deaths of the Gracchi are obvious: both killed by groups led by a senior member of the Senate after tribunates which had championed the popular cause. But the differences are significant too.[64] Gaius managed, unlike his brother, to retain a powerful position beyond a single year and appears to have had better organised support, with a base on the Aventine and some degree of armed capacity. His senatorial opponents were better organised, as well, than Tiberius' had been. They were led by a consul, and Opimius ensured the appearance, at least, of consensus by getting senatorial approval for his actions in advance. The Senate's handling of the aftermath of catastrophe was also much more confident than their horrified response in 133. Opimius forced his interpretation of events onto the fabric of Rome by building a temple to *Concordia*, Concord or Unity: its symbolism is reflected in the popular hostility it provoked as well as its use for the occasional Senate meeting.[65] An attempt to prosecute him the following year failed, and Popilius Laenas was also restored from exile. Official use of armed force had swung the balance of power back to the Senate.

Foreign and domestic politics at the end of the second century BC

The quality and range of source material decrease significantly in the decade after Gaius Gracchus' death, but some trends are visible.[66] There was little overtly *popularis* activity in the years immediately after the violent suppression of Gaius Gracchus and his supporters;[67] but his legislation was not repealed, despite Minucius' attempt. Jurors in extortion trials were now non-senatorial; citizens could claim subsidised corn doles; the Asian tax revenues were being

63. Lentulus was well into his eighties at the time; he had been suffect consul in 162 BC.
64. Flower, *Art of Forgetting*, 76.
65. M. Bonnefond-Coudry, *Le Sénat de la République romaine: de la guerre d'Hannibale à Auguste: pratiques délibératives et prises de décisions*, Rome: École Française de Rome 1989, 90–112; Clark, *Divine Qualities*, 121–3.
66. For an attempt to populate the scene, T. P. Wiseman, *Remembering the Roman People*, Oxford: Oxford University Press 2009, 33–57.
67. On *popularis* activity, see below, Chapter 2.

collected by public contractors (*publicani*); consular provinces were determined before the consular elections; and the innovation of overseas colony foundation was consolidated with the establishment, in 118, of Narbo Martius in newly conquered Gaul. On the other hand, land distribution seems to have ceased; and the extension of the citizenship had vanished from the political agenda, with what would prove to be disastrous consequences.

Popular discontent with the conduct of public affairs re-emerges in the late 110s. In 114 an appalling scandal erupted about the Vestal Virgins. One of them, Aemilia, was accused of sexual relations with a Roman *eques*; she in turn denounced two of her colleagues, Licinia and Marcia, for unchastity.[68] All three – half, that is, of the Vestals – were tried in front of the priests (*pontifices*) in December: Aemilia was convicted, the others acquitted. This was the first time that a Vestal had been found guilty of unchastity for over a century, and Aemilia's conviction was followed by her ritual burial alive near the Colline gate.[69] But the verdict of the *pontifices* did not satisfy the people and, in an extraordinary move, one of the tribunes of 113 who had just entered into office, Sex. Peducaeus, successfully proposed a plebiscite which appointed L. Cassius Longinus Ravilla as special inquisitor into the affair. Peducaeus thereby deprived the *pontifex maximus* of his ancient authority over the college of Vestals, and Longinus found both Licinia and Marcia guilty; they too, presumably, suffered the same fate as Aemilia. The episode, which marks a striking extension of popular authority over the religious sphere, is often read as the product of public anxiety in response to failures overseas, parallel with the occurrence of Vestals being buried alive in 216, shortly after the catastrophe of Cannae.[70] But there is nothing remotely comparable to Cannae in the period immediately before the trial of the Vestals. A consular army was indeed defeated in Thrace in 114, but the man in charge, C. Porcius

68. Plut. *Quaest. Rom.* 83; Oros. 5.15.
69. During the same period of time, four other humans were buried alive, two Gauls and two Greeks, in the Forum Boarium, in a ceremony which may well have been connected with the Vestals: A. Eckstein, 'Human sacrifice and fear of military disaster in Republican Rome', *AJAH* 7, 1982, 69–95; M. Beard, J. North and S. Price, *Religions of Rome*, 2 vols, Cambridge: Cambridge University Press 1998, 80–1; Z. Várhelyi, 'The specters of Roman imperialism: the live burials of Gauls and Greeks at Rome', *ClAnt* 26, 2007, 277–304.
70. E. D. Rawson, 'Religion and politics in the late second century BC at Rome', *Phoenix* 28, 1974, 193–212; A. Staples, *From Good Goddess to Vestal Virgins: Sex and Category in Roman Religion*, London: Routledge 1998.

Cato, survived to be convicted – of extortion – on his return to Rome the following year. There is no need to read this episode as the tranference to the religious sphere of anxieties arising from military failure, or indeed of struggles between different political factions.[71] The scandal of the Vestals in 114 is better seen as a genuine religious crisis, and the perceived failure of the *pontifices* to deal adequately with this crisis led to popular intervention not because the people saw an opportunity to extend their power and seized it, but because failure by the ruling elite to manage the Vestals had the potential to threaten the safety of the entire *res publica*. Certainly, the events of the previous two decades offered a model whereby the citizen body as a whole could challenge the authority of the ruling elite: but we should not assume that challenge was the end in itself.

Indeed, the crisis of the Vestals marked the start, rather than the end, of a period of military difficulties overseas. The best-documented of these is the war against Jugurtha, to which Sallust devoted a monograph. As on other occasions, the death of a ruler friendly to Rome, that of Micipsa, in 118 led to Roman involvement in disputes between potential heirs, and there was extensive diplomatic activity before war finally broke out in 111. For Sallust, the conflict foreshadows the period of conflict between Pompeius and Caesar and the state split into opposed factions: the selfishness and incompetence of the nobility created the opportunity for Marius to rise to prominence. The reluctance of the Senate to engage in conflict in Africa is presented, therefore, as the result of Jugurtha's effective bribery. But its hesitation is not exceptional. Sending ambassadors in 115 to mediate between the rival claims of Jugurtha and Adherbal was a normal response to a situation where foreign powers appealed to Rome; and the initial slowness to respond the following year to news that Jugurtha was ignoring the ambassadors' division of Numidia may be explained by other pressing issues. There was the consular defeat in Thrace mentioned above; and either this year or the following news came that Germanic tribes were heading for Italy.

The threat in northern Italy may also have played a part in the rapid peace made by Calpurnius Bestia, the first Roman commander sent to Africa against Jugurtha in 111: in 113 one of the consuls, Cn. Papirius Carbo, had been defeated by the Cimbri. However,

71. Rawson places Peducaeus' measure in the context of *popularis* legislation of the late second century; Münzer, by contrast, views the trials and convictions as the result of struggles between aristocratic factions (*Roman Aristocratic Parties and Families*, trans. R. T. Ridley, Baltimore: Johns Hopkins University Press 1999, 222–4).

Bestia's peace provoked outrage at Rome and the tribune Memmius persuaded the people to carry a measure sending one of the praetors to Jugurtha to investigate the allegations of bribery.[72] In the following year, the tribune Mamilius set up a special tribunal, the *quaestio Mamilia*, to investigate these allegations, which found no fewer than four ex-consuls and a priest guilty: the five concerned went into exile.[73]

The vigour of the *quaestio Mamilia* may well have been increased by continuing bad news from Africa. But it should not necessarily be seen as the product of a more general panic; Romans had in fact witnessed three triumphs over the previous two years, and although the Cimbri and Teutones remained a threat, this did not translate itself into imminent crisis until 109.[74] Rather, it was a demonstration by the Roman people that it was willing to intervene directly in specific aspects of foreign affairs if the Senate appeared to be neglecting the interests of the *res publica*. In Africa, the situation was retrieved, from the Roman perspective, over the following years by the campaigns first of Q. Metellus (cos. 109) and then, from 107, by Marius, consul that year, who eventually captured Jugurtha and brought the war to an end in 105. One attendant circumstance was the utter transformation of the Roman army by Marius' decision, in his preparations for this campaign, to enrol in the army any citizen, regardless of property qualification.[75] Marius himself was a new man, a *nouus homo*, lacking senatorial ancestors, and his consular ambitions were opposed by Metellus; his election, and subsequent supersession, through a popular vote, of Metellus as commander in Africa suggests that suspicion about senatorial competence was widespread.

In Gaul the Romans suffered a series of military disasters once the conflict with the Cimbri resumed in 109. M. Junius Silanus was defeated in 109 or 108; his successor L. Cassius Longinus was killed

---

72. Sall. *Iug.* 30
73. They were L. Opimius (cos. 121); C. Porcius Cato (cos. 114); L. Calpurnius Bestia (cos. 111); Sp. Postumius Albinus (cos. 110); and C. Sulpicius Galba, who may have been either a *pontifex* or an augur. According to Cicero (*Brut.* 128) this was the first time a member of a priestly college had been convicted on criminal charges.
74. Triumphs: in 111 M.Caecilius Metellus, from Sardinia, and C. Caecilius Metellus Caprarius, from Thrace; in 110, M. Livius Drusus, over the Scordisci and Macedonians. These triumphs did not, however, mark the end of fighting in Thrace and Macedonia: M. Minucius Rufus celebrated a triumph over the Scordisci in 106, as did T. Didius in 100.
75. See below, Chapter 2.

Figure 1 Coin of Faustus Sulla, 56 BC: L. Sulla receiving the surrender of Jugurtha (© The Hunterian, University of Glasgow)

in battle against another Gallic tribe, the Tigurini, in 107 along with one of his legates, the ex-consul Piso Caesoninus; Q. Servilius Caepio (cos. 106) and Cn. Mallius (cos. 105) held *imperium* simultaneously in Gaul and their failure to co-operate led to another disastrous defeat of Roman forces at Arausio (Orange, in southern France) on 6 October 105 and to the death of another consular legate.[76] The popular response was emphatic. Marius was re-elected to the consulship for 104, well before that was possible under normal rules of office-holding and before he had given up his *imperium* from the African command: he celebrated his triumph over Jugurtha on 1 January 104, the day on which he also entered upon his second consulship.[77] Moreover, he was re-elected for the four subsequent years: in effect, the Roman people as a whole had usurped the senatorial role of proroguing *imperium*. In 104 Silanus was prosecuted on the grounds that he had attacked the Cimbri without authority, though he was acquitted; in the same year Caepio was stripped of his *imperium* by a popular vote, and a tribunician law was then passed which expelled from the Senate anyone to

76. This was arguably the worst military defeat that Rome had suffered since the battle of Cannae in 216; on the date's subsequent reputation, Plut. *Luc.* 27.7
77. A striking indication of the seriousness of the situation was Marius' unsuccessful request to Nicomedes of Bithynia for military support (Diod. Sic. 36.3): only one other request for military aid from an eastern power is known during the Republic, and that is not securely attested (Kallet-Marx, *Hegemony*, 139–40).

whom this had happened. In 103 both Caepio and Mallius were convicted and exiled by a court established by the tribune Saturninus with another tribune, Norbanus, acting as Caepio's prosecutor.[78] The trial of these failed commanders split the tribunician college, with two other tribunes attempting to veto proceedings: in the riot that followed when Norbanus ignored their veto the *princeps senatus*, Aemilius Scaurus, was injured.[79]

Saturninus was also a keen supporter of Marius, proposing a law assigning land in Africa to Marius' veterans, and ensuring that Marius was re-elected to the consulship when he returned to Rome towards the end of 103 to oversee the elections. Marius then defeated the Teutones and their allies at two battles near Aquae Sextiae (Aix-en-Provence) and in the following year – declining to celebrate the triumph which he had been awarded – joined forces with the other consul of 102, Q. Lutatius Catulus, in a defeat of the Cimbri near Vercellae on 30 July. These victories decisively ended the threat in northern Italy and helped to secure for Marius a sixth consulship for 100 as well as his second triumph.

Marius now held a position of pre-eminence unparalleled since Scipio Aemilianus – who, not coincidentally, had been the last person to triumph twice. Like Aemilianus', Marius' position had been created by popular support which overruled the normal pattern of political careers. But Marius marked the transition from military to civilian leader in 100 by his support for a radical programme of *popularis* legislation, which pushed his relations with the senatorial elite to breaking point. In a murky episode, Saturninus was elected again as tribune for 100, as a substitute for a candidate, Nonius,

78. In addition, Cassius' legate Popillius Laenas had been prosecuted in 107 or 106 by the tribune C. Coelius Caldus on the charge of treason (*perduellio*), arising from the agreement which he had reached with the Tigurini to extract the survivors after Cassius' defeat and death, and convicted; Caldus also legislated to introduce the secret ballot to *perduellio* trials, a move which, according to Cicero, he subsequently rued (*Leg.* 3.36). Caepio's conviction had been preceded by an attempt to convict him of stealing gold from a temple after he captured Tolosa in 107 (Alexander, *Trials*, 33–4; the gold itself was reputed to be cursed [Gell. *NA* 3.9.7]). The trial of Caepio was replayed some years later in the Norbanus case: see below. Saturninus had been quaestor in 104 with responsibility for the corn supply and was replaced by the Senate after a rise in the price of corn; Cicero (*Sest.* 39, *Har. resp.* 43) connects his turning to *popularis* politics with the distress, *dolor*, he felt at this humiliation.

79. The year 104 also saw the extension of popular arbitration to the appointment of members of the priestly colleges, through the *lex Domitia*: see J. North, 'Family strategy and priesthood in the late Republic', in J. Andreau and H. Bruhns, eds, *Parenté et stratégies familiales dans l'antiquité romaine*, Rome: École Française de Rome 1990, 527–43.

who had been elected and was then killed during disturbances which broke out as the election continued. Saturninus was collaborating with Servilius Glaucia, who had been tribune in 101 and had managed to be elected praetor for 100; they joined forces with Marius to put forward a wide range of legislative proposals.[80]

Saturninus' legislative programme recalled, quite deliberately, aspects of the younger Gracchus': it included a grain law, an agrarian law and the foundation of a number of colonies overseas. However, he went significantly beyond Gracchus. His grain law appears to have set the price at a level a quarter of that set by Gracchus, making plausible the claims of his opponents that it would bankrupt the treasury; and his colonies were indisputably *ad hominem*, since they were for Marius' veterans, and Marius was given the opportunity to enfranchise three non-Romans as part of the foundation of each. Even more innovative was the clause in Saturninus' agrarian law (which redistributed the territory of the Cimbri) demanding that all senators must take an oath to obey the law within five days of its passage, and that failure to do so would lead to loss of senatorial position and a fine of 20 talents. Metellus Numidicus, Marius' predecessor in the war against Jugurtha, refused to swear and went into exile.[81] This may also be the year of the *lex Appuleia de maiestate*, which defined – imprecisely, to judge from subsequent trials – a new offence of 'diminishing the majesty of the Roman people'. This was intended to control the military actions of magistrates, and should thus be related to earlier moves to extend the popular oversight of foreign policy.[82] However, it is noticeable that there was no attempt to emulate Gracchus' concern with citizenship;

80. Glaucia had put forward a *repetundae* law as tribune, which returned the juries to the equestrians after Caepio, as consul in 106, reintroduced senatorial jurors: J-L. Ferrary, 'Recherches sur la législation de Saturninus et de Glaucia, II', *MEFRA* 91, 1979, 85–134; A. Lintott, 'The *leges de repetundis* and associated measures under the Republic', *ZRG* 98, 1981, 162–212.
81. G. Kelly, *A History of Exile in the Roman Republic*, New York: Cambridge University Press 2006, 29–30, 84–8; he had already clashed with Glaucia and Saturninus in his attempt as censor in 102 to expel them from the Senate and, as augur, had been involved in imposing height restrictions on the design of Marius's temple to *Honos et Virtus*.
82. R. Bauman, *The Crimen Maiestatis in the Roman Republic and Augustan Principate*, Johannesburg: Witwatersrand University Press 1967; Brennan, *Praetorship*, 366–7; J. Harries, *Law and Crime in the Roman World*, Cambridge: Cambridge University Press 2007, 72–7. A law on the allocation of eastern commands preserved on an inscription from Delphi (M. Hassall, M. Crawford and J. Reynolds, 'Rome and the eastern provinces at the end of the second century B.C.', *JRS* 64, 1974, 195–220; Crawford, *Statutes*, 231–70) is not necessarily Saturninus' (Kallet-Marx, *Hegemony*, 237–9), though it contains a provision for magistrates' oaths.

the provision for enfranchisement in his colonies was on such a small scale that it can only be understood as a means for Marius to promote his personal prestige. The extension of the Roman citizenship was still off the political agenda.

Saturninus' laws provoked violent opposition, but were passed; he also secured re-election to the tribunate along with at least two close supporters.[83] His downfall, and that of Glaucia, came from Glaucia's candidacy for the consulship of 99 and the murder (in which they were widely considered to be implicated) of Memmius, who was also standing for the consulship.[84] At this point, the Senate looked back to 121 and instructed the consuls to see that no harm came to the *res publica*. Marius obeyed, and led the forces which gathered against his former allies. Saturninus, Glaucia and their followers were besieged on the Capitol; when they surrendered, Marius imprisoned them in the Senate house. What Marius might have hoped would then happen is unclear; in fact the prisoners were stoned to death by the crowd: 'they lifted the Senate House roof-tiles and kept throwing them at Appuleius and his followers until they killed them, a quaestor and a tribune and a praetor, still wearing their insignia of office'.[85]

These events continued to reverberate in the years immediately following. Furius, one of the tribunes for 99, proposed that Saturninus' property be confiscated by the state; but he and Marius are also recorded in this year opposing attempts to recall Metellus Numidicus from exile, and the posthumous attack on Saturninus may have been an attempt by Marius to dissociate himself from his former allies. In 98, an attempt to prosecute Furius in the courts failed, and the prosecutor himself was convicted after he expressed regret for Saturninus' death; but another attempt to prosecute Furius, through the assembly of the people, failed only because the assembly lynched him instead.[86] Metellus Numidicus was recalled

83. L. Equitius, trading on the popularity he claimed as the son of Gracchus; and Sex. Titius.
84. Saturninus could cite the example of Gracchus for consecutive tribunates, but to move from praetorship directly to consulship would have been unprecedented:
85. App. *B Civ.* 1.32; E. Badian 'The death of Saturninus: studies in chronology and prosopography', *Chiron* 14, 1984, 130–40. The quaestor was L. Saufeius.
86. On the complexity of alliances and policies during these years, A. Russell, 'Speech, competition and collaboration: tribunician politics and the development of popular ideology', in C. Steel and H. van der Blom, eds, *Community and Communication: Oratory and Politics in Republican Rome*, Oxford: Oxford University Press 2013, 101–15.

from exile by a tribunician law, and the consuls were responsible for the *lex Caecilia Didia*, which specified the interval between the announcement of a legislative measure and the vote on its passage in a clear attempt to disrupt the tempo of popular legislation. What must be avoided is any straightforward division of the citizen body into rigid groupings: the recall of Numidicus appears to have commanded very wide support, for example, and it is surely possible for supporters of that measure nonetheless to have differed in their attitudes to Saturninus. What does seem clear, however, is that Marius had destroyed his position of pre-eminence by supporting and then abandoning Saturninus and by his attack on Numidicus. In a move reminiscent of Nasica's thirty years earlier, he went to Asia Minor, ostensibly to fulfil a vow he had made to the Magna Mater; he was almost sixty, and most must have assumed his political career was now over.

For Plutarch, however, Marius had a second motive in going east: he hoped to provoke conflict between Rome and Mithridates VI, the king of Pontus, and be chosen himself as leader in that war.[87] This interpretation is may well be retrojection from subsequent events, but it is nonetheless possible that Marius recognised Asia Minor as a potential and imminent conflict zone for Rome and was engaged in semi-formal investigations.[88] The Romans had largely ignored the eastern Mediterranean for a quarter of a century, preoccupied by Gaul and Africa and by internal affairs; but the consequences of the emergence of Pontus as a major power under Mithridates VI, who had become king in 120, were beginning to impinge.[89] In 108 Mithridates and Nicomedes III of Bithynia co-operated in the invasion and occupation of Paphlagonia: the Senate sent an embassy to investigate, which was ignored. But Rome's role in the region was acknowledged by embassies from both Bithynia and Pontus over subsequent years, and Diodorus (36.13) notes the presence of Mithridates' envoys towards the very end of the second century BC,

87. Plut. *Mar*. 31.1.
88. Plutarch (*Mar*. 31.2–3) records a meeting between Marius and Mithridates at which Marius said, 'Either try to be greater than the Romans, or do what you are told in silence.' The story is good, but may not be untrue; something is required to explain the resurrection of Marius' reputation so that he was elected augur in his absence.
89. On Mithridates' policy and activity, Sherwin-White, *Foreign Policy*, 102–8; B. McGing, *The Foreign Policy of Mithridates VI Eupator King of Pontus*, Leiden: Brill 1986; J. Hind, 'Mithridates', *CAH* 9², 1994, 129–64; Kallet-Marx, *Hegemony*, 239–60; B. McGing, 'Mithridates VI Eupator: victim or aggressor?', in J. Højte, ed., *Mithridates VI and the Pontic Kingdom*, Aarhus: University of Aarhus Press 2009, 203–16.

when Saturninus insulted them. Subsequent to Marius' trip, the Senate was called on to adjudicate the claims of both Bithynia and Pontus to Cappadocia; it rejected them, declaring Cappadocia free, and then supported the Cappadocians' choice of Ariobarzanes as their king. Ariobarzanes was soon deposed by Tigranes, the new king of Armenia and an ally of Mithridates, and restored by the Roman commander in Cilicia, which had been declared praetorian as part of the ongoing struggle against piracy.[90] Not only was this the resumption of land campaigning east of the Aegean after a gap of some decades and a firm move against Mithridates' ambitions; it also marked the first direct contact between Rome and the Parthians, with negotiations between Sulla and the Parthian king's representative Orabazos.[91] Although these did not generate any formal outcome, they do mark the point at which the interests of both powers were acknowledged to impinge on each other. In these years, too, with the end of the threat from the Cimbri and Teutones, the Spanish provinces became consular for the first time since Numantia.[92]

The outbreak of the Social War

Domestic politics during the 90s are not well attested, and the episodes which are recorded are, as a result, not easy to interpret. There is some evidence for strained relations with the non-Roman communities in Italy: in 95 the consuls Crassus and Scaevola passed a law, the *lex Licinia Mucia*, which prevented non-Romans from acting as though they were citizens.[93] It is not clear what actions followed from this measure: Cicero (*Off.* 3.47) draws a distinction between this measure and those which physically expelled non-Romans from the city. It is possible that it was a response to a request from, or at least aimed at assisting, the ruling elites in Italian

90. Diod. Sic. 36.15.1 (who notes that the tribune Saturninus insulted the envoys). The Roman commander was L. Cornelius Sulla (Plut. *Sull.* 5.3); the date of this command cannot be securely fixed, though Sulla had returned to Rome by 90.
91. Livy, *Per.* 70; Plut. *Sull.* 5.4–5; Vell. Pat. 2.24.3; see C. Lerouge, *L'image des Parthes dans le monde gréco-romain*, Stuttgart: Steiner 2007, 44–9; R. Shayegan, *Arsacids and Sasanians: Political Ideology in Post-Hellenistic and Late Antique Persia*, Cambridge: Cambridge University Press 2011, 315.
92. Richardson, *Hispaniae*, 156–60. There had been a resumption of campaigning in Spain under praetorian governors from 109, with triumphs in 107 and 98.
93. MRR 2.11; O. Baehrends, 'La "lex Licinia Mucia de ciuibus redigundis" de 95 a. C.', in S. Ratti, ed., *Antiquité et citoyenneté*, Besançon: Presses Universitaires Franc-Comtoises 2002, 15–33.

towns concerned about the erosion of their tax and recruitment base by migration to Rome. But its passage will have fostered division, both in the appeal to Roman voters' appreciation of citizenship as an exclusive privilege and in the resentment of those directly affected. The decision three years later by the censors – one of whom, Crassus, had been consul in 95 – to issue a joint decree expressing their displeasure at the existence in Rome of 'schools of Latin teachers of rhetoric', during a censorship otherwise notorious for the lack of co-operation between censors, also defies simple explanation.[94] But given the prominence of *Latini* in their decree, some link with the wider question of relations with non-Romans is possible. In the middle of the decade, recent history was re-examined when Norbanus was prosecuted, under Saturninus' *maiestas* law, for his actions during Caepio's trial in 103. The prosecutor, P. Sulpicius, was an ambitious and talented young orator closely linked to the *nobiles*;[95] but Norbanus was defended, successfully, by the consular M. Antonius, who, if we can believe Cicero, exploited the difficulty in defining the offence and placed Norbanus' actions in a long sequence of popular assertions of authority.[96] The case's outcome implied that violence was a legitimate aspect of Roman political life, which the *res publica* could absorb. Another important trial was that of the consular Rutilius Rufus on *repetundae* charges arising from his conduct as legate to Scaevola, who had governed Asia with conspicuous probity, to the disadvantage of Roman tax-collectors. Rutilius' conviction was widely understood as revenge, by the equestrian jury, on Scaevola, whose reputation and position made him immune.[97]

These scattered indications of tension between different groups coalesce in the year 91, which saw another tribune propose a systematic and ambitious programme of reform and face disastrous personal consequences. Unlike earlier examples, however, the tribune, Livius Drusus (son of C. Gracchus' rival in 122), was not clearly *popularis* in his sympathies, and although he died by violence during

94. Edict preserved by Suetonius: R. A. Kaster, *C. Suetonius Tranquillus De grammaticis et rhetoribus: edited with a Translation, Introduction, and Commentary*, Oxford: Oxford University Press 1995, on 25.2.
95. See below, Chapter 2.
96. Cicero made the Norbanus case the (literal) centrepiece of *De oratore* (2.197–204); see below, Chapter 2.
97. E. S. Gruen, *Roman Politics and the Criminal Courts, 149–78 B.C.*, Cambridge, MA: Harvard University Press 1968, 204–6; cf. R. M. Kallet-Marx, 'The trial of Rutilius Rufus', *Phoenix* 44, 1990, 122–39.

his year in office the catastrophe he engendered was external. In the autumn of 91 many of Rome's Italian allies revolted; the subsequent conflict, the Social War, engulfed much of the peninsula and was exceptionally destructive; its consequences arguably destroyed the *res publica* as it then existed. Despite its importance, it is extraordinarily difficult to identify the stages through which this crisis developed and the links between Drusus' extensive legislative programme and war with Italy. Many of the sources on Drusus connect him very firmly with the outbreak of the Social War, and after his assassination in the autumn of 91 he may well have become a convenient scapegoat for the conflict without necessarily having been responsible for its development.[98] Moreover, there is little opportunity to observe his laws in operation since they were repealed shortly before his death. However, an overall framework for Drusus' activities does emerge: as his father had done, he used the position of tribune in support of the Senate.[99]

The particular issue which Drusus attempted to address in favour of the Senate concerned the composition of juries at trials for extortion.[100] Resentment on the part of senators at being deprived of their forensic role in favour of the equestrians is easy to understand; and a number of specific trials had led senior figures, including the *princeps senatus* Scaurus, to seek change.[101] Less clear is the form that Drusus' solution took. Appian says that he proposed to enrol 300 equestrians in the Senate, and draw the new jurors from this greatly enlarged body.[102] This proposal is, however, suspiciously similar to Sulla's expansion of the Senate a decade later, a change that was accompanied by the creation of exclusively senatorial jurors, and it is difficult to see how a huge expansion of the Senate

98. See below, Chapter 4, for the Varian commission and Drusus' reputation.

99. Cicero sums up Drusus' tribunate as one 'undertaken on behalf of the Senate's authority' (*pro senatus auctoritate susceptus*, De or. 1.24); cf. *Mil.* 16; Diod. Sic. 37.10; Suet. *Tib.* 3.

100. P. A. Brunt, *The Fall of the Roman Republic and Related Essays*, Oxford: Oxford University Press 1988, 204–10.

101. In addition to the trial of Rutilius, Scaurus himself was prosecuted by the younger Servilius Caepio, and counter-prosecuted; Asconius links this directly with his support for Drusus (Asc., 21C). Cicero identifies both Scaurus and Crassus as Drusus' advisers at *Dom.* 50. The great orator Hortensius had begun his career in 95 with an (unsuccessful) *repetundae* prosecution (of L. Marcius Philippus).

102. App. *B Civ.* 1.35. Appian's narrative requires this move, since he understands Drusus' strategy to be the provision of equally balanced rewards, and this is the reward for the equestrians.

could have been welcome to its current members.[103] It is more likely that Drusus proposed mixed senatorial and equestrian juries.[104]

In order to gain popular support for a law on juries, Drusus put forward a land law, which appears to have revived earlier plans for citizen colonies, in Italy and Sicily, involving the redistribution of *ager publicus*.[105] The popular character of this measure is clear, and it may be through confusion with other tribunician programmes of reform that one source suggests he also passed a grain law.[106] These two or three pieces of legislation together make a coherent programme, with its aim being the enhancement of senatorial power through a reform of the courts, and the people's support elicited through land redistributions.[107]

Could a law extending the franchise to the Italians also have been part of this programme? Appian thinks it was, as an element in a balanced package, in which every group – senators, equestrians, allies and the Roman people as a whole – made gains in return for concessions.[108] But there are grounds for scepticism about Appian's narrative at this point.[109] Extending the franchise was deeply unpopular, as Gaius Gracchus had discovered, in a more limited context, thirty years previously: it is difficult to see how it made

103. I argue this point, in the context of Sulla's radicalism, at greater length below.
104. Livy, *Per.* 71. It is also difficult to understand Cicero's claim that equestrians became liable to prosecution for judicial bribery under Drusus' law (*Clu.* 153, *Rab. Post.* 16) if all Drusus' jurors were to be senators (albeit in some cases of very recent standing).
105. App. *B Civ.* 1.35–6.
106. Livy, *Per.* 71. Rickman, *Corn Supply*, 161–5, discusses the relationship between a possible *lex Liuia* and the *lex Octauia*.
107. Drusus' legislation was invalidated on the grounds that it breached the *lex Caecilia Didia* (Cic. *Dom.* 41), and included a ban on laws which included unrelated proposals. Drusus may have fallen foul of this law because he had put forward his measures together to ensure all parts passed; but other faults (such as failure to observe necessary time delays) may also have been involved; A. Lintott *Violence in Republican Rome*, 2nd edn, Oxford: Oxford University Press 1999, 142–3.
108. App. *B Civ.* 1.35. A late epitomator summarised Drusus' actions thus: 'The tribune of the people offered citizenship to the Latins, land to the poor, senatorial membership to the equestrians, and the law courts to the Senate. He was excessively generous, as he himself acknowledged, saying that he had left no one anything to distribute except the sky and the earth' (*De vir. ill.* 66) This passage raises the possibility that Drusus did offer citizenship to the Latins, a hypothesis which Mouritsen accepts (*Unification*, 120–2). The failure of such a law (there is no evidence that it passed) would then explain the plot to assassinate the consuls at the Latin festival (see below, n. 114). But it is not clear that even a limited citizenship proposal fits with Drusus' aims at the start of 91, and its presence in these sources can be explained as another example of the post mortem reception of Drusus.
109. These are articulated in detail in Mouritsen, *Unification*.

sense for Drusus to revive the issue as he attempted to win support for a judiciary law in the interests of the Senate. Moreover, the enfranchisement of Italy would have radically transformed the Roman state, not simply in terms of a massive increase in citizen numbers but also in the fundamental organisation of the army, taxation and law.[110] Its consequences, in fact, took over a generation to be worked out and implemented. Giving citizenship to the whole of Italy was simply too substantial a move to make sense in the context of Drusus' attempt to reinforce the Senate's power in relation to the equestrians.

If this is the case, then we need to explain the resolute connection in the sources between Drusus' tribunate, proposals to enfranchise the allies, and the outbreak of the Social War.[111] We can reasonably assume that Drusus began his planned legislative proposal as soon as he could, and that the judiciary and agrarian laws, at least, were therefore passed early in 91. By September, a crisis had developed, of which Cicero's De oratore provides a vivid glimpse.[112] The consul Philippus attacked Drusus' legislation at a contio during the Roman Games; Drusus in response summoned the Senate to meet on 13 September, at which Crassus attacked Philippus in a speech which, according to Cicero, brought on the fever that killed Crassus a few days later. The terms in which the dispute was articulated were much broader than the validity of Drusus' legislation: Philippus claimed that he could not work with the Senate he had, and needed another; Crassus, perhaps in response, called Philippus' status as consul into question.[113] When and how had this situation developed? Shortly before Philippus' contio he was, according to Cicero (De or. 1.24), attacking the position of the principes, and Drusus' tribunate was seriously weakened: but Cicero does not indicate how long Philippus' attacks had been going on. Something had changed to enable Philippus to launch a powerful campaign against legislation which had passed only a few months earlier. The intervention of the allies in domestic politics may provide the necessary factor.

There are some scraps of evidence to suggest increasing dissatisfaction at this time among Rome's Italian allies with their relation-

---

110. Mouritsen, Unification, 109–13.
111. App. B Civ. 1.35–7; Vell. Pat. 2.13–15; Livy, Per. 71 – notwithstanding significant differences of emphasis between these accounts.
112. Esp. Cic. De or. 1.24–6; 3.1–6.
113. Quint. Inst. 8.3.89, recording Crassus' comment to Philippus, 'Should I consider you a consul, when you don't think that I am a senator?'

ship with Rome. There are references to a plot to murder the consuls at the Alban mount during the Latin festival in the spring;[114] and to an embassy from Etrurian and Umbrian communities complaining about the agrarian law, because it threatened their use of *ager publicus*.[115] On their own, these are not robust. More solid is the deduction that, by late summer of 91, a number of allied communities were organising themselves for war against Rome. This is partly a matter of chronology: the allies were able to mobilise rapidly for war, and send an embassy to Rome before the end of the year. Their actions depended upon negotiations about co-operation and the exchange of hostages, which must have been going on for weeks, if not months, before the riots in Asculum at the end of the year which triggered the conflict. The other evidence for preparations is the presence of praetors or legates across Italy during 91: in addition to Servilius, who was killed at Asculum, a meeting between Domitius and a Marsic delegation, and the capture and escape of Sulpicius Galba in Lucania, are attested.[116] Their despatch is best explained as a response to rumours about allied discontent. If we reject the Appianic tradition that the allies wanted citizenship, then the most plausible cause of their discontent is the confiscation of *ager publicus* which allied communities – Latin and non-Latin – had been using. If Drusus' land commissioners had started work as soon as his law passed, then the anger of those dispossessed would have emerged over the summer: in time to initiate rebellion in the autumn.[117]

If we are prepared to follow this speculative line further, it is possible to suggest the issue which generated the internal debate at Rome in September 91: rumours of Italian sedition. This threat provides a context for the highly charged atmosphere that Cicero records. Drusus' position was already weakened, presumably because the Italian disturbance was regarded as his fault; Crassus' death removed from him a major supporter. Velleius, in his brief account of the events leading up to the Social War, places Drusus' citizenship proposal at this point in the narrative: 'Then, when things which had

---

114. Flor. 2.6.8; *De vir. ill.* 66; the latter ascribes the plot specifically to the Latins, plausibly given the location and event.
115. App. *B Civ.* 1.36.
116. Diod. Sic. 37.13 (Domitius; the only known Domitius of this period is the consul of 96, *MRR* 3.83); Livy, *Per.* 72 (Galba).
117. Mouritsen, *Unification*, 142–51, sets out this hypothesis in detail, and suggests that evidence of ill-feeling between Latins and Romans may have contributed to the Italian decision to act at this point. See also Roselaar, *Public Land*, 280–4.

started well were turning out badly, Drusus turned his attention to granting citizenship to the allies.'[118] This is a more convincing framework for a citizenship law, with the motive for so extreme a measure being the collapse of the rest of Drusus' programme. Perhaps he gambled that the allied threat would get the measure through the assembly, and he could then resurrect his programme, and his standing, on the support of a vast new client base. Such a move also offers a motive for his assassination.[119]

But a hypothetical citizenship proposal should not distract us from the central issue in 91, which was the way that a domestic issue engendered the collapse of Rome's system of Italian alliances.[120] In the fog which surrounds the outbreak of the Social War, Cicero provides welcome guidance. In *De officiis* (2.75) during a discussion of beneficence, he notes the vital importance of avoiding greed in the conduct of public affairs, exclaiming

> It is not yet 110 years since a law on *repetundae* was passed by Lucius Piso, there having been none before. But since then, there have been so many laws, each more stringent than the last, so many defendants, so many convicted, such a huge war stirred up through fear of the courts, such pillage and plunder of the allies in the absence of laws and courts, that we flourish through the weakness of others, not our own virtue.

Fear of the courts is, for Cicero, the cause of the Social War. His words are elliptical – we need to understand a train of thought in which this fear led Drusus to propose a change in the composition of the jury, which he made attractive by an agrarian law, which proved intolerable to the allies – but not unconvincing. The Social War thus emerged as the unintended and unforeseen result of internal conflict at Rome. It was an appalling consequence, and its destructiveness transformed the *res publica*.

118. Vell. Pat. 2.14: *tum conuersus Drusi animus, quando bene incepta male cedebant, ad dandam ciuitatem Italiae.*
119. Suspicion fell upon Philippus and Caepio: *De vir. ill.* 66
120. The link between Drusus and the extension of the citizenship may only have developed after his death; see below, Chapter 4.

CHAPTER 2

Domestic politics: violence and its accommodation

The formal elements of the Roman state, sketched above in the Introduction, provided the framework for political life; but it is evident that their operation in practice was neither smooth nor uncontentious, and that these faultlines exacerbated the conflicts of policy which emerged in this period. One source of instability was the internal dynamics of the senatorial class, whose competitiveness was constantly seeking new forms of expression. Another was the frequently uneasy relationship between the senatorial class as a whole and the Roman people.

Elite competition

The members of Rome's governing class were intensely competitive. Although birth was enormously important – to the extent that the phrase 'the Roman aristocracy' is not only meaningful but even useful – the prizes of public life did not spring directly from ancestry: they depended upon repeated electoral success, glittering performance in the roles thus allotted, and the appropriate expression of the admiration which should follow these achievements. The central paradox of Roman electoral politics was that the Roman people bestowed executive power on only a tiny proportion of itself, a group which showed a high degree of continuity from one generation to the next; but members of this group had no individual guarantee of personal success.

One way of ensuring the ongoing dominance of an elected oligarchy is to restrict who is eligible to stand for election; another is to control the voting patterns of the electorate. Both methods seem to have played a role at Rome, and both ultimately depended upon the way that public understanding of what constituted fitness to hold office was structured around experience of serving the *res publica* over generations. Formal hereditary qualifications had almost, though not quite, vanished by the second century: the patriciate retained exclusive access only to the priesthood of Jupiter and to the position of *princeps senatus*.[1] Eligibility to stand for other offices appears to have depended upon the decision of the presiding officer at the election, and almost certainly involved a criterion of equestrian wealth.[2] The pool of potential candidates was therefore small, and relatively stable from one generation to another. This is not to say that there is no change at all over time in the composition of the senatorial elite; families were vulnerable to eclipse because of male mortality, and inheritance law, which made equal distribution among surviving children the norm, complicated the preservation of senatorial wealth over time.[3] These difficulties in securing family dominance from one generation to the next meant that there was always room for men from families which had hitherto not participated in politics, but who had been enrolled by the census in the equestrian class, to stand for election and secure junior magistracies, but that further progression up the *cursus* to *imperium* holding offices was a rare achievement for such men; their sons were more likely to succeed.

The bias among the electorate towards candidates with senatorial ancestry is difficult to demonstrate directly, because evidence for the identities of those who were defeated is limited. In addition, few junior magistrates are directly attested: we can assume that praetors had held the quaestorship, but their colleagues in that office who did not progress further are generally not known, and it is precisely at this level that we would expect to see the success of 'new men', that is, those without senatorial ancestry. But if men from non-senatorial families did stand for election, albeit not in huge numbers, then their failure, in general, to reach the highest positions needs to be explained in terms of the voting patterns of the electorate. Why did voters prefer candidates whose male relatives had held office?

One answer to that question is the embeddedness of the past as

1. In relation to the consulship, indeed, patrician status was a potential disadvantage, since at least one consul each year had to be of plebeian standing. The tribunate of the plebs was restricted to those of plebeian standing.
2. This appears to have been 400,000 sesterces. Slight hesitation is appropriate, because the property qualification relates to membership of the Senate; nonetheless, given what appears to be a strong convention in this period that the censors included magistrates in the roll, one must assume that candidates met it.
3. J. Andreau and H. Bruhns, eds, *Parenté et stratégies familiales dans l'antiquité romaine*, Rome: École Française de Rome 1990; on adoption, H. Lindsay, *Adoption in the Roman World*, Cambridge: Cambridge University Press 2009, 169–73.

a positive model within Roman culture.[4] A reverence for antiquity, or what could be constructed as antiquity, was a powerful element in Roman culture, characterised most economically as an adherence to *mos maiorum*, the custom of the ancestors; and that general framework was supplemented by the claims of individual families to particular characteristics and distinct contributions to the *res publica*. Men who were descended from those who had held office in the *res publica* could appeal to the public aspects of their family's history, relying both on assumptions about the hereditability of successful public service and more prosaically on the advantage of name recognition among voters. The value of a political pedigree is indirectly attested by the existence in Roman political language of the term *nobilis*, which was used to describe a man whose ancestors had held high office, regardless of his own achievements.[5] The etymology of *nobilis*, indeed, connects the term with being known. At its simplest, this kind of popularity worked through the memories and experiences of the living: voters might be inclined to support the brothers and sons of those they had experienced as magistrates within Rome or as army commanders outside it. These memories were supplemented through public ceremonies which exposed the inhabitants of Rome to historically based narratives. Funerals were one important location for these exchanges: distinguished men were granted the privilege of a public funeral, which rehearsed not only the achievements of the dead man but also the contribution of his entire family through a speech delivered in the forum and through a procession of his male ancestors, impersonated by family members, or actors, wearing the robes associated with the highest office achieved and the relevant funeral mask.[6] More generally, stories

4. B. Linke and M. Stemmler, eds, *Mos Maiorum: Untersuchungen zu den Formen der Identitätsstiftung und Stabilisierung in der römischen Republik*, Stuttgart: Steiner 2000; A. Wallace-Hadrill, *Rome's Cultural Revolution*, Cambridge: Cambridge University Press 2008, 213–58.

5. There is debate over the precise qualifications for *nobilitas*, and its relationship to political *nouitas*: M. Gelzer, *The Roman Nobility*, trans. R. J. Seager, Oxford: Blackwell 1969; P. Brunt, 'Nobilitas and novitas', *JRS* 72, 1982, 1–17; D. R. S. Bailey, 'Nobiles and novi reconsidered', *AJPh* 107, 1986, 255–60; F. Goldmann, 'Nobilitas als Status und Gruppe – Überlegungen zum Nobilitätsbefriff der römischen Republik', in J. Spielvogel, ed., *Res publica reperta: Zur Verfassung und Gesellschaft der römischen Republik und des frühen Prinzipats*, Stuttgart: Steiner 2002, 45–66.

6. H. Flower, *Ancestor Masks and Aristocratic Power in Roman Culture*, Oxford: Oxford University Press 1996, is the fullest treatment. The development of personalised issues of coinage under the direction of young officials who might be planning subsequent electoral campaigns indicates the importance of identifiable family histories, even if the practical impact of coinage on opinions is hard to gauge.

attached themselves to the heroic figures of the past.[7] The gradual development of gladiatorial combat as a possible accompaniment to funeral ceremonies allowed personalised access to the popularity that could follow from organising public spectacles, a task otherwise linked with the tenure of office. And the presence within Rome of buildings identifiably linked with named individuals may also have advantaged their descendants. Nonetheless, the power of *mos maiorum* could be contested. In political culture, there was clearly also a rhetoric of newness which those without senatorial ancestry could employ, which emphasised individual virtue and the genuineness of achievement secured without the aid of family.[8]

Moreover, ancestry, even when present, needed to be supplemented by individual performance.[9] The aedileship attracted candidates, despite its not being an essential part of the *cursus honorum*, because it provided its holders with the opportunity to impress the electorate through the quality of display at the public festivals which constructed the Roman year.[10] The tribunate of the plebs provided an unparalleled opportunity to engage with the people on an individual basis, relying on the tribune's duty to help and protect individual citizens.[11] Personal valour was an esteemed quality: Scipio Aemilianus started his exceptional career through his willingness to serve as military tribune in Spain, and Tiberius Gracchus brought to the challenges of his tribunate a reputation from his conduct at Carthage and Numantia. And candidates drew on personal favours generated within the unequal hierarchical relationship of a patron and his clients.[12] The scope and coverage of patronage in Roman society can reasonably be debated, and could not have straight-

7. T. P. Wiseman, *Roman Drama and Roman History*, Exeter: Exeter University Press 1998; N. Horsfall, *The Culture of the Roman Plebs*, London: Duckworth 2003.

8. Cato the Elder was himself a powerful model of how to be 'new': E. Sciarrino, *Cato the Censor and the Beginnings of Latin Prose: From Poetic Translation to Elite Transcription*, Columbus: Ohio State University Press 2011. See also G. Farney, *Ethnic Identity and Aristocratic Competition in Republican Rome*, Cambridge: Cambridge University Press 2007.

9. Val. Max. 7.5, a collection of *repulsae*, electoral defeats, from the Republic, emphasises flaws of character and behaviour.

10. H. Flower, 'Spectacle and political culture in the Roman Republic', in H. Flower, ed., *The Cambridge Companion to the Roman Republic*, Cambridge: Cambridge University Press 2004, 322–43; F. Bernstein, *Ludi Publici: Untersuchungen zur Enstehung und Entwicklung der öffentlichen Spiele im republikanischen Rom*, Stuttgart: Steiner 1998.

11. Only a small proportion of each year's ten tribunes put forward legislation.

12. J-M. David, 'L'exercice du patronat à la fin de la République', in K-J. Hölkeskamp, ed., *Eine politische Kultur (in) der Krise?*, Munich: Oldenbourg 2009, 73–86.

forwardly explained or predicted the outcome of elections. But such networks existed, and were a factor influencing the way that individuals voted; opposition to the introduction of the secret ballot is difficult otherwise to explain. Candidates could and did also attempt to influence the outcome of votes by targeting the units within which votes were aggregated.[13] Although political discourse relied on a single homogenous *populus* (people), votes were secured in electoral and legislative contexts by knowing the characteristics of the citizen body in more detail.[14] And conduct during the election itself was vital. Candidates were expected to interact personally with their voters, displaying a genial openness and affability to all.

There were a number of limits on electoral competition. Public speech was not encouraged as means of campaigning, despite the importance of oratory in public life generally.[15] Bribery was illegal, and the limits on personal consumption embodied in various sumptuary laws may have been motivated in part by the Senate's collective desire to control spiralling competition between its members. Prior military defeat was surprisingly unimportant in determining progress to the consulship.[16] An additional factor in understanding the dynamics of electoral competition was the absence of political parties. Personal identity, however constructed, was essential precisely because there were no party identities for candidates to adopt. But in practice Roman politicians were not entirely atomised, and horizontal collaboration underpinned many electoral successes. The existence of such collaboration and its description as *amicitia*, 'friendship', cannot be disputed.[17] But the circumstances which contributed to the formation and duration of such bonds, the extent to which family and marriage connections determined political

13. The 35 tribes, in which every citizen was enrolled and which were the voting unit for tribunes of the people, quaestors and plebeian aediles, could be perceived to have distinct characteristics; cf. Lucilius 1131W–3W. On Tiberius Gracchus' innovative use of networks to mobilise voters in legislative assemblies, see H. Flower, 'Beyond the *contio*: political communication in the tribunate of Tiberius Gracchus', in C. Steel and H. van der Blom, eds, *Community and Communication: Oratory and Politics in Republican Rome*, Oxford: Oxford University Press 2013, 85–100.
14. On ancient analyses of the urban population in different groups, N. Purcell, 'The city of Rome and the *plebs urbana* in the late Republic', *CAH* 9², 1994, 644–88.
15. W. J. Tatum, 'Campaign rhetoric', in Steel and van der Blom, *Community and Communication*, 133–50.
16. N. Rosenstein, *Imperatores Victi: Military Defeat and Aristocratic Competition in the Middle and Late Republic*, Berkeley: University of California Press 1990.
17. On *amicitia* and Roman historiography, J. North, 'Democratic politics in Republican Rome', *P&P* 126, 1990, 3–21.

affiliations, the contribution made by intellectual and emotional sympathy to the existence of political friendships and the effectiveness of *amicitia* as a political tool were all extremely varied.[18] There were clearly moments at which a single group was able to exert a high degree of influence over the results of elections, as well as years in which contests were much more unpredictable.[19]

Elections mattered: they made and broke the careers of individuals and they asserted, every year, the place of the Roman people as the arbiter of public life. But the pursuit of personal distinction by members of the elite was not exhausted by electoral campaigning. Indeed, there were only a limited number of times that an individual would stand for election. Even a consul might only have had to be successful in three elections – that is, for quaestorship, praetorship and consulship – even if many also sought a more junior position such as a military tribuneship or a position with the mint before the quaestorship. Neither the aedileship, nor the tribunate of the plebs, for those who were eligible, was an essential part of the *cursus*, despite the obvious attractions of both offices. Re-election was not the normal practice; once an office had been secured, that was, or should have been, the end of the affair, and there were conventional limits, too, on the number of times someone could keep on trying despite electoral failure. Politicians eventually became free of dependence on the people for the continuation of their careers: hence the move away from *popularis* views discernible in so many careers. There was also a social and cultural value to *otium*, leisure, in contrast to *negotium*, the lack of leisure which arises from activity. But there were nonetheless both opportunities and expectations for the most senior ex-magistrates.

One of the striking features of Roman political life was the rela-

18. P. A. Brunt, *The Fall of the Roman Republic and Related Essays*, Oxford: Oxford University Press 1988, 351–81.
19. Münzer's exhaustive gathering of the material (*Roman Aristocratic Parties and Families*, trans. Ridley, R. T., Baltimore: Johns Hopkins University Press 1999) remains a valuable resource, even though many of the detailed conclusions he draws are deeply suspect. Models of electoral behaviour at Rome suffer from a lack of data, particularly after the end of Livy's surviving narrative, but it seems obvious that contests must have varied enormously from year to year, particularly those for the consulship. Sometimes two men will have emerged early as front-runners and the campaign will have been largely routine; on other occasions it will have gone to the last few centuries (with the further complication that a bitter contest for the one patrician slot may have gone along-side a clear plebeian favourite). One intriguing question is whether the aristocracy – and perhaps particularly the patriciate – attempted to stitch up contests, and avoid expensive campaigning, by agreeing on a candidate in advance.

tively small proportion of time that those in public life spent actually holding office. Our hypothetical consul described above would have held office for three years out of a public career, or at least of membership of the Senate, that could potentially last for a half-century or more. Within this confining framework, the intense competitiveness of the elite continually sought means of expression. Although the term of individual offices was a year only, the tenure of *imperium*, which accompanied the praetorship and consulship, could be extended: the device of prorogation was in regular use throughout the second century, particularly in the case of those whose *imperium* was exercised outside Italy. But prorogation was not automatic and required a decision by the Senate: individual distinction was constrained by the collective will. Intervention by the people in this process was possible, but unusual; to set against Marius' continued re-election to the consulship at the end of the second century we should compare the people's refusal to grant *imperium* to Aemilianus in 131, when war broke out with Aristonicus: a proposal to do so got the support of only two of the thirty-five tribes.[20] It is true that the situation in 131 was complicated by the fact that both consuls held religious positions which would normally have prevented the holder from leaving Rome: Crassus was *pontifex maximus*, and Valerius Flaccus priest of Mars (*flamen Martialis*). Crassus, indeed, as chief priest, threatened Flaccus with a fine if he abandoned his duties. Even in these circumstances, however, the people did not take the opportunity to intervene, and Crassus himself took the command.

Even with the possibility of prorogation, however, the tenure of *imperium* was necessarily brief and interrupted; hence the importance of personal *auctoritas*. If *imperium* was the right to command, guaranteed by the *res publica*, *auctoritas* was what ensured that a private individual's advice was followed and gave him a pre-eminent position within the Senate. It is in the formation and maintenance of *auctoritas* that the ongoing public prominence of individuals must be located. If *auctoritas* arose most straightforwardly from electoral success leading to public office, it was enhanced by achievements, particularly military ones. The most glamorous of these was the triumph, a ceremonial procession through Rome which displayed to the citizens both the means by which military victory had been won, in the presence of the army, and the results of that victory, with the

20. Cic. *Phil*. 11.18.

piles of booty and hordes of captives, and culminated in religious thanksgiving.[21] The triumph itself was both magnificent and ephemeral; the disposition of booty acquired in foreign campaigns could be given a permanent memorialising role, whether in the form of new buildings or by the public display of plundered works of art.

Another arena for the acquisition and display of prestige was membership of the various priestly colleges.[22] These positions arguably conferred more distinction even than reaching the consul-ship: they were limited in number and, since they were tenable for life, turnover was slow and irregular.[23] Moreover, until 104 entry was by co-option by existing members. Co-option appears to have ensured that the prizes of the priesthood were shared out in a way that was regarded as fair by those who might aspire to membership, whilst maintaining a system which made priesthoods more exclusive than even the highest magistracies, and thereby defined an inner core of the elite.[24]

None of these aspects of competition was new in the second half of the second century BC, despite constant if gradual inflationary pressure. The novelty of this period was the development of partici-pation by the people, which in turn depended on the willingness of some members of the elite to champion popular demands within the existing structures of elite competitiveness. The role of the people in the *res publica* was potentially very powerful because of its legisla-tive capacity, but in practice it invariably required elite leadership for its articulation. As a result, popular discontent was inseparable from divisions within the ruling elite. Conversely, the existence of widespread popular grievances became irresistible to members of a competitive elite searching for personal advantage. To that extent, we can sidestep unanswerable questions of personal conviction and look instead at the formal aspects of the *res publica* which facilitated

21. On the triumph, T. Itgenshorst, *Tota illa Pompa: Der Triumph in der römischen Republik*, Göttingen: Vandenhoeck & Ruprecht 2005; J-L. Bastien, *Le triumph romain et son utilisation politique à Rome aux trois derniers siècles de la République*, Rome: École Française de Rome 2007; M. Beard, *The Roman Triumph*, Cambridge, MA: Harvard University Press 2007; I. Östenberg, *Staging the World: Spoils, Captives and Representations in the Roman Triumphal Procession*, Oxford: Oxford University Press 2009.
22. G. Szemler, *The Priests of the Roman Republic: A Study of Interactions between Priesthoods and Magistracies*, Brussels: Latomus 1972.
23. A factor compounded by the young age of some of those co-opted, as is evident from J. Rüpke, *Fasti Sacerdotum*, Oxford: Oxford University Press 2008.
24. J. North, 'Family strategy and priesthood in the late Republic', in Andreau and Bruhns, *Parenté et stratégies familiales*, 527–43.

popularis political action. One possible narrative of the end of the Republic is of a century of attempts to translate popular support and *popularis* agitation into secure power within the state, and thus dislodge the authority of the collective senatorial elite, a narrative which culminated in Caesar's dictatorship; one revealing aspect of such an interpretation is the high status and political embeddedness of almost all those who pursued this approach. The Roman people was dependent on its rulers for its leaders.

The nature of the relationship between mass and elite is an important element in the current debate over the extent of democracy at Rome in the republican period. For Polybius, analysing the *res publica* as though it were a Greek city-state, the legislative and electoral role of Roman citizens, combined with their capacity to declare war and peace, established the democratic element in the Roman constitution. The Polybian analysis provided the starting point for Millar's seminal reinterpretation of Roman politics during the second century, which in turn generated an intense and ongoing debate on democracy and the Roman Republic.[25] What provides this debate with its vigour and importance is precisely the elusiveness and ambiguity of popular participation and the ways in which the role of the people was modified and controlled by the elite through a variety of formal and informal mechanisms. Thus, citizen assemblies passed laws and declared war: but an assembly, whether a formal voting assembly or an informal information-providing *contio*, could only be summoned by an elected official.[26] The results of legislative and electoral votes were determined not by a simple majority of votes, but by a majority of voting units, in a complex system which assigned citizens to different units for different kinds of votes according to age, residence and wealth. *Contiones* could only be addressed by individuals whom the presiding official had

25. F. Millar, 'The political character of the classical Roman Republic, 200–151 B.C.', *JRS* 74, 1984, 1–19, and 'Politics, persuasion and the people before the Social War (150–90 B.C.)', *JRS* 76, 1986, 1–11; M. Jehne, ed., *Demokratie in Rom? Die Rolle des Volkes in der Politik der römischen Republik*, Stuttgart: Steiner 1995; H. Mouritsen, *Plebs and Politics in the Late Roman Republic*, Cambridge: Cambridge University Press 2001; E. Flaig, *Ritualisierte Politik: Zeichen, Gesten und Herrschaft im Alten Rom*, 2nd edn, Göttingen: Vandenhoeck & Ruprecht 2004; R. Morstein-Marx, *Mass Oratory and Political Power in the Late Roman Republic*, Cambridge: Cambridge University Press 2004; K-J. Hölkeskamp, *Reconstructing the Roman Republic: An Ancient Political Culture and Modern Research*, Princeton: Princeton University Press 2010.
26. F. Pina Polo, *Contra Arma Verbis: Der Redner vor dem in der späten römischen Republik*, Stuttgart: Steiner 1996; D. Hiebel, *Rôles institutionel et politique de la contio sous la république romaine*, Paris: de Boccard 2009.

called on to speak, and an assembly could vote only on what was put to it: amendments from the floor simply did not happen. Citizen assemblies elected magistrates; but the choice was from those whose candidacy was approved by the presiding officer. One way of under-standing popular participation in this system that has been put forward is as an element in a process which demonstrated consen-sus: free choice between limited options confirmed the status quo of narrow aristocratic government whilst enacting the importance of the people.[27]

The consensus model explains a lot about Republican political culture: its emphasis on display and performance, the way in which the search for distinction is expressed by individual members of the elite through competition in well-defined genres, and even the apparent reluctance of many politicians to differentiate themselves in ideological terms from their competitors and the capacity of the system to withstand for so long a period the absence of anything which could be described as a 'government'. Arguably it encapsu-lates the aspiration of the ruling elite rather than the reality: this is how that elite wished political life to operate, and often it succeeded in making it happen. But there are enough occasions between 133 and 91, and again after 70, when consensus was replaced by clashes, often violent, between the Roman people and members of the Senate, to show that the people could not always successfully be constrained.[28] There were expected forms and outcomes for encoun-ters between people and elite which did indeed confirm that the contingent events of political life matched a natural order in which magistrates acted, the Senate advised and the people approved. But as we saw in the previous chapter, encounters frequently went wrong. The argument of this chapter is that these challenges to sena-torial government arose from widespread discontent among Roman citizens; but it is undeniable that the public and unscripted nature of many of the elements of public life enhanced opportunities for the unexpected and unwelcome. Public speech, in particular, was an unavoidable task for the political classes, and the process of address-ing an audience of citizens created space in which enthusiasm, hostility and everything in between could be displayed. When

---

27. Flaig, *Ritualisierte Politik*, 181–212; K-J. Hölkeskamp, *Senatus Populusque Romanus: Die politische Kultur der Republik*, Stuttgart: Steiner 2004 (cf. M. Crawford, 'Reconstructing what Roman Republic?', *BICS* 54, 2011, 105–14).
28. R. Morstein-Marx, '"Cultural hegemony" and the communicative power of the Roman elite', in Steel and van der Blom, *Community and Communication*, 29–47.

Scipio Aemilianus returned from Numantia, Papirius Carbo cross-examined him at a *contio* in the hope that Aemilianus would express regret for the death of Tiberius Gracchus. But Aemilianus confounded Carbo's expectations and claimed that Gracchus had been killed lawfully. The audience reacted with anger; Aemilianus dismissed it with the words, 'Let those to whom Italy is a stepmother be silent ... you cannot make me fear people whom I imported in chains.'[29] In 129, the meeting ended at this impasse; we might suspect that later, violence would have been the response.

It is also significant that despite a powerful rhetoric of constitutional stability, many aspects of political practice underwent change during the latter part of the second century. The secret ballot was introduced; standing courts, with senatorial or equestrian juries, increasingly replaced trials in front of the whole citizen body; and military service was separated from the possession of property. These changes do not form a narrative which privileges one element of the state over another, but rather indicate the variety of pressures and interest groups that were moulding the *res publica* during this period.

In 146, all voting was public. Between 139 and 107, a series of tribunician laws introduced the secret ballot.[30] In addition, in 119 the physical environment in which voting took place was altered, apparently to reduce the opportunities for those not voting to stand nearby and attempt to influence voters' choices.[31] These inevitably undermined the direct and testable influence of the elite on voting practices, and thereby seemed to undermine the dominance of the elite.[32] In Cicero's dialogue *De legibus*, his brother Quintus follows

29. Val. Max. 6.2.3; Vell. Pat. 2.4.4, *De vir. ill.* 58.8 is similar; Cicero knew the 'justly killed' (*iure caesum*) response (*De or.* 2.106, *Mil.* 8).
30. Four laws were involved, each introducing the secret ballot to a different kind of voting: 139, *lex Gabinia* (elections); 137, *lex Cassia* (all popular trials except *perduellio*); 131 or 130, *lex Papiria* (legislation); 107, *lex Coelia* (*perduellio*); these are listed and briefly described in Cicero's *De legibus* (3.35–6). See further A. Yakobson, 'The secret ballot and its effects in the late Roman Republic', *Hermes* 123, 1995, 426–42; F. Salerno, *Tacita libertas: l'introduzione del voto segreto nella Roma repubblicana*, Naples: Edizioni Scientifiche Italiane 1999.
31. The proposer was Marius, during his tribunate, and this law provoked the opposition of both consuls, whom Marius then threatened with imprisonment: Plut. *Mar.* 4.2–4.
32. The failure to repeal the ballot laws is hardly to be taken as evidence that the elite were indifferent to their passage: once in place, it is difficult to see how repeal could have won support (cf. Yakobson, 'Secret ballot', 427–9). Crawford, 'Reconstructing what', 110, draws attention to the capacity of the secret ballot to conceal divisions within the electorate.

a description of the ballot laws at Rome with a reminiscence of the Cicerones' grandfather, who resisted (unsuccessfully) the introduction of the secret ballot at Arpinum, and was commended for his efforts by Aemilius Scaurus: 'I wish, Marcus Cicero, that with your courage and virtue you preferred to operate at the top of politics, with us, than in a small town.'[33] However, it is difficult to see any obvious changes in the character of those elected in subsequent years.[34] The emergence of standing courts contributed to the Senate's capacity to control the individual ambition of its members; and one eventual consequence of military reform, intended as a popular measure, was to compel commanders to gain popular support as a means to successful agrarian legislation.[35]

Another important development in constitutional practice was the so-called 'last decree'. This measure is first attested in 121 when the Senate instructed the consul Opimius to see that the state suffered no harm. In that context, it can be seen as a correction to the disorder of 133, when the Senate was split between the consul and the *pontifex maximus*; Opimius ensured that this repression of a Gracchus emerged from the authority of the Senate and reaffirmed that body's collective responsibility for the *res publica*. In so doing, he created a powerful addition to the Senate's arsenal in a struggle to extend its collective authority at the expense of both people and magistrates. If it is plausible to see the development of the emergency decree as a replacement, in some sense, for the emergency powers of the dictator, then we have here a shift from individual to collective, albeit one whose legitimacy remained contested throughout the period.[36] In that respect, the 'last decree' can be linked to the various measures the Senate introduced to control competition and displays of pre-eminence, including legislation on consumption and extortion. An ideology of individual distinction was balanced, in Roman political culture, against the collective *auctoritas* of the Senate.

33. Cic. *Leg.* 3.36. At *Amic.* 41 Cicero has Laelius exclaiming at the 'disaster', *labes*, caused by changes in voting.
34. E. S. Gruen 'The exercise of power in the Roman Republic', in A. Molho, K. Raaflaub and J. Emlen, eds, *City States in Classical Antiquity and Medieval Italy*, Ann Arbor: University of Michigan Press 1991, 251–67, at 259.
35. In addition, a modified form of voting was introduced in 104 to choose new members of the priestly colleges: 17 of the 35 tribes voted, and candidates could only be nominated by an existing member of that college. This *lex Domitia* also prevented more than one member of family from belonging to the same college.
36. T. W. Hillard '"Res publica" in theory and practice', in K. Welch and T. Hillard, eds, *Roman Crossings: Theory and Practice in the Roman Republic*, Swansea: Classical Press of Wales 2005, 1–48, at 22.

One particular aspect of senatorial self-regulation that deserves attention is the censors' failure to renew the status of existing senators. Expulsion was a striking event, triggered by criminal conviction, or to be justified by notable moral failing: but it was at the discretion of the censors. There were eleven pairs of censors between 149 and 91 and five of them are recorded as removing senators: the most extensive such exercise was in 115, when Metellus Diadematus and Domitius Ahenobarbus expelled 32, or some 10 per cent of the total body.[37]

Issues and ideology

In 123 BC during his first tribunate Gaius Gracchus addressed the Roman people at a *contio*:

> Quirites, if you wish to employ your wisdom and courage, you will find, even if you search, that none of us comes forward here without his price. All of us, who make speeches, are looking for something, nor does anyone, for any reason, come before you unless he may take something away. I myself, who am making a speech to you in order that you may increase your tax revenue, and thereby be able to manage your benefits and the state better, do not come forward free of charge; but I am seeking from you not money, but a good reputation, and advancement. Those who come forward to speak against the measure are looking not for advancement from you, but for money from Nicomedes; and those who speak in its favour are looking not for a good reputation with you, but for reward and a return for their personal affairs from Mithridates; and those who, from the same order and group, are silent – well these are the cleverest of all: for they are getting a reward from everyone, and are deceiving everyone. You offer them your good opinion, since you think they have no part in these affairs, and the embassies from the kings offer them huge quantities of cash, because they think they are keeping quiet on their behalf – just as, in Greece, when a tragedian thought he was

37. Their expulsions included one of the previous year's consuls, C. Licinius Geta, who was himself censor in 108; on Geta, see T. P. Wiseman, *Remembering the Roman People*, Oxford: Oxford University Press 2009, 33–57. Other expulsive censors were Scipio Aemilianus in 142 (Cass. Dio fr. 76, suggesting that his colleague Mummius prevented some; there was open disagreement between the two censors [Val. Max. 6.4.2, Cic. *De or.* 2.268]); Metellus Macedonicus in 131 (who attempted to expel the tribune Atinius Labeo, who counter-attacked vigorously); Metellus Numidicus in 102, who attempted to expel Saturninus and Glaucia; and Valerius Flaccus and Antonius in 97, who expelled the tribune Duronius. These incidents are recorded because there was resistance; how far censors regularly eliminated individuals in a quieter fashion is difficult to tell.

doing extremely well when he got a talent for one play, and Demades, the best speaker in his community, is said to have replied to him: 'Does it seem wonderful to you, to have got a talent by speaking? I got ten talents from the king – for keeping quiet.' And so now those men get the greatest rewards by keeping quiet.[38]

This quotation would deserve attention simply as one of the longest of the surviving non-Ciceronian fragments of oratory from the Republican period; but it also shines a revealing light on the nature of political interaction and debate towards the end of the second century. Gaius' presentation of the relationship between *populus* and politician is firmly practical: the Roman people vote self-interestedly and choose between competing options on that basis. He assumes that the Roman people should have direct access to the benefits of imperial rule, the *commoda*; and that its task is 'to run the state', *rem publicam administrare*. It was a brave, and probably unsuccessful, politician who directly challenged either assumption: popular sovereignty was always the basis of legitimate activity. But, as we have seen, the organisation of political life left scope in practice for elite control. The development of a politics of genuine engagement with popular grievances, in distinction from the long-standing tradition of aristocratic benevolence, is a crucial reconfiguration of this period, and one led by the Gracchi.[39]

The dominant features of this form of political action, which can be described as *popularis*, were legislation offering material benefit to the people as a whole, and direct popular action, particularly over matters which were normally dealt with by the Senate. It provoked violent repression, on occasion, from Senate and magistrates, and as a result violence became emblematic of *popularis* activity.[40] *Popularis* described a technique of political action and a belief about the practical location of authority; it was not a party or even a faction, though *popularis* tribunes were aware of their predecessors

38. Gell. NA. 11.10. On the background to these events, R. M. Kallet-Marx, *Hegemony to Empire: The Development of the Roman Imperium in the East from 148 to 62 B.C.*, Berkeley: University of California Press 1995, 110–11.
39. Wiseman, *Remembering*, 5–32. Tiberius Gracchus was, of course, not the first politician to assert popular sovereignty or put forward legislation unwelcome to the majority of the Senate. But the nature of his death did create a new model. On the definition of *popularis*, M. Robb, *Beyond Populares and Optimates: Political Language in the Late Republic*, Stuttgart: Steiner 2010.
40. A. Lintott, *Violence in Republican Rome*, 2nd edn, Oxford: Oxford University Press 1999; W. Nippel, *Public Order in Ancient Rome*, Cambridge: Cambridge University Press 1995.

and planned their actions accordingly. There are examples of politicians who adopted *popularis* methods early in their careers – at precisely the point where they were seeking electoral success in the tribal assembly – before moderating their views and ascending further up the *cursus*.[41] We might, indeed, wish to distinguish between such activity and the systematic programmes of a much smaller number of tribunes, which tended to end in fatal violence because their attempts to solve major problems provoked the opposition of powerful vested interests.[42] The attractiveness of *popularis* measures was related to the success of the *res publica*; many of the assertions of popular sovereignty arise at precisely the times when senatorial decisions produced bad consequences. But care is needed in employing binary divisions. One of the most striking moments of the period is the stripping of Cn. Servilius Caepio's *imperium* in 105 BC by the people. Yet such a move required a vote by the centuriate assembly (*comitia centuriata*), which voted in groups determined by property ownership and could not be summoned by a tribune of the plebs; the measure must therefore have been proposed and the assembly summoned by the consul, P. Rutilius, whose sympathies were not *popularis*.[43] We are not dealing with a 'senatorial party' versus a 'popular party', and the dynamics of an individual senator's relationship with the people was a matter of choice, and likely to change over time.

The material benefits which *popularis* politicians offered the Roman people were, above all, land and food. Land was the issue which dominated Tiberius' tribunate, and agrarian legislation became a marker of *popularis* politicians. The ownership of public land was contentious because it put at odds those who found themselves competing for this resource; but what was at stake, and can be presented as relevant to the debate, went much further than the economic self-interest of different individuals and classes. Given that the Roman army was a citizen militia, and service in it was dependent until Marius' reforms upon meeting a property qualification, Tiberius could present his action as a response to a pressing matter

41. For example, the elder M. Livius Drusus (cos. 112) or L. Licinius Crassus (cos. 95). Indeed, there is nothing to suggest that that was not Tiberius Gracchus' plan.
42. A distinction drawn implicitly by Wiseman, *Remembering*, 30: 'One might have thought that the deaths of Tiberius and Gaius Gracchus, Saturninus, Livius Drusus, Sulpicius, and Clodius were prima facie evidence that being a *radical tribune* [my italics] was not likely to bring you to the consulship'; Livius Drusus is arguably the odd man out here.
43. Münzer, *Roman Aristocratic Parties*, 275.

of public safety, namely the difficulty in recruiting soldiers. Thus demography is crucial: an increasing population, or one which is too large for its resources, generates a quite different set of social and economic conditions from one which is shrinking or has access to adequate resources. The difficulty in the case of Rome is that it appears to be impossible to establish the size of the population, even in the broadest terms: although the census figures survive, their interpretation cannot securely be established. The latest figure for the Republican period gives around 900,000 citizens in the census of 70-69 BC; Augustus' *Res Gestae* records over 4 million in 28 BC. Since it is inconceivable that the Roman population quadrupled over this period, the method of counting must have changed between censuses, or one or more censuses contained gross inaccuracies. However, we have no solid evidence to support any particular explanation for these anomalies: consequently, it remains unclear whether we should accept a 'low' or a 'high' population count or, indeed, something in between.[44]

Many of the problems of the second half of the second century can appear as problems generated by a shortage of manpower, particularly free rural manpower: difficulties in recruitment, leading ultimately to the abandonment of a land qualification for army service; rural depopulation, as allegedly witnessed by Tiberius Gracchus; and a marked increase in the population of Rome itself. Behind this, it has been argued, are the consequences of extended overseas campaigning, which bankrupted free peasant proprietors, driving citizens from the land to Rome and out of the pool of potential army recruits and consolidating rural landholding in the hands of the wealthy.[45] Various aspects of this picture, including the increasing dependence on large slave-run estates, the connection between army recruitment and overall population, and the reliability of the census figures, have been challenged.[46] More recently, the

---

44. W. Scheidel, 'Roman population size: the logic of the debate', in L. de Ligt and S. Northwood, eds, *People, Land and Politics: Demographic Developments and the Transformation of Roman Italy, 300 BC–AD 14*, Leiden: Brill 2008, 17–70, offers an introduction to the problem; see also E. lo Cascio, 'The size of the Roman population: Beloch and the meaning of the Augustan census figures', *JRS* 84, 1994, 23–40; N. Morley, 'The transformation of Italy, 225–28 B.C.' *JRS* 91, 2001, 50–62.
45. See Brunt, *Fall*, 240–80.
46. Army recruitment, J. Rich, 'The supposed Roman manpower shortage of the later second century A.D.', *Historia* 32, 1983, 287–331; L. de Ligt, 'Roman manpower resources and the proletarianization of the Roman army in the second century B.C.', in L. de Blois and E. lo Cascio, eds, *The Impact of the Roman Army (200 B.C.–A.D. 476)*,

whole model has been systematically scrutinised by Rosenstein, who reaches a radically different conclusion. High mortality in the second century wars of conquest enabled high levels of fertility, which in turn produced a rising population overall; war did not bankrupt peasant proprietors, but it did, by abstracting labour in the form of their sons, squeeze their capacity to accumulate surpluses over time. The rural population was growing, and becoming poorer.[47] Rosenstein's argument explains both why Tiberius Gracchus' proposals received such support, and why they turned out to be so ineffective and, ultimately, destructive. The calculations of Tiberius and his aristocratic supporters were based on perceptions of a declining rural population, perceptions fuelled by difficulties in recruitment, lower census figures in the recent past, and the vast growth in the size of Rome, as people moved from the countryside to the city. But the deeply unattractive nature of the war in Spain may explain the census figures, as individuals evaded the census in order to avoid military service; and an increasing population could support the growth in Rome as well as maintain pressure on resources in the countryside. There was an appetite for land; to such an extent, as rapidly became clear, that the resources of the Roman state would be stretched to breaking point in attempting, and failing, to meet them.

Furthermore, the use of public land had profound implications for the relationship between Rome and its allies in Italy. The action of the commissioners was deeply resented by the allies, as their appeal for help in 129 testifies. The precise nature of their grievance is less clear, but one plausible scenario is that the commissioners were over-zealous in designating land as 'public land' and that they preferred to dispossess Italian occupiers rather than Roman ones. The pitiful state of our knowledge about *ager publicus* makes it rather difficult to go further. But the appeal in 129 appears to have been successful; the relationship between Roman and other Italian elites was still effective. In 91, however, such levers appear not to have been effective.[48]

Tiberius Gracchus' land law was motivated by what he regarded as the needs of the *res publica*. His solution involved offering

Leiden: Brill 2007, 3–20; on agricultural slavery, U. Roth, *Thinking Tools: Agricultural Slavery between Evidence and Models*, London: Institute of Classical Studies 2007.
47. N. Rosenstein, *Rome at War: Farms, Families and Death in the Middle Republic*, Chapel Hill: University of North Carolina Press 2004; see also L. de Ligt 'Poverty and demography: the case of the Gracchan land reforms', *Mnemosyne* 57, 2004, 725–57.
48. See below, Chapter 3.

commoda to the Roman people, and the provision of material benefits continued to be a key element in *popularis* programmes. Widespread poverty and inequality meant there was always a supportive audience for ameliorative proposals.[49] But it is not obvious that all adult male citizens would have wished to take up land allotments, and it is likely that this awareness contributed to Gaius Gracchus' corn law. By making subsidised grain available in Rome, Gaius was ensuring that all citizens could benefit from his proposals; and by so doing he created another staple of *popularis* politics. Moreover, the provision of *commoda* could now be used to ensure support for other proposals which did not need to have a *popularis* flavour. Such is its role in 122, when Drusus' colony proposals helped to draw support away from Gaius Gracchus, and in 91, when his son used a land law to create support for senatorial juries. L. Licinius Crassus' support for the foundation of Narbo in 118 is similarly identified as a *popularis* move; Crassus went on to hold the consulship and censorship, and eloquently articulate the case for senatorial government.[50] A good example of the complexity of *popularis* politics is the trial of Norbanus in the *maiestas* court in the 90s for his violence at the trial of Caepio in 103 when he was tribune, including an attack on two other tribunes. Thus his offence – under Saturninus' law on diminishing the majesty of the people – could be presented by his prosecutor Sulpicius as an assault on popular rights. Norbanus was defended by M. Antonius, consul in 99 and censor in 97, who had as consul taken a firm line against the *popularis* tribune Titius; and Sulpicius himself would in a few years move decisively to a *popularis* stance himself.[51]

The role of the people, in practice, developed significantly during

49. On living standards at Rome, A. Scobie, 'Slums, sanitation and mortality in the Roman world', *Klio* 68, 1986, 399–433; J. Toner, *Popular Culture in Ancient Rome*, Cambridge: Polity 2009, 62–74. Personal benefit could, and did, sit alongside appeals to group identity and reputation: see M.Jehne, 'Feeding the plebs with words: the significance of senatorial public oratory in the small world of Roman politics', in Steel and van der Blom, *Community and Communication*, 49–62.

50. Cic. *Brut.* 160; *Clu.* 140; *De or.* 2.223. On Crassus' career, E. Fantham, *The Roman World of Cicero's De Oratore*, Oxford: Oxford University Press 2004, 26–48; in addition to Crassus' contribution in 91, he supported Caepio's law on senatorial juries in 106.

51. Cic. *De or.* 2.48; the account of the Norbanus case emphasises Antonius' personal link to Norbanus (who had been his quaestor) to justify the defence. On Titius, A. Russell, 'Speech, competition and collaboration: tribunician politics and the development of popular ideology', in Steel and van der Blom, *Community and Communication*, 101–15, at 111–12; on Sulpicius, see below, Chapter 4.

this period: *popularis* politics emerged both as a consistent set of principles and actions and as an effective technique. Conflict between the people (and their leaders) and the Senate was frequent, and the Senate developed new mechanisms to control the people through force, when peaceful attempts to maintain consensus failed. Foreign policy failures by the Senate contributed to the people's confidence in asserting its role and responsibilities. The figure of Marius pointed forward to the close relationship between voters and leaders that was to re-emerge as a significant factor after Sulla; and his decision to enrol soldiers without regard for their census qualification broke the connection between property-ownership and the military safety of the *res publica*, only to recreate it in a new form with the prospect of land for veterans. His alliance with Saturninus is the first example of a trend which becomes very significant towards the end of the Republican period.

Another major challenge to the Senate in these four decades was the development of the equestrian class as a group with distinct political aims. This had its origins in two of Gaius Gracchus' innovations: the establishment of non-senatorial juries for *repetundae* trials, and the sale of the right to collect tax in Asia to tax-farming companies. The context of these measures is discussed in Chapter 3, below; the domestic consequence was to turn the equestrians into a distinct group with its own interests.[52] With this change comes a change in the dynamic of *repetundae* trials. Whereas defendants, by virtue of their seniority, could offer other senators a wide range of potential favours in exchange for acquittal, the possibilities with equestrians were much fewer; and bribery, or at least allegations of bribery, now become much more frequent in judicial contexts. And whilst only a small proportion of the equestrian class is likely to have been directly involved in Asian tax-farming, grievances formed there could take on a much wider relevance. There is a strong tradition that Rutilius, who was convicted of extortion in 92 BC, was the victim of an equestrian jury because he aided the governor of Asia, Q. Mucius Scaevola, in stopping abuses by tax-farmers. Gracchus may well simply have been seeking to establish a check on senatorial corruption without any intention of creating a third force in political life, but his changes contributed to the prestige of the equestrian class, and gave individuals new opportunities to enrich themselves.

---

52. Polyb. 6.17 emphasises the importance of public contracting, but does not distinguish the equestrians as a group particularly affected by it.

The development of a tripartite instead of a bipartite political system was arguably even more important than the tensions between people and Senate; the Senate's reluctance to have the behaviour of its members judged by outsiders led directly to the miscalculations which sparked the Social War.

The common thread to domestic politics in this half-century is the reaction of the Senate to perceived threats to its authority. (Whether or not they are judged to be overreaction depends more on the historian's assumption of the ideal location of power than on any objective measure.) The fundamental role of the people, in theory, in the organisation of the *res publica* was not subject to debate; and the Senate's resort to violence in 133, 121 and 100 was triggered by the attempts of the Gracchi and Saturninus to retain their power, rather than directly by the passage of the legislation they proposed. However much members of the Senate may have disliked the sharing of *commoda* and the content of *popularis* programmes, their real fear was the combination of popular power with identifiable leaders and the threat of monarchical rule. Thus we should not be surprised at the attentiveness of many members of the ruling elite to the popular will, or at their use of *popularis* techniques. When Crassus led the opposition to Glaucia's law on equestrian juries, he exclaimed to the Roman people at a *contio*: 'Take us from our wretched state, take us from the jaws of those whose cruelty cannot be satisfied by our blood; do not allow us to serve anyone, except all of you as whole, whom we both can and should serve.'[53]

The novelty that disturbed Crassus was the power of the equestrian class; by contrast, the authority of the people over the Senate was acceptable. But citizenship – that is, belonging to the Roman people – was an exclusive privilege. The acquiescence of the Senate in that model, and its failure to extend the citizenship during this period or revisit the nature of its relationship with non-Roman Italians, turned out to be serious errors of judgement.

53. Cic. *De or.* 1.225.

CHAPTER 3

Imperial power: failure and control

When Mummius, the conqueror of Corinth, was organising the transport back to Italy of the plundered works of art, he included in the movers' contracts a notable clause: if anything got lost in transport, the contractors were liable to replace it new. So the story goes.[1] The point of the story and the reason to keep telling it might seem obvious: it encapsulates, in neat comic form, the appalling ignorance of the Romans when faced with Greek cultural and aesthetic achievements, through the exemplary figure of a conquering Roman general who does not understand that the value of a work of art inheres in its unique history and identity. On this level, the joke serves as a form of resistance, and it is effective enough in such terms to survive even when stripped of a geographical and historical context.

But the story is perhaps doing slightly more than poking fun at stupid Romans. The context in which Velleius tells it is revealing: he uses it to contrast Mummius with the other great conqueror of 146, Scipio Aemilianus. Scipio was a cultivated man, devoted to learned activities; the writers Polybius and Panaetius were part of his entourage. But Velleius concludes his comparison by exclaiming that it would have been more advantageous to the *res publica* if ignorance about such matters had continued to be the norm. Mummius' failure to engage with Greek culture protects him from its corrupting effects; on Velleius' presentation, therefore, he is an unlikely hero, willing to pay the price, in terms of the loss of aesthetic gratification, of preserving true Roman character.

Mummius' own views about the value of the booty he was having crated up is hardly, therefore, likely to emerge from this freighted cultural context. But we know enough about what he *did* with his spoils to suspect that we are in fact dealing with a man skilled in

---

1. Vell. 1.13; it surfaces, minus names and with Mummius transformed into the ubiquitous *skholastikos*, in the *Philogelos* (78).

negotiating such testing interactions – or with skilled advisers. Some of the booty of Corinth did not even leave Greece: Mummius commemorated his campaigns by a number of dedications in cities in Achaea and Boeotia as well as at major and minor sanctuaries. As Kallet-Marx notes, this liberality served two functions: Mummius was demonstrating Rome's participation in the Hellenistic world, whilst leaving stark – and untouchable – memorials throughout mainland Greece of the expectations which Rome had of its participation and of the actions it was prepared to take if disappointed.[2] In Italy, too, Mummius spread the spoils around after their presentation at his triumph: surviving inscriptions testify to dedications in many towns outside Rome, including some which did not have Roman citizenship.[3] Much, too, remained spectacularly in Rome.

Mummius' keen awareness of the impact of giving booty away should alert us to another context in which his alleged concern over transport can be located, namely a debate over the appropriate use of the objects which Rome acquired through conquest. The tension between personal gain and public participation runs right through the division of the spoils: booty belonged in some sense ultimately to the *res publica*, but the *imperium*-holder had great freedom to do as he saw fit with his share, including giving it away to those who deserved reward.[4] Public display of captured artworks was not its only possible destination. By choosing to make gifts to communities rather than individuals, and to have the giving publicly commemorated, Mummius was also making a statement about where he stood on this issue. Not for him the private and exclusive enjoyment of such artefacts in the manner of some of his contemporaries. And we can connect the shipping joke to this stand, if we see here demonstration of a scrupulous concern for what belongs to the *res publica*. Everything must be accounted for; restitution must be forthcoming in case of loss.[5] The possessions of the Greeks are, for Mummius,

2. R. M. Kallet-Marx, *Hegemony to Empire: The Development of the Roman Imperium in the East from 148 to 62 B.C.*, Berkeley: University of California Press 1995, 89–90.

3. L. Yarrow, 'Lucius Mummius and the spoils of Corinth', *SCI 25*, 2006, 57–70.

4. J. B. Churchill '*Ex qua quod vellent facerent*: Roman magistrates' authority over *praeda* and *manubiae*', *TAPhA 129*, 1999, 85–115.

5. We can compare here the alleged loss of the Tolosa treasure in transit to Rome later in the century, and the younger Cato's meticulous concern over the transport to Rome of the treasure of the king of Cyprus in 58–56. I. Östenberg, *Staging the World: Spoils, Captives and Representations in the Roman Triumphal Procession*, Oxford: Oxford University Press 2009, 89, notes that all spoils of war, including works of art, were regarded as having a cash value, and that this may have been the point of Mummius' conditions.

a way to demonstrate Roman control over Romans as well as over others.

Mummius can emerge, then, from the spoils of Corinth, not as a bumbling ignoramus, but as an alert political communicator, aware of the significance of his decisions in this field and consciously locating himself within an established tradition of the handling of the spoils of war. We may suspect the importance of the elder Cato as a role model in opening up this path through the labyrinth of the relationship between Rome and the Hellenistic world; and we can see how it is modified and challenged by competing approaches to the problem. Military victory, for a Roman commander, generated a series of choices about what to do with the material that came, as a result, into Roman possession. Large-scale transfer of property was a normal consequence of military victory in antiquity, but it was a particularly pronounced aspect of Roman practice because of the phenomenon of *deditio in fidem*, a form of surrender which involved the universal transfer of property from conquered to conqueror. The quantities involved could be astonishing. The consequences of Rome's expansion were not simply a transformation of power in the Mediterranean; they included massive movement of people and things, which in turn had profound effects on the economy, society and culture of the areas affected as well as on the internal politics of Rome itself.

The parameters of Roman foreign policy

In comparison with the breathtaking expansion of Rome as a Mediterranean power between 220 and 167, and with the equally breathtaking conquests of Pompeius and Caesar between 66 and 51, the intervening century can appear to be a dull interlude in the history of Roman imperialism. The relative absence of great campaigns is in itself worthy of analysis, and though the area over which Rome exercised some form of control did increase, particularly in Asia and Africa, the degree of expansion was modest in comparison with both earlier and later periods. But this was a period of significant change in how Rome managed its empire. New methods of exploiting provinces through taxation were introduced; there was considerable debate about what was and was not acceptable behaviour on the part of magistrates, which produced legislation; and widespread opposition occurred to Roman rule across the Mediterranean, culminating at the end of the period with the catastrophic collapse of the alliance with other Italian communities. This was a period in which the tempo of Roman foreign policy was often dictated by Rome's enemies.

The question with which Polybius famously starts his history is relevant to a much longer period than that which he considered.[6] What kind of an answer we might give remains disputed. One approach is to consider what made the Romans different from the people they fought, in ways which led to military success, whether that consisted of innate character, social and political structures, economic resources or a combination of these factors.[7] Another is to consider the processes of decision-making which led to war and then to lasting hegemony over conquered territories: that is, the extent to which the Romans *intended* to turn a capacity to win wars – whatever the origins of that capacity – into a Mediterranean empire. Inherent in both these approaches is a conviction that the phenomenon of Roman imperialism is explicable and not simply the result of chance; which is not to exclude the possibility that luck does take a hand at key moments.

Two aspects in particular of Roman society deserve consideration in an explanation of what made Rome different from the Hellenistic kingdoms, not least because they were identified by Greek contemporaries as distinctive aspects of Rome. One of these is manpower. Rome had access to much greater human resources for the fighting of wars than its rivals. In part this was due to the distinctive legal framework of Roman citizenship. Freed slaves took the legal status of their former owners: so any slave freed by a Roman citizen became himself or herself a citizen, and this status was passed onto

---

6. Polyb. 1.1.5: 'Who is so miserable or idle as not to want to know how and by what kind of state practically the whole of the inhabited world came, in less than fifty-three years, under the rule of a single state, that of the Romans ...?'
7. W. V. Harris, *War and Imperialism in Republican Rome*, Oxford: Oxford University Press 1979, 9–53, argued for the inherent disposition of the Romans towards war and for their conscious desire for imperial control, in an attempt to refute the 'defensive imperialism' thesis; his work continues to dominate the debate on Roman imperialism. See further J. Rich, 'Fear, greed and glory: the causes of Roman war-making in the middle Republic', in J. Rich and G. Shipley, G. eds, *War and Society in the Roman World*, London: Routledge 1993, 38–68; K. Raaflaub, 'Born to be wolves? Origins of Roman imperialism', in R. Wallace and E. Harris, eds, *Transitions to Empire: Essays in Greco-Roman History, 360–146 B.C., in Honor of E. Badian*, Norman: University of Oklahoma Press 1996, 273–314; A. Eckstein, *Mediterranean Anarchy, Interstate War, and the Rise of Rome*, Berkeley: University of California Press 2006, 181–243; C. J. Smith and L. Yarrow, eds, *Imperialism, Cultural Politics and Polybius*, Oxford: Oxford University Press 2012.

any legitimate children born after manumission.[8] In addition, citizenship had as early as the third century become decisively separated from geographical location, through the development of Roman colonies sited across the Italian peninsula.[9] The size of Rome's citizen body was not, therefore, limited to the numbers which lived in Rome and its immediate hinterland.

Re-engineering the concept of citizenship so that its possession could be separated from living in Rome, or its adjacent territory, had produced a far greater number of Roman citizens than was the case in otherwise comparable Mediterranean city-states.[10] This in turn allowed Rome to raise a large citizen army: on average, between forty thousand and fifty thousand citizens were serving as soldiers each year in this period. In addition, the network of alliances through which Rome expressed its hegemony over the other communities in Italy demanded troops rather than taxation; a year with no conflict was a year in which Rome was not exploiting its power to the full. War was a means of collecting tax, and not simply a drain on revenue, as was the case with those of Rome's Mediterranean rivals which used mercenaries.

Another factor in Rome's tendency towards war was the value placed on military success in Roman culture. Polybius discusses the aspects of Roman behaviour which promoted this value in book 6, as the complement of the nature of the constitution in explaining Roman distinctiveness. His account combines the practical details of army organisation with a fascination with the social *mores* which cherished military glory: 'Given their concern and engagement with military reward and punishment, it is not surprising that their military activities end gloriously and successfully.'[11] Naturally, some care is needed in interpreting Polybius' picture. The logic of his overall project demanded that he emphasise what was different between Rome and the Greek-speaking world, rather than points of simi-larity; and, arguably, his experience of Roman culture was slanted towards the glorification of military achievement, given his

8. An aspect of Rome which impressed Philip V of Macedon (in a letter of 214 to the city of Larissa: *SIG*³ 543).

9. E. T. Salmon, *Roman Colonization under the Republic*, London: Thames and Hudson 1969; A. N. Sherwin-White, *The Roman Citizenship*, 2nd edn, Oxford: Oxford University Press 1973, 58–95.

10. P. A. Brunt, *Italian Manpower, 225 B.C.–A.D. 14*, Oxford: Oxford University Press 1971.

11. Polyb. 6.19–42, quotation from 6.39.11.

friendship with Scipio Aemilianus, son of the conqueror of Greece and himself a man who defined his contribution to Roman politics in terms of his successes in war. Roman militarism did not break in during the second century upon a peaceful Hellenistic world; war was the natural state here, too.[12] But Polybius' analysis should not be entirely disregarded. And in addition to the aspects of Roman culture that he identified in book 6, we can add the fact of Rome's political structure. The annual cycle of magistrates generated an impulse towards war because magistrates had only one chance at seizing military glory.

Finally, we should not underestimate the significance of Roman self-belief in perpetuating a cycle of military activity. A fragment of Lucilius distils a particular ethos: 'as the Roman people are conquered by force, overcome often in many battles, but never in war – in which all is involved'.[13] War was the natural state of Rome, and victory the inevitable outcome. This belief was validated by the nature of Rome's relationship with the gods. Roman self-image as a peculiarly religious people is already evident in Polybius (6.56.6–15), who claims that 'fear of the gods', δεισιδαιμονία, was the most important way in which the Roman state was superior to others: it enabled the masses to be controlled and ensured the probity of magistrates. Recent scholarship has emphasised the concept of Rome's 'civic religion', the subset of its religious practices which directly concerned political life. We have already seen in Chapter 1 examples of the workings of civic religion, in, for example, the Senate's response after it had murdered Tiberius Gracchus or in the popular horror at Vestal unchastity.[14] The intersection between religious practice and foreign affairs is illustrated at the very start of this period in the actions of Scipio Aemilianus at Carthage: Macrobius (3.9.6–11) records the formulae which he used to

12. Eckstein, *Anarchy*.
13. Lucilius 708–9 (W): *ut Romanus populus uictus uei, superatus proeliis / saepe est multis, bello uero numquam, in quo sunt omnia*. Lucilius articulates this idea in the context of the war against Viriathus, yet the sentiment may go back to the war against Hannibal.
14. On Roman religion in general, M. Beard, J. North and S. Price, *Religions of Rome*, 2 vols, Cambridge: Cambridge University Press 1998; J. Scheid, *An Introduction to Roman Religion*, Edinburgh: Edinburgh University Press 2003; on 'civic religion', A. Bendlin, 'Looking beyond the civic compromise: religious pluralism in late Republican Rome', in E. Bispham and C. Smith, eds, *Religion in Archaic and Republican Rome: Evidence and Experience*, Edinburgh: Edinburgh University Press 2000, 115–35, with useful comment in I. Gildenhard, *Creative Eloquence: The Construction of Reality in Cicero's Speeches*, Oxford: Oxford University Press 2011, 246–54.

dedicate Carthage to the gods of the underworld and to undertake the *euocatio* of its protecting gods; that is, to entice them to abandon Carthage and join the Roman side.[15] What exactly Aemilianus might have thought he was doing is unclear, but the very possibility of this ceremony demonstrates how competence in religious practice was an integral part of Roman leadership. There is a supernatural dimension to Roman diplomacy as well, illustrated particularly clearly by the events surrounding Hostilius Mancinus in 137. His handover to the Numantines followed as a necessary consequence of the repudiation of his treaty, and involved the fetials, that is, the group of religious officials who supervised the declaration of war. Mancinus had reneged on an oath, and the potential ill-consequences of that for the Roman state were negated by his handover to the Numantines 'naked and with his hands tied behind his back'.[16]

The Mancinus episode also demonstrates the difficulty of bringing wars to an end with anything less than total surrender by the enemy. In many of Cicero's references to it, he contrasts Mancinus' conduct, and willingness to collaborate in the repudiation of the treaty and his own surrender, with that of Pompeius, who had two years previously presented a negotiated settlement with the Numantines as their unconditional surrender: when the truth emerged, the Senate rejected his agreement and Pompeius himself became an *exemplum* of treachery. The situation in Further Spain is not exactly parallel, since the treaty which Servilianus had made with Viriathus was not formally repudiated; but the encouragement Servilius Caepio received from members of the Senate to ignore it and renew the war shows that many regarded it as an unsatisfactory conclusion to the conflict. These parameters of military success did not necessarily mean the utter destruction of the enemy, though that was a possible outcome; the key point was rather that the enemy should be entirely at the Romans' disposal, who guaranteed in turn the fitness of their own behaviour by an appeal to their *fides*, 'good faith'. *Fides* imposed no real limitation on what the Romans might proceed to do to their

15. E. Rawson, 'Scipio, Laelius, Furius and the ancestral religion', *JRS* 63, 1973, 161–74, at 168–74; Beard, North and Price, *Religions*, 1.111.
16. Vell. Pat. 2.1.5; M. Crawford, '*Foedus* and *sponsio*', *PBSR* 41, 1973, 1–7; J. Rich, *Declaring War in the Roman Republic in the Period of Transmarine Expansion*, Brussels: Latomus 1976. On the role of the fetials, F. Santangelo, 'The fetials and their *ius*', *BICS* 51, 2008, 63–93; L. Zollschan, 'The longevity of the fetial college', in O. Tellegen-Couperus, ed., *Law and Religion in the Roman Republic*, Leiden: Brill 2012, 119–44.

defeated enemies, but it did establish a conceptual framework for activity after the end of the war, in which the defeated community owed its continued existence entirely to the Romans.[17]

These aspects of Roman society and culture form the essential background to understanding its military activity; but they cannot explain on their own the sequence of decisions which created an empire. Nor can we place sole responsibility on the talents of individual commanders: some were, undoubtedly, brilliant, but Rome was also remarkably resistant to individual failure, and its voters very forgiving of it. Its success was not the result of having consistently better generals than its opponents. As important are the ways in which decisions about how to deal with Rome's neighbours, whether in peace or in war, were reached. The Senate was the location of most decision-making relevant to external affairs. It decided the tasks to be allocated to consuls and praetors and the resources which they were to be given; and it listened to embassies from allied and other states and took whatever action in response it deemed necessary. How far its decisions represent consistent or sustained policy is not easy to ascertain. If we look at the conduct of wars, the pattern is variable: there were occasions when the Senate authorised ongoing campaigning, even in unfavourable circumstances, and others where it hesitated over involvement. These apparently contradictory impulses can, however, be seen as aspects of one phenomenon, namely the difficulty of making the transition from peace to war, and from war to peace.

The practical consequences of this approach to international relations can clearly be seen in the Spanish wars. It is apparent, too, in the early stages of the war against Jugurtha. It did not, of course, mean that a commander would never surrender. But it did impose an expectation that conflict would continue until the Romans decided that it would end, on their terms. This expectation informs those moments at which the Romans hesitate to declare war, such as in the years prior to the Jugurthine war: a hesitation which need not be the product of a reluctance to engage in overseas conquest, but rather that of an awareness of the resources required. It also provides a framework in which setbacks and single defeats are an expected part of the process.

According to Sallust, however, the Senate's failure to move against

17. A. Ziolkowski, 'Urbs direpta, or how the Romans sacked cities', in Rich and Shipley, War and Society, 69–91; K-J. Hölkeskamp, Senatus Populusque Romanus: Die politische Kultur der Republik, Stuttgart: Steiner 2004, 105–35.

Jugurtha had another cause: bribery.[18] A corrupt and incompetent Senate is an integral part of Sallust's narrative: it is one of the aspects of the war against Jugurtha which makes it an instructive precursor of the catastrope which overwhelmed Rome in his own time. But the fragment of Gaius Gracchus' speech on the Aufeian law, discussed in Chapter 2, provides an interesting comparison, with its depiction of a diplomatic world in which every decision is financially motivated. In addition to showing that the debate on how best to exploit Asia financially carried on during the 120s, Gracchus' words give us a rare oratorical glimpse of the diplomatic environment at Rome. This is a world of intense public debate combined with vigorous private lobbying, in which the capacity to intervene decisively commands the avid and lucrative attention of embassies. It is also a world in which the assumption of corruption among the senatorial class can plausibly be made to the people: Rome's imperial successes made men rich. The implication of such suspicions was that the people needed to resume direct control over foreign policy through the medium of tribunician legislation, which is of course precisely what Gaius Gracchus did with his proposal to sell the rights to collect taxes in Asia and what his brother had done with his law over the allocation of the revenues from Attalus' bequest.

The other manifestation of popular involvement in foreign policy concerned broader issues of overseas administration. From this perspective, the period 146–91 is marked by increasing limits on the freedom of the Senate and magistrates to make decisions about foreign affairs. The establishment, with the passage of the *lex Calpurnia* in 149 BC, of a standing court to try extortion marked in one sense an increase in senatorial power, since senators accused of extortion were now tried by their peers. But it controlled, or attempted to control, senators' behaviour as magistrates; and it was superseded by Gaius Gracchus' extortion law, which took adjudication of such cases away from members of the Senate. Moreover, his law on consular provinces enabled the people, in theory at least, to relate consular candidates to a pair of defined tasks, as well as reducing to some extent opportunities for those elected to intrigue for command. Although, in practice, the Senate seems to have been able to override annual allocations under this law in times of emergency, it remained in force until the end of the Republic. Another important development was Saturninus' *maiestas* law, which was

18. Sall. *Iug.* 8.1 ('everything is for sale at Rome', *Romae omnia uenalia esse*); 15–16.

intended to provide a framework for punishing the incompetence of individual commanders (even if its drafting permitted its use in domestic matters).

Thus the overall framework in which external affairs were administered underwent some changes during this period. But direct intervention in foreign policy decision-making by tribunician legislation remained the exception: the Senate remained the normal location for the hearing of embassies and for decisions about the conduct of foreign policy.[19] Moreover, it would be a mistake to see struggles as solely a two-sided affair between Senate and people; the Senate, too, was concerned with magistrates who failed to obey its orders.

War and imperial expansion

The capture and destruction of Corinth and of Carthage in 146 make it a periodising date. These two events made a huge impression on both the Romans and the rest of the Hellenistic world, as evidence for the nature and extent of Roman power. They were nonetheless signs of a change which had already occurred, rather than decisive moments of change in themselves. Rome was already, by 146, the dominant power in the Mediterranean.[20] Eckstein formulates the change in terms of a shift from a system of many competing powers to one which contained a single dominant power: 'By the 180s BC, although there still remained in existence several important states other than Rome, the Mediterranean finally had only one political and military focus, and only one dominant actor; there was a preponderance of power in the hands of a single state. In political-science terminology, a system of unipolarity had replaced the long-standing multipolar anarchy.'[21] Eckstein's concern is both to elucidate the nature of foreign affairs in the Mediterranean, as a challenge to an account of Roman expansion which sees Rome as an exceptionally aggressive and militarised society, and to identify the characteristics which promoted its eventual success. If we accept that 146 is the symbolic marker of a fundamental shift in Mediterranean geopolitics, then the interesting question in the subsequent period is not primarily the external threats which the Romans faced but the

19. On the mechanics of Roman diplomacy, see further C. Eilers, ed., *Diplomats and Diplomacy in the Roman World*, Leiden: Brill 2009.
20. See further N. Rosenstein, *Rome and the Mediterranean*, 211–39.
21. Eckstein, *Anarchy*, 1–2.

manner in which they handled their new position. However, a degree of caution is required in extrapolating from Rome's conquest of the Hellenistic world to a wider state of calm. In *De officiis* (1.38), Cicero drew a distinction between wars fought about *imperium* – dominance – and those which concerned survival. His examples of the latter category are the Spanish wars and those with the Cimbri. For Cicero, the most dangerous challenges to Rome occurred after the apparent watershed of 146.

Rome's further expansion in the Hellenistic world during this period with the incorporation of Asia is something of a special case. After the defeat of Antiochus III at Apamea in 180, Roman activity in Asia Minor was purely diplomatic for over half a century; even when ambassadors were ignored, there was no indication that there was any willingness to deploy force.[22] Its decision to accept Attalus' bequest thus demands explanation. But its hand had been forced by Tiberius Gracchus' law appropriating the new revenues; and once the proconsul Crassus had been killed, control had to be asserted. Elsewhere, though, this is a period of pressure to maintain existing power and of limited successes. The Spanish wars ended with the sack of Numantia, but only after two decades of defeats and humiliations, and left no appetite for further major campaigns. The war in north Africa brought triumphs to two of its commanders but only after their predecessors' notable failures. And the major conflict of this period was the desperate war with Germanic invaders. A reactive attitude in the Senate, made cautious by frequent reverses, may also explain its failures to respond aggressively, particularly towards the threat from Mithridates and the collapse of Syrian power.[23]

The administration of peace

Rome did not necessarily require its power to assume a territorial form; the expansion of its empire, first in Italy and then overseas, was marked by a flexibility over the ways in which its power was expressed. Local self-government was acceptable, provided that it was combined with an unquestioning willingness to obey Roman

22. E. S. Gruen, *The Hellenistic World and the Coming of Rome*, Berkeley: University of California Press 1984, 569–92; A. N. Sherwin-White, *Roman Foreign Policy in the East, 168 B.C. to A.D. 1*, London: Duckworth 1984, 18–57.
23. R. Sheldon, *Intelligence Activities in Ancient Rome*, London: Cass 2005, 68–85, emphasises the lack of organised intelligence gathering.

commands; this model often involved ongoing Roman involvement because Rome was the natural location of binding and stable arbitration.[24] Nonetheless, there was no reluctance to send magistrates to specific places if circumstances demanded. Sicily and Sardinia had become such places after the first Punic war, each regularly receiving a praetorian governor; and the establishment of two provinces in Spain at the beginning of the second century led to an increase in the number of praetors to accommodate the extra demand on *imperium*-holders.[25] In the immediate aftermath of the events of 146, senatorial commissions were sent to Mummius in Greece, and to Scipio in Africa, to determine how these areas should subsequently be organised. Though there was no presumption that a regular territorial allocation for a magistrate would follow the commission's decision, that was in fact the outcome in both cases: the commissions' conclusions included the establishment of Africa as territory which then regularly received a Roman governor, and confirmation of that as the case in Macedonia.

How far could Rome be considered a part of the Hellenistic world by 146? Polybius' account gives the impression of a deep gulf between him and his hosts, with Roman habits of warfare and their ethical convictions making them profoundly alien, however far shared interests and mutual respect might bring together individuals, such as Polybius himself and Aemilianus. But Polybius' position as a self-conscious interpreter between cultures should not be disregarded: his didactic focus may perhaps lead him to material which needs explanation. And the mobility of individuals is a good place to start when considering the cultural impact of Rome's engagement with the Hellenistic world.

Polybius himself is an example, albeit of an exceptional and privileged kind, of widespread involuntary mobility from the eastern Mediterranean to Italy in the second century BC. His social status had made him a hostage; thousands of others were brought to Italy as slaves.[26] The legal consequences of manumission, in creating new citizens (even though only some slaves were likely to be freed),

24. A. Lintott, *Imperium Romanum: Politics and Administration*, London: Routledge 1993, 22–42; J. S. Richardson, 'The administration of the Empire', *CAH* 9², 1994, 564–98.
25. T. C. Brennan, *The Praetorship in the Roman Republic*, New York: Oxford University Press 2000, 164–73.
26. W. Scheidel, 'Human mobility in Roman Italy, II: the slave population', *JRS* 95, 2005, 64–79, who estimates an average annual supply of 15,000–20,000.

meant that the ownership of slaves would in time alter the composition of the citizen body. Such a process was presumably happening
on a considerable scale during the second century, fuelled by conquest and a lucrative slave trade; and it could provoke hostility, as
in Scipio Aemilianus' dismissal of an audience by impugning the
genuineness of their citizenship.[27] Some Greek-speaking slaves,
and freedmen, were occupied within elite households as teachers,
contributing to widespread though variable levels of bilingualism
among the elite.[28] There was a market, too, for practitioners of medi-
cine and for artists and craftsmen. As wealth poured into the hands
of the Roman elite, so the outlets for its expenditure developed. We
can see this trend in the thunderous denunciations of private luxury;
more prosaically, we should imagine that Rome was increasingly a
magnet to the talented and ambitious.[29] Not all Greek speakers in
the city would have made the journey there unwillingly. Nor was all
the traffic in talent in an east–west direction. Antiochus IV had
employed a Roman citizen, D. Cossutius, to complete the Olym-
peion in Athens in the 170s or 160s BC; it is not known where he
trained, but members of his family and their freedmen begin to crop
up in inscriptional evidence from the Aegean from the middle of the
second century, members of a growing community of Romans, and
non-Roman Italians, who emigrated from Rome to pursue the
opportunities for wealth-creation which the expansion of Roman
power provided.[30] Gaius Gracchus' law on the Asian taxes was a
major if unwitting impetus to the development of a Roman presence
in Asia Minor: the process of tax-farming required agents on the

27. See above, Chapter 2.
28. A. Wallace-Hadrill, 'To be Roman, go Greek: thoughts on Hellenization at Rome',
in M. Austin, J. Harries and C. Smith, eds, *Modus Operandi: Essays in Honour of
Geoffrey Rickman*, London: Institute of Classical Studies 1998, 79–91; J. N. Adams,
Bilingualism and the Latin Language, Cambridge: Cambridge University Press 2003,
308–10.
29. See, for example, the fragments of Aemilianus' speeches as censor, against Sulpicius
Galus and against Tiberius Gracchus' 'judiciary law': ORF4 122–34.
30. J-L. Ferrary, 'La création de la province d'Asie et la présence italienne en Asie
Mineure', in C. Müller and C. Hasenohr, eds, *Les italiens dans le monde grec: IIe siècle
av. J.-C.–Ier siècle ap. J.-C. Circulation, activités, intégration*, Paris: École Française
d'Athènes 2002, 133–46; on the Cossutii, E. Rawson, 'The activities of the Cossutii',
PBSR 43, 1975, 36–47; J-L.Ferrary, 'The Hellenistic world and Roman political patronage', in P. Cartledge, P. Garnsey and E. Gruen, eds, *Hellenistic Constructs: Essays in
Culture, History and Historiography*, Berkeley: University of California Press 1997,
105–19. P. Horden and N. Purcell, *The Corrupting Sea*, Oxford: Blackwell 2000,
342–400, places Roman examples within a wider framework of a highly mobile Mediterranean world.

ground. The figure of 80,000 for the number of Romans and Italians slaughtered by Mithridates in 88 is presumably exaggerated, but there were clearly large and distinct communities of immigrants from Italy in the cities of Asia Minor by the end of the 90s BC, with much of this growth having occurred over the previous thirty years.

Alongside mobility in pursuit of economic opportunities, public affairs promoted contact between elites. Rome was now firmly part of the Hellenistic diplomatic nexus, the recipient of embassies from city-states and kingdoms and the sponsor itself of frequent diplomatic travel. No single embassy to Rome in the period 146–91 appears to have made quite the impact of the one from Athens in 155, with contained three distinguished philosophers. But the traffic was regular, and promoted individual ties between ambassadors and their Roman hosts. In turn, the Senate dispatched embassies to investigate and adjudicate in areas where Rome's authority extended. Some, such as Galba's embassy to Crete, are known only from inscriptional evidence; others made an impact on the literary record, because of either the prominence of the ambassadors (as with Aemilianus' tour of the east, probably in 140–139) or the circumstances of the despatch (so Nasica's departure for the kingdom of Pergamum in the aftermath of Tiberius Gracchus' death). Given that we do not have Livy's record for this period, some caution is needed in assessing the intensity of activity: if it is indeed less prominent now than earlier in the century, that may well reflect a shift in Roman priorities to the western Mediterranean, but regular connections remain.

Members of the elite were also travelling for reasons other than official business; that is, for study, or having chosen Greece or Asia Minor as the location for exile. Titus Albucius' prominence in the record probably guarantees that he was exceptional in his engagement with Hellenistic learning: nonetheless, we can place him, on Cicero's evidence, in Athens and studying philosophy at the end of the 120s.[31] Metellus Numidicus, who attended Carneades' lectures in Athens, may have been there even earlier.[32] Albucius elected to

31. Cic. *Fin.* 1.9, quoting Lucilius; Scaevola's encounter with Albucius is probably from 120, which would fit with Cicero's description in the *Brutus* (131) of his being a young man (*adulescens*) when studying in Athens.
32. Cic. *De or.* 3.68. Panaetius may have played a part in promoting Athens as a destination for philosophically curious Romans: he had spent time in the entourage of Scipio Aemilianus before returning to become head of the Stoa (A. Erskine, *The Hellenistic Stoa: Political Thought and Action*, London: Duckworth 1990, 211–14).

return to Athens and continue his studies when he was exiled, on extortion charges, after his praetorship.[33] Nonetheless, the manner of his engagement with Greek culture deserves note: his quarrel with Scaevola arose because Scaevola addressed him, in Greek, in an official context. Lucilius' telling of the story indicates that Scaevola did so in order to humiliate Albucius and that he was successful in so doing: even a philhellene Roman wanted to ensure that his activities took place within the context of an acknowledged Roman identity. The attractive opportunities for private pleasure and public display which the ongoing encounter with the Hellenistic world generated always required careful handling.[34]

There was also considerable exchange with the western Mediterranean which contributed to Rome's distinctive development as an imperial capital: it is only if the focus is exclusively on elite literary culture that the Greek-speaking Mediterranean is the only area of interest. (And we should note the senatorial commission to translate from the Punic Mago's work on agriculture immediately after the conclusion of the third Punic war.) War brought many to Rome as slaves and in the opposite direction, Rome looked westwards, not east, for its first citizen colonies outside Italy: Gracchus' settlement of Carthage was a failure, but Narbo, founded soon after in southern Gaul, was a success. There was a politically significant settlement of Italians in Africa by the 110s BC as well as veteran settlements in Spain.

Rome and the rest of Italy

Arguably, *the* major foreign policy issue that Rome faced in the later second century – however much Romans themselves were aware of it – was its relationship with the other communities in Italy. The Italian peninsula was in 91, as it had been in 146, a patchwork of different entities, politically, culturally and linguistically distinct but at the same time ordered into some kind of a whole by the existence and behaviour of Rome. The nature of that whole is one question; another concerns the processes of change which, over the course of the last century of Republican government, elided the differences and thus contributed to the formation and recognition of 'Italia'

33. Cic. *Tusc.* 5.108.
34. The bibliography on this topic is enormous: A. Wallace-Hadrill, *Rome's Cultural Revolution*, Cambridge: Cambridge University Press 2008, is an invaluable introduction.

alongside 'Roma' in the political and intellectual lexicon.[35] These changes moved at varying speeds and manners in different areas: whereas, for example, a clear political and legal transition occurred between 90 and 88, linguistic and cultural homogenisation, though attested by its end product in Augustan Italy, resists clear and decisive chronology.[36]

The political patchwork of pre-Social War Italy reflected not only Rome's military pre-eminence, but also centuries of its audacious experiment with remote citizenship, which had created a kind of political organisation difficult to parallel in the ancient world. Some Italian communities were Rome's allies, their relationship determined by treaty; others were inhabited by Roman citizens, whether these were descendants of colonists from Rome, or from indigenous populations who had become Roman through a grant of citizenship; and others had the status of Latins.[37] Moreover, each of these categories was capable of further subdivision. The political patchwork was matched by a range of languages in addition to Latin: a range of Italic languages in central Italy, Greek widespread in southern Italy, Etruscan north of Rome, and others. In this complex environment, as Wallace-Hadrill has recently emphasised, behaviour cannot be captured by as simple a term as 'Romanisation'; Italian cultural choices were influenced by the Greek world as well as by Rome, and the value of Rome varied greatly for different communities and for different individuals within those communities.

The subsequent history of Roman Italy, as well as the value of possessing Roman citizenship within the empire, conspired to create a historiographical tradition which emphasised the desire for citizenship as the key element, and the failure of legislation to extend the franchise as the trigger for war. Individual episodes in this story, and the difficulties associated with them, are discussed in Chapter 1; it is very important not to assume that Roman citizenship had the same value for Italian allies in the later second and early first

35. M. Torelli, *Tota Italia: Essays in the Cultural Formation of Roman Italy*, Oxford: Oxford University Press 1999; M. Pobjoy, 'The first *Italia*', in E. Herring and K. Lomas, eds, *The Emergence of State Identities in Italy in the First Millennium* BC, London: Accordia Research Institute 2000, 187–211; O. De Cazanove, 'Some thoughts on the "religious Romanization" of Italy before the Social War', in Bispham and Smith, *Religion in Archaic and Republican Rome*, 71–6.
36. Wallace-Hadrill, *Cultural Revolution*; M. Crawford, *Imagines Italicae*, London: Institute of Classical Studies 2011.
37. E. Bispham, *From Asculum to Actium: The Municipalization of Italy from the Social War to Augustus*, Oxford: Oxford University Press 2007, 74–160.

centuries BC as it clearly did later under the emperors.[38] The extension of Roman citizenship through Italy before the Social War was
associated with conquest, particularly through the planting of
colonies on defeated territory, and a community which received
Roman citizenship wholesale lost its own civic identity. To become
Roman under such circumstances was not necessarily to receive
something that would be perceived as a benefit. It is also important
not to assume that the Italian allies were a homogenous group, with
identical shared aspirations and plans, either between different
communities, or between different members of one community. The
Social War was largely an Oscan-speaking revolt; the Etruscans (and
Umbrians) became involved later, and their outcome was different.
Nonetheless, the Italian allies were alike in being the allies of a more
powerful state; and Rome was willing to ignore the terms of the
treaties which it had with its allies if advantage so dictated.[39] We
know that there was widespread resentment about interference with
their landholdings following Tiberius Gracchus' law. A few years
later, Gaius Gracchus gave a vivid description of the arbitrary and
sometimes brutal punishments which some Roman magistrates
dispensed in Italy, in a speech 'Concerning the promulgated laws':[40]

> Recently, the consul came to Teanum Sidicinum. His wife said
> she wanted to wash in the men's baths. The Sidicine quaestor,
> M. Marius, was given the job of clearing the baths of those who were
> washing. The consul's wife announced to her husband that the baths
> had been put at her disposal insufficiently quickly and were not clean
> enough. As a result, a stake was set up in the forum and M. Marius
> – a very noble member of that community – was led there. His
> clothes were removed and he was beaten with rods. When they heard
> this at Cales, they announce that no one was to wash in the baths
> when a Roman magistrate was present there. At Ferentinum, for the
> same reason, our praetor ordered the quaestors to be arrested: one
> threw himself off the walls, the other was taken and beaten with
> rods.

In the absence of direct testimony, it is difficult to assess how far
other manifestations of Roman power, such as military service, or
the periodic expulsions of foreigners from Rome, were a source of
anger or bitterness, but we should be careful, again, of assuming a

---

38. H. Mouritsen, *Italian Unification: A Study in Ancient and Modern Historiography*,
London: Institute of Classical Studies 1998, 5–22.
39. Bispham, *Asculum*, 159 n. 205.
40. Gell. *NA* 10.3.2.

uniformity of views. The relationship with Rome brought opportunities for some, whether it be through profitable military service, or access to foreign markets. It is perfectly plausible to imagine that for some individuals, the experience of such opportunities also made their lack of Roman citizenship a characteristic to be resented. But such disadvantages arose fundamentally from subject status. Citizenship would be one way of securing a greater say in their treatment; but so would a change in the relationship they had with Rome, and the latter option would also preserve identities. The Social War happened because Rome's allies had become bitterly discontented with the nature of their relationship with Rome; but the outcome, of universal Roman citizenship, and with it the transferral of Italian affairs from the foreign into the domestic column, was not the obvious solution to that issue.

CHAPTER 4

The Social War, civil war and the imposition of a new order

The Social War

The Social War began with the violent deaths of two Roman officials at Asculum towards the end of 91 BC or at the beginning of 90. The date of its end is less easy to establish, because the Romans concluded peace treaties with different members of the coalition they faced at different times; one could argue that the war was effectively over as early as 89, or that it lasted in one form or another until the battle of the Colline Gate in November 82.[1] Nor is it immediately obvious who won; the terms and conditions of the ends of the various conflicts can be interpreted both as a victory for either side and as a stalemate. The Social War was a perplexing struggle even for its contemporaries to understand, though its destructiveness was obvious to all, as were its reverberations in Roman political and social life thereafter.

Velleius puts the death toll for the war at 300,000.[2] Even if the figure is exaggerated, the scale of carnage can more impressionistically be assessed from a list of Roman commanders who died during the war. As well as the death of the praetor Servilius at Asculum, a consul, a praetor, a proconsul and a legate of praetorian standing were killed in 90; in 89, one of the consuls, and two consular legates. The only parallel for this scale of loss is the second war against Carthage, over a century earlier, which was also the most recent occasion when there had been fighting in Italy. Livy devoted five books to the war (72–6), a rate of coverage over three times as dense as that for the second Punic war.

At the outset, however, the Romans appeared to be overwhelmingly stronger. The anonymous rhetorical treatise *Ad Herennium*

---

1. For modern narratives of the war, see E. Gabba, 'Rome and Italy: the Social War', *CAH* 9², 1994, 104–28; E. T. Salmon, *Samnium and the Samnites*, Cambridge: Cambridge University Press 1967, 340–89. Appian and the *Periochae* of Livy are the major ancient sources.
2. Vell. Pat. 2.15. See also Diod. Sic. 37.1–2.

includes – as an example of the 'Middle' style of speaking – a passage
from a speech which is clearly discussing the allies' decision to attack
Rome. The speaker argues that the allies are at such a disadvantage
in conventional military terms when compared with the Romans
that their decision to revolt proves they were relying on some other
form of support:

> When they had made the decision to fight us, what, I ask you, were
> they relying on when they tried to undertake war – given that they
> knew that by far the larger part of our allies remained loyal? Given
> that they saw that they did not have ready hordes of soldiers, suit-
> able commanders, or a public treasury – in short none of the things
> necessary for waging war? ... have they then, in taking up arms,
> depended on no motive or hope? Who would believe that insanity
> could seize hold of anyone to the extent that they would dare, with
> no resources at all, to challenge the *imperium* of the Roman people?
> They must, therefore, have had some motive.[3]

The speaker's implied answer to his conundrum is support from
within Rome. Whether or not this particular fragment is part of a
speech actually delivered, the context appears to be the passage of
the *lex Varia* at the beginning of 90, a treason law which investigated
'those through whose help or advice the allies had taken up arms
against the Roman people'.[4] This passage shows that early in 90, at
least, it was plausible to present allied resources as so weak that only
illicit encouragement from influential Romans could explain the
allies' action.[5] The presence of Scaurus among those accused under
this law, with Varius as prosecutor, supports the hypothesis that
those whom Varius suggested were responsible for offering this
encouragement were the associates of Drusus.[6] We can connect the

---

3. *Rhet. Her.* 4.13. The work's author denies that he has used real speeches in this book
(4.1–10), but see P.Martin, 'Sur quelques thèmes de l'éloquence *popularis*, notamment
l'invective contre le passivité du peuple', in G. Achard and M. Ledentu, eds, *Orateur,
auditeurs, lecteurs: à propos de l'éloquence romaine à la fin de la République et au début
du Principat: actes de la table ronde de 31 janvier 2000*, Lyon: Centre d'Études et de
Recherches sur l'Occident Romain de l' Université Lyon III 2000, 27–41.
4. Asc. 22C. The proposer was Q. Varius, a tribune of the plebs; Val. Max. 8.6.4
provides a (hostile) biographical sketch, which includes the detail that his law was
carried despite tribunician veto. See further E. S. Gruen, 'The *lex Varia*', *JRS* 55,
1965, 59–73; R. Seager, '*Lex Varia de maiestate*', *Historia* 16, 1967, 37–43; E. Badian,
'Quaestiones Variae', *Historia* 18, 1969, 447–91.
5. H. Mouritsen, *Italian Unification: A Study in Ancient and Modern Historiography*,
London: Institute of Classical Studies 1998, 136.
6. M. Alexander, *Trials in the Late Roman Republic 149 BC to 50 BC*, Toronto: University of Toronto Press 1990, 53.

law with other attempts to ascribe blame to Drusus. Diodorus
(37.11) preserves the text of an oath of personal allegiance to him,
which the allies are alleged to have sworn; this includes a reference
to a citizenship law of Drusus, and evokes the idea of a personal relationship between him and those who benefit under such a law. We
also have an anecdote about the four-year-old younger Cato (who
lodged with Drusus, his maternal uncle, as a child) refusing to be
suborned by the allied leader Poppaedius Silo when the latter was
visiting Drusus, despite the threat of defenestration.[7] The story
enabled biographers to demonstrate the consistent steadfastness of
Cato's character; but it relies on the perception of Drusus at the
centre of a pro-Italian movement. And Cicero records hearing the
tribune Carbo at a *contio* in 90 attack the younger Drusus for his
assault on the *res publica*.[8] After Drusus' death, and with Crassus
also dead, it is easy to see how partisan attempts by Drusus' opponents to explain the sudden outbreak of war should create a scenario
in which Drusus had encouraged the allies to launch an attack. This
group had a clear motive for supplementing the legal activity under
the *lex Varia* with speculation and rumour.[9]

A number of other prosecutions, or threatened prosecutions,
under the *lex Varia* are known.[10] The accused included Q. Pompeius
Rufus, L. Memmius, M. Antonius and C. Aurelius Cotta, and the
heterogeneity of this group is a sign of the confusion of these
months. Cotta was, according to Cicero, a close friend of Drusus,
and Memmius is described by Sisenna as Drusus' adviser, '*con-
siliarius*'; but to bring the others into a close-knit faction on the basis
of these prosecutions risks circularity. Pompeius Rufus may have
found himself under suspicion simply because, as *praetor urbanus* in
91, he seemed one of those responsible for the events.[11] Philippus

7. Val. Max. 3.1.2; Plut. *Cat. Min.* 2.
8. Cic. *Orat.* 213.
9. Further traces of a struggle to assign blame emerge in Appian (*B Civ.* 1.37) and
Valerius Maximus (8.6.4), where Varius' law becomes, impossibly, itself a cause of the
outbreak of war. After Varius himself had been convicted and exiled under the *lex Varia*,
he too became a potential scapegoat.
10. Alexander, *Trials*, 54–8.
11. Cotta and Drusus: Cic. *De or.* 1.25. Cotta failed to be elected tribune of the people
for 90; this may reflect the same suspicions as those behind his prosecution under the *lex
Varia*. On L. Memmius, see T. P. Wiseman, 'Lucius Memmius and his family', *CQ* 17,
1967, 164–7; we cannot build much on Crassus' calling Pompeius his *familiaris* in
De or. 1.168. Appian's inclusion (*B Civ.* 1.37) of Calpurnius Bestia (cos. 111) among
the victims is probably through confusion with Bestia's conviction by the *quaestio
Mamiliana*.

gave evidence against Pompeius and Memmius, but we cannot tell what mix of conviction, personal hostility, and desire to bolster his own credibility and innocence fuelled his involvement. Moreover, few of the prosecutions ended in conviction.[12] The Romans were struggling in the early months of 90 BC to understand why they were at war with their former allies: many individuals could be presented, with greater or less plausibility, as the culprits, but there was, in the end, no wholesale purge.[13]

Rome's opponents had formed themselves into a united political entity, with a name ('Italia'), a capital (at Corfinium, renamed 'Italica'), a federal structure, and a coinage.[14] That this was in place to support diplomatic activity in the late autumn of 91, and fighting at the end of the winter, is further evidence that the Italians had begun planning months before the violence at Asculum. And since these arrangements were far more elaborate than the kind of alliance required to support joint military activity, they may point to ambitions, however unrealistic, on the part of the Italians for a radical overhaul of the way Roman power operated in Italy, or even for their independence from Rome. The immediate consequences can be seen in the course of the war, which involved a complex series of different armies, commanders and campaigns. The Italians' strategy was to capture Roman enclaves; the Romans', to split the Italians' territory in two, and then deal with opposition piecemeal. Both consuls of 90 were sent to fight: this was the first time since 203 that both consuls had been fighting in Italy. P. Rutilius Lupus received the northern theatre, to the east of Rome; L. Julius Caesar the southern, in Campania, Samnium and further south. In addition, Sex. Julius Caesar (cos. 91) had his *imperium* prorogued and was sent north, and a number of experienced commanders were sent out as legates, among whom were Marius (who would receive *imperium* by a decree of the Senate later in the year), Lutatius Catulus (cos. 102) and P. Licinius Crassus (cos. 97).[15]

12. Apart from Varius, convicted under his own law in 89, the only certain conviction is Cotta's.
13. As Mouritsen notes (*Unification*, 136–7) the obscurity, to contemporaries, of the cause of the Social War is further evidence against an obvious trigger, such as the defeat of a citizenship bill.
14. A. Burnett, 'The coinage of the Social War', in A. Burnett, U. Wartenburg and R. Witschonke, eds, *Coins of Macedonia and Rome: Essays in Honour of Charles Hersh*, London: Spink 1998, 165–72; M. Pobjoy, 'The first *Italia*', in E. Herring and K. Lomas, eds, *The Emergence of State Identities in Italy in the First Millennium BC*, London: Accordia Research Institute 2000, 187–211.
15. For a full list, see *MRR* 2.27–30. Philippus is notable by his absence.

Figure 2 Italian coin from the Social War: Italian bull goring Roman wolf
(© The Trustees of the British Museum)

In the north, a major battle was fought in the valley of the river Tolenus on 11 June; the Romans were victorious, but Rutilius was killed, and such was the grief when his body was returned to Rome that the Senate decreed that in future war casualties should be buried where they fell.[16] Further north, the legate Pompeius Strabo was defeated and took refuge in Firmum, where he was besieged; and Servilius Caepio, who succeeded Rutilius, fell for the Marsian leader Poppaedius Silo's pretend surrender, and was killed in the subsequent ambush.[17] But thereafter the Romans, now under the command of Marius, began to dominate the northern front. Marius inflicted a serious defeat on the Marsi (with Sulla among his legates), and Sex. Caesar was able to join forces with Strabo, inflict a defeat on those besieging Firmum, and then pursue the survivors to Asculum. Asculum was itself then besieged by the Romans and became the major focus for the remaining campaigning in the northern area

Further south, the Italians began their campaign by besieging and seizing towns loyal to Rome. In Samnium, Venafrum was captured

16. App. *B Civ.* 1.43.
17. Strabo and Caepio were both of praetorian standing, though the dates of their - praetorships are uncertain.

early in the year by Marius Egnatius, and Aesernia besieged; and Papius Mutilus, the Samnite leader, raced through Campania. Nola fell into his hands, despite (or because of) the presence there of the praetor Postumius with a sizeable detachment of Roman troops, who defected to the Italian side when faced with a choice between that and death; the officers, including Postumius, were executed.[18] Papius then took Herculaneum, Stabiae, Surrentum and Salernum and settled down to the siege of Acerrae, which lay between him and the key Roman town of Capua.[19] L. Caesar attempted to relieve Aesernia, but was defeated by Egnatius, and retreated towards Acerrae, where he and Papius spent the remainder of the summer in indecisive skirmishing.[20] Aesernia fell to the allies later in the summer, together with its legate M. Claudius Marcellus. In Lucania, the legate P. Licinius Crassus was defeated and Grumentum captured.

Towards the end of 90, a third front threatened to open in Umbria and Etruria.[21] The impulse behind this revolt was presumably the successes of Italia, and the Marsi sent a large force to support the uprising, despite the winter and the difficulty of the intervening terrain. This was intercepted by Strabo and was largely destroyed in battle and the succeeding retreat; had it reached the other side of the Appennines, it would have found that the revolt been brought to an end. The Roman success was in part due to military action, with L. Porcius Cato operating in Etruria and A. Plotius in Umbria; but this was backed up by diplomacy. The Senate passed a decree offering Roman citizenship 'to the Latins and the allies', and the surviving consul L. Caesar, who had returned to Rome to hold the consular elections, oversaw its passage into law.[22] The *lex Iulia* marks a major shift in policy. Rome was in crisis in the autumn of 90, after a summer of fighting marked by notable disasters, including the death of a consul in battle, and facing a new threat to the north; Appian records that, for the first time, freedmen were enlisted in the army.[23] In such circumstances, the entire basis of the relationship between Rome and other communities in Italy could

18. Appian (*B Civ.* 1.42) ascribes its fall to treachery.
19. M. Frederiksen, *Campania*, Rome: British School at Rome 1984, 264–80.
20. App. *B Civ.* 1.45; but Livy records a victory of sufficient scale for the Romans to have put off military dress (*Per.* 73).
21. App. *B Civ.* 1.49; Livy, *Per.* 74; W. V. Harris, *Rome in Etruria and Umbria*, Oxford: Oxford University Press 1971, 212–29.
22. Cic. *Balb.* 21; Vell. Pat. 2.16 is probably also describing the *lex Iulia*.
23. App. *B Civ.* 1.49.

be revisited, and a previously unpalatable proposal find support.

It is unclear whether the *lex Iulia* simply offered citizenship or also addressed the complex range of issues that would arise when a previously independent political entity became a community of Roman citizens; but on balance it is likely that it did only the former.[24] This was an emergency measure, primarily intended to prevent the further spread of fighting. One particularly urgent question which it appears to have avoided was the distribution of new citizens into the Roman voting units called tribes: this distribution would determine how much influence the new citizens potentially had over tribunician legislative assemblies, as well as the elections for more junior magistrates. But it seems to have surfaced soon afterwards, with proposals to put the new citizens into a small number of new tribes which were perhaps also to vote last.[25] In fact, these tribal allocations were not implemented; but it is clear, if unsurprising, that the Romans were well aware that implementing the enfranchisement of a large number of new citizens had serious consequences for voting practices and thus for political life. It may not be a coincidence that censors were elected in 89 (though the censors of 92 had abdicated early, so a symbolic cleansing [*lustrum*] was overdue), since one of their responsibilities was the citizen roll; or that one of those elected was L. Caesar. (His colleague was P. Licinius Crassus, returned from unsuccessful campaigning as legate in Lucania.) In fact, though these censors *did* complete the *lustrum*, they did not tackle the question of enrolling new citizens.[26]

The consuls for 89 were two of the war heroes of the previous year: Pompeius Strabo and L. Porcius Cato.[27] Strabo sponsored

24. E. Bispham, *From Asculum to Actium: The Municipalization of Italy from the Social War to Augustus*, Oxford: Oxford University Press 2007, 162–72.
25. App. *B Civ.* 1.49 posits ten new tribes, Vell. Pat. 2.20 eight; Sisenna fr. 17P refers to two, created by a *lex Calpurnia*.
26. Our source, admittedly, is Cicero's speech *Pro Archia*, in a passage (11) in which he is explaining away the fact that Archias – allegedly a citizen for over a quarter of a century by 62, the date of his trial – has never been recorded in a census: he missed those of 70 and 86 through absence from Italy (with Lucullus, in both cases) and 'during the first one of Iulius and Crassus no part of the people was enrolled'. But even with the considerable lapse of time it is difficult to believe that Cicero would have risked a patent falsehood. Festus (366L) records a procedural irregularity in the census, as a result of which the census was 'rather unlucky' (*parum felix*); in the light of what happened subsequently, the verdict is easy to understand.
27. The dating of the elections in relation to campaigning is not entirely clear; if they followed Cato's military action in Etruria, his success would become very easy to understand. Strabo's victory over the Marsian relief force is more likely to be after his election.

a consular law which granted the 'Latin right' to communities in Cisalpine Gaul; this supplemented the *lex Iulia* and conciliated Rome's allies there.[28] Strabo then continued the siege of Asculum: it fell in the late autumn.[29] Cato fought against the Marsi, and defeated them in a battle in which he was killed.[30] Sulpicius Galba, one of Strabo's legates, subdued the Vestini and Marrucini, and Italia's capital was forced to move from Corfinium south to Bovianum. Another legate, Cosconius, marched south along the Adriatic coast and captured Salapia, Cannae and Ausculum. And at some point during these northern campaigns in 89, the Samnite leader Egnatius was killed. In the southern war, Sulla emerged as Rome's leading general (even allowing for the distortion which his *Memoirs* have effected on the surviving sources). With the assistance of a fleet, he recaptured the towns which Papius had captured the previous year, with the exception of Nola, and then moved east, forcing the surrender of Aeclanum, and then north to Bovianum, which he captured; Italia's capital was now shifted again, to Aesernia. The southern campaigns were not without cost. Postumius Albinus (cos. 99), who was serving among Sulla's naval commanders, was assassinated by his own troops; and T. Didius (cos. 98 and twice a *triumphator* [celebrator of a triumph]) died in battle on 11 June, the anniversary of Rutilius' death the previous year.[31] But by the time that Sulla returned to Rome to seek the consulship for 88, the Romans were clearly dominant in the south. Many of their opponents may by now have surrendered, though the war was not over: the Samnites and Lucanians continued to fight, and six Roman legions continued to besiege Nola.

Losing the peace: the transition to civil war

In the early months of the Social War, the Senate had dispatched an embassy, led by the consular Aquillius, with instructions to C. Cassius, the governor of Asia, to restore Nicomedes, the king of Bithynia, and Ariobarzanes of Cappadocia, both of whom had been

28. Asc. 3C; he is probably wrong in implying that the 'Latin right' brought with it at this period the opportunity to acquire Roman citizenship through local office-holding (Mouritsen, *Unification*, 99–108). See further Bispham, *Asculum*, 173–5.
29. Sex. Caesar had died of disease during the siege.
30. For reasons which are unclear, Marius' *imperium* had not been renewed.
31. Albinus: Plut. *Sull.* 6.9, Polyaenus, *Strat.* 8.9.1 (Sulla declined to investigate, demanding instead that the perpetrators recoup their reputations through victory); Didius' death: Ov. *Fast.* 6.567–8.

deposed by men who had Mithridates' backing. The Roman ambassadors were successful; subsequently, Nicomedes invaded Mithridates' territory.[32] Mithridates sent an envoy to the Romans in Asia to protest; he was ignored, and he then invaded Asia, defeated Nicomedes and began to force the Romans west towards the coast. For Appian, this is a story of Roman greed and expansionism: it is they who encourage Nicomedes to attack Mithridates.[33] But, as Kallet-Marx points out, Appian's ultimate source here is probably Rutilius Rufus, in exile in Mytilene and with his own grievances about provincial government to air.[34] We need not believe that the Romans were bent on setting off a major conflict in the east at a time when they were struggling with a deteriorating situation in Italy; they may well have expected Mithridates to acquiesce in their demonstration of power. But, if so, they miscalculated, and news from Italy may have encouraged Mithridates to pursue a more aggressive policy than he might otherwise have judged safe. News of Mithridates' attack reached Rome in time for the Senate, in 89, to declare Asia one of the consular provinces for the year 88 in advance of the consular elections, which were presumably held in December.[35] It was forty years since the Romans had last sent legions east of the Aegean; since then, the province of Asia had made *publicani* and businessmen rich.

This Mithridatic command precipitated a domestic crisis. It was initially, and unsurprisingly, allocated to Sulla, presumably with

32. A. N. Sherwin-White, *Roman Foreign Policy in the East, 168 B.C. to A.D. 1*, London: Duckworth 1984, 108–20; J. Hind, 'Mithridates', *CAH* 9², 1994, 129–64, at 140–3; R. M. Kallet-Marx, *Hegemony to Empire: The Development of the Roman Imperium in the East from 148 to 62 B.C.*, Berkeley: University of California Press 1995, 247–50.

33. App. *Mith.* 11–14.

34. Kallet-Marx, *Hegemony*, 250–4.

35. Prior to Sulla's changes, elections appear to have fallen late in the year (A. Lintott, *The Constitution of the Roman Republic*, Oxford: Oxford University Press 1999, 12 n. 4); thus the surviving consul of 89, Pompeius Strabo, could have been back in Rome in time to hold them at the usual time; he can be placed at Asculum on 30 November (*ILS* 8888) but his triumph on 25 December presumably took at least a few days' organisation. T. Mitchell, 'The volte-face of P. Sulpicius Rufus in 88 B.C.', *CPh* 70, 1975, 197–204, queries this timetable, arguing for earlier consular elections, and suggests that the initial consular province that Sulla received was the ongoing war in Italy; but there is no reason to think that, in this period, December was a late date for elections. Stronger is Mitchell's argument from Sulla's presence with his army outside Nola early in 88; but this can be explained as Sulla's preparing to take the army which he had commanded as a legate with him to Asia. The fall of Asculum late in 89 and Pompeius Strabo's triumph *de Asculaneis Picentibus* was a powerful closural symbol of Rome's successes in the Social War, though the other consular province for 88 was certainly the ongoing war in Italy.

both his and his colleague Pompeius' approval.[36] Its existence may
have encouraged Pompeius Strabo's unfulfilled ambition for an
immediate second consulship.[37] And then one of the newly elected
tribunes of the plebs for 88, P. Sulpicius, successfully proposed a law
to transfer it from Sulla to Marius.

Sulpicius was also responsible, during his tribunate and in collaboration with another tribune, Antistius, for vigorous opposition to
an attempt by Julius Caesar Strabo to stand for the consulship
despite the fact that he had not held the praetorship; and Sulpicius
put forward laws permitting the return of exiles, limiting senatorial
indebtedness, and allocating new citizens and freedmen to all existing tribes.[38] His tribunate was also notable for its shift in direction:
Cicero remarks that 'the popular breeze carried Sulpicius, who had
set out from an excellent position and was opposing Gaius Julius as
he sought the consulship against the laws, further than he wished';
and, as tribune, Sulpicius quarrelled with his great friend, the consul
Pompeius, to the astonishment and upset of their friends.[39] Sulpicius'
tribunate was full of action, and consequence; but many details of
chronology and motivation remain opaque.

The first question which arises is the timing of Caesar Strabo's bid
to become consul. None of the sources which notes the episode

36. The Social War gave Sulla's career, hitherto only moderately successful, decisive
impetus; in a sign of its consolidation, he married (Plut. *Sull.* 6.10–11) Caecilia Metella,
daughter of the former *pontifex maximus* Metellus Delmaticus and widow of Aemilius
Scaurus; P. Tansey, 'The death of M. Aemilius Scaurus (cos. 115 B.C.)', *Historia* 52, 2003,
378–83. The Metelli had been the most successful family in Roman politics in the
last quarter of the second century and, despite a generational and demographic dip (see
R. Syme, *The Roman Revolution*, Oxford: Oxford University Press 1939, 570),
remained wealthy and politically alert. Pompeius Rufus had no known military experience, and he and Sulla were friends (his son was married to Sulla's daughter).
37. Vell. Pat. (2.21) says, 'foiled in his hope of continuing to hold the consulship'
(*frustratus spe continuandi consulatus*) and moves directly to the Octavian war (see
below). We do not know if Strabo stood and was defeated, or found his candidacy
blocked in some way (an intriguing question since, as the only surviving consul, he
presumably conducted the elections).
38. Sources in *MRR* 2.41–2.
39. Cic. *Har. resp.* 43: *Sulpicium ab optima causa profectum Gaioque Iulio consulatum
contra leges petenti resistentem longius quam uoluit popularis aura prouexit.* J. Powell,
'The tribune Sulpicius', *Historia* 39, 1990, 446–60, at 457–8, points out that *ab optima
causa* means 'from a very good cause' or 'case', which Powell takes to be his opposition
to Strabo's candidature; it does not have automatic political implications. The ancient
sources are gathered in A. Greenidge and A. Clay, *Sources for Roman History 133–70
B.C.*, 2nd edn, rev. Gray, E., Oxford: Oxford University Press 1960, 160–4; the break
with Pompeius is used by Cicero, in his *Laelius*, as the starting point for the whole
dialogue.

specifies the year of his attempt; the involvement of Sulpicius, as tribune, places it either in 89, and the campaign for the consulship of 88, or in 88 and the consulship of 87, but the choice remains contentious.[40] The implication of Cicero's words at *De haruspicum responso* 43 is that Sulpicius began his tribunate as someone who was not regarded as *popularis* in his sympathies. That is not inconsistent with the rest of our evidence for his actions before his tribunate, though most of the evidence comes through Cicero's writings. He presents Sulpicius as an outstanding orator; and Sulpicius' first moment of public prominence was his prosecution of Norbanus in 95.[41] How far he actually was close to Licinius Crassus, Antonius and the other speakers is unclear; and of course the kind of friendship, based on strong shared interests in oratory, that involved holiday visiting did not imply a great deal about shared political outlooks or willingness to co-operate. But his exceptionally close friendship with Pompeius Rufus suggests that it was not a coincidence that he sought the tribunate for 88, the year in which Pompeius hoped to hold the consulship; and that implies that Sulpicius expected to work harmoniously with Sulla, too.[42]

In addition to the situation in Asia Minor, the major issue at Rome at this moment was the means by which the transition to peace in Italy was to be managed. A crucial aspect was the registration of the new citizens and as the war approached its end, the size and urgency of the problem increased: it may already have been apparent that the censors were not making progress in citizen enrollment. Sulpicius' law on tribal allocations was favourable towards the new citizens, and a possible interpretation is that Sulpicius intended, in alliance with the consuls, to use his tribunate to resolve the 'Italian question', despite opposition from many existing citizens, and hasten the end

40. Badian, '*Quaestiones*'; A. Lintott, 'The tribunate of P. Sulpicius Rufus', *CQ* 21, 1971, 442–53; B. Katz, 'Caesar Strabo's struggle for the consulship – and more', *RhM* 120, 1977, 45–63; Mitchell, 'Volte-face'; B. Marshall, *A Historical Commentary on Asconius*, Columbia: University of Missouri Press 1985, 144–5; Powell, 'The tribune Sulpicius'.
41. See above, p. 59. Sulpicius' participation at the Norbanus trial made him an obvious character for Cicero's dialogue, given the prominence of the case in *De oratore*; but he also contributes to the sense of wasted promise and impending disaster which is so marked a feature of the dialogue's *mise-en-scène*, particularly in the opening of the third book.
42. Apart from Pompeius Strabo and, possibly, Caesar Strabo – both of whose candidatures were anomalous – no other consular candidates are known; that supports the hypothesis that Pompeius Rufus and Sulla would in normal circumstances have been confident of victory.

of the Social War on terms that had a reasonable prospect of being lasting. Success in this project, whether via a *lex Sulpicia* or a *lex Pompeia Cornelia*, would have generated substantial and lasting popularity for its instigators among the new citizens. Other men may plausibly have hoped to acquire such popularity for themselves, and the issue provides a context for Caesar Strabo's seeking the consulship for 88. Strabo's elder brother was the consul of 90 (and censor in 89) who had sponsored the *lex Iulia*. Strabo himself was another fine orator and a popular figure, who had used his position as aedile in 90 to speak frequently to the people; he had not, as far as we know, fought during the Social War.[43] His candidature in 89 would then be an attempt by the Caesares to consolidate their position in relation to the new citizens, made urgent by the emergence of a rival bloc with the same ambitions – and thus justifying the accelerated candidature. (It may even have had the support of a senatorial decree.[44]) Moreover, it would have been in direct competition with Sulla's ambitions, given that two patricians could not hold the consulship in the same year; its implications for the plebeian Pompeius Rufus would have been much less severe. Thus one implication of putting Caesar Strabo's attempt in 89 is that Sulpicius was, in effect, working in support of Sulla. If so, Sulpicius surely expected reciprocal support from Sulla for his own legislation, including the tribal distribution of the new citizens. If – and this remains speculative – Sulla made it clear to Sulpicius, after entering office as consul, that he had no intention of so supporting him, and if Pompeius Rufus indicated that he would not break with his consular colleague, then we have a context for Sulpicius' change of direction, his break with Pompeius Rufus, and the extraordinary aggression directed at Sulla personally with his law on the Mithridatic command.

This reconstruction makes citizenship, and the end of the Social War, a dominant issue in Rome in December 89.[45] It also provides a personal context for Sulpicius' actions, and gives Sulla good reason to distrust the Senate. But its basis is fragile, and the evidence on Caesar Strabo could equally support a consular attempt in 88. To move it to 88, for the consulship of 87, resolves the chronological difficulties involved in trying to fit Sulpicius' opposition to Strabo into the last weeks of 88, and explains why none of the sources tell

43. Cic. *Brut.* 305; Strabo's half-brother Lutatius Catulus, Marius' colleague in the defeat of the Cimbri, may have been a source of further support.
44. That appears to be the implication of Cic. *Phil.* 11.11.
45. For a suggested chronology of enfranchisement, see Bispham, *Asculum*, 175–87.

us that Strabo was defeated in the elections for 88.[46] The later date
makes the Mithridatic command a much more likely spur to Strabo's
ambition than the citizenship question.[47] Since opposition to Strabo
is presented as a part of Sulpicius' tribunate from the outset this
date also implies that Strabo began his campaigning early in 88; this
may have been unusually early in the pre-Sullan political calendar,
but perhaps explicable if Strabo was intending to legitimate his
campaign with formal senatorial approval.

The removal of Strabo's candidature as a factor in Sulpicius' initial
activity, which follows if Strabo was attempting to be elected for 87,
still leaves tribal distribution as the central element in the legislative
programme which Sulpicius put forward during his tribunate. This
law was highly controversial: it provoked strong opposition from
existing citizens, whose electoral influence it diminished. Sulpicius
responded to that opposition by organising gangs. So serious did the
disturbances become that the consuls authorised the suspension of
public business, which Sulpicius challenged violently: in the fighting
which followed, the consul Pompeius' son was killed.[48] Appian
makes Sulpicius an ally of Marius from the outset, and presents
their alliance as a quid pro quo: Marius supported Sulpicius' tribal
distribution in return for Sulpicius' support over the Mithridatic
command, with the added advantage that the gratitude of the new
citizens could be turned into immediate support for Sulpicius' law on
the command. The very familiarity of an alliance between a tribune
and a military leader may make us sceptical of Appian's account,
or at least of its chronology; it is easier to account for Cicero's
emphasis on a change during Sulpicius' tribunate if Sulpicius joined
forces with Marius only once it became apparent that he could not
rely on the consuls.[49] Sulpicius' preoccupation – whether or not in
competition with other groups at Rome – was with the structure of
post-war domestic politics.

Sulpicius' law on the command against Mithridates had two
elements: it took away the command from Sulla, and it gave it by
name to Marius. The latter part, the popular bestowal of *imperium*,

46. If Strabo did stand in 89, then defeat, or withdrawal of candidature, are the only
explanations for Sulla's election.
47. A fragment of Diodorus (37.2) makes Strabo and Marius rivals for the command
against Mithridates.
48. App. *B Civ.* 1.55; Plut. *Mar.* 35; *Sull.* 8.
49. This view keeps tribal distribution at the centre of Sulpicius' plans; the alternative,
to make that a means to secure Marius' end of the Mithridatic command, is less attractive.

did have precedents.[50] So did popular removal of *imperium*: this happened to Servilius Caepio after his defeat at Arausio in 105, and the possibility was enshrined in a *lex Cassia* of 104, which expelled from the Senate anyone whose *imperium* the people had abrogated. Marius himself had received Metellus' command against Jugurtha in 107. But such moves had taken place only in response to failure, and with an individual whose *imperium* had been prorogued: there is no parallel for ending a command in this way before it had begun.[51]

Sulla was thus faced with an unprecedented challenge. His response was to return to the army which he had commanded the previous year, which was still encamped at Nola. Sulla persuaded his troops to support his position as consul, and leaving one legion at Nola under the command of App. Claudius Pulcher he returned with the remainder to Rome.[52] The siege of Nola remained in stalemate, and the Italian capital at Aesernia had not yet been attacked. Elsewhere, though, in southern Italy, the Italian position was collapsing under the attacks of Metellus Pius, who had taken over Cosconius' forces in Apulia and captured the symbolically and strategically important town of Venusia.[53] His opponents appear to have fallen back to Bruttium, where a plan to cross over to Sicily was foiled by the governor of Sicily, C. Norbanus. The Romans were emerging decisively as the victors in the Social War just as their internal affairs were progressing from political violence to open civil war.

Accounts of Sulla's march on Rome use the language of war against foreign enemies.[54] According to Appian, he justified his action on the grounds that he was acting to free the state from tyrants; but although his army was willing to follow him, only one of his officers was.[55] Once news of his imminent armed arrival

---

50. None recent, however. Scipio Africanus in 210 is the clearest parallel, since he was *priuatus* at the time of the vote; more recent examples of the people overriding senatorial decisions on *imperium*, such as Aemilianus and Marius himself, involved men who had been elected to the consulship, albeit in irregular fashion.

51. Sulpicius' law did not remove Sulla from the consulship.

52. App. Claudius Pulcher had held the praetorship in 89, and the easiest way to explain his presence in Campania is that he had been appointed as Sulla's successor.

53. Venusia was the only Latin colony to join the Italians; G. Bradley, 'Colonization and identity in Republican Italy', in G. Bradley and J-P. Wilson, eds, *Greek and Roman Colonization: Origins, Ideologies and Interactions*, Swansea: Classical Press of Wales 2006, 161–87, at 176–7. Its capture may provide the context for the enslavement of Horace's father.

54. App. *B Civ.* 1.57–9; Livy. *Per.* 77; Plut. *Sull.* 9; Vell. Pat. 2.19.

55. App. *B Civ.* 1.57: ἐλευθερώσων αὐτὴν [sc. τὴν πατρίδα] ἀπὸ τῶν τυραννούντων. The officer is usually, following E. Badian ('Waiting for Sulla', *JRS* 52, 1962, 47–61, at

reached Rome, the Senate sent envoys and attempted to negotiate. Sulla ignored these and continued his advance: the alleged bad faith of these envoys, which is found in Appian's account, presumably goes back to Sulla's own account in his memoirs. Despite his superiority in numbers, equipment and training, he had considerable difficulty in securing the city, not only because of opposition from the troops which Marius and Sulpicius had gathered but also from the civilian population. But once in control Sulla, together with Pompeius Rufus (who had joined his forces before the attack on Rome), proceeded to implement measures which responded to the attempt to deprive him of the command against Mithridates. All of Sulpicius' laws were annulled on grounds of illegality, since they had been passed during a suspension of public business. Marius, Sulpicius and ten others were declared enemies of the state and condemned to death.[56] Popular legislative activity, and the capacity of tribunes, were curtailed in some way, possibly by ensuring that the *comitia centuriata*, which tribunes could not summon, was the only assembly which could pass laws. No steps were taken about the new citizens. Pompeius Rufus was put in charge of the forces which Pompeius Strabo still commanded; thus Sulla left an ally behind him, in charge of the one of the most significant armies left in Italy.[57] And consular elections were held, with Cn. Octavius and L. Cornelius Cinna being elected.[58] Sulla attempted to control events after his departure by ensuring that Cinna, one of the consuls for 87, swore

54–5), identified as L. Licinius Lucullus, but see P. Thonemann, 'The date of Lucullus' quaestorship', ZPE 149, 2004, 80–2.

56. The other ten included Marius' son; Appian (B Civ. 1.60) also lists a Junius Brutus (presumably Damasippus, the urban praetor in 82) and Publius Cethegus, Gaius and Quintus Granius, Publius Albinovanus and Marcus Laetorius; Cicero (*Brut.* 168) adds Q. Rubrius Varro, which leaves two unknowns. An Albinovanus surfaces switching sides in 82 (App. B Civ. 1.91) and is probably the same man; little is known of the others. The fact that we do not know what the men other than Marius, his son and Sulpicius had done in 88 to earn the enmity of Sulla and Pompeius Rufus is an indication of the poverty of our evidence.

57. Strabo's position at this point is something of a puzzle. Technically, his *imperium* had come to an end on the day of his triumph. But he returned with and to his army in Picenum. Was he given an exceptional grant of *imperium*, to consolidate Rome's victory in the north? Or was his position illegal? And, since Pompeius Rufus' province must have been in Italy, to continue military operations against those Italians who remained under arms, was this in fact a change to the Senate's initial dispositions?

58. Little is known of Octavius' career prior to his consulship; he may have missed most of the Social War, since an inscription puts him in an eastern province for his praetorship. Cinna served as a legate, probably in Pompeius Strabo's army. Neither had Sulla's support (Plut. *Sull.* 10.3).

an oath of loyalty to him in a striking public ceremony on the Capitol: Cinna took a stone in his hand and, wishing that if he failed to remain on good terms with Sulla he would be cast out from the city as the stone was cast from his hand, threw the stone onto the ground.[59] It was only late in 88 or early in 87 that Sulla left Rome for the east: the dissensions between him and Marius had delayed the response to Mithridates by a year, a failing which Mithridates had exploited by invading Greece.

Sulla acted as though he hoped to return to the situation prior to Sulpicius' law; there were many reasons why this did not happen, not least the fact that the consuls of 87 were unable to co-operate, and substantial forces remained in Italy which provided the material to transform political dissension into civil war. App. Claudius had a legion near Nola, the forces which Sulla had left behind when he marched on Rome; Metellus Pius was continuing his campaign in Lucania; and Pompeius Strabo's army remained in Picenum, under his command. (When Pompeius Rufus had arrived to take command, he had been killed by the soldiers, possibly with Strabo's encouragement.[60]) As soon as the consuls had taken office, Cinna abandoned his support for Sulla. He was behind a tribune's attempt to prosecute Sulla; in so far as *imperium*-holders were immune from prosecution, this may have implied that Sulpicius' law of the previous year was still in force.[61] Cinna also put forward a law to distribute the new citizens in all the tribes. This law was vetoed by the tribunes, and there were violent confrontations between rival groups of citizens, with Octavius personally leading the opposition. Cinna left Rome and the Senate, led by his colleague Octavius, deprived him of the office of consul. In fresh elections to fill the consular vacancy the priest of Jupiter (*flamen Dialis*), L. Cornelius Merula, was elected.[62] Cinna went to Campania and took control of

---

59. Plut. *Sull.* 10; cf. Cass. Dio fr. 102. We do not know whether Octavius was compelled to do likewise; the story of Cinna, the oath-breaker, is clearly the more memorable anecdote.

60. Livy, *Per.* 77; Vell. Pat. 2.20; Appian (*B Civ.* 1.63) reflects a tradition more sympathetic to Strabo.

61. Plut. *Sull.* 10; Cic. *Brut.* 179.

62. App. *B Civ.* 1.64–5; Livy, *Per.* 79; Vell. Pat. 2.20; *Schol. Gronov.* 286St. The relative chronology of Cinna's departure from Rome and the passing of a *senatus consultum* sacking him from the position of consul is unclear: Appian's view – that the Senate passed its measure as a response to Cinna's abandonment of the city and promise of freedom to slaves – may simply represent the anti-Cinnan tradition which became canonical after Sulla's victory. According to Granius Licinianus (35.15), the Senate approved, for

the legion there commanded by Appius Claudius. He marched them back towards Rome, and news of his initiative encouraged Marius to return to Italy from Africa, where he had fled the previous year; Marius landed in Etruria and raised a force there. Rome now found itself between two opposing armies. The Senate instructed Pompeius Strabo to move his troops to Rome, to support the consul Octavius; Strabo obeyed, but slowly. The Senate also instructed Metellus to negotiate a truce with his opponents in the south and bring his army to Rome. Metellus attempted to do so but was unable to agree to the demands which he faced: not simply citizenship, but also the retention of all the booty which had been seized during the war and the return of captives.[63] Faced with a stalemate, Metellus left A. Plotius as his legate in Campania and departed for Rome.[64] Cinna and Marius moved into this vacuum and sent Flavius Fimbria to negotiate with the Samnites and Lucanians: Fimbria agreed to all their demands, and in return the Italians sent some forces to join Cinna's army.

The civil war which now erupted, sometimes called the Octavian war, involved the collaboration of Cinna and Marius against forces whose commanders, in theory at least, were following the orders of the Senate.[65] The picture was, however, complicated by the ambiguous behaviour of Strabo, who was allegedly negotiating with Cinna during the war, with the object of achieving the second consulship he had been hoping for at the end of 89. Fierce fighting took place around Rome and nearby in Latium. Marius captured and sacked Ostia; the Cinnan forces were driven back from the Janiculum hill, with heavy losses on both sides, and Marius then took the towns of Antium, Aricia and Lanuvium.[66] This enabled the Cinnan forces to threaten Rome's food supply; moreover, the senatorial forces were weakened by disease. (One of the victims may have been Strabo; his death is variously ascribed to plague and to a lightning strike.[67])

the first time, the publication of a part of the Sibylline books which was interpreted to mean that Cinna's banishment would lead to peace and security.

63. Dio Cass. fr. 102. 7.
64. Plotius was soon after defeated and killed by the Samnites (Livy, *Per.* 80).
65. Marius had no formal position during this civil war but regained *imperium* later in the year once he resumed the command against Mithridates; Strabo's position was technically dubious: see above.
66. This is the order of events given in Livy (*Per.* 79–80).
67. Whatever the actual cause, the persistence of the lightning story underscores his unpopularity (Plut. *Pomp.* 1), presumably connected with his failure decisively to protect Rome from attack; see T. W. Hillard, 'Death by lightning, Pompeius Strabo and the people', *RhM* 139, 1996, 135–45.

Strabo's death, if anything, strengthened the senatorial side, since the remainder of his army was taken over by Octavius; but the Senate began negotiations with Cinna, and though it was unable to secure significant concessions, it oversaw the rescinding of the law which had banished Marius, and opened the city gates to them.

Cinna and Marius marked their return by a purge of their opponents: among those killed or forced to commit suicide were the consuls Octavius and Merula, the orator Antonius, Caesar Strabo and his brother Lucius Caesar, Q. Lutatius Catulus, P. Licinius Crassus and C. Atilius Serranus.[68] Metellus Pius retreated to Africa; App. Claudius went into exile, and had his *imperium* abrogated, after he failed to obey a tribune's summons.[69] Cinna and Marius then declared themselves consuls for 86 BC.

Domestic politics and foreign affairs in the 80s BC

Assessing the five years during which Cinna and his immediate supporters dominated the political life of Rome is difficult: not only are the sources limited, but the period was also subject to a sustained rewriting once Sulla had returned to Italy.[70] Cinna was regarded as a tyrant, and Marius and Cinna's return to Rome as comparable to the sacking of a city. They undoubtedly started their regime with terror: in executing their opponents, they had Sulla's declaration of some of them as *hostes* the previous year as a precedent, but the purge of 87 BC was noticeably more effective and wide-ranging. Just as the boundaries between political dispute and military conflict collapsed, so the penalty for being on the losing side in a political quarrel

68. As with the enemies (*hostes*) identified by Sulla the previous year, it is surprisingly difficult to identify the precise actions which made these men the enemies of Marius and Cinna, and there is a danger in allowing purges to simplify politics in rigid blocs. Simplest is the hypothesis that these five consulars, and the influential Caesar Strabo, were prominent in the Senate in support of the consul Octavius. Whereas Sulpicius alone among Sulla's enemies was killed, Marius and Cinna were effective in turning political enmity into death, and we can trace here the beginnings of a literature of enforced political deaths which culminated in the anecdotes of the proscriptions. Thus we have the record of Octavius refusing to flee (Diod. Sic. 38.2) and being cut down whilst sitting on the curule chair (App. *B Civ.* 1.71), the display of heads on the speakers' platform (Cic. *De or.* 3.8–10) and macabre anecdotes about the deaths of other victims (App. *B Civ.* 1.72–7).
69. Cic. *Dom.* 83. Badian, 'Waiting', demonstrates, however, that there was no wholesale departure by the aristocracy from Rome.
70. For a recent attempt, M. Lovano, *The Age of Cinna: Crucible of Late Republican Rome*, Stuttgart: Steiner 2002.

became death, even for those men, such as Merula, who had not been involved in the fighting.[71] The consequences of opposition were underscored by the public display of the victims' heads on the speakers' platform. But it would be an oversimplification to dismiss the entire period down to Sulla's return as a terrorist interlude; there is some evidence for attempts to re-establish peaceful civic life in radically changed circumstances, attempts that failed, and are obscured in our evidence, largely because Sulla's subsequent invasion of Italy was successful and his own solutions for Rome's problems were of a very different nature.

When Sulla finally arrived in Greece in 87, he found a military situation which had become considerably more serious than it had been when the Senate first decreed Asia a consular province in 89. Mithridates' forces had during 88 overrun Asia, forcing the governor Cassius to flee first to Apamea and then to Rhodes. Romans and Italians had been massacred, including the former consul M'. Aquillius whose capture and execution reverberated as a grisly *exemplum*.[72] Many cities had declared their support for Mithridates, and the normal flow of revenues to Rome was now seriously disrupted. Moreover, Mithridates had taken advantage of the Romans' failure to act swiftly by sending troops to mainland Greece under his general Archelaus.[73] He had already received overtures from a faction at Athens, which now sided firmly with Mithridates, and became the first focus of Sulla's campaign; he captured the city on 1 March 86. Sulla then moved his troops north in pursuit of those of Mithridates, and over the summer of 86 he defeated them near Chaeronea and then destroyed a second force at Orchomenus.

Marius' aim was still the Mithridatic command, but he died within a fortnight of taking office on 1 January 86 and the province

---

71. F. Hinard, 'La terreur comme mode de gouvernement', in G. Urso, ed., *Terror et Pavor: Violenza, Intimidazione, Clandestinità nel Mondo Antico*, Pisa: ETS 2006, 247–64; Merula and Catulus, unlike the others, were prosecuted and committed suicide before the verdicts (Alexander, *Trials*, 60–1). E. Weinrib, 'The prosecution of Roman magistrates', *Phoenix* 22, 1968, 32–56, at 41–3, notes the exceptional frequency of tribunician prosecutions in the opening part of the Cinnan period and speculates that tribunician attempts to abrogate *imperium* (attempted in the case of Sulla and achieved in that of App. Claudius Pulcher) may be a Cinnan innovation.
72. He was executed by having molten gold poured down his throat, in a symbolic demonstration of the Roman greed which Mithridates presented as the cause of the war.
73. Sherwin-White, *Foreign Policy*, 132–48; F. Santangelo, *Sulla, the Elites and the Empire*, Leiden: Brill 2007, 33–9.

of Asia passed to the suffect consul L. Valerius Flaccus with immediate effect.[74] On arrival in Greece, Flaccus bypassed Sulla and took his two legions across the Hellespont with the intention of attacking Mithridates directly; but his forces mutinied, and he was killed by his legate Flavius Fimbria. The epitomator of Livy records that Flaccus was disliked because of his greed, but his death is more likely to be the a consequence of the tripartite division in internal Roman politics – between Sulla, the followers of Cinna and the late Marius, and those who were attempting to remain separate from both groups. Memnon records, in his history of his home town Heraclea in Pontus, instructions to Flaccus, from the Senate, to investigate the possibility of collaborating with Sulla against Mithridates. Fimbria, a staunch supporter of Marius, may have been acting to forestall this prospect.[75] Fimbria took control of the army and continued into Asia Minor, where he laid siege to Mithridates at Pergamum.

Sulla's victories at Chaeronea and Orchomenus during 86 were decisive for the campaign in Greece, and demonstrated the calibre of his troops. But his lack of naval forces prevented him from capitalising on these successes. Mithridates' ships were still in control of the Aegean, and he, so far, secure in Asia Minor. Sulla opened negotiations with Mithridates; but he also sent his quaestor Lucullus to collect naval forces from Egypt and elsewhere in north Africa. Lucullus brought the fleet he gathered up the Aegean coast of Asia Minor, bringing a number of communities back under Roman control. Whilst he was so doing, he received messengers from Fimbria, asking for co-operation in capturing Mithridates, who had escaped from Pergamum south to Pitane on the coast. Since Fimbria was in control of the hinterland, Mithridates' only possible escape was by sea.[76]

Lucullus, however, refused to co-operate with Fimbria in captur-

---

74. This man must be distinguished from his homonym, who was consul in 100 and appointed *princeps senatus* by the censors of 86. The son of the suffect consul of 86 (*pr.* in 63) was defended by Cicero, though the section of *Pro Flacco* dealing with the defendant's early life, and touching on his father's career, is fragmentary. One minor puzzle is the patrician status of both consuls after the election of Flaccus.

75. Livy, *Per.* 82; Memnon, 24. In addition to acting as Marius and Cinna's negotiator with the Samnites during the Octavian war, Fimbria appears to be implicated in Cinna's domestic policy through his (abortive) prosecution of Scaevola in 86. A. Lintott, 'The offices of C. Flavius Fimbria in 86–85 B.C.', *Historia* 20, 1971, 696–701, argues that he was Marius' quaestor in 86 BC, subsequently transferred to Flaccus.

76. Plut. *Luc.* 2–3.

ing Mithridates (who escaped), and after naval engagements with Mithridates' fleet further north he took Sulla's army across the Hellespont. The presence of two mutually hostile Roman armies gave Mithridates scope to negotiate in 85 an exceptionally lenient peace treaty with Sulla, the peace of Dardanus, by suggesting that he might instead join forces with Fimbria.[77] As Sherwin-White points out, Mithridates was not required to make a formal surrender to the Romans, and although he gave up his recent conquests he kept his original kingdom intact. Sulla's troops were thus deprived of any opportunity for looting, though Mithridates was required to pay a substantial indemnity; that lack may have contributed to Sulla's decision to extract five years of back taxes from Asia as a single lump sum (of 20,000 talents), an imposition which left the area in a financially parlous state for years to come.[78] Once peace had been secured, Fimbria's leverage was greatly diminished. Sulla brought his army up to Thyateira, where Fimbria was encamped; the two forces fraternised, and Fimbria, on seeing this, committed suicide.[79] Sulla spent most of 84 in Asia dealing with its organisation and then returned, via Athens, to Italy, landing with his army at Brundisium during the winter of 84–83.[80]

Neither the Senate nor Cinna and his followers had much success in their attempt to exercise control over the eastern empire; and Rome's internal divisions compromised its military capacity. Metellus Pius held Africa after the Octavian war until it was recaptured by Fabius Hadrianus.[81] And for some reason the governor of Gaul and Hispania Citerior, C. Flaccus, was never replaced.[82] There were other high-profile absentees from Rome: App. Claudius, whose troops Cinna had seized at Nola, was deprived of his *imperium* and exiled; the young Marcus Crassus (whose father and brother were among those killed by the Marians) fled to Spain; and Sulla's wife Metella escaped to Athens. But the picture of a

77. Sherwin-White, *Foreign Policy*, 142.
78. Santangelo, *Elites*, 111–27.
79. Fimbria's troops remained in Asia, forming part of Murena's army and then Lucullus'; they were eventually recalled to Italy only in 67.
80. Brundisium welcomed Sulla, for which it was rewarded by immunity from taxation.
81. Fabius Hadrianus' cruelty and greed provoked an uprising by Roman citizens in 82, during which he was burned alive in the governor's residence at Utica, becoming thereby exemplary of bad government: Cic. *Verr.* 2.1.70, 2.5.94.
82. E. Badian, 'Notes on provincial governors from the Social War down to Sulla's victory', in E. Badian, *Studies in Greek and Roman History*, Oxford: Blackwell 1964, 71–104, at 88–96; he appears to have been governor for 13 years.

Rome deserted by the nobility given in some sources must be dismissed as a gloss which emerged after Sulla's victory.[83] Civilian life resumed: the law courts functioned, legislation was passed, and new censors were elected in 86.[84] And the war in Italy was over: the terms that Fimbria negotiated held. In one striking respect, however, normality was not achieved, since Cinna secured his re-election to the consulship for 85 and 84, and his colleague in 85, Cn. Papirius Carbo, was also re-elected for 84. The circumstances of the elections for 85 are unclear; the following year, the elections took place as preparations to respond to Sulla's return quickened. Despite the precedent of Marius – and the military threat from Sulla was presumably the justification offered for the repeated holding, if justification were required – this seizure of the consulship marked a radical break in practice. This must have been a source of considerable chagrin to those who would otherwise have expected the opportunity to stand for that office; we simply cannot tell what Cinna might have intended to do in this respect in the medium term.[85]

The treatment of the Italians remained the major domestic issue, and Cinna had promised distribution among the 35 tribes as he gathered support for his campaign against Octavius in 87. A law to this effect may have been passed as soon as the Marians took control of Rome, in which case the actual allocation to tribes is likely to have been part of the job of the censors elected in 86.[86] How far Cinna tried to influence the censorial elections is unclear, but it is striking that L. Marcius Philippus, who had as consul opposed Livius Drusus so vigorously, was one of those successful; he was unlikely to be pro-Italian.[87] But there were not many possible candidates, and perhaps fewer willing to engage with such a contentious issue. The actual distribution of the new citizens into tribes seems to have combined recognition of loyalty or disloyalty during the war with adherence to the overall principle of a wide distribution as well as some attempt

---

83. Vell. Pat. 2.23; Badian, 'Waiting'.
84. 'For about three years the city was not at war' (Cic. *Brut.* 308): Cicero describes the years 86–84, during which he was in Rome.
85. See further below, Chapter 5.
86. Bispham, *Asculum*, 189–99.
87. His colleague, M. Perperna, is a fascinating nonentity: he leaves barely a scratch on the surviving sources, but at his death, at the age of 98, in 49 BC, only seven of the men he had enrolled in the Senate as censor were still alive: a curiosity noted by Valerius Maximus (8.13.4) and the elder Pliny (*HN* 7.156).

to keep numbers balanced between the different tribes.[88] That is, whilst the censors did not eschew the opportunity for reward and punishment, they were also concerned to establish a system which might actually work.

A second major problem was finance, both public and private. During the Social War, the cost of the fighting and a drop in revenues due to the disruption created a financial crisis, one consequence of which was that debtors were unable to service their loans.[89] The urban praetor for 89, Sempronius Asellio, attempted to provide relief to debtors; he was lynched whilst sacrificing at the temple of Castor and Pollux in the forum, and no action was taken against those suspected of orchestrating the violence.[90] Sulpicius' law limiting senatorial debt should be understood in this context, and a late source ascribes to Sulla and Pompeius in 88 a measure regulating interest payments.[91] In 86 the suffect consul Flaccus passed a law which allowed debtors to settle their debts by the repayment of just a quarter of the principal, and in the following year the praetors issued an edict confirming the rate of exchange between the *as* and the denarius, which had been fluctuating since the official value of the bronze *as* was greater than its metal value. The importance of this measure can be gauged from the popularity which Marius Gratidianus gained in his attempt to claim sole credit for it. The measures brought back a degree of stability to the financial system but the state's finances more generally remained a problem.[92]

After Flaccus' disaster, no further attempt was made to appoint a commander for the war against Mithridates in succession to Sulla, and by 85, at least, Cinna and Carbo were concentrating on preparing for Sulla's return to Rome. They intended to meet Sulla in Greece and to that end Cinna started to gather troops, but was stoned to death when a mutiny broke out due to his forces' unwillingness to embark and to fight other Romans.[93] Carbo was unable to hold elections for a suffect consul due to religious objections from the

88. L. R. Taylor, *The Voting Districts of the Roman Republic: The Thirty-Five Urban and Rural Tribes*, Rome: American Academy in Rome 1960; Bispham, *Asculum*, 196–8.
89. Cic. *Leg. agr.* 2.80; Lintott, 'Tribunate', 451–2, on the costs of the Social War.
90. App. *B Civ.* 1.54; Val. Max. 9.7.4; Livy, *Per.* 74.
91. Festus, 464L.
92. M. Crawford, 'The edict of M. Marius Gratidianus', *PCPhS* n.s. 14, 1968, 1–4; D. Hollander, *Money in the Late Roman Republic*, Leiden: Brill 2007, 28–9.
93. Livy, *Per.* 83; App. *B Civ.* 1.77–8; *De vir. ill.* 69. Plut. *Pomp.* 5 has Cinna as the victim of a centurion who believes him to have killed Pompeius; see R. Seager, 'Sulla', *CAH* 9², 1994, 165–207, at 184.

Figure 3 Temple of Castor and Pollux (Photo courtesy of Elizabeth Moignard)

augurs and remained sole consul for the rest of 84; later in the year Gaius Norbanus and Scipio Asiagenes were elected consuls. Whereas Cinna had been and Carbo remained determined to oppose Sulla by force, conscious that they would not survive a Sullan victory, a group within the Senate, led by its *princeps* L. Valerius Flaccus, hoped to engineer a peaceful settlement. The trigger was a letter that Sulla sent the Senate from Asia in 84, announcing his successes against Mithridates and promising vengeance on his enemies; the Senate sent a delegation to Sulla and instructed the consuls not to raise any troops until Sulla replied, an instruction which was ignored. Nor did Sulla show any desire to negotiate, telling the senatorial delegation that he was in a better position to provide safety than it was, since he had an army.[94] Nonetheless, the senatorial initiative should not be regarded as inevitably futile; military violence was not yet a normal tool of political life, and there must still have been hope that Sulla's actions in 88 would turn out to be an anomaly rather than a precedent. The episode also demonstrates the limits on the power of Cinna and his supporters; he and Carbo could secure their re-election to the consulship, but they could not prevent other members of the Senate from acting independently. Sulla, too, needed to manage the fears of those in Italy, and his success in so doing, and

94. App. *B Civ.* 1.79. Livy, *Per.* 84, has a much more conciliatory Sulla.

thereby ensuring that he did not face opposition from a unified peninsula, was crucial in paving the way to his final victory.[95]

Sulla rejected the senatorial overtures and he and the consuls moved to open preparation for fighting. The numbers involved were enormous: Norbanus, Scipio and Carbo had the equivalent of 20 legions between them, and Sulla's forces were supplemented first by those under the command of Metellus Pius, and then with others supplied by M. Licinius Crassus and Strabo's son, Gnaeus Pompeius. Pius had some claim to legitimate authority, since the *imperium* which he had held since his praetorship in 89 had not lapsed; Crassus was perhaps motivated by revenge; Pompeius' motives are less clear.[96] The fighting continued for the best part of two years, from Sulla's return to Italy during the winter of 84–83 until his final victory in the battle of the Colline Gate on 1 November 82, and took place across much of central and northern Italy, compounding the devastation due to the Social War.[97] Sulla himself defeated Norbanus in Campania early in 83 and subsequently persuaded Scipio's army to abandon him (earlier negotiations between Sulla and Scipio to end the war were wrecked by the praetor Sertorius, who captured Suessa during the truce).[98] The war continued largely under the guidance of Carbo, who was based at Ariminum, where he faced the forces that Pompeius was recruiting in Picenum. Meanwhile, at Rome catastrophe struck, with the destruction by fire on 6 July of the temple of Capitoline Jupiter. The connection with the unhappy state of the *res publica* was obvious.

At the consular elections towards the end of 83 the conflict hardened further: Carbo secured election to a third consulship, and his colleague was Marius' 26-year-old son. At least four of those elected to the praetorship were also active opponents of Sulla.[99] Carbo,

---

95. B. W. Frier, 'Sulla's propaganda and the collapse of the Cinnan Republic', *AJPh* 92, 1971, 585–604; Santangelo, *Elites*, 67–87.

96. He had spent the Cinnan period in Rome, not without difficulty, and Carbo attempted to incorporate him into the forces he was preparing against Sulla; R. Seager *Pompey the Great*, 2nd edn, Oxford: Blackwell 2002, 25–6.

97. Seager, 'Sulla', 187–97.

98. Cic. *Phil.* 12.27 uses the meeting as an example of negotiations – unlike those with Antonius – which took place without violence (*uis*) or danger (*periculum*), though the terms were not kept.

99. C. Carrinas and Brutus Damasippus had already been involved in the fighting as legates. Q. Antonius Balbus failed to hold Sardinia against Sulla's forces, and M. Perperna (presumably the son of the consul of 92) escaped eventually to Spain after he was driven out of his province of Sicily by Pompeius.

furthermore, had those senators who had joined Sulla declared *hostes*. At the same time, splits were visible with Carbo's followers, most obviously in the figure of Sertorius, who abandoned the fighting in Italy in order to go to his province of Spain.[100] The fighting paused during the winter of 83–82; when it resumed, Sulla sent Metellus to face Carbo, while he moved north to meet the consul Marius. He crushed Marius' forces at the battle of Sacriportus, near Signia, twenty-five miles or so east of Rome; the survivors, including Marius, took refuge in Praeneste, where they were besieged. The remainder of the war was effectively dominated by the siege of Praeneste, since it drew Carbo south, leaving Norbanus behind in Cisalpine Gaul to deal with Metellus. Sulla himself left the siege of Praeneste under the command of Lucretius Ofella and went initially towards Rome, where he faced no opposition; he summoned an assembly (presumably outside the city boundary) where 'he regretted unavoidable current circumstances and urged confidence, as these would come to an end and things return to what they should be'.[101] He arrived in a city which had just witnessed another round of killing: on Marius' orders, the urban praetor Brutus Damasippus had arranged for the deaths of four men who were regarded as Sulla's supporters: Carbo Arvina (tr. pl. 90), P. Antistius (tr. pl. 88), L. Domitius Ahenobarbus (cos. 94), and, most shockingly of all, the *pontifex maximus* Mucius Scaevola.[102] Too little is known of these men's careers and affiliations to determine whether their murders were motivated by personal enmity, fear that they would hand over the city to Sulla, or some mixture; in fact, Damasippus and Sulla's other opponents had then left Rome, and Sulla faced no opposition at this point.[103]

100. P. Spann, *Quintus Sertorius and the Legacy of Sulla*, Fayetteville: University of Arkansas Press 1987, 37–9.
101. App. *B Civ*. 1.89. On Ofella, A. Keaveney, 'The short career of Q. Lucretius Afella', *Eranos* 101, 2003, 84–93.
102. Scaevola had already been attacked and wounded by Fimbria at the elder Marius' funeral in 86. He is consistently treated by Cicero as a peace-maker, whose neutrality provided a possible model for Cicero's own position in 49 (e.g. *Att*. 8.3.6; 9.15.2; see J. Harries, *Cicero and the Jurists: From Citizens' Law to Lawful State*, London: Duckworth 2006, 11–26); but his caution in relation to the Marians is apparent in e.g. his failure to inaugurate a *flamen Dialis* to replace Merula and, perhaps, involvement in the manoeuvres which prevented the election of a suffect consul during the summer of 84 (I am grateful to John Bollan for letting me see his as yet unpublished work on Scaevola). Many sources put Scaevola's death in the highly symbolic location of the temple of Vesta.
103. The account of his welcome (App. *B Civ*. 1.88) may derive from Sulla's own

He then marched north into Etruria and met Carbo's forces near the town of Clusium. Their encounter was inconclusive, but a large detachment that Carbo sent towards Praeneste under the command of Marcius Censorinus was defeated by Pompeius, and although Censorinus escaped back towards Carbo, most of his troops deserted. The stalemate near Clusium was interrupted by news of an army of Samnites and Lucanians marching north to relieve Marius, in response to Sulla's decision to execute the Samnites whom he captured after the battle of Sacriportus.[104] Sulla returned south and prevented the two forces from uniting. Meanwhile, the conflict in Cisalpine Gaul was at an end: another of the 12 *hostes* of 88, Albinovanus, had changed sides, assassinating most of his fellow commanders as the price of his welcome by Metellus (though Norbanus himself escaped). Carbo sent Damasippus (who had joined him on leaving Rome) in another attempt to relieve Praeneste; when this failed, Carbo gave up the struggle, and his army, and escaped to Africa. Carrinas, who had been defeated near Spoletium by Pompeius and Crassus, took over what remained of Carbo's army and marched it to join those of Damasippus; when it became clear that there was stalemate at Praeneste, they and the Samnites co-ordinated a march towards Rome. Sulla followed, and outside the Colline Gate, on 1 November, he destroyed his opponents.[105]

Sulla's revenge after the Colline Gate was extensive, with the number of victims among the senatorial and equestrian classes running into the hundreds; the hideous device of the proscription lists introduced a legal basis for a massive exercise in the expropriation of property and in the transformation of the membership of the governing elite.[106] But he offered an apparently indiscriminate welcome to those willing to change sides, and the ranks of the

account; Appian also notes that Rome was short of food, presumably because the granaries had been emptied by the departing Marians (P. Garnsey, *Famine and Food Supply in the Graeco-Roman World: Responses to Risk and Crisis*, Cambridge: Cambridge University Press 1988, 199–200). The contrast with the violence with which Sulla was met in 88 is noticeable.

104. The reasons for this decision, which ran counter to Sulla's attempts in general not to alienate the inhabitants of Italy, are obscure; Salmon, *Samnium*, 382–5, suggests that he was exploiting Roman fear of the Samnites to rally his own support.

105. App. *B Civ.* 1.93; Plut. *Sull.* 29; the pattern of near-disaster followed by total victory may derive from Sulla's own account, as – probably – does the presentation of the Samnites as bent on the destruction of Rome.

106. F. Hinard, *Les proscriptions de la Rome républicaine*, Rome: École Française de Rome 1985; Santangelo, *Elites*, 78–87.

successful were full of prudent late recruits.[107] The inner circle of
those who had been his adherents since his departure from Rome
in 88 was too small to implement his plans and of necessity, the
victorious coalition was broad, and heterogenous.

Following his victory, Sulla terrorised the Senate by having his
prisoners executed within earshot whilst it was meeting, and then
had L. Valerius Flaccus elected as *interrex* (temporary presiding
officer), to whom he suggested that a dictator should be appointed
to bring order to the state. Sulla took that office towards the end of
82; it had not been used for over a century, but it offered the advantage of constitutional power unconstrained by a colleague or the
threat of veto. The terms of the law Flaccus proposed for Sulla's
appointment freed him from the one significant constraint on a
dictator, the office's usual time limit of six months or less; and it gave
blanket approval for his current and future acts.

The Sullan *res publica*

Sulla had secured for himself autocratic power, and from now until
his return to the status of a private individual at the end of 80 BC
the Romans were exposed to a baffling and unpredictable mix of the
traditional and the unprecedented. One of his first acts as dictator
was to hold consular elections; little is known about the successful
candidates, M. Tullius Decula and Cn. Cornelius Dolabella, though
the latter had commanded some of Sulla's naval forces.[108] We should
probably assume that Sulla required, in some haste, two individuals
of appropriate standing and loyalty who would not seek to interfere
with his overall control; Dolabella's patrician status may have been
an added attraction. The prospect of normal government embodied
in the election of consuls was overshadowed by Sulla's position as
dictator, rammed home to every spectator by his 24 lictors, and by
the ongoing slaughter of his opponents. The elections may also have
been clouded by the execution of Lucretius Ofella, a legate of Sulla
who had just brought the seige of Praeneste to a successful conclusion. He attempted to stand for the consulship, though not a
member of the Senate, and Sulla had him killed in the forum; these

107. Among these were Ofella; L. Marcius Philippus, who took Sardinia from its
governor Antonius Balbus; P. Cornelius Cethegus and Albinovanus, both among the
12 declared *hostes* in 88; and C. Verres.
108. E. S. Gruen, 'The Dolabellae and Sulla', *AJPh* 87, 1966, 385–99, at 386.

events are probably better placed at the end of 82, before Sulla had begun to implement his programme, and with relative nonentities standing for the consulship, than a year later, when the other candidates included Sulla himself and Metellus Pius, and Sulla's legislation on the *cursus* was in place.[109] Against this background of violence and unpredictable innovation, the reforms which Sulla introduced may not have immediately appeared to offer a return to traditional government; and, although that is the way in which his programme is often interpreted, aspects of it marked a striking break with the past.[110]

His programme contained a number of different elements, including a wholesale overhaul of the criminal law, major changes to the role and function of the tribunate of the people and a transformation in the articulation of magistracies with the organisation of foreign affairs and with the composition of the Senate. The legal reforms built on what was already established practice, namely standing courts for specific offences, each under the presidency of a magistrate and with large juries drawn not from the citizen body as a whole but from a restricted group of the wealthy: Sulla drew his jurors from among senators only. Most of his courts dealt with offences for which there was already a legislative framework, which the relevant *lex Cornelia* developed (in some cases, such as extortion, the only change may have been in the composition of the jury); one new offence concerned forgery, of coins and wills.[111]

The sources agree that the capacities of the tribunate of the people were severely limited, though the precise details are not entirely secure: probably, tribunes were unable to introduce legislation, and their capacity to veto legislation may have been restricted (use of the veto to protect citizens remained).[112] Just as importantly, Sulla barred those who had held the tribunate from subsequently holding magistracies; at a stroke, he made it impossible for those who

109. Keaveney, 'Afella'.
110. E. S. Gruen, *The Last Generation of the Roman Republic*, Berkeley: University of California Press 1974, 7–12; K. Christ, *Sulla: eine römische Karriere*, Munich: Beck 2002; A. Keaveney, *Sulla: The Last Republican*, 2nd edn, London: Routledge 2005; H. Flower, *Roman Republics*, Princeton: Princeton University Press 2010, 117–34, puts the argument for disjunction.
111. E. S. Gruen, *Roman Politics and the Criminal Courts, 149-78 B.C.*, Cambridge, MA: Harvard University Press 1968, 248–78; D. Cloud, 'The constitution and public criminal law', *CAH* 9^2, 1994, 491–530.
112. L. Thommen, *Das Volktribunat der späten römischen Republik*, Stuttgart: Steiner 1989, 207–16.

wanted an ongoing role in public life to use the tribunate as a means to that end. The number of praetorships rose to eight each year and the number of quaestors to 20. The rise in the number of praetorships was in response to the increasing number of foreign territories which required governors; the shortage of of ex-praetors and ex-consuls to take on *prouinciae* had led to some very lengthy terms of provincial command. As Brennan notes, Sulla himself had had his command in Cilicia prorogued repeatedly after he held the praetorship in 97.[113] At the same time, the increase in numbers provided, at least in theory, enough court presidents of praetorian rank for all the standing courts established under Sulla's legislation. Similarly, the increase in the number of quaestors provided one to assist each provincial governor as well as supplying those required for duties in Rome, without the need to prorogue the position beyond a year.

The quaestorship now brought with it membership of the Senate; consequently, the size of the Senate would over time increase greatly, and Sulla chose to anticipate the effects of time by enrolling 300 new senators immediately, though the effects of war had reduced the size of the Senate so extensively that the immediate result was probably a body of 450.[114] Rules covering the rest of the *cursus* as well were stated, or restated; a fixed order in which offices should be held, minimum ages for office-holding, and a minimum interval of ten years between tenures of the same office. This last was of particular relevance to the consulship: holding it year after year, as Marius had done, and more recently Cinna and Carbo, was forbidden. And it now became the practice for consuls and praetors to remain in Rome for most or all of their year in office, proceeding to their overseas territory only towards the end of the calendar year or in the early months of the next.[115] Sulla did not abolish the censorship, but neither did he arrange for a census to be held, although one was due in 81 or 80; consequently, the registration of the new citizens remained partial. In addition, the position of *princeps senatus* fell into abeyance.

These were enormous changes to the way that public life in Rome operated and their effects over the remaining thirty years of the

113. T. C. Brennan, *The Praetorship in the Roman Republic*, New York: Oxford University Press 2000, 390.
114. F. Santangelo, 'Sulla and the Senate: a reconsideration', *Cahiers du Centre Gustave-Glotz* 17, 2006 [publ. 2008], 7–22.
115. F. Pina Polo, *The Consul at Rome*, Cambridge: Cambridge University Press 2011, 225–48.

Republic were profound. Two consequences in particular should be noted; the intensity of competition for the consulship increased, since the success rate for praetors suddenly dropped from one in three to one in four; and the authority of the Senate – more than half of whose members would now hold no further office after their initial year as a quaestor – was significantly diluted.[116]

Sulla introduced other changes, some of which were a return to earlier practice: thus subsidised corn-doles were abolished, co-option replaced election for filling vacancies in the priestly colleges (which were also increased in size to 15), and new laws restricting conspicuous consumption were passed. He also returned to the issue of the enfranchisement of the new citizens: whilst there was no attempt to reverse the extension of the citizenship in general, or to upset the tribal arrangement which had already been made, some individual communities were deprived of the citizenship and many lost territory, which was confiscated to establish colonies of Sullan veterans. Loss of rights and of territory were punishments for failure to support Sulla on his return to Italy; other new citizens benefited, the most prominent by elevation to the Senate and others through the opportunities for profit which the proscriptions, and more general lawlessness, offered.[117]

Whilst Sulla remained in Rome, overseeing his reform programme, his generals were dealing with military opposition across the Mediterranean. In the east, Licinius Murena, whom Sulla left in charge of Asia, with Fimbria's troops, provoked the so-called second Mithridatic war by invading Cappadocia in 83. Mithridates complained to Rome, and in 82 a senator, C. Calidius, arrived with instructions from the Senate to Murena to stop, which Murena ignored (perhaps with Calidius' private support). Later that year, Mithridates defeated Murena's forces and expelled them from his territory; subsequently, a further envoy from Rome, Aulus Gabinius, arrived with instructions to Murena to return to Rome, which he did, celebrating a triumph later in 81. The situation is murky: the basis of Murena's authority is unclear (he may not have held the praetorship) and his troops, who had acquiesced in the murder of one commander and deserted their next, were presumably keen on an opportunity to enrich themselves at the expense of Mithridates.

116. Sulla's constitutional changes are discussed in more detail in Chapter 5.
117. Santangelo, *Elites*, 134–91.

What is clear, however, is that Sulla took steps as soon as he was able
to regularise the situation.

Closer to Rome, the threat came from those unwilling to come to
terms with Sulla, or not offered that option. The fighting in Italy did
not come to an end until 80 BC, when Volaterrae and Nola finally
surrendered. Carbo had fled to Sicily and was captured there by
Pompeius and executed; Brutus Damasippus, who had joined Carbo,
committed suicide.[118] Pompeius then took his forces to the province
of Africa, which he won back from another refugee from Sulla, Cn.
Domitius. Spain, however, remained partially outside the control
of the government in Rome until 72 BC under the command of
Sertorius.[119] The Roman empire was in a fragile, and fissile, state.
The pressure of other challenges may be one factor explaining the
Senate's caution over Egypt, when news arrived in 80 that Ptolemy
XI had left his kingdom to Rome.[120] He had received assistance, and
money, from Rome earlier in the 80s, and the will seems to have
been collateral to the loan, with room for considerable doubt over
its very existence. Instead of attempting to take up the inheritance,
the Senate sent an embassy to Tyre to recover the loan; but the possibility that Rome had a legal claim on Egypt, in place of Ptolemy XI's
successor, Ptolemy XII 'Auletes', surfaced from time to time thereafter.[121]

At Rome, Sulla faced a dilemma of his own making. He intended
to re-establish orderly government, which involved limiting the
opportunities for individuals to consolidate power. Hence the pre-
vention of iteration in office, and *maiestas* and *repetundae* legislation
to control the activities of magistrates and promagistrates. But
Sulla's own career offered a seductive model of what could be gained
by ignoring such limitations; moreover, he sent out mixed messages
about what would happen to those who tried to emulate him. Ofella
was executed because he tried to stand for consulship without
the necessary career history. But Pompeius was encouraged and
promoted and after his victory in Africa demanded, and received, a
triumph.[122]

118. So Livy, *Per.* 89; the fragment of Helvius Mancia (Val. Max. 6.2.8) suggests otherwise, but may be embroidered.
119. See below, pp. 136–8.
120. D. Braund, 'Royal wills and Rome', *PBSR* 51, 1983, 16–57, at 24–8; *contra*,
E. Badian, 'The testament of Ptolemy Alexander', *RhM* 110, 1967, 178–92.
121. L. Marcius Philippus was an advocate of action, it seems, during the 70s, and it
provided the basis for Crassus' proposal when censor in 65. See below, pp. 178–9.
122. E. Badian, 'The date of Pompeius' first triumph', *Hermes* 83, 1955, 107–18; Seager,

The problem of Pompeius would lurk, unresolved, intensifying and occasionally flaring up, for the next three decades, but initially Sulla's reforms appeared to have been successful. He took the consulship with Metellus Pius in 80; in 79, the successful candidates were Servilius Vatia and Appius Claudius Pulcher.[123] That these men were 'Sullan' is hardly surprising, or notable: the civil war had imposed identities on those in public life, and there was nothing novel in factional politics. What is interesting, however, is the prominence of Rome's old aristocracy among those successful in the new regime. To underscore the return to normality, too, Sulla himself returned to private life early in 79 BC.[124] His death, early in 78 BC, was met with unprecedented ceremony; it also left a gaping hole and potential opportunities for the ambitious. A chance notice has Julius Caesar, then in his early twenties, returning hot-foot to Rome from Cilicia, where he was on the governor's staff, 'in the expectation of a new disturbance';[125] such sentiments, whether optimistic or otherwise, were likely to be widespread. It was not obvious that Sulla's reforms, as opposed to his actions, would set the parameters for subsequent events.

The first challenge to Sulla's dispositions came from M. Aemilius Lepidus, who held the consulship in 78 with Q. Lutatius Catulus. Not a great deal is known about Lepidus' earlier activities: he may have been the legate of Sulla who captured the town of Norba in 81 BC (though the consul of 77 BC, another Lepidus, is also a possibility) and was governor of Sicily in 80.[126] His election was opposed by Sulla, whose acts he may have begun to attack even before Sulla's death; he also opposed, unsuccessfully, the plans for an elaborate public funeral for Sulla. But he did not move into open opposition to the *res publica* until late in his consulship or even early in the following year. He was assigned Transalpine Gaul as his province; and both he and Catulus were despatched by the Senate during 78 to Etruria, where the settlement of Sullan veterans had provoked an

Pompey, 29. This was the point at which Pompeius assumed the cognomen *Magnus*, 'the Great'.

123. Servilius Vatia may have been the man who failed to be elected to a consulship in 87, despite Sulla's support (*Plut.* Sull. 10.3, Servaeus).

124. The remaining year of his life is the obvious location for the composition of his memoirs: C. J. Smith, 'Sulla's memoirs and Roman autobiography', in C. J. Smith and A. Powell, eds, *The Lost Memoirs of Augustus*, Swansea: Classical Press of Wales 2008, 65–85.

125. Suet. *Iul.* 3.

126. App. *B Civ.* 1.94.

uprising by existing inhabitants. It was only after he had taken the field that he decided to use the uproar in Etruria as the springboard for an attempt to seize power in Rome by force. In fact, Lepidus was quickly defeated, and fled to Sardinia, where he died soon afterwards; but the Senate took the threat extremely seriously, passing the 'last decree' and giving Pompeius a grant of *imperium*.[127] Once the revolt was over, Pompeius refused to disband his forces: the standoff was resolved – presumably to Pompeius' satisfaction – by sending him to Spain to join Metellus Pius in the ongoing and as yet unsuccessful attempt to win back the peninsula from Sertorius' control.[128]

In the eastern Mediterranean, the immediate priorities were to consolidate Rome's authority by land and to address the problem of piracy.[129] Servilius Vatia secured a series of land and sea victories between 77 and 74 in Cilicia, which secured him a triumph and the title 'Isauricus'; piracy nonetheless remained endemic. In 74, probably in response to the disruption of Rome's grain supply, the Senate attempted to deal with the problem by identifying piracy as a praetorian command and assigning it to M. Antonius.[130] He began in the west, before moving to tackle pirates based on Crete, where he sustained a serious defeat in 72 or 71, was forced to negotiate a treaty, and died shortly afterwards.[131] The alarm at Rome provoked by piracy is clear from Cicero's *Verrines*: Verres' successes against the pirates of the coast of Sicily, including the capture of a number of ships, is a major element in the fifth speech of the second hearing,

---

127. Sall. *Hist.* 1.77.22M, Plut. *Pomp.* 16.

128. Domitius Calvinus, proconsul in Nearer Spain, had been killed in battle in 79 and Pius had suffered a number of defeats: Spann, *Sertorius*, 56–82. Pompeius' dispatch was the subject of Philippus' quip that he was sent *non pro consule sed pro consulibus* (Cic. *De imp. Cn. Pomp.* 62), 'not as a proconsul but in place of the consuls'; neither consul of 76 wished to be sent.

129. D. Magie, *Roman Rule in Asia Minor to the End of the Third Century after Christ*, Princeton: Princeton University Press 1950, 278–301; Sherwin-White, *Foreign Policy*, 152–8; Kallet-Marx, *Hegemony*, 291–9.

130. Antonius was the son of the orator, who had celebrated a triumph over pirates in 100; Vell. 2.31.3–4 describes his *imperium* as *infinitum*, and compares it directly to Pompeius' position in the 60s; modern sources note the lack of territorial basis as a novelty (Kallet-Marx, *Hegemony*, 304). But if the unbreakable link between *imperium* and territory is a development of the 60s, as J. S. Richardson (*The Language of Empire: Rome and the Idea of Empire from the Third Century* BC *to the Second Century* AD, Cambridge: Cambridge University Press 2008, 106–16) argues, Antonius' position merely represents the older understanding of a *prouincia* as a task.

131. P. de Souza, *Piracy in the Graeco-Roman World*, Cambridge: Cambridge University Press 1999, 141–8; J. Linderski, 'The surname of M. Antonius Creticus and the cognomina *ex victis gentibus*', ZPE 80, 1990, 157–64.

forcing a sustained counter-attack from Cicero.[132] In addition, serious campaigning resumed in Thrace, with three consular commanders during the decade.[133]

A little later, the war with Mithridates was resumed. The precipitating factor appears to have been the Roman annexation of Bithynia: following the bequest of the kingdom to Rome by Nicomedes, who died in 75 or 74 BC, the governor of Asia, Junius Juncus, began its organisation as a province. Mithridates responded by invading Bithynia early in 73, but it appears, despite chronological obscurities, that the Romans had already made substantial preparations for war even before this. One of the consuls of 74, Lucullus, persuaded the Senate to override its earlier dispositions and assign him Cilicia; his colleague, Marcus Cotta, received Bithynia, as its first governor. Lucullus' action is presented in most of the sources as a shady intrigue, but whatever the negotiations behind the scenes, a strong case of imminent threat from Mithridates must have been put to the Senate to justify its sending both consuls east of the Aegean, unprecedented in itself and particularly striking given the continuing success of Sertorius in Spain.[134] Lucullus' campaigns were, at first, overwhelmingly successful: by the end of 71, he had compelled Mithridates to flee his kingdom and take refuge with his son-in-law Tigranes, king of Armenia.[135] During 70, Lucullus completed the conquest of Pontus with the capture of a string of coastal towns, including Amisus, which was sacked.[136] On his return to Asia (where he attempted to resolve the chronic indebtedness of the cities, which dated back to Sulla's impositions during the first war against Mithridates) he announced his victory to the Senate, and asked for a commission of ten to assist in the organisation of captured territory. This served to mark the end of the campaign, as well as Lucullus' adherence to the traditions of senatorial oversight.[137]

---

132. Cic. *Verr.* 2.5.42–145; R. Nisbet, 'The orator and the reader: manipulation and response in Cicero's Fifth Verrine', in A. Woodman and J. Powell, J., eds, *Author and Audience in Latin Literature*, Cambridge: Cambridge University Press 1992, 1–17.
133. App. Claudius Pulcher, C. Scribonius Curio and M. Terentius Varro Lucullus: Kallet-Marx, *Hegemony*, 296–9.
134. Cilicia had become available through the fortuitous death of Octavius (cos. 75).
135. Sherwin-White, *Foreign Policy*, 165–74; B. McGing, *The Foreign Policy of Mithridates VI Eupator King of Pontus*, Leiden: Brill 1986.
136. Plutarch (*Luc.* 19) reflects a tradition in which Lucullus sought to minimise damage; the distinguished scholar Tyrannio was enslaved and brought to Rome.
137. In fact, the failure to capture Mithridates would lead over the next few years to the unravelling of most of Lucullus' successes: see below, pp. 141–2.

Another military threat emerged unexpectedly in 73 BC, when a group of gladiators escaped from their training barracks in Capua under the leadership of a Thracian called Spartacus and, recruiting followers from among slaves in Campania, established a fortified base on Mount Vesuvius.[138] The Senate's initial response was to send forces under praetorian command, which strikingly failed to resolve the problem. A number of Roman defeats are recorded, though there is some confusion over the names of the commanders, and the slave forces moved out of Campania and raided a number of towns in southern Italy. In a remarkable sign of the emerging seriousness of the situation, the consuls of 72, Gellius Poplicola and Cornelius Lentulus Clodianus, were both despatched, with four legions between them. Gellius succeeded in destroying part of the opposition in a battle near Mount Garganus in Apulia. Subsequently, however, both consuls were defeated, and during this year the slave forces are also attested in Cisalpine Gaul, where they inflicted a defeat on the governor Cassius Longinus. This continued humiliation of Roman power led the Senate to recall both consuls and give the command to M. Licinius Crassus, who received a further six legions.[139] The reasons for the choice of Crassus are not very clear. He had at least had successful experience of command; in addition, in ways that we cannot fully map, he had wide networks of support within the Senate itself.[140]

Crassus joined his new forces with those already in the field, reviving the ancient tradition of decimation as an eye-catching punishment for those who had been defeated. Spartacus had returned south, through the length of Italy, towards the straits of Messina,

138. Appian (*B Civ.* 1.116–20), Plutarch (*Crass.* 8–11) and Livy (*Per.* 95–7) are major ancient narratives of the revolt; modern discussion in J-C. Dumont, *Servus: Rome et l'esclavage sous la République*, Rome: École Française de Rome 1987, 271–96; K. Bradley, *Slavery and Rebellion in the Roman World, 140 B.C.–70 B.C.*, London: Batsford 1989, 83–101; T. Urbainczyk, *Slave Revolts in Antiquity*, Stocksfield: Acumen 2008, 64–73.

139. In contrast to Pompeius, whose early career as a Sullan adherent his resembled, Crassus had pursued a conventional *cursus honorum* through the 70s. The nature of his appointment against Spartacus is debated; he must have held the praetorship during the 70s (since there is no suggestion that his election to the consulship – unlike that of Pompeius – was irregular), with 73 BC the latest date which would make his consulship fit Sullan rules. His appointment in 72 then becomes difficult to explain as something other than an exceptional grant of *imperium* (his appointment came after the end of that year's campaigning season, but there is no evidence of another propraetorian command during the interval). It may be easier to assume that Crassus was praetor in 72, and secured an irregularly early consulship on the back of his success against the slaves.

140. Gruen, *Last Generation*, 66–74.

hoping to cross to Sicily; but he was unable to secure boats for the crossing, and Crassus pinned him down in Bruttium during the winter of 72–71. Spartacus eventually escaped with at least some of his forces eastwards towards Brundisium, but found himself between the armies of Crassus and of Terentius Varro Lucullus, who was returning via Brundisium from his proconsular command in Thrace and Macedonia to assist. The slave force turned back towards Crassus, and was decisively defeated. Spartacus was killed in the battle and those of his supporters who were captured were executed in very public crucifixions along the road between Capua and Rome. By this point, however, the threat had led the Senate to recall Pompeius from Spain (where he and Metellus had finally reasserted control) to help with operations, and Pompeius' adroit claims to have brought the campaign against Spartacus to a close inflamed existing ill-feeling between him and Crassus.

This revolt, and its leader Spartacus, have become powerful moments in the modern historiography and reception of Rome. Indeed, the Spartacus story often floats free of its context in the 70s, or is treated primarily as an episode in the relationship between Pompeius and Crassus. But it demonstrated ongoing disruption within Italy. Spartacus' huge force travelled widely in Italy south and east of the Appennines: it is attested from Lucania to Cisalpine Gaul, at various points during the two years of its existence. The sources posit various motives for its journeys, but the main reason was surely logistical: it needed to be fed. The consequence was widespread plundering and destruction among the areas through which it passed.[141] In addition, the growth in the slave forces from a small group of gladiators into a body capable of regularly defeating Roman armies implies an extensive capacity to recruit. These recruits included agricultural slaves, whose departure presumably had a negative impact on the rural economy. They seem also to have included at least some free men.[142] Their presence points, at the very least, to severe ongoing social and economic disturbance in southern Italy: joining a slave-led revolt was a desperate act. It is plausible, too, to assume that hostility to Rome motivated some free recruits:

141. Florus (2.8.5): 'not satisfied with the destruction of villas and villages, they plundered Nola, Nuceria, Thurii and Metapontum with appalling violence'; Sall. *Hist.* 3.96–8; Oros. 5.24.
142. Z. Rubinsohn, 'Was the *Bellum Spartacium* a servile insurrection?', *Rivista di filologia* 99, 1971, 290–9; P. Piccinin, 'Les Italiens dans le *Bellum Spartacium*', *Historia* 53, 2004, 173–99.

it was less than a decade since Sulla had concluded the war against the Samnites. But there is less evidence to support the idea that Spartacus' forces were reviving the Social War, or entertained serious hopes of challenging Rome's power.

At Rome, the role of the Roman people in political life was the major issue, and Sulla's restrictions on the tribunate proved unsustainable. There was regular tribunician agitation for change; and in 75 the consul Cotta sponsored a law to remove the ban on holding further office after the tribunate. Pressure for a full restoration of tribunician power provided the background for the consular elections in 70.[143]

The consulship of Pompeius and Crassus: a fresh start?

During the closing months of 71 BC, the ends of two long wars were publicly marked in Rome. Crassus celebrated an *ovatio* (a more modest version of a triumph) at the end of his successful campaign against Spartacus' revolt, and Metellus Pius and Pompeius both triumphed from Spain.[144] In addition, Terentius Varro Lucullus (cos. 73) celebrated a triumph over the Bessi, a Thracian tribe; his haul of booty included an enormous statue of Apollo which he dedicated on the Capitol.[145] After a period of uncertainty, both Pompeius and Crassus undertook to dismiss their forces once the military celebrations were over, and the two co-operated in ensuring their election as consuls for 70. The message appeared to be one of restoration and stability: crises in Spain and Italy had been contained and the commanders in these conflicts reintegrated into civilian political life. Given that the opponents in these Spanish campaigns were Romans, and that the slave revolt involved fighting in Italy, these celebrations also marked the end of the period of civil war which had begun in

---

143. On tribunician activity in the 70s, B. Marshall and J. Beness, 'Tribunician agitation and aristocratic reaction 80–71 B.C.', *Athenaeum* 65, 1987, 361–78; on Licinius Macer (tr. pl. 73), T. P. Wiseman, *Remembering the Roman People*, Oxford: Oxford University Press 2009, 59–80.

144. Crassus was denied a triumph and received the less spectacular *ovatio* because his opponents were slaves, but his receipt of a laurel wreath (rather than the *ovatio*'s myrtle wreath) suggests active lobbying within the Senate to boost his profile (Gell. *NA*. 5.6.20–3). For details of the triumphs, see the catalogue in T. Itgenshorst, *Tota illa Pompa: Der Triumph in der römischen Republik*, Göttingen: Vandenhoeck & Ruprecht 2005.

145. Plin. *HN* 4.92, 34.39; for Pliny, Varro Lucullus counts among the great Roman statue accumulators (*HN* 34.36).

Figure 4 Coin commemorating Pompeius' triumph in 71 BC (© The Trustees of the British Museum)

88. In Pompeius' case, his election to the consulship marked too the end of the anomaly by which a man who had never held public office or been a member of the Senate commanded the *res publica*'s forces. His candidature was shockingly irregular, given his age and lack of previous offices, and required senatorial dispensation, but his tenure of the position suggested that the answer to the question of what Pompeius would do at the end of civil wars was a peaceful one. This impression was perhaps one which Pompeius consciously promoted: his commission to his former legate Terentius Varro to write a handbook on senatorial procedure may have been a deliberate signal that he had no intention of breaching senatorial norms of behaviour during his consulship.[146]

Pompeius had indicated in a speech which he delivered as consul-elect that he intended to remove the last remaining restrictions on the tribunate: whether or not this was a long-standing ambition, the restoration of the tribunate was clearly an overwhelmingly popular move.[147] Crassus wanted his share of this popular approval, too: this was the only measure on which the consuls co-operated, although they staged a public display of amity late in the year.[148] Neither consul accepted a provincial command at the end of the year: presumably neither man felt the need for an immediate military appointment, and Crassus felt his interests were better served by

146. Gell. *NA* 14.7.
147. Pompeius' *contio*: Cic. *Verr.* 1.45.
148. *MRR* 2.126.

cultivating his connections in Rome.[149] Another important alteration to the Sullan system also took place in 70, with a change to the composition of juries: only one-third of jurors would now be senators, with the other two-thirds equestrians and *tribuni aerarii*.[150] Non-senators, albeit wealthy ones, were once again allowed a role in the state beyond that of electoral and legislative voter to which they had been restricted since 82. But the law, proposed by the praetor L. Cotta, does not appear to have provoked significant opposition.[151]

The restoration of the tribunes' capacity to legislate increased the number of methods of law-making. Consuls and praetors, who since Sulla's dictatorship had alone had the capacity to bring a *lex* to an assembly, retained that right, and from 70 down to the end of the Republic both routes were regularly used, side by side.[152] The first piece of tribunician legislation following the *lex Pompeia Licinia* may date from 70, if Plautius' law restoring citizenship to those followers of Lepidus who had fled to Sertorius dates from this year. Although tribunician, this measure appears to have had wide support; it was another sign that the civil wars were now firmly in the past.[153]

The year 70 was also that of the first censorship since Marcius Philippus and Perperna had held the office in 86, with the consuls

149. Consuls who did not go to a province were a common phenomenon in the post-Sullan period, though one which seems to increase in frequency after Pompeius and Crassus; of the 14 consuls who are known not to have gone to a province in the period 79–53, only one did so before 70 (P. Cornelius Lentulus Sura, cos. 71), though this may reflect in part better information for the later part of the period (four of the ten uncertain cases fall before 70: see J. P. V. D. Balsdon, 'Consular provinces under the late Republic, I: general considerations', *JRS* 29, 1939, 57–73, at 63 nn. 46–7). We may nonetheless be dealing with a shift in practice, in which the model of Pompeius was relevant.

150. The precise definition of *tribuni aerarii* remains unclear, but they possessed a census rating equivalent to the equestrians'.

151. Cicero suggests in the *Verrines* that the measure could be resisted, but he was using the threat of change to try to persuade his all-senatorial jury to convict Verres; cf. J-L. Ferrary, 'Cicéron et la loi judiciaire de Cotta (70 av. J.-C.)', *MEFRA* 87, 1975, 321–48.

152. C. Williamson, *The Laws of the Roman People: Public Law in the Expansion and Decline of the Roman Republic*, Ann Arbor: University of Michigan Press 2005, provides a catalogue; Pina Polo, *Consul*, 290–307.

153. Caesar spoke on behalf of the measure (Suet. *Iul.* 5, Gell. *NA* 13.3.5) but his interest was personal: his brother-in-law, the younger L. Cinna, was among those who stood to benefit. For the Senate's support, see Gruen, *Last Generation*, 37. Plautius may be behind two other pieces of legislation: *lex Plautia de ui*, and an agrarian law (E. Gabba, *Republican Rome, the Army and the Allies*, trans. P. Cuff, Oxford: Blackwell 1976, 151–3). The name is too common, and the date of both pieces of legislation too uncertain, for any confidence, though both measures would make sense as part of a self-conscious reassertion of popular authority in this year.

of 72, Cornelius Lentulus Clodianus and Lucius Gellius, being elected.[154] Their registration of 910,000 citizens arguably completed the enfranchisment of Italy.[155] They also conducted a review of senatorial membership notable for its rigour: 64 senators, over 10 per cent of the total membership, were expelled. A complete list of expulsions cannot be compiled, but the identity of some is known: astonishingly, they included one of the previous year's consuls, Lentulus Sura, as well as at least two jurors from a notorious recent example of judicial corruption, the trial of Oppianicus in 74.[156] Cicero suggests, when he discusses this censorship in his defence of Cluentius in 66, that the censors were responding to 'a popular wind'; we need not accept his implication that their decisions were unfair to see the severity of their choice as a public demonstration that the Senate was capable of policing itself. We also know of a review of the equestrian class during 70, which was carefully stagemanaged to let Pompeius display to the people his combined status of consul and equestrian.[157] The completion of the *lustrum*, presumably in 69 after the normal 18-month duration of the censorship, marked an important symbolic regularisation of the *res publica* and its members in relation to the gods and with itself.[158]

154. Both Clodianus and Gellius were among Pompeius' legates in the 60s, and both had served in Pompeius Strabo's army during the Social War, but there is no secure evidence that they were open Pompeians at the time of their election. On the other hand, relations between both men and Crassus were unlikely to be good, following their shared debacle against Spartacus in 72 and replacement by Crassus, and they permitted Pompeius his display at the review of the equestrians (see below).

155. G. Pieri, *L'histoire du cens jusqu'à la fin de la République romaine*, Paris: Sirey 1968, 163–72; T. P. Wiseman, 'The census in the first century B.C.', *JRS* 59, 1969, 59–75; A. Coşkun, '"Civitas Romana" und die Inklusion von Fremden in die römische Republik am Beispiel des Bundesgenossenkrieges', in A. Gestrich and R. Lutz,eds, *Inklusion/Exklusion: Studien zu Fremdheit und Armut von der Antike bis zur Gegenwart*, Frankfurt: Lang 2004, 85–111.

156. Livy, *Per.* 98; Asc. 84C; Cic. *Clu.* 119–34.

157. Plut. *Pomp.* 22.

158. D. Dzino, '*Annus mirabilis*: 70 B.C. re-examined', *Ancient History* 32, 2002, 99–117; A. Vasaly, 'Cicero, domestic politics, and the first action of the *Verrines*', *Classical Antiquity* 28, 2009, 101–37, at 108–10, notes the clustering of public spectacle in the summer of 70: in addition to the activities associated with the census and with elections, Pompeius' victory games for his Spanish campaign were celebrated from 16 August to 1 September, and his dedication of a temple to Hercules in the Forum Boarium, and Crassus' public feast there, may also date from this period.

CHAPTER 5

The limits of autocracy

In Livy's history of Rome, books 51–70 covered the years 146–91 BC; books 71–97 the years 91–70; and books 98–116 the years 70–44.[1] Thus he used 27 books (that is, books 71–97) to cover just 21 years. The only areas of comparable density are the civil war between Caesar and Pompey (8 books, 109–16, for a little over 5 years) and its continuation between 44 and 30 BC (17 books for 14 years). The common thread linking these three periods of detailed analysis is obvious: civil war. Romans fighting Romans demanded an intense level of attention, a factor that becomes even clearer if one further subdivides Livy's account: the period from the tribunate of Drusus in 91 down to Sulla's death at the beginning of 78 required a full two decades of his history. Not coincidentally, civil war is the chief interest of Appian, our most detailed surviving narrative source for the years 91–78. Yet the vagaries of transmission have acted in the opposite direction, to push us away from these two decades towards the subseqent two.[2] The consequence has been to obscure these crucial two decades, whilst suggesting, by contrast, that the answers to our questions lie in the following thirty years, brightly illuminated for us, or so we think, by Cicero's logorrhea.

During these two decades, the Roman state was engaged in a series of wholesale transformations. These changes involved shifts in the distribution of power between different factions within the elite and between different groups within Roman society with a speed and range difficult to parallel in earlier political history; they also affected the nature of power and its sources, and the identity of Roman society. The Rome which emerged in 70 BC from these trans-formations was not only radically different from the Rome of 91 BC; it also represented the triumph of one model of political organisation

1. Coverage is recorded in the *Periochae*.
2. We have lost, in addition to Livy's narrative, the memoirs of Sulla and the histories of Rutilius Rufus, Licinius Macer, Cornelius Sisenna and Sallust himself.

among a number of competing possibilities. The experimentation of these years was wide-ranging: army, citizenship and leadership were all subject to modification and scrutiny.

Power and armed force

Essential to many narratives of the end of the Republic is the irruption into political life of military force: soldiers replace citizens as the arbiters of power. Sulla conventionally features as a key figure in this process: his decision to respond to a political challenge – Sulpicius' law to move the command against Mithridates from him to Marius – by military force is seen as the decisive moment of change, which extended the bounds of the possible, and acted as an example to his successors. A vital element in the equation was Sulla's personal ability to convince his troops – though not his officers – to attack Rome, and our sources agree that a key stage in the process was a speech that Sulla gave to his troops. But two other factors facilitated his decision. One was the change in army recruitment which Marius had introduced in preparation for his campaign against Jugurtha, which appears to have thereafter become standard practice.[3] Sulla's legions were part of an army that was rapidly professionalising, consisting of volunteers who expected financial reward from their service. The model of military service as an integral element in land-owning citizenship had been replaced by one based on the exchange of goods for services; and Sulla presented himself to his forces as a guarantor that their service would adequately be rewarded.

The very unusual situation of 88 BC was also an element in enabling Sulla to apply armed force to a domestic political dispute. The Social War had involved the first serious military action in Italy since the second war against Carthage, over a century earlier. The scale of the levies, of both sides, was enormous, and many of these troops were still under arms in 88, since the war had by no means been concluded at this point. When Sulla told his men that they would be replaced by other forces in the war against Mithridates if he was replaced as commander, his argument had genuine plausibility. The moment of transition, from an intense and demanding war to peace, presented an unusual possibility of choice among different legions. Some would be disbanded; others redeployed,

---

3. E. Gabba, *Republican Rome, the Army and the Allies*, trans. P. Cuff, Oxford: Blackwell 1976, 20–69.

and Sulla was able to exploit an element of uncertainty that was normally not present. Furthermore, the outbreak of the Social War superimposed widespread military mobilisation upon intensely competitive domestic politics. The Italian problem had broken unexpectedly upon internal conflicts concerning a range of issues; the resolution of relations with Italy did little to resolve these other problems. Indeed, the *lex Varia* seems to have exacerbated internal divisions. Sulla's march on Rome was only the first of a sequence of violent encounters between Romans. Sulla's colleague as consul in 88, Pompeius Rufus, was unable to take control of an army previously commanded by Pompeius Strabo: the soldiers lynched him. Independently of Rufus' disaster, the consuls of 87 fell out over domestic matters and Cinna followed the example that Sulla had set; Cinna left Rome to take control of the forces commanded by Pulcher, and used them to win back power in Rome. The civil wars of the 80s required the build-up of military forces which the demands of the Social War had created; at the same time, the existence of so many armies proved an irrestistable temptation to a number of politicians as a decisive means of controlling domestic politics.

Sulla's march on Rome, however, should not be treated as a phenomenon entirely without precedent. The use of force was, by 88, a well-established technique in political life, and politicians were alert to the possibilities of organising violence to ensure desired outcomes to domestic political activity: at precisely this moment, for example, Sulpicius was successfully attempting to control the passage of his legislative programme by deploying gangs of his supporters. Nor was violence only a *popularis* technique. The attack on Tiberius Gracchus in 133 was led by the Senate, and in 121 the consul Opimius secured formal agreement from the Senate to use military force to suppress Gaius Gracchus: the justification for this was to prevent harm coming to the *res publica*. Marius also received senatorial authorisation to use force against Saturninus and his followers. Sulla's action can be placed within this emerging tradition of direct violent and extra-legal action, undertaken by magistrates and justified by an urgent need to protect the *res publica*. He did not, of course, have senatorial backing for his action; but it is easy to see how an argument could be constructed that the Senate was constrained by the tribune Sulpicius.

The troops who followed Sulla to Rome in 88 and those involved in the Octavian war the following year were men who had been

Roman citizens before the Social War. After the Social War, the new Roman citizens were also eligible to serve. Cinna's death may have been connected to the incorporation of new citizens into the army; but, in so far as the evidence exists, it seems that the amalgamation of new and old citizens into a single army was rapid and thorough. This process did, however, consolidate the end of a citizen militia. Rome's new legionaries were not, after 85, men whose first language was necessarily Latin; they might have their origins in communities which had fought against Rome in the Social War, and they themselves might have taken part in that conflict on the Italian side. Even before the Social War, the distributed nature of Roman citizenship must have meant that some soldiers had never been to Rome, or exercised their vote; but this tendency was now surely greatly strengthened. The extension of the citizenship, coming on top of the changes to military organisation implemented by Marius, decisively marked the end of the citizen militia as an ideal underpinning Roman military activity.

Experiments in autocracy

There were three distinct experiments with personal authority during the 80s: the changes which Sulla introduced in 88; the period of Cinna's and Carbo's repeated consulships in the mid-80s; and the period of Sulla's dictatorship from 82 onwards. The first set should be seen as a quick fix to enable Sulla to depart for the campaign against Mithridates. Cinna and Carbo's actions may have simply been a pragmatic attempt to keep power, but their profound implications for the *res publica* would have been unmistakable: without the circulation of the highest offices, there was no recognisable Roman elite. It freed the Roman people from the constraint of pandering to elite competition; there was, after all, no inescapable reason why iteration of office was incompatible with many aspects of the existing *res publica*. Sulla's dictatorship, by contrast, took an existing, though disused office and re-engineered it to offer a legal basis for military autocracy.[4]

Thus what had in origin been a factional conflict between Marius, Cinna and their followers on the one hand and their opponents,

4. F. Hurlet, *La dictature de Sylla: monarchie ou magistrature republicaine?*, Brussels: Institut Historique Belge de Rome 1993; C. Nicolet 'Dictatorship at Rome', in P. Baehr and M. Richter, eds, *Dictatorship in History and Theory: Bonapartism, Caesarianism and Totalitarianism*, Cambridge: Cambridge University Press 2004, 263–78.

Sulla prominent among them, on the other, with the grounds of
dispute being competition for personal success, developed into a
profound re-examination of the nature of political organisation.
In consequence, care is needed in assuming a continuity of aims
and identity between those who opposed Marius in 88, and those
who supported Sulla in 82. It was a period of complex and shifting
loyalties, which a bipartite model cannot fully capture. A relatively
trivial problem in nomenclature illustrates the difficulty: what are we
to call those whom I described above as 'Marius, Cinna and their
followers'? 'Marians' and 'Cinnans' are found in modern accounts,
but *Mariani* and *Cinnani* not before the imperial period. The group
clearly had a cohesion beyond that given by the elder Marius and
Cinna, as its continuation after the latter's death demonstrates. But
whom did it contain? What, for example, was the relationship
between Scipio and Norbanus, the consuls of 83, and Carbo? They
followed the instructions of the Senate and led their armies against
Sulla and his followers; do we adopt a Sullan mode of thinking when
we identify them not as the leaders of the *res publica* but as Marian
or Cinnan partisans? The Senate in the mid-80s was not under the
control of Cinna, and it consistently pursued a more pacific stance
towards Sulla than Cinna and subsequently Carbo and Marius did.[5]

This group was responsible for substantial achievements during its
five years or so of dominance, despite preparations for Sulla's return,
and the civil war which followed, as is apparent even with the relentless hostility towards them as tyrants in subsequent pro-Sullan
sources. The censorship of 86/5 and its enrolment of new citizens,
though partial, was a major achievement; and Crawford raises the
intriguing possibility that Cinna sponsored legislation to provide a
framework for the municipalisation of Italy following the extension
of Roman citizenship.[6] When Sulla returned to Italy, he could not
gainsay the principle of enfranchisement.[7] In Rome itself, 86–84 was
a period of peace, with the resumption of forensic activity and
attempts to resolve financial difficulties. There is also some evidence
for integration into political life at the highest levels of the new citizens: Burrienus (pr. 83) and Carrinas (pr. 82) may have been newly

5. Cf. App. *B Civ.* 1.82, describing the popularity of Scipio and Norbanus because they
had the 'pretext of the state', πρόσχημα τῆς πατρίδος.
6. M. Crawford, 'How to create a *municipium*: Rome and Italy after the Social War',
in M. Austin, J. Harries and C. Smith, eds, *Modus Operandi: Essays in Honour of
Geoffrey Rickman*, London: Institute of Classical Studies 1998, 31–46, at 40.
7. F. Santangelo, *Sulla, the Elites and the Empire*, Leiden: Brill 2007, 67–77.

enfranchised, and Velleius' two forebears, who held the praetorship in the 80s, certainly were.[8] These form a not negligible proportion of all praetors between 87 and 82. For members of the nobility at Rome, a regime change must have seemed attractive if only to permit them career progression.[9]

The Sullan *res publica*

The restoration of 'normality' seems to have been a priority for Sulla and was marked by a sequence of events with symbolic as well as actual importance: the proscription lists were closed, elections for magistracies were held and Sulla himself resigned his office of dictator. This apparent return to a status quo ante went alongside deeply rooted changes in Rome's politics and society. Sulla attempted to transform the *res publica* by limiting locations of power. The equestrians, who had only recently become a political force, were removed from the directly political sphere through their loss of jury activity: they returned to what they had been prior to 123, a group of wealthy citizens not engaged in the business of the *res publica*, whose standing was recognised through their privileged position at the census and in the centuriate assembly. *Imperium*-holding magistrates remained supremely powerful executive officers; but Sulla attempted to ensure that they were genuinely answerable to the Senate. He revived earlier rules on office-holding which ensured that it was always punctuated by breaks as a private individual, and put a ten-year interval between one tenure of the consulship and another. This was a clear reaction to recent events, namely the repeated consulships of Gaius Marius and his emulators Cinna and Carbo. It can also be seen as a restriction on the prerogatives of the Roman people, who were now prevented from demonstrating their opinion of military commanders through the direct and repeated bestowal of *imperium*, as they had done in the case of Marius during the war against the Cimbri. Sulla's other attempt to control magistrates was his *maiestas* law: not in itself a novelty – the *lex Appuleia de maiestate* was a predecessor – it appears to have laid clear limits on what provincial governors could and could not do in a military

8. T. P. Wiseman, *New Men in the Roman Senate 139 B.C.–A.D. 14*, Oxford: Oxford University Press 1971, 217, 222, 239; Vell. Pat. 2.16.3, emphasising their citizenship as a personal reward.
9. Cicero's euphemism in his early speeches for Sulla's side is *nobilitas* (*Rosc. Am.* 16, 135, 138, 141, 149; *Verr.* 2.1.35, 37).

sphere. The *lex de maiestate* emerges in the post-Sullan period most frequently as a second line of attack against provincial governors, if prosecution on *repetundae* charges failed; in its intent, it put the Senate firmly in control of decisions over foreign policy, which magistrates were, in theory, supposed to implement. It is, however, a curiosity of Sulla's reforms that he left the *lex Sempronia de provinciis consularibus* in place; even though other aspects of his programme made this law even more unwieldy than it had been in 123. Although it is clear that there was nothing in the post-Sullan period to prevent consuls from leaving for their province during their year in office, it became unusual for them to do so until late in the year (some, such as Julius Caesar in 59, did not depart until the following year). And the increase in the number of praetors meant that the centuriate voting assembly had to take place in high summer if it was to have time to get through its business in daylight. Consequently, the Senate would take a decision on consular provinces almost two years before those consuls would arrive in their provinces to begin campaigning at the end of the winter following their year in office. No satisfactory explanation has, to my knowledge, been offered for this peculiarity.[10]

A third group whose powers Sulla curtailed was Roman citizens as a whole. The construction and meaning of citizenship within Sulla's version of the *res publica* was significantly different, and greatly weakened, from its pre-Social War form. In part this was because of a factor independent of Sulla, namely the huge increase in the number of citizens because of enfranchisement after the Social War. The importance of an individual's vote was correspondingly reduced. In addition, however, citizens after Sulla were deprived of many of the opportunities for action and influence which had existed prior to 82. Sulla achieved this end economically, through his transformation of the role of the tribunes of the people, which amounted to the near-destruction of an office which had been integral to the state for centuries. He drove talented individuals away from it, by banning former tribunes from holding any other offices: it could no longer serve as a means for the ambitious plebeian *nobilis*, or aspirant, to introduce himself as a political force to the Roman people. And Sulla prevented those who did hold it from undertaking positive political action through the removal of the office's legislative

---

10. Maintaining the *lex Sempronia* did prevent intrigue by consuls; that may have seemed to Sulla a benefit worth keeping, particularly if, in practice, the *lex Sempronia* could be ignored at times of crisis.

capacity. The tribunate was reduced to a negative position: tribunes could protect citizens by preventing the actions of others, but could not initiate. As a result, the Roman people's participation in the *res publica* was limited to voting for magistrates, and voting on consular or praetorian legislation. The trend of Sulla's thinking here seems easy to grasp, namely that every episode of domestic violence over the previous half-century had at its heart a tribune of the people putting forward profoundly divisive legislative proposals: the Gracchi, Saturninus, Drusus and finally, and personally, Sulpicius. By removing the capacity for tribunician legislation, Sulla presumably hoped to eliminate the possibility of such internecine upheavals. The people's approval was still required for the passage of laws, but these could now only be proposed by the highest magistrates, dependent for their election on the approval of the centuriate assembly.[11]

Sulla, therefore, eliminated the equestrians from the political sphere, severely limited the contribution of the Roman people, and placed some barriers in the way of magistrates' freedom of action. In addition, he radically transformed the nature of the Senate. His enrolment of an additional 300 senators, and the increase in the number of quaestors which maintained the new larger size, are often read as attempts to shore up the body's authority. This is debatable. The new senators were, presumably, men who had previously been enrolled among the equestrians: there is no sign that the property qualification was relaxed, and little evidence of an influx of the recently enfranchised.[12] Whatever Sulla intended by increasing the size of the Senate, it was not to hasten the integration of the new citizen communities of Italy, or to represent the massive increase in the total number of citizens. Some of Sulla's new senators were demonstrably personal adherents; none is likely to have been drawn from among his opponents. To that extent, then, the ranks of the

11. One aspect of Sulla's limitation on the role of people was to reduce the differential between citizens who lived in Rome and those who did not – the latter category having, of course, increased massively in the previous few years, even though not all were yet registered as such. If the major moment of civic participation was now the elections then it was presumably more straightforward for citizens across Italy, at least the wealthier among them, to plan their participation than it was in an environment in which legislation could be proposed at any point in the year, and voting on it taken rather sooner than the news could spread throughout Italy and those interested plan and complete a trip to Rome. There is, however, no evidence that Sulla had the equality of the new citizens in mind when he introduced these changes.
12. F. Santangelo, 'Sulla and the Senate: a reconsideration', *Cahiers du Centre Gustave-Glotz* 17, 2006, 7–22 [publ. 2008].

new senators, meeting in their new Senate house, would have acted as a pledge for the continuation of Sulla's reforms and a check on any moves to change that later magistrates might have introduced.

The massive increase in the number of senators changed the role of individual senators as well as the overall impact of the Senate. Prior to Sulla's changes, 300 senators were enrolled at each census, with the number dipping slightly, through death, until the next *lustrum*. Around 10 per cent of senators would be holding an elected magistracy, or prorogued *imperium*, at any one point; a slightly higher proportion would be priests, on the assumption that most, though not all, members of the four priestly colleges were also senators; there were embassies to fill, commissions to man, and laws to draft and juries to compose. It seems reasonable to think, therefore, that before Sulla's reforms a senator in good health, even if he had risen no further up the *cursus* than the aedileship, would be engaged, with reasonable frequency, on a wide range of judicial, legislative, executive and sacral functions. Sulla's reforms increased the number of entry-level positions; but there was a corresponding increase in only one aspect of the Senate's work, namely its provision of jurors. The post-Sullan senator was, overwhelmingly, a juryman. At the same time, Sulla effectively removed the checks on judicial corruption which had previously been present: the laws still existed, but without tribunes of the people capable of pursuing abuses, the post-Sullan legal framework was a licence for senators to print bribe money.

The Sullan Senate was, therefore, very different in its functions from the pre-Social War body of the same name. Moreover, the new senators joined a Senate that was deeply marked by the violent transfer of power to Sulla. There had been executions ordered by the urban praetor Damasippus in the last days of the previous regime: the number of victims was small in comparison with those who died later, but the appalling presence among them of the *pontifex maximus*, Mucius Scaevola, made the event notorious. Sulla had terrorised the Senate into granting him the dictatorship by letting the sounds of the execution of prisoners act as a backdrop to the meeting; and senators had been prominent among those proscribed and those executed as Sulla's officers mopped up the remaining opposition.[13] There were losses at all levels of experience and seniority,

13. F. Hinard, 'La terreur comme mode de gouvernement', in G. Urso, ed., *Terror et Pavor: Violenza, Intimidazione, Clandestinità nel Mondo Antico*, Pisa: ETS 2006, 247–64.

though they are most easy to trace among men who had held the consulship. When Sulla assumed the dictatorship in 82 BC, he was also the most junior surviving consular: of the nine men who had held that office since his tenure in 88 BC, eight were already dead, and Carbo was soon to be executed by Pompeius. The impact of the Social War had reduced still further the number of consulars: only four are known still to have been alive when Sulla captured Rome.[14] L. Valerius Flaccus, consul in 100, had led the senatorial negotiations with Sulla, and been appointed *interrex* after Sulla's victory in November 82; he then became master of horse to Sulla's dictator. C. Valerius Flaccus (cos. 93) was – still – governor of Gaul; he returned to a triumph in 81. Neither Flaccus was notably active after 81. Nor do we know of any action from M. Perperna (cos. 92): unsurprisingly so, perhaps, if the Perperna who opposed Sulla, joined with Lepidus in 78, and then made his way to Sertorius was his son. Among pre-Sullan consulars only L. Marcius Philippus (cos. 91), that great survivor, was prominent in the Senate of the 70s.[15] Earlier Senates might have contained thirty or forty consulars; Sulla's seems initially to have had, at most, four, including himself. The Sullan Senate was separated from its pre-Social War incarnation – little more than a decade earlier – by a deep gulf of violence, and marked by the absences of those who had died in the Social War and been killed in internecine violence.

In the context of the late Republic, this violent hollowing out of the state's leaders can be set alongside similar episodes later: the civil war between Caesar and the governing class in 49–46, and the struggles from 43 onwards between Caesar's potential heirs.[16] These comparisons should not, however, occlude the novelty at the end of 82. Violence at Rome over the previous fifty years had killed many people; and there were casualties among senior magistrates during war, with a strikingly large number of fatalities during the Social War. But nothing, not even the second war against Carthage, had a comparable effect on the group of senior senators. The leading men

14. R. Evans, 'The *consulares* and *praetorii* in the Roman Senate at the beginning of Sulla's dictatorship', *Athenaeum* 61, 1983, 521–8; see also J.Hawthorn, 'The Senate after Sulla', *G&R* 9, 1962, 53–60.
15. J. van Ooteghem, *Lucius Marcius Philippus et sa famille*, Brussels: Palais des Académies 1961, 133–57.
16. On the losses of 49–46, see below; for the triumviral period, J. S. Richardson, *Augustan Rome, 44 BC to AD 14: The Restoration of the Republic and the Establishment of Empire*, Edinburgh: Edinburgh University Press 2012, 34–8.

in the *res publica* (*principes ciuitatis*) had been almost completely wiped out.

It is much more difficult to trace the rate of attrition among more junior members of the pre-Sullan Senate, but they were clearly still present in some numbers: Sulla's Senate is not an entirely clean slate, and in addition to the continuity provided by individuals there was also the powerful image of the senator within Roman society, whose marks of distinctiveness remained unchanged for its new holders. Nonetheless, a profound shift had taken place. The Sullan Senate contained a large number of men who were new to political activity, and had not entered the political sphere through engagement with the Roman people in an electoral contest. Many of them had profited very substantially from their loyalty to Sulla: they did not wish to see their gains vanish, and they were faced with a system which gave them substantial further opportunities to exploit their new status as senators for material gain. The events of the 70s can be seen as a conjunction of senatorial competitiveness and incompetence with the growing rage of the Roman people at their exclusion from the *res publica*.

Rome, Italy and the Mediterranean

A transformation had occurred with the *lex Iulia* and the other enfranchising laws at the end of the Social War: the dividing line, for Rome, between home and foreign affairs now lay distantly at the boundary with Cisalpine Gaul. Italy itself now contained no allies of the Roman *res publica*, but only communities of Roman citizens. This development was all the more startling because it occurred immediately after the first conflict in Italy south of the Appennines since the war against Hannibal more than a century earlier. Men whom Roman citizens had fought alongside as auxiliaries had become, over the course of just a few years, first their opponents in the Social War and then in turn citizens who could serve on equal terms in the same legions. The mechanisms by which citizenship was extended across Italy in the aftermath of the Social War are only incompletely documented, but indicate that a degree of uniformity in the administrative constitution of newly Roman communities was combined with continued local variation in the handling of particular issues.[17] The questions that arose appear to have been adminis-

17. Crawford 'How to create'; E. Bispham, *From Asculum to Actium: The Municipal-*

trative rather than ideological: that is, after 89, the principle that peaceful free inhabitants of Italy were Roman citizens appears to have held, albeit with some exceptions and debate in particular cases. The long-standing existence of citizen colonies across the Italian peninsula meant that this extension of citizenship did not involve any major conceptual shift: it had long been possible to be a Roman citizen whilst permanently domiciled in a location so distant from Rome itself that regular presence in Rome was impossible. The lived experience of Roman citizenship was already, prior to 89, deeply varied.[18] The challenge lay rather in processes of incorporating the hundreds of thousands of new citizens into the *res publica*'s organisational structures and the unfolding consequences of an Italy now unified through the legal equality of its free inhabitants.

The extension of the citizenship had cultural as well as political implications, the speed and nature of which are much debated.[19] It is undeniable that by the Augustan period a profound shift had occurred, which involved the spread of the Latin language and the development of an idea of Italy which encompassed rather than excluded Rome. Enfranchisement was one of the major steps in this process, but the complex and contested background to the extension of the citizenship, and the extent of other developments during this period, must act as a caution against straightforward expectations of how Roman citizenship may then have engendered further changes. We have already seen that there was no immediate flood of new citizens entering the Roman Senate, for example; the integration of Italians into the political elite was a process lasting more than a generation. Languages other than Latin were still widely spoken in Italy in 90: their disappearance from the record took place over the next century or so.[20] The extension of the citizenship made it possible for colonisation and the army, in particular, to transform individual and community identities, but the disruption of the 80s

ization of Italy from the Social War to Augustus, Oxford: Oxford University Press 2007, 205–404.

18. C. Nicolet, *The World of the Citizen in Republican Rome*, trans. P. Falla, London: Batsford 1980, 17–47.

19. M. Crawford, 'Italy and Rome from Sulla to Augustus', *CAH* 10[2], 1996, 414–33; A. Wallace-Hadrill, *Rome's Cultural Revolution*, Cambridge: Cambridge University Press 2008, 73–143; G. Bradley, 'Romanization: the end of the peoples of Italy?', in G. Bradley, E. Isayev and C. Riva, eds, *Ancient Italy: Regions without Boundaries*, Exeter: Exeter University Press 2007, 295–322.

20. M. Crawford, *Imagines Italicae*, London: Institute of Classical Studies 2011.

and the prolonged civil war after 49 were essential enabling factors in this process.[21]

Even before 49, however, disturbances in parts of Italy, directed at Roman power, continued for many years after the ostensible end of fighting at the battle of the Colline Gate. An armed rising in Etruria in 78 was the starting point for Lepidus' attack on the *res publica* in that year; Etruria was also the site of the battle in 62 which ended Catiline's rising. The confiscations of land for the benefit of Sullan veterans left a mark on communities whose bitterness would take decades to fade; and individual property-owners had been erased from the landscape through the proscriptions. The uprising which started in Campania in 73, and is associated above all with Spartacus, involved free men as well as slaves, a mix which points to antagonism towards Rome as a unifying force as well as desperation among some of Rome's new citizens. The destruction that this force inflicted on the areas through which it passed was serious, and Roman failure to deal quickly with the problem is unlikely to have endeared Roman power to those who suffered. Moreover, Crassus' victory in 71 did not absolutely mark the end of the problem. The proconsul C. Octavius was active near Thurii in 60 in clearing out remnants of Spartacus' and Catiline's followers.[22] This is a chance notice in the biography of his son, the emperor Augustus; the scale of the problem is better seen in the Senate's decision, in the same year, and taking advantage of an apparent lull in overseas demands, to make clearing up the Italian countryside the consular province for the following year. This allocation, which has become enmeshed in questions of Caesar's ambition and the opposition which it provoked, nonetheless reflected a genuine and continuing problem.

Glimpses of these issues as they affected specific communities emerge from Cicero's early forensic oratory, with his clients including men from Umbria, Etruria, Latium and Apulia.[23] Some of the problems which his clients were attempting to resolve – or withstand – were ongoing aspects of a largely unpoliced society; the need to secure possession of property through violence, for example, was

---

21. On the movement of people with Italy, see W. Scheidel, 'Human mobility in Roman Italy, I: the free population', *JRS* 94, 2004, 1–26.

22. Suet. *Aug.* 3.1, 7.1; Octavius had been given this task as an extra on his way to Macedonia, his province.

23. For a summary, K. Lomas, 'A Volscian Mafia? Cicero and his Italian clients', in J. Powell and J. Paterson, eds, *Cicero the Advocate*, Oxford: Oxford University Press 2004, 97–116.

unlikely to have been confined to the 70s and 60s. But elsewhere the direct effects of recent war are evidence. In the defence of Sextus Roscius of Ameria, delivered in 80 BC, the effects of Sulla's coup resonate. The elder Sextus Roscius, a substantial land-owner in the Tiber valley near Ameria in Umbria, had been included in the proscription list; and he died by violence. That was a story which must have been played out across Italy. What makes the Roscius case different is that one of his sons was subsequently accused of his murder, and Erucius, the prosecutor, had the support of two of Roscius' relations; the case was the first to be held in the newly constituted standing court to try offences under the *lex Cornelia de sicariis et veneficiis*.[24] Beyond those facts, little about the actual case is clear, not least the problem of how anyone could be prosecuted for murdering a victim of the proscriptions.[25] Nonetheless, the speech does give us a glimpse of how Italian communities reacted to the period of upheaval, plausible in its picture of how local rivals seized opportunities to acquire property and enhance status, of the power which associates of Sulla wielded, and of the network of connections with the Roman elite which wealthy members of Italian communities used for protection and support. The elder Roscius – who died in Rome – was on friendly terms with members of the Roman elite. Indeed, one reading of *Pro Sexto Roscio Amerino* is to see it as a contest between two models of influence and power: autocracy, where proximity to the tyrant is key, and the traditional networks of patronage which put the great families of the elite at the top of the pyramid. At the time of this speech, it was not yet clear that the second model would win out.

One of the many questions that the Roscius case leaves unanswered is the fate of the elder Roscius' 13 farms. The younger Roscius was acquitted; but that verdict would not bring him his property back, and one suspects that any subsequent attempt to regain it through the courts might well have failed in the face of the unalterable fact of the proscription lists. *Pro Cluentio* offers us a comparable narrative for Larinum. This was the largest town in the territory of the Frentani, in Apulia, at the eastern edge of Samnium;

24. For the case and its background, A. Dyck, *Cicero: Pro Sexto Roscio*, Cambridge: Cambridge University Press 2010.
25. W. Stroh, *Taxis und Taktik: die advokatischen Dispositionskunst in Ciceros Gerichtsreden*, Stuttgart: Teubner 1975, 55–79; M. Alexander, *The Case for the Prosecution in the Ciceronian Era*, Ann Arbor: University of Michigan Press 2002, 149–72; A. Lintott, *Cicero as Evidence*, Oxford: Oxford University Press 2008, 425–7.

it was an Oscan-speaking area, though Greek and Latin are both found on its pre-Social War coinage.[26] It fought against Rome during the Social War, was overrun by Cosconius' forces as he marched south in 89, and appears to have been enfranchised soon afterwards.[27] Cicero's speech, delivered in 66 BC, concentrates on the tortuous relationships between his client Cluentius and Cluentius' relatives, and on the complex judicial prehistory of the case, but it also sketches out the town's recent history. By the time of Sulla's return, it was a town (*municipium*) with a governing body of four elected magistrates, who found themselves deposed and replaced by a pro-Sullan group of four, with proscriptions following.[28] Cicero makes his client's stepfather (and alleged victim) Oppianicus the instigator of these events: Oppianicus' allegiance to Sulla was, according to Cicero, a strategy to resolve an internal dispute at Larinum in his favour. He fled to Metellus Pius' army in the face of hostility at Larinum, and he returned with armed force to take control of town: Sulla appears in the narrative only to have his name used by Oppianicus. A less slanted analysis is to see an intersection of local and Roman politics, to the advantage of the victors in both arenas.

Another issue onto which *Pro Cluentio* throws oblique light is the fragility of free status. The starting point for Cicero's narrative of events is the fate of Marcus Aurius: 'as a young man he was captured during the Italian war at Asculum and fell into the hands of Q. Sergius, a senator (this is the man who was convicted in the murder court), and was on his property in a slave camp'.[29] Later in the speech Cicero notes that Cluentius returned a slave-woman, whom he had bought, to her husband Ceius, 'a Samnite', as soon as he found that she was of free status, without waiting for judgement.[30] Unfortunately, Cicero does not tell us how the woman found herself enslaved; date and ethnicity might suggest that this, too, is a consequence of the Social War. It is unclear whether or not any wholesale measure was passed at Rome to address the position of

26. G. Barker, ed., *A Mediterranean Valley: Landscape Archaeology and Annales History in the Biferno Valley*, Leicester: Leicester University Press 1995, 181–253; Lomas, 'Mafia', 108–10.
27. App. *B Civ.* 1.52.
28. Cic. *Clu.* 25.
29. Cic. *Clu.* 21. Aurius' relatives discovered his location, but before they could secure his freedom he was – according to Cicero – murdered by his brother-in-law Oppianicus' agents.
30. Cic. *Clu.* 162.

those Italians who were captured during the course of the Social War; but even if it was, implementation would have depended upon the information and energy of the friends and relatives of the enslaved. One can suspect that many Italians captured during the war remained in agricultural slavery until their deaths.

Sulla's coup thus speeded up the integration of Italy after the Social War. He himself appears to have been less interested in addressing the consequences of enfranchisement than his opponents, but the terms of his victory embedded the power of men who had become his supporters. The extensive transfer of land, property and power as a result of Sulla's dictatorship dramatically confirmed the importance of Rome to the newly enfranchised communities: if Larinum and Ameria are remotely representative, the ruling classes across Italy after 80 were firmly committed to the status quo in Roman political life, and the benefits which it provided them.

If civil war drove the evolving relationship between Rome and its former allies in Italy, it also had profound consequences for Roman choices around foreign policy. The 80s BC mark the first point at which Rome's political fracturing played out across the Mediterranean, and Sulla's victory thus involved extensive fighting outside Italy. The campaigns in Sicily, Gaul and north Africa were rapid, but eliminating anti-Sullan forces in Spain took nearly a decade from 82, demanded substantial forces, and generated a leadership crisis whose solution – Pompeius – created its own set of problems.

The independence of the Iberian peninsula from senatorial rule under Sertorius' command was brief but highly significant. In a sense, Sertorius was following Sulla's actions in Greece and Asia Minor, which had shown the practical capacity of a Roman general to ignore instructions from the Senate and operate independently. Of course, their cases had important differences: Sertorius' position had become that of an enemy of Rome once Sulla was in power, whereas Sulla himself was never formally disowned by the Roman *res publica*. But both demonstrated how Rome's foreign conquest could provide the forces to maintain internal discord, a model which would drive the next civil wars almost to the point of dissolving the unity of Roman power. As importantly, preoccupation with internal affairs interfered significantly with foreign policy. Sulla left the war with Mithridates unfinished; Metellus and Pompeius' campaigns in Spain took their tempo from Sertorius and then Perperna. The period reinforces the message of the late second century, that Roman foreign policy was heavily contingent upon domestic affairs.

Figure 5 Pompeius: a bust in the Ny Carlsberg Glyptotek, Copenhagen (© Ny Carlsberg Glyptotek)

In other respects, however, Sulla was a deeply innovative figure in the development of Roman imperialism. As Santangelo has argued, Sulla pioneered the systematic use of punishment and reward to control the cities of Asia Minor, and their governing elites: those which had supported Rome during the Mithridatic war were privileged in the post-war period, within an administrative framework which facilitated contact between the Roman governor and all provincial communities. As a result, the advantages for the political classes in the Asian cities of personal relationship with leading Romans became significant, and led to the establishment, and recording, of networks of patronage.[31] In this, as in so many other matters, Pompeius was Sulla's attentive pupil. A consular law in 72 gave him rights to enfranchise provincials in Spain, which he used to reward service and create lasting obligations.[32] Over two decades after he had left Spain, the gratitude that communities felt towards him as a result of his actions during the war with Sertorius became

31. Santangelo, *Elites*, 50–66, 107–33.
32. Among those who received citizenship in this way was L. Cornelius Balbus, the agent of Pompeius and later of Caesar.

a factor in the fighting between his legates and Caesar's forces during the next round of civil war.[33]

Internal conflict thus appears to have pushed forward a shift in the mechanics of Roman imperialism, as the desire for competitive advantage in domestic politics led individuals to exploit the inhabitants of the empire. This shift increased the resources available for Rome's civil wars, with disastrous consequences for their length and intensity; and through personal contacts it supported the cultural integration of elites across the empire. Both consequences were to have profound effects on the nature of Roman power long after the collapse of Republican government.

Causes of change

Competition between members of the elite remained central to politics in the period after Sulla's settlement. An immediate example is in the use of images of ancestors: Appius Claudius Pulcher, consul in 79, dedicated shields bearing images of his ancestors in the temple of Bellona, and Aemilius Lepidus developed the idea by placing them in the Basilica Aemiliana as well as in his house.[34] Wax images were replaced by metal; at the same time, a private memorial was made public.[35] Pliny does not date these innovations, though the date of Aemilius' death suggests that both men were celebrating their achievement of the consulship, and they therefore date immediately after Sulla's return to private life. It may not be coincidence that these men were – as Sulla also was – patrician: at precisely the point at which the Senate was expanding to include men with no previous family history of participation in it, tenure of the highest offices was dominated by a post-Sullan aristocracy of patricians and of old established plebeian *nobilis* families. For these men, packaging the past was an enduring concern.

Competition between members of the elite through the display of resources, as a means towards achieving tangible political success through election to office is, then, a continuing feature in the political landscape. But the parameters within which competition now

---

33. Caes. *B Civ.* 1.61. On Pompeius' personal connections in the east, see below; they arguably contributed to his death, by leading him to believe that Egypt would provide him with a safe haven after his defeat at Pharsalus.
34. Plin. *HN* 35.12–13.
35. H. Flower, *Ancestor Masks and Aristocratic Power in Roman Culture*, Oxford: Oxford University Press 1996, 75–7; Wallace-Hadrill, *Cultural Revolution*, 223.

operated had changed. The Roman people – whose chief remaining function in the Sullan *res publica* was to elect magistrates – was vastly extended from its pre-Social War form. The length of time that it took to register all the new citizens, a process which appears only to have been completed by the censorship of 70, may well reflect the potential of this change, since registration involved allocating new citizens to tribes, which in turn determined the effect that their votes would have in elections. Until this process was completed, the capacity of Rome's new citizens to play a political role was limited; once it had been, the gap between the citizen body in legal fact and the citizen body in voting practice posed an interesting challenge to the ruling elite. The gap had of course existed to some degree from the point at which Rome extended its citizenship beyond the bounds of a city-state to communities too distant to permit regular participation in activity in Rome; but the extension of citizenship following the Social War very greatly increased its size, and consequently made elections much more unpredictable, at least in theory, to those attempting to secure victory for themselves or their friends. Complex questions, concerning the identity of those who would be present in Rome, the factors which would affect their decision, and the processes by which favours might effectively be distributed to them, now became urgent. The unpredictability of the composition of the electorate on any particular occasion may have contributed to the increasing concern with electoral bribery in the post-Sullan period. But the change in the composition of the electorate, and the increase in competition for higher offices, did not lead to an increased number of new men reaching the consulship.[36]

The result of Sulla's innovations was, then, to make the political system more difficult for its participants to understand and predict. New voters did not belong to existing systems through which voting patterns could be predicted; new senators were not necessarily part of networks of obligation and favour. New measures had to be devised, in an attempt to control this strange new environment. At the same time, citizens' demand for the restoration of their role proved irresistible to individual politicians. But deep suspicion, generated by poverty, attempts at repression, and senatorial greed and incompetence, remained even after 70 between the people and its rulers. These suspicions, never resolved, dominate the course of politics over the remaining years of the Republic.

36. There are none in the decade after Sulla.

CHAPTER 6

The end of the Republic, 70–44 BC

In comparison with the rapid changes and destructive violence of the years from the Social War to the first consulship of Pompeius and Crassus, the following two decades were a period of relative calm and political stability. There was only one episode of major conflict within Italy itself, the short-lived and easily defeated uprising led by Catiline in 63–62 BC. And, broadly speaking, magistrates and tribunes of the plebs were elected in the same way and to do the same tasks in 50 BC as they had been in 70 BC.[1] But conventions were bent to breaking point and beyond, and violence frequently disrupted political life. Caesar's invasion of Italy in the first weeks of 49 BC had, as its background, his own transgressive career and that of Pompeius, Crassus and others who with greater or lesser success attempted to transcend the constraints of collective power. Caesar's invasion sparked a new civil war, in which he was victorious; his dictatorship, which began during this war and lasted for less than a year after its conclusion, revealed a new range of problems, few of which had reached any kind of solution by the time of his assassination.

The continuing problem of Mithridates

If the consulship of Pompeius and Crassus marked an end to a period of experimentation in domestic political life, it offered the illusion of similar closure in foreign affairs. Pompeius and Crassus were themselves responsible for much of the apparent peace, with the restoration of unitary Roman rule in Spain, and the final defeat of Spartacus' uprising. Mithridates had fled ahead of a victorious Lucullus, whose request to the Senate for a commission to arrange

---

1. There was nonetheless much legislation during the period, which modified various of the *leges Corneliae*: C. Williamson, *The Laws of the Roman People: Public Law in the Expansion and Decline of the Roman Republic*, Ann Arbor: University of Michigan Press 2005, 367–414.

for Mithridates' former possessions to be brought under Roman control arrived during the year 70.[2]

Nonetheless, the sense of an ending was undermined over the following years. Lucullus had sent App. Claudius, one of his legates, to Tigranes to negotiate the handover of Mithridates.[3] When Tigranes refused, Lucullus invaded Armenia: a development which took Roman forces across the Euphrates into new territory, and was difficult to bring into alignment with Lucullus' original instructions.[4] Initially, Lucullus was successful, defeating Tigranes near Tigranocerta on 6 October 69, in a battle which became exemplary for the disparity in size of the forces involved on each side and the overwhelming nature of the victory.[5] He then captured and destroyed Tigranocerta, and over the winter of 69–68 was engaged with the diplomatic consequences of his victory. These included negotiations with the Parthian kingdom, securing Parthian neutrality.[6] In 68, Lucullus continued his campaign against Tigranes, taking his forces north and winning another victory by the river Arsanias towards the end of the summer. But he failed, again, to capture Mithridates; and his troops' discontent forced him to abandon the pursuit and return over the Taurus mountains again to the headwaters of the Tigris, where he captured and overwintered in the city of Nisibis. Here, his brother-in-law Publius Clodius exacerbated the hostile feelings among Lucullus' army, concentrating particularly on those men who had originally been sent to the east as part of Valerius Flaccus' army in 86.[7] Moreover, Mithridates had escaped behind Lucullus and by 67 was attacking the forces which Lucullus had left behind in Pontus. Lucullus responded by marching back towards Pontus, but did not arrive in time to prevent the battle of Zela, at which Mithridates comprehensively defeated the Romans under the legate Triarius. Lucullus was unable to persuade his troops to continue fighting, and they encamped over the summer of 67 in Cappadocia.

Part of Lucullus' difficulty by this point was that his command

---

2. See above, p. 114.

3. This man was the son of the consul of 79, elder brother of Publius Clodius (see below) and Lucullus' brother-in-law.

4. A. N. Sherwin-White, *Roman Foreign Policy in the East, 168 B.C. to A.D. 1*, London: Duckworth 1984, 173–6.

5. Plut. *Luc.* 28.7–8.

6. This may or may not have involved a formal treaty: Sherwin-White, *Foreign Policy*, 180–1.

7. W. J. Tatum, *Publius Clodius Pulcher: The Patrician Tribune*, Chapel Hill: University of North Carolina Press 1999, 44–9.

was now coming to an end: a *lex Gabinia*, proposed by one of the tribunes of 67, had appointed the consul Glabrio to the command against Mithridates, and news of this had reached Lucullus by the summer of 67.[8] Other changes to his command had already taken place: Asia had been allocated to one of the praetors of 69, and Cilicia had been identified as consular under the *lex Sempronia*. How far these allocations should be seen as an attack on Lucullus is debatable: he had, after all, announced his victory in a letter to the Senate in 70, and Cilicia had become an important base for the fight against piracy.[9] There were good arguments to be made in favour of new commanders in these two areas, given Lucullus' decision to move south and east, even if we may suspect that those pressing for the changes were not necessarily Lucullus' friends. But the *lex Gabinia* was a different matter; it assigned to another not only Bithynia and Pontus, the last territorial areas over which Lucullus had *imperium*, but also the war against Mithridates.[10] This law was passed before news of Zela reached Rome: even without renewed crisis, Lucullus' failure, two full years after he had announced victory over Mithridates, actually to end the war had made his position untenable.[11] Moreover, Gabinius' law, unlike consular provinces allocated under the *lex Sempronia*, had immediate effect.

Another ongoing problem, and one with more direct effects on Rome itself, was piracy.[12] This was not a new problem; it appears

---

8. R. Williams, 'The appointment of Glabrio (cos 67) to the Eastern Command', *Phoenix* 38, 1984, 221–34.

9. R. M. Kallet-Marx, *Hegemony to Empire: The Development of the Roman Imperium in the East from 148 to 62 B.C.*, Berkeley: University of California Press 1995, 311–14; T. C. Brennan, *The Praetorship in the Roman Republic*, New York: Oxford University Press 2000, 564–5; Lucullus had allegedly become unpopular in Rome among creditors due to his debt refinancing in Asia during the winter of 70 (Plut. *Luc.* 20.5; Cass. Dio 36.2) but the direct effects of this on senatorial decisions are unclear. On piracy, see below.

10. Cicero's account of Lucullus' campaigns in his speech *De imperio Cn. Pompei* is tactfully vague in many parts, but the language of chapter 26 ('on your orders, who thought that, in line with tradition, an end should be placed to the length of *imperium*') seems clear: the Roman people ended Lucullus' tenure of *imperium*. Gabinius' law also discharged the Valerian legions (Sall. *Hist.* M 5.13), which implies that he thought serious campaigning was over.

11. Gabinius attacked Lucullus' lavish lifestyle in *contiones* (Cic. *Sest.* 93), presumably to construct an argument that it was his search for booty that was delaying the conclusion of the campaign. After Lucullus returned to Rome he became exemplary of a morally dubious type of luxury (R. Evans, *Utopia Antiqua: Readings of the Golden Age and Decline at Rome*, London: Routledge 2008, 93–108).

12. P. de Souza, *Piracy in the Graeco-Roman World*, Cambridge: Cambridge University Press 1999, 43–148; P. Horden and N. Purcell, *The Corrupting Sea*, Oxford: Blackwell

with more frequency and vividness in our sources at about this time than earlier, but this in part reflects a political environment in which piracy had become an object of crisis as other threats diminished. Crete was an important base for the pirates, and appears to have been designated as a consular province before the elections for 69: this provoked intense diplomatic effort from the Cretan communities in an attempt to avert an attack. Initially, these efforts were successful, resulting in a senatorial decree confirming the terms of Antonius' treaty; but a tribunician veto appears to have followed, and the Senate changed its policy, with the dispatch of an ultimatum whose terms were, presumably intentionally, unacceptable to the Cretans.[13] Fighting resumed with the arrival of Q. Metellus, to whom the command had been allocated, and he besieged a number of Cretan towns.[14] But his actions appeared to have little effect on piracy in the western Mediterranean and its direct consequences on Rome. Cicero paints a picture of an Italy terrorised by pirates in his speech of 66 *De imperio Cn. Pompei* (31–3), with the capture of two praetors and attacks at the harbours at Caieta, Misenum and Ostia.[15]

This was the background to Gabinius' other major law, which established a three-year command for an ex-consul, with *imperium*, including the capacity to override other *imperium*-holders within 50 miles of the sea, and extensive resources of men, ships and money. It did not name Pompeius, but he was immediately understood to be the intended beneficiary. Its passage involved violent confrontation. Dio records a Senate meeting at which Gabinius was first almost killed, and then, as his supporters rushed the building in retaliation, the consul Piso was captured and himself only saved from assault by the intervention of Gabinius (36.24). Subsequently, Gabinius' opponents attempted to derail his law through a tribunician veto, applied by L. Trebellius. In scenes reminiscent of Tiberius Gracchus' encounter with Octavius, Gabinius interrupted voting on this law to get the people to vote on deposing Trebellius from office; but, once 17 tribes had voted in support, and the eighteenth was about to vote,

2000, 387–8; M. Tröster, 'Roman hegemony and non-state violence: a fresh look at Pompey's campaign against the pirates', *G&R* 56, 2009, 14–33.
13. Kallet-Marx, *Hegemony*, 309–11.
14. The command fell initially to the other consul of 69, Hortensius, who declined it; we do not know which province Metellus had initially drawn.
15. Plut. *Pomp*. 24 also records the capture of praetors, with their names.

Trebellius decided to withdraw his veto, and the measure on piracy passed.

According to Velleius (2.31.3–4), the actual powers which Pompeius gained under this law were comparable with those that M. Antonius had had seven years previous for *his* piracy campaign. Velleius' interpretation, that it was fear of Pompeius' power and automomy which caused the very different response from the Senate, is surely correct, but we can supplement his account by noting differences in procedure and substance which tended to enhance Pompeius' position. Antonius' command came via the Senate, involved him alone, and does not seem to have been generously resourced. Pompeius was the beneficiary of a tribunician law which gave him startlingly large resources and the patronage inherent in the appointment of numerous legates. The law was also a much more direct challenge to senatorial control of military activity: by identifying a former consul as its beneficiary it implied that existing magistrates were not capable of responding to the problem (in contrast to Gabinius' law on the Mithridatic command, which identified one of the consuls as the commander and was therefore in effect an updating of that year's *lex Sempronia*). It also suggested that the Senate's own attempts to deal with piracy through the command of Metellus were inadequate.[16]

Gabinius' laws were part of a burst of tribunician legislative activity during this year, which not only pitted Senate against people but also split the tribunician college very publicly into opposing groups. The tribune Cornelius put forward a variety of measures: whereas Gabinius' focus was on foreign policy, Cornelius concentrated on procedure and governance.[17] Most contentious was his measure which made the people the only source of exemption from the laws; that is, to stop the Senate from voting its own members exemptions. In confrontations reminiscent of those surrounding Gabinius' piracy law, this was vetoed by Servilius Globulus, and

16. Cicero suggests that the price of wheat dropped dramatically on Pompeius' appointment (*De imp. Cn. Pomp.* 44): 'on the day on which he was appointed by you as commander in the maritime war the price of wheat dropped so much – in a situation of extreme shortage and expense of grain – as scarcely happens with extended peace and abundant harvest'. Anxiety over the food supply is likely to have been a major factor in generating popular support for the measure: P. Garnsey, *Famine and Food Supply in the Graeco-Roman World: Responses to Risk and Crisis*, Cambridge: Cambridge University Press 1988, 204–6.

17. M. Griffin, 'The tribune Cornelius', *JRS* 63, 1973, 196–213; T. P. Wiseman, 'The Senate and the *populares*, 69–60 B.C.', *CAH* 9², 1994, 327–67, at 329–38.

although Cornelius attempted to circumvent the veto he withdrew his proposal in order to avoid further violence.[18] A compromise, to allow the Senate to grant exemptions, but only if 200 senators were present, passed subsequently without dissension. Cornelius also successfully put forward a measure to compel praetors to follow their own edicts; two other unsuccessful measures of his are known, one to forbid loans to foreign states and another on bribery, though the latter prompted one of the consuls to put forward a bribery law with less stringent penalties. Finally, another tribune, Roscius Otho, carried a law which reserved 14 rows of seats at theatrical shows for members of the equestrian class.

How should we interpret this sudden burst of activity? Pompeius himself, a private individual since the end of his consulship, is one factor: it is implausible that he was not deeply involved in the attempt to give him the command against the pirates. This move, in turn, may have been triggered by a realisation that he could no longer rely on the Senate to grant him opportunities outside the normal *cursus* as had happened earlier in his career; or perhaps that he no longer needed to do so, since the restoration of the tribunician powers now made it possible for him to turn his popularity with the people directly into military commands. Despite Pompeius' nods towards senatorial authority during his consulship, the restoration of tribunician powers that year allowed him now to step around that authority. The command against the pirates also had the attraction of being distinctively different from the kind of territorially based provincial command which had become the norm in the post-Sullan period, and thus did not compromise Pompeius' carefully maintained separation from the normal *cursus*, which he had most recently emphasised by refusing a consular province.

The legislation of 67 also suggests that the Senate was perceived to be abusing its powers on a grand scale. Asconius notes, in the introduction to his commentary on Cicero's defence of Cornelius in 65, that restrictions on the granting of exemptions were unwelcome because senators had used them to do favours to their friends, and praetors who were looking for votes ignored their edicts to obtain

---

18. C. Steel, 'Tribunician sacrosanctity and oratorial performance in the late Republic', in D. Berry and A. Erskine, eds, *Form and Function in Roman Oratory*, Cambridge: Cambridge University Press 2010, 37–50. These events were the basis for the *maiestas* charges which Cornelius faced in 66; he was defended by Cicero, and Asconius' commentary on Cicero's (lost) speech is the major source for Cornelius' actions along with Dio's narrative (36.38–40).

influence. He gives part of the wording of Cornelius' measure on loans: 'since loans were being made to the legates of foreign states at high rates of interest, and scandalous profits being made from them, no one should lend money to the envoys of foreign states'.[19] The indebtedness of provincial communities is attested elsewhere, and a number of successful *repetundae* prosecutions took place during these years.[20] Whilst some of our evidence on senatorial abuses is undoubtedly tendentious, it is difficult to escape the conclusion that senators had been using the freedom from external scrutiny that Sulla had given them to maximise their personal profits both in Italy and abroad. How far Pompeius sought to exploit this anti-senatorial feeling in promoting his own interests is unclear, though personal integrity was undoubtedly a part of his public persona: the young man accused of embezzlement had been replaced by an irreproachable defender of the public good.

The events of 67 are also the first recorded occasion since the restoration of the tribunate when the ten tribunes were split. A model of tribunician power which involved a process of negotiation with the people throughout the year, and was not an absolute, emerged very clearly from the violence of 67; this realisation provided renewed impetus to the move towards organised violence as a political tool.[21] Finally, the consul Piso contributed significantly to the outburst of factional confrontation. He took a lead in opposing Gabinius, and subsequently tried to interfere with Pompeius' levying of troops; and Asconius' account (51C) suggests he was physically in the midst of Cornelius' encounter with Globulus. It is plausible to suspect that he was involved in persuading other tribunes to oppose Cornelius and Gabinius, and he sponsored the bribery law which reduced the urgency of Cornelius' more stringent proposal. He also refused to accept the candidature for the consul-

19. Asc. 57C–59C.
20. L. Migeotte, *L'emprunt public dans les cités grecques*, Paris: Les Belles Lettres 1984; Santangelo, *Elites*, 111–26. *Repetundae* convictions from 78 include those of Cn. Cornelius Dolabella (pr. 81), Q. Calidius, P. Septimius Scaevola and C. Verres, with a number of other cases which ended in acquittal or whose outcome is unknown: see M. Alexander, *Trials in the Late Roman Republic 149 BC to 50 BC*, Toronto: University of Toronto Press 1990.
21. A. Lintott, *Violence in Republican Rome*, 2nd edn, Oxford: Oxford University Press 1999, 187–200; W. Nippel, *Public Order in Ancient Rome*, Cambridge: Cambridge University Press 1995, 47–69.

ship of Lollius Palicanus, in the face of fruitless opposition from at least some of the tribunician college.[22]

Pompeius' campaigns, 67–62 BC

Pompeius' campaign against the pirates proceeded rapidly: starting at the western end of the Mediterranean, he and his legates swept eastward, driving the pirates before them and concluding the campaign within forty days with a major sea-battle off the coast of Cilicia, near Coracesium.[23] Not everything went smoothly. Pompeius faced opposition from Piso when he passed through Rome between the western and eastern parts of his campaign, and later he clashed over jurisdiction with Metellus in Crete. His elimination of piracy was, moreover, only temporary.[24] But the news in Rome was of glorious success. Cicero's speech *De imperio Cn. Pompei*, from early in 66, offers a particularly vivid glimpse of Pompeius as a quasi-divine being, whose exceptional qualities as a military leader have brought about spectacular success: 'Good heavens above! Has the unbelievable and god-like virtue of any one man ever brought such light, so quickly, to the state – with the result that you, who only recently saw the fleet of your enemies at the mouth of the Tiber, now hear that no pirate ship is within the Mediterranean?' (33). Cicero's discussion of the pirates – and Pompeius' earlier campaigns – is in support of a new law to put Pompeius in charge of the campaign against Mithridates and Tigranes.[25] This was proposed by one of the tribunes, Manilius, and it allocated to Pompeius Cilicia,

22. Val. Max. 3.8.3; Lollius' co-operation with Pompeius in 71, when Lollius had held the tribunate, may alone explain Piso's hostility (and Pompeius had departed from Rome by the time of the elections) but a more general demonstration by Piso of his power, in the face of the provocations and disappointments of the first half of the year, is also plausible.

23. Plut. *Pomp.* 27.2–28.4; de Souza, *Piracy*, 167–12; Tröster, 'Hegemony'.

24. Pompeius in Rome: Plut. *Pomp.* 27.1–2. Livy, *Per.* 99 records an exchange of letters between Metellus Creticus and Pompeius, with Creticus complaining that 'the glory of his achievements had been taken from him by Pompeius, who had sent *his* legate to Crete to receive the surrender of the cities' There is evidence of renewed pirate trouble in the 50s: de Souza, *Piracy*, 179–85.

25. On the speech, J. Gruber, 'Cicero und das hellenistische Herrscherideal: Überlegungen zur Rede *De imperio Cn. Pompeii*', WS 101, 1988, 243–58; P. Rose, 'Cicero and the rhetoric of imperialism: putting the politics back into political rhetoric', *Rhetorica* 13, 1995, 359–99; C. Steel, *Cicero, Rhetoric, and Empire*, Oxford: Oxford University Press 2001, 114–56.

Bithynia and Pontus, superseding their existing commanders; it does not appear to have set a duration for his command.

The rationale for Manilius' measure was clear. The war against Mithridates was still not over, and Roman prestige had received a serious blow the previous year in the defeat at Zela; there was no report of decisive action by either Glabrio or Marcius Rex; and Pompeius was already present in the eastern Mediterranean, having successfully completed one major campaign and with the resources to undertake a new task. Moreover, Pompeius' record in bringing to a conclusion intractable problems such as Sertorius, Spartacus and the pirates made him an attractive candidate to deal with Mithridates, who had first challenged Rome over twenty years previously. Pompeius had presumably seen the opportunity, and begun planning for it, late in the previous summer as he concluded the pirate campaign. Effecting the command through a law, rather than through the Senate, gave him the opportunity to reassert his direct link with the people; it also evaded the opposition from two senior consulars, Hortensius and Catulus.[26]

Pompeius moved north to Galatia where he met Lucullus, and took over from him most of his troops; the meeting between the two ended in blunt recriminations, and Pompeius ignored the decisions taken both by Lucullus and by the senatorial commission of ten requested by Lucullus.[27] He then set out after Mithridates, whom he defeated in battle later in 66; Mithridates, however, escaped north towards Colchis and thence to the Crimea. Pompeius turned aside to deal with Tigranes (who had now refused further aid to his father-in-law and was facing a revolt led by his son). Tigranes capitulated to Roman power in a powerfully symbolic meeting, which may or may not have been stage-managed; the terms included the handover

26. Cic. De imp. Cn. Pomp. 51, 59–60; cf. Plut. Pomp. 30.4. On the contional debate, R. Morstein-Marx, Mass Oratory and Political Power in the Late Roman Republic, Cambridge: Cambridge University Press 2004, 182–3; B. S. Rodgers, 'Catulus' speech in Cassius Dio 36.31–36', GRBS 48, 2008, 295–318. The consulars openly in favour of the measure (Cic. De imp. Cn. Pomp. 68) were Servilius Vatia (cos. 79), Curio (cos. 76), C. Cassius (cos. 73) and Cn. Lentulus (cos. 72). Manilius had begun his tribunate with an unsuccessful attempt to allocate freedmen to all tribes; his motives in supporting Pompeius are unclear. Serious forward planning by Pompeius much earlier than late summer 67 is unlikely, since it was only during this year that the weaknesses of the Senate's response to Lucullus' perceived incompetence (i.e. his supersession) became clear.
27. On Pompeius' campaigns in 66–62 see Sherwin-White, Foreign Policy, 186–226; Kallet-Marx, Hegemony, 320–34; R. Seager, Pompey the Great, 2nd edn, Oxford: Blackwell 2002, 53–62.

to Rome of recent conquests, including Syria, and a fine of 6,000 talents.[28] Tigranes himself retained his kingdom of Armenia; initially, Pompeius proposed to install Tigranes' son as ruler of Sophene, but then took him to Rome as a hostage.[29] Pompeius also renewed the treaty with the Parthian ruler Phraates which Lucullus had negotiated. He then continued north, but his route suggests that his aim was initially, at least, the demonstration of Roman power in the areas which had been under Tigranes' sway rather than pursuit of Mithridates.[30] Late 66 and 65 were taken up with fighting the Albanian and Iberian tribes in the eastern Caucasus; he also founded a city, Nicopolis, for discharged veterans.[31] He then moved to Amisus, where he spent the winter of 65–64 in the organisation of Bithynia, leaving Mithridates undisturbed in the northern Black Sea region. Pompeius appears, in fact, to have decided to abandon active pursuit of Mithridates and late in 64 turned south towards the former Seleucid kingdom of Syria, which he organised as a province.[32] He then intervened in Judaea, capturing Jerusalem in October 63 and installing a Roman nominee as high priest. Meanwhile, the problem of Mithridates had solved itself: his son Pharnaces had rebelled successfully against him, and Mithridates had committed suicide. Pharnaces sent to Pompeius the embalmed body of Mithridates, hostages, and the men who had captured and killed M'. Aquillius twenty-five years earlier. Pompeius received them at Amisus, having returned to Pontus for the winter of 63–62. With the announcement at Rome of the death of Mithridates – which was marked by a ten-day thanksgiving (*supplicatio*) – the task entrusted to him under the *lex Manilia* was completed; but he did not immediately return to Rome. He undertook extensive administrative arrangements of the areas now under Roman control, which included new organisational structures in Pontus and the confirm-

28. The scene, with Tigranes' prostration (*proskunesis*) to Pompeius and Pompeius' restoration of his diadem, is described by Dio (36.52.1–4), Plutarch (*Pomp.* 33.2–5), Appian (*Mith.* 104–5) and Velleius (2.37.3–4).
29. The younger Tigranes was exhibited at Pompeius' triumph in 62 and remained in custody at Rome until 58, when he was freed by Clodius: see Tatum, *Clodius*, 170.
30. Sherwin-White, *Foreign Policy*, 195–206.
31. This was the first official community of Roman citizens in the Greek east.
32. Pompeius' eastern conquests probably mark the point at which *prouincia* acquired a decisively territorial sense, and we can therefore talk of his 'provincial organisation': see J. S. Richardson, *The Language of Empire: Rome and the Idea of Empire from the Third Century BC to the Second Century AD*, Cambridge: Cambridge University Press 2008, 106–14.

ation of the power of numerous local rulers, as well as the imposition of direct Roman rule in Syria. In the spring of 62, he set out for
Rome: his route, down the coast of Asia Minor via Mytilene and
Ephesus to Rhodes, and then across the Aegean to Athens, was not
surprising, but it enabled him to arrange impressive public acknowledgement of his achievements at each of these stopping points.[33]

Italian crises

Pompeius was returning to a Rome preoccupied by issues other than
his spectacular conquests, and the fallout from the resulting clash of
interests directed much of Rome's domestic politics over the next
decade. Early in 62, as Pompeius was organising his return, a consular army defeated and largely destroyed forces under the command
of an ex-praetor, L. Sergius Catilina, in battle near Faesulae in
Etruria, in the first large-scale violence between citizens, in Italy,
since Lepidus' uprising fifteen years earlier.

Catiline was from a patrician family (*gens*), not recently prominent.[34] He was born around 110 BC; he is first recorded in the army
of Pompeius Strabo during the Social War (where it is likely that he
met both Pompeius Magnus and Cicero) and emerges as an adherent
of Sulla after the latter's return to Italy in 82.[35] It is probable that
he benefited financially from the proscriptions, and that this access
of wealth supported his political career; we must assume that he
followed the *cursus honorum* during the 70s.[36] He is next attested
as governor of Africa in 67–66, implying that he had just held a
praetorship. He was prosecuted for extortion on his return, by
P. Clodius Pulcher; Cicero, in one of his earliest surviving letters (*Att.*
1.2.1), is contemplating defending him, though in the end he did not.
Catiline was acquitted, but the prosecution delayed his consular
candidacy and he first stood in the summer of 64 for the consulship
of 63.

33. He gave Mytilene its freedom in honour of his friend and historian Theophanes (this
might be the occasion of his grant of citizenship to Theophanes) and was spectator at a
poetry competition (the poetry in his honour); at Rhodes, he listened to disputations,
including one by Posidonius which was subsequently published; at Athens, he listened to
the philosophers, and gave the city 50 talents (Plut. *Pomp.* 42.4–6).
34. A. Dyck, *Cicero: Catilinarians*, Cambridge: Cambridge University Press 2008, 1.
35. *ILS* 8888; Sall. *Hist.* 1.46M; Asc. 82C–4C. Much of the evidence about Catiline's
early life is filtered through the invective of Cicero and others and is thus suspect: see
B. Marshall, 'Catilina and the execution of M. Marius Gratidianus', *CQ* 35, 1985,
124–33.
36. He was *not* expelled from the Senate in the censorial purge of 70.

Electoral competition had reached unprecedented levels: in addition to the increase in competition following from Sulla's expansion in the number of magistrates, some of those expelled from the Senate in 70 were attempting to restart their political careers. The organisation and manipulation of voting were of urgent concern.[37] Manilius' first measure as tribune, before the law on the Mithridatic command, was a revival of Sulpicius' plan to distribute freedmen among all 35 tribes: the voting took place on 29 December, which in 67 was the day of the Compitalia festival, and consequently a day on which voting assemblies could not legally be held. The law was passed, and annulled the following day, 1 January 66, by a decree of the Senate passed during the normal first meeting of the year; lethal violence accompanied these events.[38] In 65, the censors, Catulus and Crassus, clashed over the enrolment of Transpadanes as citizens: this quarrel was probably one of the reasons that they resigned the office before the census was completed. In the same year, the tribune Papius passed a law which expelled all non-Italians from the city; its purpose was apparently to prevent the illegal assumption of citizenship. In addition, bribery was a widespread electoral tactic, and in 67 the tribune Cornelius forced the consul Piso to put forward a bribery law which imposed stiffer penalties than those under the *lex Cornelia de ambitu*. The following year both men elected to the consulship (one of them a nephew of Sulla) were convicted under the *lex Calpurnia* and stripped of office.

If Cicero's letters are a reasonable guide, campaigning could begin as much as a year before the elections, with candidates taking advantage of the gathering of voters for the previous year's elections to test the waters. Thus, as early as the summer of 65 Cicero was reviewing his chances and rivals, and as a result we know, relatively, a lot about

37. A. Yakobson, *Elections and Electioneering in Rome: A Study in the Political System of the Late Republic*, Stuttgart: Steiner 1999, 141–7; C. Rosillo Lopez, *La corruption à la fin de la République romaine*, Stutttgart: Steiner 2010, 57–69.
38. Asc. 45C, 65C–6C. It seems implausible that Manilius was not aware of the conditions for a legal vote: did he hope that overwhelming popular support would override them? The Compitalia was a notably popular festival, with a 'bottom-up' organisation; a consequence of the banning of *collegia* (associations) in 64 was that the Compitalia was suspended. It was also a movable feast, its date set by the magistrates: when was the date (apparently, quite early within the possible range) set? It would be intriguing if Manilius were using the symbolism of the Compitalia to support the enactment of an alternative popular festival. Asconius locates the violence, with Manilius' opponents being led by Domitius Ahenobarbus, on the steps of the Capitol: is it possible that it took place on 1 January, and was an attempt to communicate with the Senate as they processed to the sacrifice at the temple of Jupiter Optimus Maximus?

Catiline's first attempt. There were two other serious candidates: Gaius Antonius and Cicero himself.[39] Antonius was a member of a distinguished plebeian family, son of the great orator Marcus Antonius, who had celebrated a triumph in 100 BC; the commander against the pirates in the late 70s was his elder brother. This Antonius' career had so far been less distinguished; one of Sulla's prefects in Greece in the mid-80s, his actions are subsequently un-attested until his expulsion from the Senate by the censors of 70.[40] Cicero was a 'new man', from a prosperous Italian family with connections among the Roman aristocracy; he was a diligent lawyer, who was challenging the supremacy of Hortensius as Rome's greatest orator, and had demonstrated his support for Pompeius with the brilliant speech in support of Manilius' law two years earlier.[41] On most occasions, a patrician and a *nobilis* would have defeated a *nouus homo*; but Cicero was lucky in facing opponents with disreputable and even dangerous reputations, and Catiline and Antonius were unlucky in finding an opponent who had pains-takingly been working for years to compensate for his lack of ancestral distinction. Catiline and Antonius co-operated in their campaigning, and the three candidates clashed in the Senate shortly before the elections, during a debate on electoral bribery: Asconius records that the only charge that Catiline and Antonius could bring against Cicero was his birth. If accurate, this is a testament to Cicero's care in constructing his public persona up until this point, not least his decision not to take a province after his praetorship. The fragments of Cicero's speech on this occasion, by contrast, evoke a shadowy world of secret meetings, murderous plans and dissolute behaviour.[42] Hard work and scare tactics succeeded: Cicero was elected at the head of the poll. Antonius took second place, by a narrow margin.

Had the voting gone otherwise, Cicero and Catiline might well

---

39. Cic. *Att.* 1.1.
40. Asc. 84C, recording the reasons for his expulsion: 'because he had plundered the allies, rejected a court judgement, and as a result of his great debts had sold property and held none in his own name'.
41. E. Rawson, *Cicero: A Portrait*, 2nd edn, London: Bristol Classical Press 1983, 1–43.
42. Asc. 82C–94C; R. Lewis, *Asconius: Commentaries on Speeches of Cicero*, Oxford: Oxford University Press 2006, 289–304; J. Crawford, *M. Tullius Cicero: The Fragmentary Speeches*, Atlanta: Scholars Press 1994, 163–203. The speech contains the first articulation of Cicero's magnificently deceptive fiction, namely the existence of a 'First Catilinarian Conspiracy' in 65: D. Berry, *Cicero Pro Sulla oratio*, Cambridge: Cambridge University Press 1996, 265–72.

have shared a peaceful consulship, despite the temperature of the campaign; after all, Cicero and Antonius managed to co-operate, particularly when Cicero helped Antonius to a lucrative proconsulship. Catiline still had support: when he was prosecuted in the autumn of 64, on the charge of murdering Marius Gratidianus in 82, ex-consuls provided testimonials, and he was again acquitted.[43] He stood in 63 for the consulship of 62: the field was stronger than the previous year, with at least three other plausible candidates. L. Licinius Murena's immediate family had not produced a consul, though his father had celebrated a triumph; his own lengthy military record included service with Lucullus and he could expect support from Lucullus' veterans, now returned to Italy. D. Junius Silanus was, like Catiline, trying a second time for election; he had failed two years earlier (when Cicero described him as lacking in friends and reputation) and little else is known of his earlier career, but his family was noble, he was a member of the pontifical college, and his wife Servilia was extremely well connected; one consequence for Silanus was the energetic support of M. Cato, Servilia's half-brother, only quaestorian in rank but already making himself heard on the political scene.[44] Servius Sulpicius Rufus was, like Catiline, a patrician from a family not recently prominent; he was a noted jurist and a friend of Cicero, whom he persuaded, in advance of the elections, to propose a more rigorous bribery law. The election was, therefore, very open, and the intensity of the competition may have played a part in Catiline's decision to present himself as the 'leader and standard-bearer of the wretched'. He was alleged to have said this and made other inflammatory remarks at a private meeting, and on that basis Cicero secured a delay in the elections so that a meeting of the Senate could be held.[45] At this meeting, Catiline said that

43. Alexander, *Trials*, 108–9.
44. On Servilia, see R. Bauman, *Women and Politics in Ancient Rome*, London: Routledge 1992, 73–6. Servilia's son from her first marriage was M. Brutus, one of Caesar's assassins; her three daughters from the marriage with Silanus would all marry prominent men (the youngest, Cassius' widow, lived until AD 22, when her funeral procession contained the funeral masks (*imagines*) of 20 noble families, though not those of Brutus or Cassius [Tac. *Ann.* 3.76]).
45. Cic. *Mur.* 50: 'he said that a faithful defender of the wretched could not be found, except a man who was wretched himself; the damaged and wretched ought not to trust the promises of the prosperous and fortunate; those who wished to recoup what they had consumed and get back what had been taken from them should consider what *his* debts, *his* possessions, and *his* daring ...'. Cicero was supporting Servius Sulpicius; since two patricians could not be elected, Catiline was the most significant threat to Servius' campaign, and Cicero later claimed, in his defence of Murena, that Servius' distraction

'the *res publica* had two bodies, one weak, with a feeble head, the other strong, but lacking a head; so long as he lived he would be its head, providing it deserved him'.[46] This account comes from Cicero, from a speech given four months later when Catiline was in open revolt; but the force of his argument is weakened if the catch-phrases he ascribes to Catiline were not recognised as such. At the very least, Catiline was presenting a deeply divided *res publica*, and claiming to represent those financially oppressed and ignored by existing authority.[47] How far these claims were developed into anything resembling a programme is much less clear, and the account of Catiline's private meeting, and its suggestion, perhaps, of debt cancellation and a reversal of previous expropriations, is liable to have been the product of his electoral rivals.[48]

Catiline's analysis of a double state can be linked to other episodes before the elections.[49] A tribunician land law had been proposed at the start of the year, which gave a commission of ten wide-ranging powers to acquire land in Italy for distribution by selling overseas *ager publicus* as well as to distribute remaining Italian *ager publicus*.[50] It was an attempt to translate Pompeius' spectacular commands into popular benefit; but it did not come to a vote, largely

from campaigning to pursue bribery terrified the Roman people (*Mur.* 48) because it made Catiline's election more likely.

46. Cic. *Mur.* 51. In a slightly earlier Senate meeting, Catiline had promised to put out the fire threatening his position with destruction, not water.

47. Cicero's reference to *qui consumpta replere, erepta reciperare uellent* ('those who wished to replenish what they had used up and get back what they had had taken away') is a reference both to those who benefited from Sulla (the former group) *and* those who suffered from him (the latter); similarly, *Cat.* 2.20–1 identifies both groups among Catiline's followers (cf. Sall. *Cat.* 28.4; Cass. Dio 37.30.5). They would be uneasy partners; the presence of the latter may largely be a Ciceronian fiction, drawing on existing fears about the consequences of unpicking Sulla's actions, and Catiline's troops were largely ex-Sullans (though see W. V. Harris, *Rome in Etruria and Umbria*, Oxford: Oxford University Press 1971, 289–94). On the state of Italian agriculture, N. Rosenstein, 'Revolution and rebellion in the later second and early first centuries BC: Jack Goldstone and the "Roman revolution"', in L. de Ligt and S. Northwood, eds, *People, Land and Politics: Demographic Developments and the Transformation of Roman Italy, 300 BC–AD 14*, Leiden: Brill 2008, 605–29.

48. Similarly, Cicero's public appearance wearing a breastplate, in response to an alleged assassination attempt (*Mur.* 52), should be seen as a further attempt to prevent Catiline's election.

49. F. Millar, *The Crowd in Rome in the Late Republic*, Ann Arbor: University of Michigan Press 1998, 94–108; A. Drummond, 'Tribunes and tribunician programmes in 63 B.C.', *Athenaeum* 87, 1999, 121–67.

50. J-L.Ferrary, '*Rogatio Servilia Agraria*', *Athenaeum* 66, 1988, 141–64; M. Crawford, *Roman Statutes*, 2 vols, London: Institute of Classical Studies 1996, 757–60; A. Drummond, 'Rullus and the Sullan *possessores*', *Klio* 82, 2000, 126–53.

through the opposition of the consul Cicero. He attacked the speech in the Senate on 1 January and then, having weakened the measure's senatorial support, attempted to persuade the people that it was a tyrannical threat to their well-being.[51] He also secured the promise of a tribunician veto, and in response the proposer, Rullus, withdrew the measure.[52] The debate not only points to poverty and discontent among the urban population, but also shows the impact of Pompeius, as men manoeuvred to exploit his conquests and position themselves advantageously for his return. Pompeius' veterans were probably among the intended beneficiaries, and Cicero invokes Pompeius' disadvantage under the proposal as a reason for opposition.[53] Cicero prided himself on defusing another potential clash, when he persuaded the Roman people to abandon a demonstration of hostility to the former tribune Roscius Otho, whose law of 67 reserved the front rows at theatrical performances for equestrians.[54] Cicero also opposed a proposal to restore the right to office-holding among the descendants of the proscribed.[55] Perhaps most striking of all was the revival of pre-Sullan history with the prosecution of a senator, Gaius Rabirius, for *perduellio* (a charge of treason now almost obsolete through the development of *maiestas*) which arose from his actions during 100. He had been, it was alleged, one of the crowd who got onto the Senate house roof and stoned Saturninus and his companions to death. The prosecution was initiated by one of the tribunes, Labienus, and took place in front of the centuriate assembly; Rabirius was defended by Hortensius and Cicero (whose speech survives); and the trial was brought to an end, before a vote, by the raising on the Janiculum of the flag signifying an enemy attack, and hence the suspension of civilian business.[56] The point

51. The argumentative strategies of Cicero's *De lege agraria* speeches are well analysed by A. Vasaly, *Representations: Images of the World in Ciceronian Oratory*, Berkeley: University of California Press 1993, 217–43; for Cicero's use of a *popularis* stance, Morstein-Marx, *Mass Oratory*, 190–202, 207–12.

52. Cic. *Sull.* 65.

53. Cic. *Leg. agr.* 1.6; 2.23–5.

54. On *De Othone*, Crawford, *Fragmentary*, 209–14. F. X. Ryan, 'The praetorship of L. Roscius Otho', *Hermes* 125, 1997, 236–40, suggests that the games were the *ludi Apollinares* in July, with Otho presiding as urban praetor, and queries the link usually drawn between Otho's law of 67 and the demonstration in 63.

55. Cic. *Att.* 2.1.3 includes a speech *de proscriptorum filiis*, 'on the children of the proscribed', among his consular orations; see Crawford, *Fragmentary*, 201–7; N. Marinone, *Cronologia Ciceroniana*, 2nd edn, Rome: Centro di Studi Ciceroniani 2004, 85.

56. On Rabirius' trial and Cicero's speech, W. Tyrrell, *A Legal and Historical Commen-*

was, evidently, not the conviction or punishment of Rabirius per se, but the demonstration that judicial authority lay ultimately with the people, and that senatorial decrees, even in the form of instruction to the consuls to see that the *res publica* suffered no harm, did not provide protection against capital charges.[57] But the abandonment of the trial left matters still indeterminate, emphasising the profound gap between different views of the location of authority and the difficulty of reaching a compromise solution.

Catiline's pronouncements in the summer of 63 were attempts to win support for what was, realistically, his last chance to become consul: Cicero's attempts to suggest a more sinister agenda did not persuade the Senate, which refused to take any action. When the elections were held, Catiline was defeated (as was Servius Sulpicius) and it was only then that he began to plan an armed uprising.[58]

Sallust (*Cat.* 35) preserves a letter from Catiline to Catulus, which the latter read out to the Senate after Catiline had left Rome later in the autumn (Orestilla was Catiline's wife):

> L. Catilina to Q. Catulus. Your unimpeachable good faith, known to me by experience and welcome to me in times of danger, guarantees confidence in my request. For that reason, I have decided not to offer a defence of my new plan; but, though not conscious of any guilt, I have decided to put forward an explanation, which, heaven help me, you may recognise as true. Provoked by injuries and insults, and because, deprived of the reward of my hard work and effort, I could not maintain my standing, I took up, in accordance with my custom, in public the cause of the wretched, not because I could not pay my own debts from my possessions – or Orestilla's generosity not meet other debts from her resources and those of her daughter – but because I saw that unworthy men were being distinguished by honourable success and I realised that I was outcast because of groundless suspicion. For this reason, I have pursued hopes, perfectly

tary on Cicero's Oratio pro C. Rabirio Perduellionis, Amsterdam: Hakkert 1978; A. Primmer, *Die Überredungsstrategie in Ciceros Rede Pro Rabirio perduellionis reo*, Vienna: Verlag der Österreichischen Akademie der Wissenschaften 1985. The trial involved C. Julius Caesar, already a popular figure through his extravagant aedilician games in 65 and well-publicised connections with Marius; he was shortly to secure election as *pontifex maximus* (defeating Servilius Isauricus and Catulus) and as praetor for 62.

57. Morstein-Marx, *Mass Oratory*, 224–8. That is not to say that Labienus might not have enjoyed conviction: his uncle had been among the dead.

58. Sulpicius responded by prosecuting Murena (unsuccessfully) on bribery charges, in the hope of election if Murena was convicted, in the way that the consuls of 65 had reached office. He would not in fact stand again for over a decade.

honourable given my position, of retaining what is left of my standing. Although I would like to write more, I have been told that
violence is being organised against me. I entrust Orestilla to you and
place her in your care; keep her safe from harm, for your children's
sake. Farewell.

This is the language of thwarted ambition and personal shame: we
do not need to deny the reality of deep social and economic problems to accept that Catiline's actions here fit within a pattern of the
resort to military violence by members of the governing elite which,
after Sulla, had become conceivable. Leaving behind letters indicating that he was going into exile in Massilia (modern Marseilles),
Catiline in fact joined an armed uprising in Etruria led by Manlius,
an ex-centurion from Sulla's army who was working on Catiline's
instructions.

The apparent ease with which this uprising was put down,
combined with Cicero and Sallust's emphasis on Catiline's
irrationality, can give the impression that his actions after failing
to be elected consul are beyond reasonable explanation. But
various considerations make his strategy appear more feasible. First,
Spartacus' uprising had taken a great deal of time and resources to
suppress; it was not implausible to think that a group of veterans
could resist for some time the limited forces which the Senate had
immediately to hand. Secondly, Catiline was negotiating with the
Allobroges, a Gallic tribe deeply dissatisfied with their treatment by
Roman power in Narbonese Gaul, with the aim of acquiring their
military support. And the whole environment was potentially going
to change in the near future, with the arrival back in Italy of
Pompeius. Did Catiline hope to play Pompeius to Pompeius' Sulla,
in an imminent military takeover of the *res publica*?

In Rome, Cicero had persuaded the Senate to pass the so-called
'last decree' in October, even before the arrival of news of Manlius'
uprising, but was unable to secure any measures directly against
Catiline until he was known to have joined Manlius, at which point
he and Manlius were declared *hostes* and the consul Antonius
was instructed to march against him.[59] The discovery of proof that
Catiline's supporters in Rome were negotiating with the Allobroges
came later. The Allobroges' envoys had approached their patron,

---

59. On chronology, Dyck, *Catilinarians*, 7–10; peace in the rest of Italy was maintained
by the prompt despatch of two of the praetors and two promagistrates, fortuitously waiting outside Rome for their triumphs.

Fabius Sanga, for advice; he in turn had passed them on to Cicero, who persuaded them to set up a meeting with the conspirators to generate written evidence. He then arranged to arrest the envoys as they left Rome, carrying letters and accompanied by one of the conspirators.[60] Cicero's actions at this point are often treated as a demonstration of his success and competence, following his own self-presentation of his actions as consul, which culminate in his acclamation by the Senate as *pater patriae*, father of the fatherland, and his salvation of the *res publica*. Cicero was aware of the impact of the Allobroges' evidence, with the dramatic staging in the Senate as the conspirators were summoned forward to acknowledge their seals on unbroken letters, and the letters were then read out.[61] But in fact he had overreached with this public display of conspiracy. It was irrelevant to dealing with the armed threat from Catiline, which was the major problem facing the *res publica*, and for which a solution was already in place; and Cicero's intelligence-gathering had neutralised the Allobroges well before their arrest. But the ambush and subsequent publicity had revealed five conspirators against the *res publica* (one an ex-consul and serving praetor, another a senator), and set up the awkward problem of what to do with the guilty men. Cicero's strategic error was compounded by the Senate's assumption of control over the conspirators' fate, in the debate on 5 December, and its decision to execute the five men.[62] Their deaths crystallised the unbridgeable gap between different understandings of the *res publica*: the message which Labienus had sent with Rabirius' trial was ignored.

Catiline's uprising was possible because of widespread economic discontent; and it relied on a belief among its participants, however tenuously based, that the political organisation of Rome remained, after Sulla, provisional. To that extent, its best point of comparison is Lepidus' uprising, fifteen years earlier. I have also suggested that it, like other events in 63, was driven in part by the imminent return of Pompeius. Certainly, the ways in which Roman politics had become increasingly polarised during 63, in large part due to the firmly

---

60. Cicero describes these events in *Cat.* 3.4–12; cf. Sall. *Cat.* 44–6.
61. S. Butler, *The Hand of Cicero*, London: Routledge 2002, 85–102.
62. On the legality of the decision, A. Drummond, *Law, Politics and Power: The Execution of the Catilinarian Conspirators*, Stuttgart: Steiner 1995, 95–113; J. Harries, *Cicero and the Jurists: From Citizens' Law to Lawful State*, London: Duckworth 2006, 190–3; on the gulf between different views, T. P. Wiseman, *Remembering the Roman People*, Oxford: Oxford University Press 2009, 12–13.

articulated views of the consul Cicero, made it more difficult for Pompeius to negotiate a satisfactory reintegration into Roman political life, and consequently forced him to make choices which had serious medium-term implications.

Factionalism, the people and the collapse of order

Lentulus Sura, Cethegus, Gabinius, Statilius and Caeparius were executed on 5 December and Cicero, who had publicly overseen the deed, was escorted home by a rejoicing crowd. 'Those famous Nones' became a key element in the Ciceronian *mythos*, and the apparent unity of the Roman people at this moment supported Cicero's post-consular policy of *concordia ordinum*, 'harmony of the orders'.[63] One reason why Cicero articulated his achievements as consul so relentlessly in the following years was that his version was not uncontested; and the challenge began almost immediately, with the entry into office on 10 December of the new college of tribunes. Two of them, Metellus Nepos (half-brother of Pompeius' wife Mucia, and former legate of Pompeius) and Calpurnius Bestia, attacked Cicero's handling of events.[64] Nepos used his veto to prevent Cicero from giving a customary end-of-office speech at the ceremony at which retiring magistrates swore that they had obeyed the laws whilst in office, and subsequently at a *contio* justified his act on the grounds that 'a man who had punished others without trial ought not himself to have the opportunity to speak'; Cicero responded by changing the formula of the oath and declaring that he had saved the *res publica*.[65] Nepos then proposed laws summoning

63. *O Nonae illae Decembres*, *Flac.* 102; *concordia* harked back to C. Opimius, the consul who in 121 had overseen the armed response to the younger Gracchus, and subsequently dedicated a temple to Concord. Cicero had prepared for the rejoicing on 5 December with his brilliant *Third Catilinarian* speech from 3 December, which explained to the people the uncovering of the conspiracy; see I. Gildenhard, *Creative Eloquence: The Construction of Reality in Cicero's Speeches*, Oxford: Oxford University Press 2011, 278–92.

64. Nepos had already indicated likely hostility to Cicero (*Mur.* 81) before he entered office, though the grounds are not known, and the younger Cato is supposed to have decided to stand for the tribunate only when he heard that Nepos was doing so (Plut. *Cat. Min.* 20–1).

65. Cicero narrates events in *Fam.* 5.2; see also *Pis.* 6–7 with Asc. 6C; for his response to Nepos, J. Crawford, *M. Tullius Cicero: The Lost and Unpublished Orations*, Göttingen: Vandenhoeck & Ruprecht 1984, 95–6, and *Fragmentary*, 215–26. On the letters between Cicero and Nepos' brother Celer (the earliest surviving in the *Fam.* collection), W. C. Schneider, *Vom Handeln der Römer: Kommunikation und Interaktion der politischen Führungsschicht vor Ausbruch des Bürgerkriegs im Briefwechsel mit*

Pompeius back to Italy to deal with Catiline, and permitting him to stand for the consulship *in absentia*.[66] The attempt to pass these measures was accompanied by violence which recalled the clashes between tribunes in 67: Cato and Minucius Thermus (another tribune) physically prevented the herald from reading the text of the law out, and when Nepos, who had the text by heart, continued the recitation, Minucius Thermus put his hand over Nepos' mouth. The audience was on Nepos' side, and drove Cato, Thermus and their supporters into the temple of Castor and Pollux; but Cato returned and attempted to disrupt the meeting again. At this point, the Senate met and instructed the consuls to see that the state took no harm; it also suspended Nepos from office, as well as the praetor Caesar, who was supporting Nepos' measures and had appeared alongside him at the disputed *contio*. Nepos responded by leaving Rome in order to rejoin Pompeius' forces.[67]

Nepos was presumably acting in what he thought were Pompeius' interests – as well as his own – by engineering a re-enactment of Pompeius' return from Spain to deal with Spartacus in 71.[68] Pompeius was still a popular enough figure with the Roman people to have made his strategy feasible, but the Senate's opposition was far more clearly articulated, not least because of Cato's energy, and Nepos may well have made a tactical error in pursuing Cicero at the same time as he attempted to transform Pompeius' situation. Cicero's friends would have found it more difficult, as a result, to support Nepos' measures, even before the outbreak of violence. So far from packaging Pompeius as a solution to a crisis, Nepos turned him into a potential further problem for the *res publica*.

The legate Petreius' success in battle against Catiline removed the possibility that Pompeius might be needed; and Pompeius' reception of Nepos is unlikely to have been friendly. It is worth speculating whether Pompeius' decision, on his return to Italy, to divorce Mucia – presented by Plutarch as a response to her infidelity during his absence – was not just as much about repudiating her brother's

Cicero, Hildesheim: Olms 1998, 85–116; J. Hall, *Politeness and Politics in Cicero's Letters*, Oxford: Oxford University Press 2009, 153–62. *Fam.* 5.2.2 is an early example of Cicero's capacity to offend through his search for a laugh – as well as clear evidence that he was well aware of the effects, and dangers, of his search for praise.
66. Cass. Dio 37.43.1; Plut. *Cat. Min.* 26; *Schol. Bob.* 134St.
67. Cass. Dio 37.43–4; Plut. *Cat. Min.* 26–29; Suet. *Iul.* 16. On the implications of violence among tribunes, Steel, 'Sacrosanctity'.
68. Seager, *Pompey*, 73.

unruly political positioning.[69] Well before he arrived, Pompeius took care to reassure the Senate by letter that his intentions were peaceful.[70] Cicero was delighted by this, if less pleased by a lack of warmth and congratulation for him personally; a benevolent Pompeius, returned to influential private life, might well have bolstered his broad coalition of 'good men'.[71] In reality, however, the political environment at Rome was now unwelcoming to Pompeius, and despite Cicero's optimism, common ground between different interest groups was not easy to find. The popular movement had become more radical since Pompeius' departure, associated now with armed uprising and violence at Rome severe enough to recall, in the Senate's response, the periods of Saturninus and Gracchus. Pompeius was clearly unwilling to join himself with this group. But many in the Senate remained hostile to his ambitions, and they had now an effective leader in the younger Cato.[72] Pompeius tried, unsuccessfully, to conciliate Cato, and then attempted for a few years to find a third way, by which his uniqueness would be recognised by the Senate; when this failed, he took up *popularis* methods once more, with destructive consequences for the political system.[73]

Pompeius arrived back in Italy, at Brundisium, late in 62 and, as a very public sign of his intentions, immediately disbanded his army. He then made his way to Rome, though he naturally had to stay outside the city until after his triumph.[74] His immediate priority was

69. Infidelity: Plut. *Pomp.* 42.7. Cicero (*Att.* 1.12.3) says that the divorce is 'very much approved of', which is compatible with either theory.
70. Cic. *Fam.* 5.7.1: 'In the letter which you sent publicly I, along with everyone else, took enormous pleasure; you demonstrate exactly the promise of peace which I, relying on you alone, have always promised to everyone.'
71. Cic. *Fam.* 5.7.
72. Cato successfully opposed an attempt by Pompeius to influence the consular elections in the summer of 62 in favour of his former legate Pupius Piso (Plut. *Pomp.* 44.1–2; *Cat. Min.* 30; Cass. Dio 37.44.3); he also showed himself alert to the threat of popular discontent, and at some point pushed for a senatorial decree authorising subsidy for the price of grain (Plut. *Cat. Min.* 26.1). It is a pity that we have only a few Ciceronian letters from 62; it would be interesting to know how Cicero assessed the emerging situation.
73. Having divorced Mucia, Pompeius looked immediately for his (fourth) wife, and decided on one of the daughters of Servilia; but their uncle Cato refused (Plut. *Pomp.* 44.2–3; *Cat. Min.* 30.2–4).
74. This was not a serious impediment to Pompeius' participation in political life; the Senate had numerous possible meeting places outside the city boundary (*pomerium*) (M. Bonnefond-Coudry, *Le Sénat de la République romaine: de la guerre d'Hannibale à Auguste: pratiques délibératives et prises de décisions*, Rome: École Française de Rome 1989, 137–51) and the *circus Flaminius* was an accessible location for *contiones* (e.g. Cic. *Att.* 1.14.1).

to bring his campaigns to a satisfactory close, which required senatorial recognition of his arrangements in the east and provision,
through land distribution, for his veterans. Not only did it become
rapidly clear that Pompeius could not deploy a supportive bloc
within the Senate to ensure these ends, and that his relationship with
the people was not entirely secure; but, just as he was re-entering
the domestic sphere, a peculiar scandal erupted, which dominated
political life throughout 61. Cicero, writing to Atticus on 1 January
61, records, 'I expect you have heard that Publius Clodius, Appius'
son, was caught in women's clothing at Caesar's house during the
public sacrifice; and was protected and got out by a slave-girl;
and that it is a frightful scandal. I'm sure you are upset by this.'[75]
Responding appropriately to this act of sacrilege at the rites of the
Bona Dea ('Good Goddess') occupied the Senate and people until
May and involved a law setting up a special tribunal to try Clodius,
which nonetheless acquitted him after substantial bribery.[76]

This affair is both trivial and profoundly serious: trivial, in so far
as there is no good explanation for Clodius' act; serious, in its threat
to the *res publica* by compromising relations with the gods and its
consequent impact on political life over the following half-year and
beyond. The split between Clodius' supporters and everyone else
exacerbated and complicated existing divisions, and the struggle
over the passage of the law under which Clodius could be tried
provided a fresh opportunity for violence, and gave Clodius a
powerful impulse to organise his supporters in ways which he drew
upon for the rest of his life.[77] Moreover, the affair jammed the Senate
(which decided in February that it would deal with no other business
until the measure concerning Clodius was passed) and did little good
to the reputation of the consul Piso. No progress on legislation in
Pompeius' interests was made in 61, though he did manage –
through extensive bribery – to ensure that his former legate Afranius
was elected to the consulship, though the other – another ex-legate –

75. Cic. *Att.* 1.12.3.
76. Cic. *Att.* 1.13.3, 1.14.1–4, 1.16.1–10; P. Moreau, *Clodiana religio: un procès
politique en 61 avant J.C.*, Paris: Les Belles Lettres 1982; Tatum, *Clodius*, 62–86.
77. On political divisions, see Cic. *Att.* 1.14.5 and 1.16.1, aligning Clodius' faction with
the Catilinarians; on Clodius' use of violence, Tatum, *Clodius*, 142–8; J. Tan, 'Publius
Clodius and the boundaries of the *contio*', in C. Steel and H. van der Blom, eds, *Community and Communication: Oratory and Politics in Republican Rome*, Oxford: Oxford
University Press 2013, 117–32. Cicero would doubtless claim that the enmity of Clodius
was an important outcome, though one risks trivialising Clodius' actions by assuming
that personal enmity was the chief cause of his legislation against Cicero in 58.

was Metellus Celer, Nepos' elder brother and, since the Mucia affair, not Pompeius' friend.

Pompeius' third triumph took place on 28–9 September 61; there is no sign that the Senate obstructed Pompeius' request, as it did most requests for triumphs in the post-Sullan period, and the delay between arrival and celebration is to be explained by the elaborate preparations required, and Pompeius' desire for his triumph to coincide with his birthday. It was a spectacular occasion, notable not just for its length and breathtaking display of wealth and conquest, but also for its recasting of Roman imperial power as territorial dominance.[78] But it did not mark a fresh start for Pompeius' political life. He had a supportive tribune, Flavius, in 60, and Cicero's (modified) support for a land law to benefit his veterans which Flavius proposed; but the consul Celer was implacably opposed and orchestrated sufficient senatorial opposition to stymie the measure for good.[79] In addition, relations between the equestrian class and the Senate were at a low ebb as a result, largely, of Cato's upright conduct: there had been a measure on bribery directed at equestrian jurors late in 61, and deadlock over requests to renegotiate tax-contracts in Asia. When Pompeius' eastern arrangements did finally come up for discussion, Lucullus joined Celer and Cato in objecting to a single vote, arguing that each measure needed separate scrutiny, a process which could well have taken years.

In consequence, Pompeius decided to change tactics. Hitherto, he had relied on – and been disappointed by – consuls who were closely connected with him. For the following year, however, he established links with an independent operator.[80] Caesar had, following his praetorship in 62, been governing Hispania Ulterior (and renewing the Spanish wars). He returned in late spring of 60, indicating his intention to stand for the consulship in that summer's elections. He

78. M. Beard, *The Roman Triumph*, Cambridge, MA: Harvard University Press 2007, 7–41; I. Östenberg, *Staging the World: Spoils, Captives and Representations in the Roman Triumphal Procession*, Oxford: Oxford University Press 2009.
79. Cic. *Att.* 1.19.4. Flavius responded to Celer's obstruction by imprisoning him (tribunician sacrosanctity made the device of sitting on a bench in front of a building in which he had placed Celer effective): in a moment of high farce, Celer had the back wall knocked down in order to permit his advisory group (*consilium*) to attend (Cass. Dio 37.50). Flavius then desisted.
80. 'Independent' is a relative term: Caesar had consistently favoured Pompeius' interests earlier in his career in the hope of reflected benefits: M. Gelzer, *Caesar: Politician and Statesman*, trans. P. Needham, Oxford: Blackwell 1968, 33–70. But Caesar had not structured his career as a follower of Pompeius.

also desired a triumph, which seemed to offer his opponents in the Senate the opportunity to put off his ambitions by delaying approval beyond the date of elections.[81] In addition, a *lex Sempronia de prouinciis consularibus* had been passed which gave the consuls the 'woods and pastures' of Italy as their province; despite genuine problems around brigandage, such an allocation to the consuls was a clear attempt to restrict the military ambitions of the successful candidates.[82] In return for a promise of laws confirming Pompeius' provincial arrangements and providing land for his veterans, Caesar received the support of Pompeius' adherents in the elections.[83] Caesar had long been a political ally of Crassus, and he kept Crassus' support despite his rapprochement with Pompeius; but there was no compact between all three until after Caesar had actually taken office.[84] Caesar attempted also to secure Cicero's support for his consulship.[85]

The novelty of Caesar's consulship lay not so much in co-operation between a consul and senior ex-consuls as in the political tactics which he used.[86] The year 59 was one of autocracy: Caesar seized control of decision-making, and rendered his opponents impotent. He was able to do so through widespread popular support, ruthless disregard for political convention, and violence, and the result was the passage of an extensive and ambitious legislative programme. Pompeius was rewarded for his co-operation by a single *lex Iulia*, which confirmed all his arrangements from his eastern campaigns. In broad terms, the consequences were the

81. In addition to general anxiety about the likely actions of a consular Caesar, Cato – who orchestrated the delay – was supporting his brother-in-law Bibulus' consular candidacy; Bibulus had throughout his career been disadvantaged by simultaneous office-holding with Caesar (Suet. *Iul.* 10).

82. *Siluae callesque*, Suet. *Iul.* 19. There was no difficulty for Bibulus' supporters in favouring such an allocation, since Bibulus was unlikely to have serious military ambitions; he had not taken a province after his praetorship and did not do so after his consulship.

83. Pompeius' bargaining position was strengthened because there was a third viable consular candidate, Lucceius. Collaboration was confirmed by Pompeius' marriage to Caesar's daughter Julia.

84. E. S. Gruen, *The Last Generation of the Roman Republic*, Berkeley: University of California Press 1974, 88–9.

85. Cic. *Att.* 2.3.3–4, without success.

86. Pollio appears to have identified 60, and the agreement between Pompeius and Caesar, as the turning point (Hor. *Carm.* 2.1 with R. Nisbet and M. Hubbard, *A Commentary on Horace Odes Book II*, Oxford: Oxford University Press 1978 ad loc.); A. Lintott, *Cicero as Evidence*, Oxford: Oxford University Press 2008, 171, cautions against overinterpretation of the despair over the *res publica* found in Cicero's letters.

substantial reorganisation and extension of the provinces of Cilicia and Bithynia-Pontus, each of which now regularly received a proconsular governor and had a garrison of two legions; the confirmation of friendly relations with a number of client kings in the interior of Asia Minor; the creation of a province of Syria, formed from the Seleucid kingdom; and the installation, in Judaea, of a pro-Roman high priest. Alongside these large-scale developments was the detailed recreation of landscape and settlement through the movement of people and the foundation of cities; and the consolidation of Pompeius' position as the major benefactor and patron of the region. Pompeius now surpassed his peers in reputation and wealth to an extent which can be difficult to grasp; and his conquests transformed the finances of the *res publica*, with revenues rising, he claimed, from 50 million to 85 million denarii.[87] In addition, the position of Ptolemy Auletes as king of Egypt was confirmed (in return, it was alleged, for a breathtaking bribe of 6,000 talents); the injudicious contracts which the *publicani* had agreed were renegotiated, in favour of the contractors; there were agrarian laws to redistribute substantial amounts of the remaining public land in Italy; and a new *repetundae* law was passed, unprecedently strict and detailed.[88] Consular legislation itself is not an unusual occurrence, particularly in the post-Sullan period, when consuls tended to remain in Rome during their year in office; but the scale and popular flavour of much of Caesar's are striking, and suggest that he was transferring to the consulship methods characteristic of the tribunate – an office from which Caesar himself, of course, had been barred by his patrician status. Moreover, this legislation was carried through despite the constant and unwavering hostility of Caesar's consular colleague, Marcus Bibulus, and frequent opposition from the Senate. The very fact that Bibulus had been elected demonstrates the limits on what Caesar's supporters could achieve: it was clear from the time of election that Bibulus would not co-operate, and he announced that he was seeking religious evidence which would preclude legislative assemblies.[89] Caesar simply ignored Bibulus and

87. Plut. *Pomp.* 45.3. Some of the diplomatic confirmation took place through Vatinian laws.
88. The tribune Vatinius' law setting limits to the size of a governor's entourage (*cohors*) can perhaps be seen as a coda to this *lex Iulia*. On Caesar's legislation, L. R. Taylor, 'On the chronology of Caesar's first consulship', *AJPh* 72, 1951, 254–68; Gelzer, *Caesar*, 71–101; Williamson, *Laws*, 376–8. Caesar also arranged for daily publication of records of senatorial and public business, the *acta diurna*.
89. Bibulus was an ally of Cato, and would later marry Cato's daughter.

the rest of the opposition; he was able to do so, and Bibulus unable to impose his views despite his position as consul, because of Caesar's adroit manoeuvring. He initially attempted to gain the Senate's support for his land law, the first measure to which he turned: Dio (38.2) describes the reluctance of members of the Senate to express either support or criticism. Dio links this to the quality of Caesar's legislative drafting, but his account reveals the working of intimidation, too, with Caesar threatening to imprison Cato, and desisting only out of shame when Petreius followed Cato from the Senate, saying that he preferred to be imprisoned with Cato than participating in the Senate with Caesar. Later in the year, another senator, Considius, remarked that he – unlike others – was not afraid to attend Senate meetings chaired by Caesar, since old age had removed his fear of death.[90] Faced with an unco-operative Senate, Caesar decided to proceed with his legislative programme without senatorial approval: this was, for consular legislation, exceptionally unusual, but did not itself render the legislation invalid.[91] Caesar was prepared to go directly to the people, with a close relationship with the tribune Vatinius and active support from at least one other member of the college.[92] But three other tribunes were hostile, and there was a showdown on the steps of the temple of Castor – the location at which Cato and Nepos had come to blows three years earlier.[93] This time, however, the focus was a clash between the consuls: Bibulus attempted to interrupt Caesar as the latter spoke from a position higher up the temple steps and declare unfavourable

90. Cic. *Att.* 2.24.4; cf. Plut. *Caes.* 14.8; J. Bellemore, 'Cato's opposition to Caesar in 59 B.C.', in K. Welch and T. Hillard, eds, *Roman Crossings: theory and Practice in the Roman Republic*, Swansea: Classical Press of Wales 2005, 225–57.
91. F. Pina Polo, *The Consul at Rome*, Cambridge: Cambridge University Press 2011, 298–300.
92. Cicero's speech *In Vatinium*, delivered in connection with the trial of Sestius in 56, is the main source for Vatinius' earlier career; all that can safely be extracted from his vituperation is some association with the tribune Cornelius, a quaestorship in 63, and subsequent service as legate with Cosconius in Hispania Ulterior; whether his agreement with Caesar predated his success in the tribunician elections is unclear. His marriage to the daughter of Antonius Creticus (and sister of Antonius the triumvir) looks like a reward (Cic. *Vat.* 28 implies that it took place after C. Antonius' condemnation in the spring of 59); Cicero, of course, claims that Vatinius' support for Caesar was merely a cash transaction (*Vat.* 38) The other tribune was C. Alfius Flavus (*Vat.* 38; *Sest.* 114) but he played a much less active role, and no legislation from him is known.
93. The hostile tribunes were Q. Ancharius, Cn. Domitius Calvinus and C. Fannius; as Cicero notes (*Sest.* 113–14), all continued to successful careers. (Calvinus showed exceptional survival skills: consul in 53, he supported Caesar during the civil war, and held a second consulship in 40: J. Carlsen, 'Cn. Domitius Calvinus: a noble Caesarian', *Latomus* 67, 2008, 72–81.)

omens: he was pushed down them by Caesar's supporters, and his *fasces* (the badge of office) were broken.[94] Bibulus responded by retreating to his house and announcing unfavourable omens for the rest of his year in office; these had no immediate effect, but left Caesar's actions liable to subsequent challenge.

Caesar resolved the difficulty over his province with a *lex Vatinia*, which gave him *imperium* in Illyria and Cisalpine Gaul. With great significance for future developments, this law innovated by shaping Caesar's command through duration rather than task: it was for five years. The Senate subsequently added Transalpine Gaul, which had fortuitously become available through the sudden death of Celer, to whom it had been allotted. And, acting as *pontifex maximus* rather than as consul, Caesar approved the adoption of Publius Clodius by Fonteius, with Pompeius assisting in his position as augur. The adoption removed Clodius' patrician status and thereby made him eligible to stand for the tribunate of the plebs. Cicero read this development through the lens of his own enmity with Clodius, and claimed later (*Dom.* 41) that the adoption was a direct response to his own criticism of the state of the *res publica* uttered earlier on the day of the adoption in his (unsuccessful) defence of C. Antonius on *repetundae* charges.[95] This solipsism can for the most part be ignored: Cicero was far from the most outspoken of Caesar's critics, the chronology is too tight, and Caesar went to some lengths to protect Cicero from Clodius, with the offer of a position on his staff in Gaul, or support for a publicly sanctioned journey abroad, both of which would have taken Cicero from Rome. Caesar's motives in supporting Clodius are not entirely clear, but must relate to his perception of how political events might develop after his departure from Rome. Clodius was unpredictable, but an active *popularis* stance could be expected; and that was likely to keep Caesar's opponents preoccupied.

Caesar consistently got his way throughout his consulship: and Cicero – whose letters to Atticus give us snapshots of events between early April and late summer this year – found therein cause for despair: 'the state is dead'; 'nothing is in a more hopeless state than the *res publica*'.[96] He derived some consolation, however, from

---

94. Suet. *Iul.* 20.1; Cass. Dio 38.2–3.
95. Crawford, *Lost*, 124–31.
96. *Att.* 2.21.1, *tota periit*; 2.25.2, *re publica nihil desperatius*. The letters (*Att.* 2.4–25) are initially responses to Atticus' reports from Rome and then from Rome to Atticus, who had left for Epirus. See Lintott, *Evidence*, 167–75.

Pompeius' unpopularity, the reactions of the audience at the *ludi Apollinares*, and the enthusiasm for Bibulus and for Curio, the son of the consul of 76 who had not yet held office but was nonetheless speaking out vigorously against Caesar and Pompeius. Curio was effective enough to be the object of a smear campaign, orchestrated by an informer, Vettius, who claimed that Curio intended to assassinate Pompeius. Whether Vettius was actually working for Caesar, or was merely at this point a hopeful freelance, Caesar would have been the beneficiary of Curio's removal and of anything which made it more difficult for Pompeius to waver from the alliance. But Curio outplayed Caesar by revealing the 'plot' in the Senate, and Vettius was imprisoned and subsequently died.[97] What does emerge from Cicero's letters is that tyrannicide was being mentioned that summer, with reference to the exemplary figures of Servilius Ahala and Brutus.

As this extraordinary year approached its end, the attitude of the new magistrates towards Caesar, and their other plans, were of vital importance. Despite earlier rumours that Pompeius and Crassus were planning to stand for the consulship of 58, Gabinius and Piso Caesoninus had been elected. Gabinius is a further example of a nominee of Pompeius (after his tribunate he had joined Pompeius as a legate) whose election depended entirely on Pompeian support, but Piso was a well-respected *nobilis*, though his decision to stand for the consulship came relatively late in the campaign. That decision was presumably linked to the alliance he made with Caesar, symbolised by Caesar's marriage to his daughter Calpurnia.[98] But the praetors-elect, who included Cato's brother-in-law Domitius

97. Cic. *Att.* 2.24.2–3; L. R. Taylor, 'The date and meaning of the Vettius affair', *Historia* 1, 1950, 45–51.
98. Piso's character and political motivations are traduced by Cicero's attacks, but a consistent pursuit of political compromise, perhaps informed by his Epicureanism, can be discerned: M. Griffin, 'Cicero, Piso and their audiences', in C. Auvray-Assayas and D. Delattre, eds, *Cicéron et Philodème: la polemique en philosophie*, Paris: Rue d'Ulm 2001, 85–99, Y. Benferhat, 'Plaidoyer pour une victime de Cicéron: Pison', *REL* 80, 2002, 55–77; H. van der Blom, 'Fragmentary speeches: the oratory and political career of Piso Caesoninus', in Steel and van der Blom, , *Community and Communication*, 299–314. Piso benefited financially and politically from the co-operation, but he brought to it distinguished ancestry and presence: we can observe the difference between Caesar's approach to friends and allies and that of Pompeius (see also C. Steel, 'Friends, associates and wives', in M. Griffin, ed., *A Companion to Julius Caesar*, Chichester: Wiley-Blackwell 2009, 112–25). A curiosity is the life of Calpurnia's much younger (half?-) brother, who survived the civil wars to follow a distinguished career under Augustus and Tiberius, dying in AD 32 (R. Syme, *The Augustan Aristocracy*, Oxford: Oxford University Press 1986, 329–45).

Ahenobarbus, were less amenable. Ahenobarbus and his colleague C. Memmius attempted to unpick Caesar's legislation at the start of 58 in a senatorial debate; Caesar participated, delaying his start for Gaul, and he and his allies were able to prevent any action.[99] More serious a potential threat to the interests of Pompeius, Caesar and Crassus was the tribune Clodius, who confirmed this year his position as a *popularis* figure. He is an exceptionally difficult figure to assess, because of the unremitting hostility of Cicero, who is the most important source for his actions. But it nonetheless seems clear that he was not anyone's agent, despite the co-operation with Caesar which had put him in the position to become a tribune; and that the elimination of Cicero from Roman politics was only a small element in a sustained and ambitious programme of reform.[100]

Many of its elements follow well-established *popularis* traditions. There was a grain law, which superseded Cato's law of 62: it made distributions free rather than subsidised.[101] There were laws on political procedure, including one which made some changes to the Aelian and Fufian laws on the use of the veto, and another which limited the censors' capacity to reprimand individuals: for Cicero, our major source, these provide further evidence of Clodius' insanity but both can be seen as attempts to ensure openness and consistency in the behaviour of magistrates. Another law re-established the *collegia*.[102] These laws were proposed as soon as Clodius entered

---

99. Suet. *Iul.* 23; Cic. *Sest.* 40; Caesar thought the matter important enough to disseminate the speeches he gave (*ORF*⁴ 393–4). His late departure from Rome has unwittingly contributed to the scholarly fantasy of a *lex Cornelia de prouinciis ordinandis* (A. Giovannini, *Consulare imperium*, Basle: Reinhardt 1983, 7–30; Pina Polo, *Consul*, 225–48); he remained close to Rome for some weeks more, and gave a carefully balanced speech at a *contio* on Cicero's situation which Clodius organised outside the *pomerium* (Cass. Dio 38.17).

100. On Clodius, Tatum, *Clodius*; A. Lintott, 'P. Clodius Pulcher: *Felix Catilina*?', *G&R* 14, 1967, 157–69, and *Evidence*, 175–82; J. Spielvogel, 'P. Clodius Pulcher: eine politische Aushahme-Erscheinung in der Späten Republik?', *Hermes* 125, 1997, 56–74; for his legislation, *MRR* 2.196. On Cicero's invective, Gildenhard, *Creative Eloquence*, with extensive bibliography; C. Steel, 'Name and shame? Invective against Clodius and others in the post-exile speeches', in J. Booth, ed., *Cicero on the Attack: Invective and Subversion in the Orations and Beyond*, Swansea: Classical Press of Wales 2007, 105–28.

101. Garnsey, *Famine*, 206–14.

102. For a censorial hearing under the *lex Clodia*, C. Steel, 'Pompeius, Helvius Mancia and the politics of public debate', in Steel and van der Blom, *Community and Communication*, 151–9. Dio (38.13.1–2) puts corn, *collegia* and the censorship together as a programme designed to appeal to all, including the Senate, and it is surely likely that senators, particularly the more junior, would have welcomed a curb on the arbitrary power of the censors. A single passing reference in Suetonius (*Dom.* 9) attests to another

office, and passed, without veto, on 4 January. On the basis of the popularity Clodius thereby gained he started on a second tranche of measures, to which phase the attack on Cicero belongs.

Cicero and Clodius had been personal enemies since Cicero destroyed Clodius' alibi at his trial for sacrilege, and Cicero's letters from the summer and autumn of 59 demonstrate constant awareness of the threat. He nonetheless confidently expected to resist whatever might come.[103] In the event, however, he did not. Clodius put forward a proposal to exile anyone who put Roman citizens to death without trial: no one was named, but the relevance to Cicero was clear. At the same time, Clodius put forward laws overriding the existing consular allocations, giving Piso Macedonia and Gabinius Cilicia. The quid pro quo was obvious. Even more disastrously for Cicero, Pompeius withdrew his support. He claimed that he was afraid of an assassination attempt planned by Cicero, but this is surely a smokescreen (and an excuse which Pompeius used at other points in his career to justify a withdrawal from public affairs). We can only assume that Pompeius had calculated that, given the strength of Clodius' position, any attempt to protect Cicero would be too expensive, both to his own reputation and in terms of potential disorder at Rome. Other senior figures, including Hortensius and Cato, urged Cicero to depart quietly, and he did so on the day on which both these Clodian laws were passed. Clodius then drew up a law which addressed Cicero's case directly, specifying that he must remain 400 miles from Rome and confiscating his property. Cicero's house on the Palatine was badly damaged by the people, and Clodius subsequently had the site dedicated to the gods and put up on it a shrine to Freedom.[104]

Cicero's hostility to Clodius is so powerful that, even if one can discount the extremes of his characterisation, it is difficult to escape from his narrative of exile as the result of a personal attack. But – though Clodius' personal dislike and desire for revenge should not be dismissed – the defence of a citizen's right to trial, and immunity from arbitrary punishment by magistrates, is at the very heart of

---

measure in less elevated circumstances: a *lex Clodia* forbade treasury clerks from engaging in business, a move presumably designed to prevent personal profiteering – though Suetonius' text also indicates that it had little practical effect.

103. Cic. *Att.* 2.18.3, 2.19.4–5, 2.20.2, 2.21.6, 2.22.1–2, 2.23.3, 2.24.5; *Q Fr.* 1.2.16.
104. On the sequence of events, W. Stroh, '*De domo sua*: legal problem and structure', in J. Powell and J. Paterson, eds, *Cicero the Advocate*, Oxford: Oxford University Press 2004, 313–70, at 316–23.

popularis politics. Cicero's departure from the scene also removed one of Rome's most effective orators, who had already demonstrated his skill in persuading the people to oppose popular measures; and, perhaps most importantly, Cicero was disliked by many in Rome. They had celebrated when Gaius Antonius had been convicted on *repetundae* charges the previous spring, and now they attacked Cicero's house. Clodius did not risk his reputation, or popularity, by removing Cicero.

The final aspect of Clodius' legislation was a series of interventions in foreign affairs. In addition to the commands allocated to Piso and Gabinius, he set up a special command to annex Cyprus. This move extended direct Roman control to the island and demonstrated Clodius' capacity to challenge Pompeius' dominance of the east; financial concerns may also have played a part.[105] In a neat move, Clodius gave the command to Marcus Cato, thus removing from Rome another influential figure and one who had already demonstrated political adroitness and an alert responsiveness to managing popular discontent. The Cyprus command also included an instruction to Cato to restore some Byzantine exiles, and Clodius unpicked Pompeius' arrangements in Galatia, replacing Deiotarus, whom Pompeius had established as king, with his son-in-law Brogitarus. Clodius also sprang the younger Tigranes from house arrest at Rome: having invited him to dinner, he refused to return him to his host-cum-captor, the praetor L. Flavius.[106] Clodius ignored Pompeius' requests that Tigranes – whom he had brought to Rome – be returned; and attacked Gabinius when he protested, with symbolically powerful breaking of his *fasces* and the threat to confiscate his property through consecration.[107] Overall it is difficult to read Clodius' foreign policy interventions as anything other than a direct challenge to Pompeius' authority, which demonstrated, in true *popularis* fashion, the people's ultimate authority as well as Clodius' own position at Rome, which made him sufficiently powerful to challenge Rome's most powerful man. If Pompeius had hoped that co-operation over Cicero's fate would protect him, he was wrong; and Cicero, watching events intensely from Thessalonica, realised

---

105. E. Badian, 'M. Porcius Cato and the annexation and early administration of Cyprus', *JRS* 55, 1965, 110–21; Sherwin-White, *Foreign Policy*, 268–70, suggests financial concerns played only a small part.
106. Asc. 47C. Tigranes' attempt to escape from Italy ended when he was shipwrecked at Antium; Flavius' attempt to capture him ended in fatalities.
107. Cass. Dio 39.30; Cic. *Pis.* 28.

the significance of the split. But we should not see Clodius' behaviour as either isolated or erratic. Back in the summer of 59, Cicero had claimed that 'Publius is our only hope'; the *nobiles* – of whom Clodius was of course one – were enjoying Pompeius' discomfiture.

Clodius' popularity was based on his unremittingly *popularis* actions, but he supplemented his position of power by the notably effective paramilitary organisation of his supporters (which drew on the revived *collegia*). This support in turn enabled him to orchestrate crowd behaviour at *contiones*, demonstrating both his own authority and the unpopularity of his opponents. And it provoked a response. Violence was not a new phenomenon, but it developed a new level of importance in the mid-fifties which almost brought the regular functions of government to a standstill. Clodius based his operation on genuine popular appeal, even if he supplemented that with cash, and his levels of violence alienated some of his core supporters; but his opponents found no difficulty in matching his forces with hired supporters.

The consuls elected for 57 were Lentulus Spinther and Metellus Nepos, both *nobiles* and both well equipped to claim the consulship on their own merits: neither appears to have owed his election to his ties with either Caesar or Pompeius.[108] For Cicero, Nepos' election was not good news: in addition to their earlier clashes, Nepos was Clodius' cousin (indeed, his own tribunate may have offered Clodius a model of how not to be a successful *popularis*). Moreover, Clodius' brother Appius was one of the year's praetors. But Spinther was a friend, and Nepos was persuaded to put away his enmity. They worked consistently on Cicero's behalf throughout 57, as did Pompeius, most of the praetors and a number of the tribunes. Among the latter, Milo and Sestius stand out, not least because of their organisation of gangs to challenge Clodius' continuing presence. But at least two of the tribunes were hostile to Cicero's return, and as a result the early months of the year were marked by violent encounters between the two groups at popular assemblies and trials. Tribunician vetoes blocked the matter in the Senate, and in the end Cicero's supporters turned to the centuriate assembly, which had legislative capacity, though – given this assembly's cumbersome

---

108. Nepos and Caesar had both attacked Cicero at the start of 62, but they do not appear to have been working in concert; and the coolness between Nepos (one of Pompeius' legates during the 60s) and Pompeius after his divorce of Mucia appears to have abated. Spinther, much later, could remind Caesar of evidence of their friendship (Caes. *B Civ.* 1.22.3–4).

structure – it was seldom used for law-making. But it was weighted towards the wealthy, and – supplemented by the presence of wealthy Italians who gathered in Rome during the summer for the elections – it passed the necessary measure overwhelmingly on 4 August. Cicero was already on his way back to Italy.

Cicero's recall has a significance beyond the personal because it demonstrated that Clodius and his popular support *could* be checked, given sufficient will and organisation; but the idea that it marked the formation of broad, solid opposition to Clodius was an illusion, however strongly Cicero based his attempt at a political revival on that idea. Roman politics remained deeply factional. Moreover, Cicero was barely back in Rome before he destroyed his credibility as a unifying figure by openly declaring himself, once more, Pompeius' man. The price of food had risen sharply during the summer of 57, and despite Clodius' free grain distributions there was widespread discontent, which manifested itself in public demonstrations. On 7 September, three days after his return, Cicero proposed in the Senate that Pompeius be given *imperium* to reorganise the grain supply, at a meeting surrounded by hostile crowds to which only two other consulars dared come. That Cicero should feel confident in the presence of baying Clodians – and indeed win transient applause from them – through his support for Pompeius showed unmistakably where his fundamental loyalties lay; it is unsurprising that he found rapprochement with the *nobiles* difficult, even though he was careful not to take part in the subsequent negotiations over the precise content of Pompeius' *imperium*.[109]

The autumn continued to be marked by violent clashes. Some related to the continuing struggle to control Cicero's symbolic value through the use of the site of his house.[110] Others arose from elections. Although those for consuls and praetors had been held at the normal time, those for the aedileship were constantly postponed as Clodius' enemies attempted to prevent his election. Cicero gives a

---

109. As he noted (*Att.* 4.1.7), he needed the support of the pontiffs, few of whom were naturally sympathetic to Pompeius' ambitions, if he was to regain the site of his Palatine house. He did, with *De domo sua*, but the compensation was disappointing, and he claimed (*Att.* 4.2.5) that it was because 'they' were jealous of his regaining his position; we can afford to be more sceptical. Cicero also took an opportunity to cement relations with Caesar when he proposed a 15-day supplication in response to Caesar's successes during his second year of campaigning (Cic. *Prov. cons.* 26–7), though given the scale of Caesar's successes Cicero may well have been the net beneficiary.
110. Cic. *Att.* 4.3.2–3 describes a series of violent encounters between Cicero's entourage and Clodius' men in early November.

vivid glimpse in a letter to Atticus of Milo's manoeuvres with the announcement of unfavourable divine signs:

> On 19 November Milo arrived at the Campus Martius with a large band before midnight. Although Clodius had a picked force of runaway slaves, he didn't dare to enter the Campus. Milo held his position until midday, to people's intense pleasure and much to his glory. A shameful struggle for the three brothers, their power broken, their madness ignored. But Metellus asked that any announcement of unfavourable signs the following day take place in the forum; there was no need to go to the Campus at night; he would be at the *comitium* (voting place) at first light. And so at the end of the night on the 20th Milo went to the *comitium*. At dawn Metellus was secretly racing to the Campus by back routes; Milo followed the man through the woods and made his declaration. Metellus took himself off to extensive foul abuse from Q. Flaccus. The 21st was market day, and there were no *contiones* for two days. Today is the 22nd and I'm writing three hours after midnight. Milo is already in position on the Campus.[111]

At the same time, Clodius' enemies were attempting to bring him to trial for violence before he received immunity through office-holding, but without success, and by mid-January the elections had finally been held.[112] Clodius then arranged the prosecutions of Milo and Sestius, and used Milo's trial as an opportunity to attack Pompeius, who was facing widespread criticism because of his support for the exiled king of Egypt (see below, pp. 178–81); he appears also to have been involved in the trial in April of Caelius, the charges against whom included attacks on the Alexandrian ambassadors which had the potential to embarrass Pompeius.[113] Clodius also continued his harassment of Cicero, seizing upon the response which the diviners (*haruspices*) had given when consulted about a strange noise heard near Rome They judged that 'rites are due

---

111. Cic. *Att.* 4.3.4–5. The 'three brothers' are Clodius, Metellus Nepos and Appius Claudius. Q. Flaccus is otherwise unknown.
112. Cic. *Q Fr.* 2.1.1–3 describes a meeting of the Senate on 15 December 57 at which Clodius' violence was discussed, and the meeting broken up by his supporters; it is clear that the consuls-elect favoured holding the elections before any judicial activity, and presumably they held the elections as soon as they entered office. By the date of *Q Fr.* 2.2 it has dropped off the agenda.
113. Cicero's defence speech *Pro Caelio* survives. It seems probable, too, that Clodius, as member of the Board of Fifteen (*Quindecimvir*), pushed for that college's decision in January on the Egyptian affair, given the block it placed on Pompeius' ambitions (see below). Clodius was one of Milo's prosecutors; his involvement in Sestius' trial is indirect.

to Jupiter Saturn Neptune Tellus and the heavenly gods' because 'games have been held carelessly and have been soiled, holy and religious places have been treated as not sacred, ambassadors have been killed contrary to law and right, promises and oaths have been ignored and ancient secret sacrifices have been held carelessly and have been soiled'.[114] The deconsecration of the shrine of Freedom was easy to identify as a holy place which had been treated as 'not sacred'; Cicero's desire to rebut this charge can be seen in his speech *De haruspicum responso*, which set out an alternative narrative of sacrilege with Clodius at its centre and which was probably disseminated very soon after the Senate's discussion.

Cicero and Clodius continued to snipe at one another until Clodius' death, but by the time they were engaged with the *haruspices* the wider political picture had changed. Pompeius' political pre-eminence and special status had been marked, since Caesar's consulship, through his grain-supply *imperium*, which was so set up that he ran the complex logistical operation from Rome, or at least his suburban base outside the city walls; and Rome itself was being changed, as his great theatre complex took shape on the Campus Martius. But Clodius continued to humiliate him publicly, the tribune Gaius Cato was attacking him, and there was no sign of rapprochement with the *nobiles*. In mid-February, Cicero described Pompeius' position in a letter to his brother Quintus in Sardinia: Pompeius had been abused by Clodius' supporters at Milo's trial, come under fire, in the Senate's discussion of the violence at that trial, from the *nobiles* and a few days later faced full-scale invective from Gaius Cato, also in the Senate. As a result, Pompeius was taking steps to protect his position by summoning supporters from the countryside, in the face of 'the contional crowd pretty much lost to him, the nobility hostile, the Senate unreasonable and the young disaffected'. 'Big things are afoot', surmised Cicero.[115] In fact, Pompeius decided to reinforce his position by standing for a second consulship – despite the fact that he would continue to hold pro-consular *imperium* to manage the corn supply. In order to make that ambition easier to realise, he renewed negotiations with Caesar, and

---

114. For the reconstructed text of the response and discussion, A. Corbeill, 'A text in Cicero's *De haruspicum responsis*', in Berry and Erksine, eds, *Form and Function*, 139–54.
115. Cic. *Q Fr.* 2.3.4. Cicero was himself trying to keep his head down, not contributing to the earlier Senate debate and deeply embarrassed by lavish praise from Gaius Cato.

the two men met in Cisalpine Gaul, at the town of Luca, in early April before Caesar's campaigning began.[116]

Pompeius' needs were obvious.[117] The immediate difficulty for Caesar was the *lex Sempronia*: the Senate was shortly to decide the provinces for the incoming consuls, and both Gauls could be considered.[118] Caesar, it appears, wanted to control the way his provincial command ended, which meant that he required an effective senatorial presence to steer that debate to other areas. The agreement held, though Pompeius and Crassus faced enormous opposition to their consular ambitions, led by the consul Marcellinus and M. Cato. They faced a particularly strong rival in L. Domitius Ahenobarbus, Cato's brother-in-law and a man whom Cicero described as 'consul-designate for as long as he has been alive'.[119] Fatal violence was required to deter Ahenobarbus' candidacy, and Pompeius and Crassus had to delay elections into 55, when the support and presence of Caesar's soldiers helped them into office. Their priority in office was their and Caesar's military ambitions: the former were secured through a tribunician law, the *lex Trebonia*, under which Crassus received Syria and Pompeius both Spains, and the latter through a *lex Pompeia Licinia* which gave Caesar a further five years in Gaul. But Pompeius and Crassus also sponsored laws on legal procedure and on bribery, and in what may have been a conscious recollection of their first consulship, arranged for the election of censors.[120] Pompeius also dedicated his theatre complex on the Campus Martius, with lavish games.

One rapid consequence of this renewed co-operation between the

---

116. Suet. *Iul.* 24; Plut. *Caes.* 21.3; *Pomp.* 51.3; *Crass.* 14.5; Caesar's *B Gall.* is silent on the meetings (he and Crassus had met earlier at Ravenna). Lintott, *Evidence*, 202, identifies the most senior attenders at Luca.

117. Crassus' motives are, as so often, difficult to discern but the desire to achieve military glory, suggested by subsequent events, may have been crucial.

118. The *lex Vatinia*, which covered Cisalpine Gaul and Illyria, may have specified 1 March 54 as its end date (Cic. *Prov. cons.* 36–7); in practical terms, therefore, another *imperium*-holder could have taken it over for the campaiging season of 54, though there would have been an anomalous period in the opening two months of the year. There seems to have been no legal impediment to the allocation of Transalpine Gaul.

119. Cic. *Att.* 4.8a.2. The previous four generations of Domitii Ahenobarbi had reached the consulship and Lucius Domitius' father had been *pontifex maximus*. See further J. Carlsen, *The Rise and Fall of a Roman Noble Family: The Domitii Ahenobarbi 196 BC–AD 68*, Odense: University Press of Southern Denmark 2006.

120. Those elected were M. Valerius Messalla and that great pre-Sullan survivor Servilius Vatia Isauricus; they did not complete the *lustrum*, but did review the membership of the Senate, to the embarrassment, in at least one case, of Pompeius (Steel, 'Mancia').

three men was the sidelining of Cicero, who resumed his adherence to Pompeius.[121] That decision turned out to be hugely important for Latin literature, since the great treatises of the 50s, *De oratore* and *De republica*, had their origins in Cicero's resulting leisure and dissatisfaction. The wider political landscape, however, proved surprisingly resistant. Cato, despite failing to be elected to the praetorship for 55, was prominent in the opposition to the *lex Trebonia*, assisted by two of the tribunes, one of whom, Ateius Capito, declared hostile omens when Crassus was departing for his province in late autumn.[122]

Foreign policy in the 50s

Crassus' departure for Syria was the culmination of his personal ambition; and it was attractive because it seemed to offer the opportunity to rival Pompeius' past conquests and Caesar's current activities by engaging with the Parthian empire, which Pompeius' annexation of Syria had brought into direct contact with Rome. Pompeius left M. Aemilius Scaurus, one of his quaestors, in charge there with propraetorian *imperium* when he returned to Rome, and neither Scaurus nor his replacement, Marcius Philippus, seems to have undertaken any serious campaigning. But Gabinius, who reached the consulship in 58, saw the area's potential and having initially received Cilicia as his province (see above, pp. 170–1) he had his *imperium* transferred to Syria, probably in response to news of raids which could serve as a pretext for war. Once in Syria, he became involved in a dynastic intrigue with the Parthian royal family, but was unable to intervene decisively because of other events. He revisited Pompeius' settlement in Judaea, transferring

121. Pompeius had gone from Luca to Sardinia, and there asked Quintus Cicero to convey to Marcus 'a request not to attack Caesar's interests and position, if I wasn't able or didn't want to support them' (Cic. *Fam.* 1.9.9). Cicero obeyed, desisted from opposition to the Campanian land law, supported Caesar's ambitions by opposing the inclusion of either Gaul in the provinces identified that year under the *lex Sempronia* (in the speech *Prov. cons.*), and later in the year defended Pompeius' and Caesar's associate Balbus on the charge of illegally assuming the citizenship (*Balb.*). Lintott, *Evidence*, 201, well describes the shift in Cicero's position in 56 as 'the close of an enormous parenthesis'.
122. Plut. *Cat. Min.* 43.4; Cass. Dio 39.33–6. For Ateius' intervention, *MRR* 2.216; it would be tempting – given what happened to Crassus – to dismiss most of this as subsequent embroidery, but Cic. *Att.* 4.13.2 contemporaneously (though perhaps with a touch of *schadenfreude*) indicates that it was an unedifying departure; K. Weggen, *Der Lange Schatten von Carrhae: Studien zu M. Licinius Crassus*, Hamburg: Kovac 2011.

authority from the high priest to five councils; once these had been established, he did turn his attention to Parthia, but very soon was distracted by developments in Egypt.[123]

Prior to examining Gabinius' intervention in Egypt, it is worth considering Rome's dealings with the Ptolemaic kingdom more generally. Before Pompeius' campaigns in the east, the Romans had been slow to take advantage of the weaknesses of the Egyptian monarchy. Cyrene had been bequeathed to them by its last ruler, Ptolemy Apion, in 96; and the Senate's initial response was to accept the bequest and leave the cities free.[124] Lucullus visited Cyrene in 86 BC whilst gathering resources for Sulla, and was called on to adjudicate internal disputes; apart from that episode, there is no evidence of Roman involvement in the area until 75 or 74, when a quaestor was sent out to impose direct rule.[125] We simply do not have enough evidence to tell what lies behind this decision: Oost suggests that the prospect of tax revenues may have been the motive at a time when pressure on the treasury was building, but, though plausible, this can only be speculation. That a quaestor was sent out may well support the idea that finance was the Senate's chief concern, but the fragment of Sallust on which we depend for this episode describes the individual sent, Lentulus Marcellinus, as an inappropriate choice; it also links his appointment to the manoeuvrings of a single figure, almost certainly the consul Cotta, which suggests that Sallust saw here an example of shady backroom dealing for personal advantage.[126] Egypt itself had allegedly been left to the Romans in the will of Ptolemy Alexander a few years after the bequest of Cyrene; unsurprisingly, given more pressing concerns at Rome in 88, nothing was done about this, and during the first war with Mithridates the Romans negotiated with his brother Ptolemy Soter, who remained in possession of the throne. After Soter's death Sulla supported the claims of Ptolemy Alexander's son, also Ptolemy Alexander, who had joined his forces during Sulla's campaigns against Mithridates; but he was murdered by a mob in Alexandria within weeks of becoming king and succeeded by Soter's son, Ptolemy Auletes. The Senate then ignored Egypt for over a decade, refusing to commit itself

123. Sherwin-White, *Foreign Policy*, 271–9.
124. Livy, *Per.* 70.
125. Lucullus: Plut. *Luc.* 2; quaestor, Sall. *Hist.* 2.43M; S.Oost, 'Cyrene, 96–74 B.C.', *CPh* 58, 1963, 11–25.
126. P. McGushin, *Sallust: The Histories*, Oxford: Oxford University Press 1992, 206–8.

to acknowledging any claimant as king;[127] but in 65 it became the second issue which the censors quarrelled over, with Crassus attempting some extension of financial control over the territory; the details are obscure, and his plan collapsed. In 59 Julius Caesar, as consul, finally arranged for the Roman acknowledgement of Auletes' position, in return for a cash payment. The following year, however, the tribune Clodius proposed a law to annex Cyprus, M. Cato being identified as the quaestor acting in place of a praetor (*quaestor pro praetore*) in charge of the process. This move appears to have fuelled the Alexandrians' existing resentment of Auletes, who was expelled the following year and took refuge in Rome, installing himself at Pompeius' Alban villa.

The official response of the Senate, confirming Ptolemy's status as friend and ally, was to add his restoration to the *prouincia* of Cilicia which had been alloted to one of the consuls of 57, Lentulus Spinther. But at the same time, Gabinius, who arrived in Syria in the spring of 57, was in contact with the Alexandrian opposition about the identity of a suitable husband for Berenice IV, Ptolemy's daughter, who had emerged as the ruler of Egypt.[128] Gabinius does not seem to have received any official instructions on this matter, but it is inconceivable that he was operating without advice from Rome, including above all that of Pompeius: the Romans were, at least unofficially, keeping their options open. These negotiations may have contributed to a sense of disappointment in Alexandria when news arrived that the Romans supported Ptolemy's restoration, and the Alexandrians' decision to send to Rome a huge embassy – 100 is the figure given in the ancient sources – led by the philosopher Dio.

This embassy provoked Ptolemy, and his supporters, into what turned out to be a counter-productive reaction. He arranged to ambush the embassy when it landed at Puteoli; and his successful attempts to prevent the survivors from addressing the Senate included the assassination of the embassy's head, Dio. There was popular outrage at Rome, orchestrated initially by Favonius, the close associate of the absent Cato, and Ptolemy left Rome and made his way to Ephesus. Despite his departure, the incoming tribune of the plebs Gaius Cato kept the matter alive with 'frequent *contiones*', in which he attacked not only Ptolemy but also the consul Spinther,

127. Two passing references in Cicero's *Verrines* (2.2.76, 2.4.61) show that the issue was on the agenda in the late 70s, with Seleucid claimants as well, and that Hortensius, consul in 69, supported Auletes.
128. Porph *FGrH* 260, F2.14; Strab. 17.1.11; Cass. Dio 39.57.1–2.

who was preparing to depart for Cilicia.[129] The Senate did not immediately respond – a letter from Cicero to Quintus shows that it was preoccupied with other matters, with its meeting on 15 December 57 devoted to the prospect of redistribution of public land in Campania, and measures to deal with the violence of the previous weeks which had held up the aedilician elections – and, depending on the force of popular feeling, might have continued to ignore C. Cato. But it was bounced into action early in 56 by the leaking, to C. Cato, of part of the Sibylline books which the *Quindecemviri* had identified in response to a lighting strike on a statue of Jupiter. This passage, which C. Cato presented to the people, stated that 'if the king of Egypt comes seeking help, do not deny him friendship, but do not help him with a multitude. Otherwise, you will have trouble and danger.' By 13 January, when Cicero wrote to Spinther, the Senate had accepted the advice's relevance to Ptolemy and that, it would seem, ruled out the use of an army.[130]

The matter preoccupied the Senate for the rest of January, with strong differences of opinion emerging between the consulars and the Senate as a whole, and contributed to the faltering reputation of Pompeius, who was regarded as attempting to manipulate events to his own advantage.[131] But in the end nothing was done, and by early summer Cicero was writing to Spinther with pragmatic encouragement to which, he claimed, Pompeius assented:

> since no *senatus consultum* exists removing from you the restoration of the Alexandrian king, and since the opinion on that matter which was recorded – you know it was vetoed – that no one should at all restore the king has the force only of an opinion of a group of angry men rather than of the advice of a firm-minded Senate, you, who are in control of Cilicia and Cyprus, should see what you can do and succeed at, and if the situation appears to be such as to allow you to take Alexandria and Egypt, it befits the dignity of your and our *imperium* that you should leave the king at Ptolemais, or somewhere else, and advance on Alexandria with your army and fleet so that, once you have secured the city peacefully with a garrison, Ptolemy may return to his kingdom; the result would be that he was restored by you, as the Senate decided at the outset, and he would be brought

---

129. Fenestella (fr. 21 Peter).
130. Cic. *Fam.* 1.1. It is worth noting that there is no sign that anxiety about Spinther's position contributed to the backlash; the outrage arose from Ptolemy's illegal behaviour in Italy and from anti-Pompeian sentiment.
131. Cic. *Fam.* 1.2–1.6; *Q Fr.* 2.2–2.5; Cass. Dio 39.12–16.

back without a multitude, as our religious men said the Sibyl wanted it.

There was, then, a way round the religious objection; but, as Cicero goes on to make clear, Spinther should proceed on this basis only if he is sure he will succeed: 'if everything were to fall out as we hope and pray it will, everyone will say that you acted wisely and bravely; if something goes wrong, the same men will accuse you of greed and recklessness'.[132] Spinther was not persuaded, and concentrated his efforts in Cilicia (his campaigning was eventually rewarded, in 51, with a triumph, the last to be held before the outbreak of civil war). Gabinius, instead, took up the task early in 55, on the instructions of Pompeius, now holding the consulship. He defeated the forces of Archelaus, Berenice's husband, put Auletes back on the throne, and left behind a small occupying force of Roman troops. In an outcome which supports Cicero's analysis, he was acquitted after his return to Rome of *maiestas*, succumbing subsequently to *repetundae* charges.[133]

Gabinius was distracted from Parthia by Egypt; his successor in Syria, Crassus, made Parthia his priority. During the first year of his command he campaigned in Mesopotamia. The following year he marched his entire force, now increased by the arrival of his son Publius, who had been one of Caesar's legates in Gaul, with a detachment of Gallic cavalry, to meet the Parthian army. The battle at Carrhae was a catastrophic defeat for Roman forces, the worst since the disaster at Arausio half a century earlier, with casualty figures, for the battle and its aftermath, given at 30,000; among the dead were both Crassus and his elder son.[134] Crassus' quaestor, Cassius (subsequently among the killers of Caesar), led the survivors back to Syria and organised its defence, remaining there in effective charge until late in 51, when Bibulus arrived.

Meanwhile in Gaul Caesar's campaigns had lost momentum.

---

132. Cic. *Fam.* 1.7.4.
133. Cicero gave evidence against Gabinius at his *maiestas* trial but was compelled to defend him on the *repetundae* charges; he did not disseminate his unsuccessful defence (Crawford, *Lost*, 188–97), but his speech in the related case of Rabirius Postumus does survive: M. Siani-Davies, *Cicero's Speech Pro Rabirio Postumo*, Oxford: Oxford University Press 2001.
134. The tragic colouring of the Carrhae campaign climaxes in the story, almost certainly a fiction, of Crassus' head being used as a prop in a performance of Euripides' *Bacchae* before the Parthian king; B. Marshall, *Crassus: A Political Biography*, Amsterdam: Hakkert 1976, 151–61; R.Sheldon, *Rome's Wars in Parthia*, Edgware: Vallentine Mitchell 2010, 29–49; Weggen, *Schatten*.

Initially, his successes had been extraordinary. He had turned back the Helvetii's migration and then, in concert with the Aedui, who were allies of Rome, he turned his attention to the German leader Ariovistus, despite the fact that only the previous year, under Caesar's guidance, Ariovistus' position in north-eastern Gaul had been acknowledged by the Senate with the title of king. By the end of the summer of 58, Caesar had defeated Ariovistus and left Roman forces to overwinter well outside the area Rome had previously controlled. The following year he appeared to complete the conquest of Gaul with a campaign against the Belgae and the negotiated submission of the inhabitants of western Gaul.[135] Caesar was on shaky legal ground, since very little of this activity could be said to have been authorised by the Senate; but it was legitimised, at least for the time being, by the acknowledgement of his success with the voting of a supplication. His conquests turned out to be on shaky ground, too: the western Gauls revolted during the winter of 57–56, disrupting Caesar's intention of turning to Illyricum. After concluding negotiations with Crassus and Pompeius, he was back in Gaul, and it remained his focus for the rest of this proconsulship. Consolidation during 56 was followed by eye-catching exploits the following year: the bridging of the Rhine and the invasion of Britain, followed in 54 by a more extended campaign which concluded with the surrendering of hostages by the southern Britons and their agreement to pay tribute. These were met in Rome in 55 by a second supplication, of 20 days. But again Caesar faced an uprising, more serious than the one three years previously. Co-ordinated attacks on Roman winter quarters led to the destruction of one force of a legion and five cohorts, with the deaths of two legates, and prevented Caesar from returning to Italy at all that winter. The following summer involved another crossing of the Rhine, but no substantial consolidation, a fact concealed in the sixth book of his *Commentarii* by his German ethnography.

The last years of the Republic

In the elections for the year 54 both Domitius Ahenobarbus and Cato were elected (to the consulship and praetorship respectively),

---

135. These campaigns are covered in Caes. *B Gall.* 1–2, which were probably sent annually to Rome (T. P. Wiseman, 'The publication of *De Bello Gallico*', in A. Powell and K. Welch, eds, *Julius Caesar as Artful Reporter: The War Commentaries as Political Instruments*, Swansea: Classical Press of Wales 1998, 1–9).

and the other consul, Appius Claudius, was not an adherent of Pompeius or of Caesar.[136] Despite Cicero's gloomy allusion to a note-book full of the names of future consuls, Pompeius' continuing influence over elections is difficult to discern.[137] Moreover, elections were a barometer of increasing political chaos. *Interreges* had been required in 55 and 54 as different candidates attempted to control the composition of the centuriate assembly by delaying elections. That pattern continued, though in 53 the cause was an enormous bribery scandal which erupted around the consular election. Compe-tition was particularly intense, since, relatively unusually, there were four credible candidates whose chances were closely balanced.[138] All were threatened with prosecution for bribery, and finally C. Memmius made a statement in the Senate detailing a pact that he and Calvinus had made with the consuls in office to secure their elec-tion in return for the allocation of new consular provinces.[139] In 54, too, the courts were very busy, with many of the cases having a direct political purpose, and by the summer the census had been abandoned.[140] The elections in the end did not take place until the summer of 53, when Messalla and Calvinus – the two candidates who appear *not* to have had Pompeius' and Caesar's support – were elected.[141] By the time they were elected, the next year's contests were under way, and here, as in 57, conflict between Clodius and Milo caused the blockage. On this occasion, Milo was a (not implausible) consular candidate and Clodius was standing for the praetorship.[142]

---

136. These elections were delayed until late autumn (Cic. *Att.* 4.13.1), which may reflect attempts to manipulate the outcome.

137. Cic. *Att.* 4.8a.2. Pompeius failed to secure the election of his consular candidate, T. Ampius Balbus (Cic. *Planc.* 25).

138. They were M. Aemilius Scaurus, Cn. Domitius Calvinius, C. Memmius and M. Valerius Messalla Rufus. On their connections and the campaign, E. S. Gruen, 'The consular elections for 53 B.C.', in J. Bibauw, ed., *Hommages à Marcel Renard*, vol. 2, Brussels: Latomus 1969, 311–21.

139. Cic. *Att.* 4.17.2–3. The delays gave rise to talk of a dictatorship (Cic. *Att.* 4.18.3; *Q Fr.* 3.6.4).

140. Alexander, *Trials*, 137–49 (compare the drought in the previous and subsequent years); Marinone, *Cronologia*, 131–4, for Cicero's involvement, which included his most reluctant, and unsuccessful, defence of Gabinius on *repetundae* charges. Census: *Att.* 4.16.8. No reason is recorded, but the juxtaposition with challenges under the *lex Clodia* suggests that Senate membership may have been the sticking point.

141. Cass. Dio 40.45 points to evolving political practice: the tribunes of 53 opposed the curule elections because they wished to preserve their (enhanced) role in the absence of praetors. It was Pompeius who, according to Dio, ensured the elections took place by publicly disavowing any dictatorial ambition.

142. Milo's rivals were Metellus Scipio and Plautius Hypsaeus (Asc. 30C), both of

Their violent encounters provoked the Senate to put on mourning garb and included a riot in which both consuls were injured; by the start of the year elections had not been held, and an *interrex* had not been appointed.[143] What Pompeius might have intended is unclear, and the situation changed abruptly after Milo's men murdered Clodius on 18 January. The Roman people burnt down the Senate house the following day (in an extension of the cremation of Clodius' body) and then attempted to appoint Milo's electoral rivals as consuls, failing which it called on Pompeius to become dictator. Two months of legal manoeuvres and continued electoral campaigning followed until, towards the end of the intercalary month, Pompeius was appointed by the *interrex* to his third consulship, this time without a colleague.[144] This broke with precedent in a variety of ways: not only did it repeat from 55 the anomaly of a consul who already held proconsular *imperium*, it ignored the Sullan framework for repeated office-holding, and it undermined the essential collegiality of the position of consul. Nonetheless, it was welcomed by a broad coalition among the Senate (though the enthusiasm may in part have been fuelled, as Asconius suggests, by a fear that Pompeius might become dictator); Pompeius had already been instructed to recruit troops across Italy when the Senate passed the 'last decree' in the days after Clodius' death and the destruction of the Senate house. This willingness to set aside precedent is a testament to the crisis which seemed to be engulfing the *res publica*.

whom had Pompeius' backing (Plautius had been his quaestor and proquaestor during the Mithridatic campaign and Pompeius had married Metellus Scipio's daughter Cornelia, after the death of Julia in 54 and after Cornelia was widowed by the death of the younger P. Crassus at Carrhae, in a move which may indicate Pompeius' attempt to solidify his position with the *nobiles*). Milo put his trust in lavish games and the support of those who opposed Clodius. Clodius' plans for his praetorship are difficult to disentangle from Cicero's scaremongering, but an interest in the civic position of freedmen (whose numbers had recently increased) is attested (Tatum, *Clodius*, 234–9). The legislative capacity of the praetorship gave its holders the opportunity to apply political pressure even though few *leges* actually resulted (Brennan, *Praetorship*, 471–5); despite Brennan's scepticism, Clodius may have intended to develop the office's potential as a medium for popular legislation as Caesar had developed that of the consulship.
143. Cass. Dio 40.46; *Schol. Bob.* 172St; Asc. 30–1C. T. P. Wiseman, 'Caesar, Pompey and Rome, 59-50 B.C.', *CAH* 9², 1994, 368-423, at 403–4, sketches the background of crisis to the year 53, with reverses in Caesar's campaigns followed by the disaster at Carrhae. It is not unreasonable to think that these may have contributed to willingness to support a Pompeius-led reform. In addition – whether by chance or because of an outbreak of disease – a number of senior figures appear to have died in 54 or 53: Nepos, Marcellinus, Curio, Gellius and Torquatus (Syme, *Augustan Aristocracy*, 22–3).
144. Asconius' introduction to Cicero's speech in defence of Milo gives a vivid and detailed picture of Rome utterly obsessed by Clodius' murder (30C–42C).

Pompeius did, to a remarkable extent, succeed in re-establishing order, albeit with the support of armed men. He passed a new law on violence, under which many of the participants in the Clodius/Milo affray – on both sides – were convicted and exiled.[145] After a few months, he presided over elections for the vacant consulship; the successful candidate was his new father-in-law, Metellus Scipio, but Pompeius' decision to ensure that there were two consuls was nonetheless a public demonstration that he did not intend any long-term derangement of normal government.[146] There was also some other important legislation. Pompeius successfully proposed a *lex Pompeia de prouinciis*, which built on a decree of the Senate of the previous year, proposed by consuls, that there should be an interval of time between holding a magistracy in Rome and proceeding to a provincial command.[147] The measure had originally been proposed the previous year by the consuls, who had lost half their year in office to scandalously delayed elections in which bribery was rife. An interest in controlling electoral competition by restricting consular candidates' access to the wealth-generating capacity of provincial government is understandable – particularly as neither consul had taken a province after their praetorship, whereas their rivals had.[148] But the implications for provincial government were considerable, and may have been of greater interest to Pompeius when he revived the measure as sole consul: his entire career had demonstrated the

145. The only other named individual in this category, apart from Milo, is Sex. Cloelius, Clodius' secretary, but Asconius (56C) claims that there were 'many' further victims, the majority supporters of Clodius; Saufeius, Milo's gang-leader, was acquitted. A further sign that order was restored may be Servius Sulpicius Rufus' willingness to risk involvement in consular elections again, 11 years after his previous attempt.

146. Indeed, perhaps the reverse: Scipio was more likely to receive the support of the centuries than the other candidate, Hypsaeus, and thus required less intervention by Pompeius.

147. Cass. Dio 40.46.2, 40.56.1–2. The law's operation in relation to the praetorship can be seen in a letter of Caelius to Cicero (*Fam.* 8.8.8), which gives the text of the decree arranging the allocation of praetorian provinces, and is consistent with Dio's account and his specifying of a five-year gap. Giovannini, *Imperium*, argued that the *lex Pompeia* did not apply to the consulship; he must be right that consular *imperium* itself did not change as a result, though it is difficult to escape the conclusion that the *lex Pompeia* attempted to alter the method by which all provinces were *normally* allocated – though it had only a brief period of operation before the outbreak of civil war. See further C. Steel, 'The *lex Pompeia de prouinciis*: a reconsideration', *Historia* 61, 2012, 83–93, and Chapter 7 below.

148. Scaurus had been governor of Sardinia (and was defended by Cicero in the autumn of 53 on *repetundae* charges; his prosecutors argued (Asc. 19C) that the trial must take place before the elections, 'so that Scaurus could not buy the consulship with the money which he'd taken from the provincials'. Memmius had been in Bithynia.

potential of splitting the two spheres.[149] Pompeius also secured
an extension for the term of his Spanish command.[150] Metellus,
meanwhile, oversaw the restoration of the censors' powers over
Senate membership, repealing the relevant lex Clodia. And, for the
first time in three years, consuls were elected in time to take office on
1 January 51.

Pompeius had thus managed to eliminate violence from political
life and re-establish the principle of orderly office-holding. Given the
events of the previous years, this was a notable achievement. But he
made little progress with another problem whose intractable outlines
were now beginning to emerge, namely the position of Caesar. The
relationship between Pompeius and Caesar is at the heart of many
accounts of the outbreak of civil war in 49, and within that framework the key question becomes the moment at which the two men
broke apart. But it is perhaps more helpful to frame the problem in
terms of Caesar's *imperium*: Caesar, and Pompeius, and indeed the
entire *res publica*, needed to find a way of managing the end of
Caesar's *imperium* in Gaul. There were two recent examples of
difficult end points for the extended tenure of *imperium*: Sulla in 83,
and Pompeius in 61. The different route which each man had taken
when faced with the moment of transition from *imperium*-holder to
priuatus established two ends of a spectrum: armed invasion as
opposed to a peaceful return to private life. Caesar's activity in the
latter part of the 50s can be seen as an unsuccessful attempt to find
a third way between these two extremes.

The first clear indication that Caesar did not wish to follow the
example of Pompeius in 61 and return to private life at the end of
his command was his effort to ensure that he could stand for office
in absentia. A request from him is first attested in the winter of 53–
52.[151] Pompeius added his support to the tribunes, and a law to this
effect was passed during 52 with the support of all ten of them.[152]
Caesar's motive is understandable: the measure was an exceptional
honour, and would protect him from his opponents' threats to
prosecute him for his actions as proconsul in Gaul as well as

---

149. See below, Chapter 8. One consequence of the law was Cicero's departure from
Rome to govern Cilicia, which in turn generated Caelius' letters to him, which unfold,
albeit with frustrating elisions, the developing crisis at Rome over Caesar's position.
150. App. *B Civ.* 2.24; Cass. Dio 40.56; Plut. *Caes.* 28.5, *Pomp.* 55.7.
151. Cic. *Att.* 7.1.4.
152. References in *MRR* 2.236; the unity is notable given the deep split in the college
after Clodius' death and suggests – in 52 – that opposition to Caesar's exceptionalism
was confined to a small group.

signalling his intention to remain at the centre of political activity. Pompeius' stance was more complicated. At some point this year, he sponsored another measure on the rights of magistrates, known as the *lex Pompeia de iure magistratuum*; its provisions included a reassertion of the principle that candidates needed to present themselves in person when seeking election.[153] The contradiction between this and the law of the ten tribunes is obvious; Suetonius (*Iul*. 28.3) suggests that Pompeius forgot that he was contradicting himself; some modern interpreters see here an attempt by Pompeius to double-cross Caesar. Neither of these views is plausible; rather we should see here a tension between two aspirations. Pompeius was trying to re-establish peaceful civil government, and understood the threat which individual ambition posed to this aim. At the same time, he did not at this point want to fall out with Caesar. The result is the acknowledgement of Caesar as an exception to normal behaviour – just as Pompeius himself was an exception. From this perspective, the rider to the law on the rights of magistrates which noted Caesar's position as an exception is better seen not as an addition, when Pompeius realised, or was informed of, his error, but as an integral part of his initial conception of the issue.[154] This conception was based on Pompeius' pre-eminence and, on this interpretation, one point of the rider was to demonstrate to Caesar Pompeius' capacity, as well as his willingness, to protect and support him. Meanwhile, during 52 Caesar was engaged with another Gallic revolt, even larger and better organised than the two previous rejections of his claim to have established Roman power throughout Gaul. It concluded with a massive Roman victory following a long siege of the stronghold at Alesia and another 20-day supplication in the autumn of 52; but Caesar himself remained in Gaul throughout the winter, and the eighth book of his *Commentarii* – written by his legate A. Hirtius – records ongoing fighting in 51.[155]

Pompeius' consulship in 52 was in many respects a striking success. He steered the *res publica* back from the brink of military dictatorship to calm and order and re-established regular elections. He sponsored a thorough overhaul of the mechanisms for office-holding, in Rome and overseas: its implications were extensive, though in fact the outbreak of civil war prevented their significance

153. Cass. Dio 40.56.
154. Seager, *Pompey*, 138–9; this was certainly Cicero's view (*Att*. 8.3.3).
155. On Hirtius' narrative, R. Cluett, 'The continuators: soldiering on', in Griffin, *Companion to Julius Caesar*, 192–205.

from becoming apparent. And he maintained good relations with Caesar. But if this was the situation at the opening of 51, we need to account for its transformation, over the next two years, into the outbreak of civil war.

The legislation of 52 had established for Caesar the *ratio absentis*, his right to stand whilst absent, but it had not addressed the ending of his command in Gaul. The date at which the command ended has been the object of extensive, and inconclusive, scholarly debate. The failure to reach a conclusion on this question is perhaps not surprising, since it is unclear whether there ever was an agreed and fixed end point to Caesar's *imperium*. Dates were not used in this way elsewhere to manage imperial government: commands ended when a successor arrived, and the imprecision that could arise from this system is well documented for us in Cicero's letters at both ends of his Cilician command. The alternative end point was the end of the task. Pompeius' commands in the 60s did not, as far as we know, have fixed terms: they were defined by the existence of a problem, by their nature out of the normal run of events, and ended when the problem had been solved. Caesar's sphere of operation was not exceptional in this way: it was natural to assume that Transalpine Gaul would continue to be an area to which the Romans wished to send commanders, and that, eventually, someone else would replace him. The point of *ratio absentis* was to ensure that, at whatever point Caesar's command ended, he could stand for office; that implied that it was not necessary to define an end date.[156]

That the appointment of a successor was the way in which Caesar's command was expected to end is apparent from Cicero's speech *De prouinciis consularibus* from 56 BC. The burning question then had been whether or not one of the consuls of the following year would receive Transalpine Gaul as his *prouincia*: if so, Caesar's command would come to an end at some point late in 55 or early in 54, when his successor arrived. The exact date is not important; the identification of a successor is. The Senate decided that Gaul would not be a consular province, but the fact of the debate does rather suggest that Caesar's five years – counted inclusively – included 59. If so, then presumably, in the normal course of events, the Senate would have revisited the question in 55, and either prorogued his

156. Another factor was the ten-year interval between consulships, which would imply that the earliest that Caesar could have held the office would have been 48 – which would fit neatly with the view that he initially received command for five campaigning seasons and that the *lex Trebonia* gave him a further five.

command, or appointed a praetor to replace him. However, the normal course of events was overturned by the second consulship of Pompeius and Crassus, who received their proconsular commands by law, and had Caesar's command extended. At this point ambiguity did arise: had the *lex Licinia Pompeia* taken effect immediately, or was it to be understood sequentially to the initial senatorial decree?[157] On any view, the campaigning season of 51 belonged to Caesar; thereafter, debate could arise.

The consuls of 51 were M. Marcellus and Ser. Sulpicius Rufus, and the former was clearly hostile to Caesar; he publicly demonstrated this in the early summer through the public flogging of a man from Novum Comum, thus indicating that he did not accept the legitimacy of Caesar's colony there. Whatever the precise legal issue, Cicero's comment makes clear that this gesture was an insult to Caesar, and likely to offend Pompeius too.[158] Marcellus attempted to bring Caesar's command to an end, apparently suggesting that 1 March 50 should be its end point.[159] Pompeius opposed him; Marcellus failed to secure enough senatorial support to pass the measure and for the time being appeared to have abandoned the attempt.[160]

Later in the summer the Senate renewed its consideration of the issue: by this point, consuls had been elected, so that the earliest that Caesar could have held the office would have been 18 months hence. On the last day of September, the Senate met in the temple of Apollo.[161] Cicero's correspondent Caelius records the meeting in some detail, including texts of the four measures the Senate passed.[162] One instructed the next year's consuls to ensure that discussion of the consular provinces should take precedence over all other public business from 1 March 50. This was not vetoed, but the other three – one which declared a vetoing of discussion of consular provinces to be against the interests of the *res publica*, one which demobilised those of Caesar's soldiers who had served their time, and one which did not include Transalpine Gaul among the praetorian provinces, thus making it an inevitable choice for a consular

157. Seager, *Pompey*, 140–2; Lintott, *Evidence*, 433–6.
158. Plut. *Caes.* 29.2; App. *B Civ.* 2.26; Cic. *Att.* 5.11.2.
159. Cic. *Att.* 8.3.3. This was the first specific end date suggested for Caesar's command.
160. Cic. *Fam.* 8.2.2 (June 51).
161. Its location on the Campus Martius, outside the *pomerium*, allowed Pompeius to attend the meeting: Bonnefond-Coudry, *Le Sénat*, 137–60.
162. Cic. *Fam.* 8.8.

province – all were. Caelius records in the same letter two obser-
vations that Pompeius made, 'which have very much given people
confidence'. Pompeius thought that discussion of Caesar's provinces,
though unfair before 1 March 50, should not be delayed after that
date; and, in response to a question, 'What if he [sc. Caesar] wished
to be consul while in command of his army?', he replied, 'What if my
son wished to beat me with a stick?'[163] This cryptic remark appears
to have combined counter-factual improbability with Pompeian
authority: it was unthinkable that Caesar would attempt to
challenge Pompeius' authority in this way, but if he were to do
so, Pompeius would inevitably prevail. Caelius says that people
interpreted this as meaning that Pompeius had *negotium* with
Caesar; this is potentially ambiguous, but in practice a positive
meaning for *negotium*, 'a deal', is more likely here than the alternative, 'trouble', in the light of the confidence which these remarks
produced. If so, then Pompeius' calm assertion of paternal dominance made people believe he had the situation under control.
Caelius' conclusion was that Caesar would take one of two courses
of action: either stay in Gaul, not standing for election in 50, or
secure election *in absentia* and then leave his province.

The Senate's debates during 51 confirmed that the end of Caesar's
command in Gaul was the major political issue facing Rome without
advancing much towards a solution; and by so doing it established
more clearly the opposition between Caesar's supporters and those
who, with whatever degree of personal animosity, wished to control
his power. Pompeius' attitude was, naturally, of great interest to both
sides, and his responses characteristically evasive: in this case, the
evasion maintained a careful balance between the interests of
Caesar's supporters and his opponents. Pompeius would welcome
Caesar's return provided that it was on Pompeius' terms. And we
should not forget that the Parthians remained a very serious threat,
to which a substantial response might soon be required. Were that to
be the case, the emerging threat of a contest between Pompeius and
Caesar might well be dissipated.

163. Cic. *Fam.* 8.8.9. Did the questioner mean Caesar's holding consular and proconsular commands simultaneously, or standing for election whilst retaining his command
and army? Standing for election whilst holding the Gallic command was precisely what
the *ratio absentis* provided for; by the spring of 50 (Cic. *Fam.* 8.11.3) Caelius can say
that Pompeius 'doesn't want, indeed fears' this prospect, but it is less clear that in the
previous autumn use of the *ratio absentis*, rather than simultaneous tenure of consular
and proconsular *imperium*, could have been described by Pompeius as though it were
unthinkable. Of course, the question may have been deliberately ambiguous.

Neither of the consuls who had been elected for 50, C. Marcellus and L. Aemilius Lepidus, was a supporter of Caesar; and Lepidus, son of the consul of 78, had an open quarrel with Pompeius.[164] This is an important reminder that Roman political life was not yet polarised into two camps; Lepidus, indeed, seems to have had ambitious plans of his own, and was actively stamping his family's name on the forum.[165] Among others elected in the summer of 51 was Curio, as tribune, at a supplementary election which was held when one of the men initially elected was convicted of bribery.[166] Velleius says of him that 'no one put a greater or more blazing torch to civil war and the quantity of evils which followed without inter-ruption for twenty years than Gaius Curio'.[167]

C. Scribonius Curio was the son of the consul of 76; he first becomes prominent in 59, with attacks on Caesar and involvement in the Vettius affair with its alleged plot to assassinate Pompeius.[168] He served under C. Claudius Pulcher in Asia, as proquaestor or, more probably, as military tribune; he is the recipient of a number of letters from Cicero during this time.[169] Caelius reported to Cicero at the time of Curio's election to the tribunate that he was announcing himself as a supporter of the *boni* (good men); by the summer of 51, that meant, in turn, opposition to Caesar.[170] His initial proposals bore out Caelius' predictions: some attempt to alter Caesar's Campanian land law and a measure to reduce expenditure by officials whilst travelling.[171] This initial phase also included more personal aims, with an attempt to have his cousin Memmius recalled

164. App. *B Civ.* 2.26 is, however, probably an exaggeration; C. Marcellus was closely aligned with his cousin M. Marcellus, but the evidence for Lepidus' hostility to Caesar is less strong (a threat to prosecute Vatinius some years earlier).

165. T. P. Wiseman, 'Rome and the resplendent Aemilii', in H. Jocelyn, ed., *Tria Lustra: Essays and Notes Presented to John Pinsent*, Liverpool: Liverpool Classical Monthly 1993, 181–9.2.

166. Cic. *Fam.* 8.4.2.

167. Vell. Pat. 2.48.

168. The younger Curio's date of birth is usually placed in 84 BC; W. McDermott, 'Curio *pater* and Cicero', *AJPh* 93, 1972, 381–411, at 387, notes a difficulty with this, suggest-ing 82 – in which case Curio would not have been quaestor in 54.

169. Cic. *Fam.* 2.1–6.

170. An index of the complexity of networks is that Marcus Antonius was among those whom Caelius identifies as opponents to Curio's tribunate: this is that same Marcus Antonius who – so Cicero tells us – used to climb through the roof tiles to visit Curio: *Phil.* 2.44–6.

171. Campanian land: Cic. *Fam.* 8.10.4; travel, Cic. *Att.* 6.1.25. This latter measure indicates the care needed in labelling policies, in so far as it can be paralleled in the legis-lation of both Clodius and Cato.

from exile. But there were no fireworks, and Caelius could, in February 50, describe his tenure of office as 'utterly congealed'. But at the end of the letter in which that phrase occurs, Caelius noted a sudden change:

> As to what I said above about Curio's total frost – he's warmed up now – being torn apart blazingly. On a total whim, because he didn't get his way about intercalation, he's gone over to the people and begun to speak for Caesar and boast about a road law, not unlike Rullus' agrarian one, and a corn law, which instructs the aediles to make distributions; he hadn't yet done this when I wrote the earlier part of the letter.[172]

It seems likely that an intervention in foreign affairs, a proposal to annex the kingdom of Juba, belongs to this second phase. Caelius' wording shows that Curio's shift included his espousal of the popular cause: if so, he cannot have been using a popular legislative programme as a reason for demand an intercalary month. The idea that Curio's shift was the result of a bribe from Caesar is prevalent in later ancient sources, but not considered by Caelius or Cicero at the time, even though Caelius regards Curio as an ally of Caesar after his change of direction.[173] Curio's actions are better seen as the result of his calculation of his own political interests, and a desire not to waste the opportunities offered by the tribunate. He remained, throughout this year, an independent figure; and in his dealings with Caesar, he appears less as a supporter and more as someone trying to prevent Caesar from renewing co-operation with Pompeius, which might have restricted his own ambitions. At any rate, from the spring of 50 he worked consistently to keep Pompeius and Caesar apart, attacking Pompeius whilst claiming to speak and act for Caesar. A crucial element in this strategy was his call for Pompeius to give up his army at the same time as Caesar did: this was hugely popular and very unwelcome to Pompeius, whose *imperium*, extended in 52, undoubtedly had a later end date than Caesar's, and who was attempting to remain the arbiter of what Caesar could and could not do.[174] Hindsight, reinforced by Curio's

172. Cic. *Fam.* 8.6.5.

173. Cic. *Fam.* 8.11.2, reporting a conversation between Curio and Cornelius Balbus, who rebuked Curio, questioning his *fides* towards Caesar. The grounds of this were Curio's opposition to Cicero's request for a *supplicatio*, which Balbus claimed was against Caesar's interests; a useful reminder of Caesar's desire to keep on good terms with everyone that he could.

174. Gruen, *Last Generation*, 470–83; Seager, *Pompey*, 144. Pompeius accused Curio of promoting quarrels between him and Caesar (Cic. *Fam.* 8.11.3).

adherence to Caesar during the civil war, is responsible for the idea that he was a Caesarian partisan throughout the year. A better model for understanding Curio is Clodius (whose widow Curio had now married); extensive *popularis* legislation and a recognition that unity between Pompeius and Caesar was inimical to that end. As the results of the consular elections for this year showed, Roman politics were not exclusively composed of Pompeians and Caesarians, and civil war was not regarded as inevitable at the start of 50. It emerged, rather, as an unexpected and unwelcome prospect, onto a stage occupied by men busy pursuing their own interests.

By late spring of 50, Pompeius had declared himself in favour of an end date for Caesar's command – 13 November 50. That implied that Caesar should stand for election as consul, using his *ratio absentis*, that year; the date may even have been chosen to fit with a subsequent journey back to Rome, preparation and celebration of a triumph before taking office on 1 January 49. That would have given Caesar what he claimed to want, though on Pompeius' terms.[175] But Caesar, though his campaigning in Gaul was extremely low-key, and consistent with immediate departure, did not stand for the consulship that summer. This was a crucial decision, putting him for the first time directly at odds with Pompeius' public position, signalling that the *ratio absentis* might not serve as the device to integrate him back into Roman political life; raising the question, in turn, of what might fulfil that function.

This decision of Caesar's has received remarkably little attention in discussions of the outbreak of civil war, merely noted as a peculiarity.[176] One explanation offered is the candidacy that year of Ser.

175. Caelius observes in the letter (Cic. *Fam.* 8.11) which records the Ides of November date: 'This is the stage set of the whole affair: Pompeius, as if he is not attacking Caesar but arranging for him what he thinks fair, says that Curio is stirring up trouble; but he really doesn't want Caesar to be consul-elect before he has handed over his army and province, and openly fears that' (*scaena rei totius haec: Pompeius, tamquam Caesarem non impugnet sed quod illi aequum putet constituat, ait Curionem quaerere discordias; ualde autem non uult et plane timet Caesarem consulem designatum prius quam exercitum et prouinciam tradiderit*). It is easiest to read *ualde* onwards as Caelius' interpretation of what is going on rather than something which Pompeius was openly saying; he is warning Cicero of potential trouble ahead. Pompeius' public behaviour and statements in early summer of 50 were consistent with his expecting Caesar to stand for election that year and give up his province as *consul designatus*.
176. Gruen, *Last Generation*, 477, 'Caesar evidently chose not to run in the elections of that [sc. 50] year. The reason, unfortunately, eludes us'; R. Morstein-Marx ('Caesar's alleged fear of prosecution and his *ratio absentis*', *Historia* 56, 2007, 159–78, at 173) notes the importance of the decision, and sees here Caesar's fears about his opponents' capacity to block his election.

Sulpicius Galba, a former legate of Caesar: given that two patricians could not be elected to the consulship, Caesar may have stood aside in favour of his friend.[177] This may or may not seem plausible; what is implausible, surely, is that Caesar made his decision, for whatever reason, without realising its effect on Rome, and on Pompeius. It was a declaration that Caesar was not prepared to re-enter domestic politics on Pompeius' terms.

The consuls elected for 49 were hostile to Caesar, and they and Pompeius moved to a position of close co-operation.[178] Censors were elected, as well; one was Caesar's father-in-law Piso, the other Appius Claudius, who began a vigorous programme of senatorial expulsions. The extent to which these were directly partisan is unclear (he did try to expel Curio, though was prevented by Piso), but unsurprisingly many of the expelled are found on Caesar's side. Among the tribunes-elect was Caesar's legate and former quaestor M. Antonius, whose election to the augurate Caesar had also secured that summer, though there were others likely to be hostile.[179] By late autumn, it was obvious that Caesar was not about to give up his command. In a senatorial debate at the beginning of December, Pompeius had majority support: a proposal that he should give up his army was defeated, whereas the same on Caesar passed. But a proposal that both Pompeius and Caesar should give up their commands passed at this meeting by 370 votes to 22.[180] This situation was unacceptable to Pompeius: he was no longer prepared to negotiate and he moved to take charge of forces in Italy. With war apparently now unavoidable, the new consuls, on taking office, were able to convince the Senate to pass resolutions against Caesar: the end to his *ratio absentis* and the appointment of a successor. Those tribunes who supported Caesar attempted to veto this; but the Senate passed the decree instructing the consuls to see no harm came

177. Galba was defeated, an outcome which Hirtius (*B Gall.* 8.50) claims was a result of his closeness to Caesar; by now, after the civil war, the 'official version' is that Caesar was planning to stand in 49 for 48.
178. They were Spinther's brother Lentulus Crus and a third Marcellus, brother of the consul of 51; they were not an inspiring pair (Cic. *Att.* 8.15.2, in March 49: 'I pay no attention to the consuls, who are more unstable than a feather or a leaf') and given the long interval since Crus' praetorship (in 58) it is tempting to wonder whether he – a patrician – was not pushed forward as a specifically anti-Galba candidate.
179. Six tribunes are known for the year; Q. Longinus was a supporter (Cic. *Att.* 6.8.2), the rest hostile. The same letter of Cicero claims three supporters of Caesar among the praetors-elect, though his information is not perfect (he assumes that the heavily indebted Crus will support Caesar).
180. App. *B Civ.* 2.118.

to the state, and the vetoes were ignored. The tribunes' departure from Rome for Caesar's camp then became the proximate cause of the war.

The civil war

Caesar crossed from Cisalpine Gaul into Italy in January 49 with three legions; a further seven remained on the other side of the Alps under the command of Trebonius.[181] He was opposed by a number of *imperium*-holders in Italy, including Pompeius; the new consuls, C. Claudius Marcellus and L. Cornelius Lentulus Crus; L. Domitius Ahenobarbus, who had been given the command in Transalpine Gaul in succession to Caesar; and Cicero, still retaining his Cilician *imperium*. Pompeius was, in practice, orchestrator of the military opposition to Caesar, but he had no formal position from which to do so: inserts in Cicero's letters show him simply requesting Cicero's co-operation.[182] The consuls joined his forces, but Cicero dithered in Campania, hoping that he might be able to mediate peace; and Domitius Ahenobarbus ignored Pompeius entirely by occupying Corfinium and levying troops for his command in Gaul.

Caesar quickly captured Corfinium and released Ahenobarbus and his officers unharmed and unransomed, demonstrating that his victories would be accompanied by mercy. But, with this exception, there was no fighting at this point in Italy, since Pompeius decided to move the conflict from Italy to Greece. His motives, and the time at which he made this decision, are not entirely clear; but the example of Sulla may well have been powerful, and Pompeius could reflect on the infinitely greater resources which he could access in the eastern Mediterranean as a result of his conquests in the 60s than those which Sulla had had at his disposal. The position of Caesar's opponents in Italy, by contrast, was not strong: Pompeius' most experienced troops were the two legions he had reclaimed from Caesar the previous year, which he was understandably reluctant to rely on against Caesar, and Caesar himself had moved with unexpected speed to establish himself in central Italy.[183] By exiting from Italy,

181. The main source for the war is Caesar's own account in his *Bellum Civile*, a relentlessly tendentious account which appears nonetheless to be accurate in most of its factual statements: see further K. Raaflaub, '*Bellum Civile*', in Griffin, *Companion to Julius Caesar*, 175–91.
182. Cic. *Att.* 8.11A, 8.11C; Cicero was not impressed by the tone of these letters, referring to their *neglegentia* (off-handedness) (*Att.* 8.11.6).
183. Seager, *Pompey*, 152–60.

Pompeius hoped to regain the initiative and dictate to Caesar where and when the decisive stages of the conflict would take place. He marched to Brundisium, whence he began shipping his forces across the Adriatic. His strategy succeeded: Caesar was delayed in his pursuit at Corfinium, and as a result he was unable to blockade the harbour at Brundisium sufficiently fast to prevent Pompeius' departure with all his forces.

Without ships, Caesar was unable, as yet, to follow, and instead turned his attention to securing the western part of the Mediterranean. He sent legates to seize Sardinia and Sicily; the senatorially appointed governors of those provinces fled to Africa. Here, Attius Varus was in control, having recently escaped from Caesar's forces at Auximum; he had been governor of Africa a few years earlier and persuaded the legate Ligarius, left in charge by the previous governor Considius, to co-operate with him. Attius refused to hand over the province to the incoming governor Tubero (who then left for Pompeius' forces) and subsequently resisted Curio, who followed up his seizure of Sicily on behalf of Caesar with a failed invasion of Africa.[184]

Caesar himself was concentrating on Spain, which was at this point firmly in the Pompeian camp after five years of Pompeius' proconsulship; his legates, L. Afranius, M. Petreius and Terentius Varro, held both provinces with seven legions between them. Before setting out, Caesar paused briefly in Rome and spoke to a meeting of the Senate on 1 April. According to his account, he expressed his willingness to negotiate with Pompeius, but no envoys could be found, because Pompeius had indicated that he would regard any senator who remained in Rome as a supporter of Caesar.[185] He refers elliptically at this point in his *Bellum Civile* also to obstruction from the tribune Metellus; we know from elsewhere that Metellus' obstruction consisted in refusing Caesar access to the treasury and its emergency reserves. Caesar's unwillingness to overrule Metellus at this point is striking.

Caesar detoured on his way to Spain via Massilia, which refused him access; he represents the city as seeking to maintain its neutrality, but Domitius took the city as his base once he arrived to assume command of his province of Transalpine Gaul. Caesar left legates and troops for a seige by land and sea and proceeded to Nearer

184. Caes. *B Civ.* 1.30–1; Cic. *Lig.* 2–3.
185. Caes. *B Civ.* 1.32–3.

Spain to face Afranius and Petreius. After indecisive fighting at
Ilerda, Caesar outmanoeuvred his opponents as they retreated south-
westwards and induced their surrender. He then moved against
Terentius Varro, who held Further Spain with two legions as a legate
of Pompeius; one of Varro's legions deserted and he negotiated his
surrender. Caesar himself then marched back to Italy, pausing briefly
to accept the surrender of Massilia, and reached Rome in December
49 BC. He had already been appointed dictator (by one of the
praetors, Aemilius Lepidus, after the Senate had passed an enabling
law) and now presided over the elections for 48, in which he was
elected consul alongside Servilius Isauricus, and the Latin festival.
This took 11 days; he then set out for Brundisium.

Pompeius had initially established his winter quarters at Thessalonica, and at some point during the winter of 49–48 was entrusted
with overall charge of the conduct of the war. The coalition facing
Caesar in the eastern Mediterranean was broad. Its *imperium*-
holders included Pompeius' father-in-law, Metellus Pius Scipio, who
had received Syria as his province in succession to Bibulus, and
brought his troops to join Pompeius'; Bibulus, whom Pompeius had
placed in charge of the fleet on his return from Syria; C. Claudius
Marcellus, the consul of 49, who was jointly in charge of the fleet at
Rhodes; the other consul of 49, Lentulus Crus; L. Domitius Ahenobarbus, who had escaped from Massilia shortly before its fall and
made his way east; the younger Cato, who had abandoned his
province of Sicily the previous year in the face of Caesarian forces;
Cicero, who had eventually left Italy; and three of the praetors of
49.[186] The senatorial side had an overwhelming advantage in terms
of *imperium*-holders, with all that that implied in terms of legitimacy, and it is clear from Cicero's letters during the early months of
the campaign that these considerations were important in Pompeius'
planning and that of his allies.[187] A large number of other senators

186. *MRR* 2.275–8; Rawson, *Cicero*, 194–201.
187. Cicero's argument later, against Marcus Antonius, that Pompeius' Senate was
legitimate included the claim that it included ten consulars (*Phil.* 13.28): these are listed
as Afranius (cos. 60), Bibulus (59), Lentulus Spinther (57), Domitius Ahenobarbus and
Appius Claudius (54), Metellus Scipio (52), Ser. Sulpicius Rufus and M. Marcellus (51)
and Lentulus Crus and C. Claudius Marcellus (49). On the particular difficulties raised
by the allegiances of the consuls of 51, see D. R. S. Bailey, 'The Roman nobility in the
second civil war', *CQ* 10 (1960), 253–67. Caesar had only three or perhaps four
supporters of consular rank: Gabinius (58), Domitius Calvinus and Valerius Rufus (53)
fought for Caesar: Gabinius certainly and Calvinus possibly were recalled from exile by
Caesar. The remaining consulars – M. Perperna (cos. 92; he died in the spring of 49),

had also come east: Dio records 200 in Thessalonica that winter, with formal mechanisms of government, including space marked out for the taking of auguries.[188] Among these senators was M. Brutus, who chose the senatorial side despite his enmity with Pompeius, who had executed Brutus' father in 77 BC in the aftermath of Lepidus' uprising. Concern with constitutional propriety marked the handling of the important formal shift on 1 January, when magistrates became promagistrates, and there were no new elected officials.[189] The Senate prorogued; clearly there was no hesitation among Caesar's opponents in regarding themselves as forming a legitimate Senate. But recreating the Roman people outside Rome was, apparently, not possible. The move from consuls to proconsuls may have facilitated a decision by the Senate's military commanders to entrust Pompeius with overall authority in the campaign.[190] Pompeius' connections in the eastern Mediterranean enabled him to supplement extensively the forces he had brought from Italy.[191]

Caesar managed to ship his forces over the Adriatic early in 48, ahead of the expectations of his opponents: he evaded the naval blockade which Bibulus was running, and took control of the towns of Oricum and Apollonia. Pompeius marched to meet him, and after an inconclusive encounter near the river Apsus, Pompeius retreated towards Dyrrachium, where he was besieged by Caesar. After some weeks of skirmishing, Pompeius inflicted a defeat on Caesar's forces, and Caesar, also suffering shortages of supplies, retreated south-eastwards into Thessaly. He joined his legate Domitius Calvinus, who had been skirmishing with Metellus Scipio, and having sacked Gomphi he based himself in the Thessalian plain. Pompeius followed, joined up with Metellus Scipio, and on 9 August 48 the two sides fought near Pharsalus: the senatorial side had around twice as many troops as Caesar, with a notable advantage in cavalry. Nonetheless, Caesar was victorious, and captured Pompeius' camp; Pompeius fled first to Larisa, and thence to Mytilene, where he was joined by his wife Cornelia.[192] He chose Egypt as the safest place

L. Aurelius Cotta (65), L. Iulius Caesar (64), C. Antonius (63), L. Calpurnius Piso (58), L. Marcius Philippus (56), C. Marcellus (cos. 50) and L. Aemilius Lepidus Paullus (cos. 50) – were neutral. In some cases relationship to Caesar may explain their stance.
188. Cass. Dio 41.43.2.
189. Cass. Dio 41.43.1–4.
190. Caes. B Civ. 3.16.4; cf. Luc. 5.44–9.
191. Caes. B Civ. 3.4–5.
192. Accounts of the campaign include Caes. B Civ. 3.85–99; Vell. Pat. 2.52; App. B Civ. 2.65–82; Plut. Pomp. 66–72; Caes. 43–6; Luc. 7; Cass. Dio 41.53–61.

to regroup: Ptolemy Auletes' son Ptolemy XIII was now monarch alongside his sister Cleopatra (VII), and Pompeius hoped that his earlier support for the father would pay dividends now. It did not: the Egyptians were afraid that support for Pompeius would lead them into war with Caesar, which they would lose, and Pompeius was assassinated on arrival.[193]

The battle of Pharsalus and Pompeius' death became iconic moments in the narrative of the civil war, turning points in what turned out to be a process of transition from republican government to monarchy.[194] For contemporaries, the first challenge posed by Pharsalus was to explain how Pompeius the Great, with his superior forces, had been defeated, and then to find a place for the outcome in the evolving story of the civil war. Cicero, reflecting in 46 – after he had been pardoned by Caesar and returned to Rome – on his decision to join Pompeius and the course of the campaign, identified the poor quality of Pompeius' troops, and Pompeius' overconfidence, deriving from his success at Dyrrachium, as the key factors:

> I regret my action not so much because of the danger it brought but because of the many faults which I encountered there: first, forces which were neither large nor war-like; then, apart from our leader and a few others – I am talking of the leading men – the rest were rapacious in war, and so cruel in their words that I shivered even at the thought of our victory; the debts of our most distinguished men were enormous. Well? Nothing good except the cause. When I saw this, I gave up hope of victory and at first began to push peace – for which I had always been an advocate; then, since Pompeius was entirely unsympathetic to that view, I began to urge him to slow down the war. He supported this sometimes, and seemed likely to favour that view, and perhaps would have done, if he had not begun to trust his soldiers after one particular fight. From that time onwards, that great man was no commander; he set recruits and a motley army to fight crack troops; defeated, he abandoned even his camp, shamefully, and fled alone.[195]

Cicero was himself not present at Pharsalus, and is not perhaps the most reliable military analyst, particularly in self-exculpatory mode; moreover, alongside his criticism of the other Pompeians we should

193. Caes. B Civ. 3.103–4; Vell. Pat. 2.53; Luc. 8.472–872; App. B Civ. 2.83–6; Plut. Pomp. 77–80.
194. On the important part played by Asinius Pollio in this process, see L. Morgan, 'The autopsy of C. Asinius Pollio', JRS 90, 2000, 51–69.
195. Cic. Fam. 7.3.2.

set the tradition, represented most clearly in Plutarch's biography, that Cicero himself did little to contribute to the harmony of his side.[196] Caesar uses a similar explanatory framework. The Pompeian side was deluded by their success near Dyrrachium: they no longer considered the *ratio belli*, the plan of campaign, and regarded themselves as already the victors.[197] Pompeius was forced to offer battle because he was under pressure from his own side; the impression of bad advice and weak leadership is underscored by the speech (*B Civ.* 3.87) given to Caesar's former legate Labienus, who had joined the senatorial side. He refers to his own experience in order to decry the quality of Caesar's forces, and is shortly to be shown to be entirely wrong. Caesar also presents the overconfidence of his opponents through the squabbles which arose among them, particularly those between Spinther, Domitius Ahenobarbus and Scipio over who would be the next *pontifex maximus* once Caesar was gone. 'In short, everyone was engaged in seeking office, financial rewards, or pursuing private enmities; their thought was not of the plans which might give them success, but how they would make use of victory.'[198] Caesar's apparent objectivity serves the presentation of Pompeius as a man succumbing to a single, fatal error, in seeking a pitched battle, and let down by his followers, who failed to apply reason to the problem in front of them and were pursuing ignoble private ends.

The value to the survivors – whichever side they had fought on – of an account which centred the dead Pompeius and ascribed blame to other senior Pompeians is understandable. Nonetheless, there may be some truth in the picture of Pompeius forced into a poor decision through pressure from senior figures in his army. Whether or not his *imperium* had been formally recognised as greater in some way at the point when the other *imperium*-holders acknowledged his authority, it nonetheless remained the case in practice that he commanded a coalition constantly vulnerable to dissension, and within which his own authoritative position provoked disquiet.[199] With his departure for Egypt, the senatorial forces faced a crisis of leadership. Cato, who had been left in charge at Dyrrachium, responded to the news by asking Cicero, as the senior *imperium*-holder, to take command; Cicero refused, so incensing Pompeius' elder son that

196. Plut. *Cic.* 38.2–6.
197. Caes. *B Civ.* 3.72.1.
198. Caes. *B Civ.* 3.83.4.
199. See e.g. Plut. *Pomp.* 67.2–5.

Cato had difficulty in preventing his murder.[200] Cicero returned
to Italy soon after, and took no further part in the war. Cato took
the command, and set out to join Pompeius; when he heard of
Pompeius' death, he moved on to Africa. As events turned out, only
two of Cicero's ten consulars, Metellus Scipio and Afranius, continued the fight after Pharsalus. Bibulus, Appius Claudius and –
probably – Gaius Marcellus were dead, of natural causes, before the
battle; Domitius Ahenobarbus died in it; Lentulus Crus was captured
with Pompeius in Egypt, and executed shortly afterwards; his
brother Spinther also died soon after Pharsalus. Sulpicius Rufus and
Marcus Marcellus, like Cicero, gave up on the war.[201]

Caesar pursued Pompeius to Egypt and there became involved
in a civil war between the siblings Ptolemy XIII and Cleopatra VII;
after defeating the forces of Ptolemy (who drowned during battle)
and securing Alexandria, he re-established Cleopatra as ruler alongside her other brother, Ptolemy XIV. He remained in Egypt well into
47, some months after the end of the fighting; the interval fuelled
ancient, and modern, speculation about his relationship with
Cleopatra, and it may be significant that the author of the *Bellum
Alexandrinum* draws a discreet veil.[202] But the situation in Egypt
was complex, and the conventions of Hellenistic diplomacy time-
consuming. Nor did Caesar return directly to Rome, despite serious
unrest there.[203] He went first to Syria, and then north towards
Pontus, which Mithridates' son, Pharnaces, had recently seized, after
defeating Roman forces under Domitius Calvinus at Nicopolis.
Caesar's success in battle against him at Zela in August 47 became
proverbial for its speed and reinscribed a site of Roman defeat with
a splendid victory; it also left Caesar free to return to Rome.[204]

Although there had not been any serious fighting in Italy, the civil
war was having a deleterious effect on the economy and stability
of the peninsula. High levels of indebtedness continued to be a
source of discontent. In 48, one of the praetors, Caelius, proposed

200. Plut. *Cic.* 39.1–2.
201. Sulpicius went to Samos; Caesar pardoned him and made him governor of Achaea
in 46; Marcellus retreated to Mytilene, whence he was unexpectedly permitted by Caesar,
in 46, to return to Rome, a decision which Cicero greeted with *Pro Marcello*. Marcellus
was murdered at the Piraeus as he returned (*Fam.* 4.12).
202. *B Alex.* 33.5
203. The author of the *B Alex.* has Caesar finding out about these difficulties only once
arrived in Syria and carefully explains why he nonetheless could not return immediately
(65).
204. *B Alex.* 72–3 stresses Triarius' defeat as he sets the scene for Caesar's success.

suspending the payment of interest and rents; this brought him into conflict with other magistrates, and after he attacked the urban praetor Trebonius, the consul Servilius suspended him from office and dragged him away from the speakers' platform when he was attempting to address a public meeting.[205] Caelius then made his way south to join forces with Milo, who had returned, unrecalled, from exile at Massilia, and was re-establishing his gladiatorial band. Their attempts to raise forces using Pompeius' name came to an end, however, when Milo died during a skirmish and Caelius was killed by some of Caesar's troops based at Thurii. But Dolabella, one of the tribunes of the people of the following year (he had managed to lose his patrician status through adoption), revived legislation to abolish debts and rents; he was opposed by another tribune, Trebellius, and by Marcus Antonius, whom Caesar had appointed as master of horse. The ongoing violence at Rome over this question ceased only when Caesar reached the city in September 47.[206] Caesar was also faced with mutinous troops, complaining of their length of service, who murdered some of their officers before he was able to defuse the situation through the promise of substantial cash bonuses.[207]

These disturbances can be connected with widespread uncertainty about the source of political authority and the prospects for the future. Servilius, left as sole consul after Caesar's departure for Greece early in 48, faced sustained opposition from other magistrates, as described above. No curule magistrates were elected in 47 until after Caesar's return in the autumn; this left Marcus Antonius, master of horse to Caesar's dictator, as the most senior figure in Rome during most of the year. There was, unsurprisingly, great anxiety among senators in Rome to respond appropriately to the developing situation; and financial pressures among the population more generally fuelled outbursts of violence. And after news of Pharsalus arrived, Caesar's followers began to confiscate Pompeian properties.

To a certain extent Caesar's safe return to Italy was alone suffi-cient to restore order. He supplemented that with moderate measures on debt relief and rent remission which restored a degree of financial stability, and he forced his associates to pay something in return for

205. Caes. B Civ. 3.20–1; Cass. Dio 42.22–4.
206. Cass. Dio 42.30.
207. Plut. Caes. 51 identifies two ex-praetors as the victims; Dio (42.52.2–55.4) has the mutineers almost killing Sallust (cf. App. B Civ. 2.92–4) and then rampaging towards Rome, killing two unnamed senators en route.

the property they had seized. He also oversaw the election of magistrates. But more systematic activity had to wait: by December he had set out again from Rome and on the 17th reached Lilybaeum in Sicily, the crossing point for Africa. The senatorial forces who had chosen to continue armed opposition to Caesar had established themselves there: Attius Varus, who had seized control of Roman-administered territory at the start of the war, accepted Cato's advice and handed over authority to Scipio. Labienus, Afranius, Sulla's son Faustus and Cato, who was in charge of Utica, were also with Scipio's forces. So too were Pompeius' two sons. The elder, Gnaeus Pompeius, had commanded part of Pompeius' fleet during the Pharsalus campaign, but had not held any elected office; Sextus had played no role so far.[208] Gnaeus was soon sent to Spain, to exploit the revolt against Caesar which the unpopularity of Q. Cassius Longinus, who had been left in charge of Further Spain, had provoked. The younger Pompeius' value lay in his father's identity. He had no constitutional position to justify the command he took on in Spain, and we can see here an early example of the dynastic principle at work, superseding a system in which authority derives ultimately from the people.

Caesar's forces were outnumbered: Scipio had ten legions, and the support of Juba, the ruler of Numidia, who had defeated Caesar's legate Curio in 49. Caesar found unexpected support from P. Sittius, a Roman who had moved to Africa after he was exiled in 57, and subsequently gathered mercenary forces with which he served Bocchus, king of Mauretania. Sittius' activities were sufficient to prevent Juba from bringing all his forces to Scipio, and after a period of indecisive skirmishing, Caesar defeated the Pompeians at Thapsus in April 46. Cato committed suicide, as did Juba and Scipio, and Afranius and Faustus were captured by Sittius and killed shortly afterwards. Labienus, however, escaped to Spain, taking with him four of Afranius' legions; so did Pompeius' younger son Sextus.

208. Pompeius' marriage to Mucia followed his brief marriage to Aemilia, itself a consequence of Sulla's return to Italy; and it is unlikely that the younger Gnaeus was born before 79 (if he had been, why was he not a quaestor in 49?). Pompeius left for Spain in 77, returning in 71; it is probable that Sextus was born after this interval, since otherwise it is difficult to explain why he sat out the Pharsalus campaign on Mytilene with his stepmother Cornelia. Their sister Pompeia was probably also born after Pompeius' return from Spain; if born in 70, she would have been just old enough to be betrothed in 59, when she became involved in the negotiations over a marriage alliance between Caesar and Pompeius; if her conception predated Pompeius' Spanish command, it is odd that she was not yet married in 59.

The tally of deaths at the end of this African campaign gave it a myth-making potential only a little less than that of Pharsalus itself. The anonymous author of the *Bellum Africanum* records Scipio's cruelty (46) and un-Roman subordination to the odious Juba (57), and Scipio's promise of Roman Africa to Juba may be a Caesarian fabrication;[209] but Scipio's dying words survived as an example of Republican nobility.[210] And Cato's suicide at Utica after the battle of Thapsus transformed him into a potent symbol of resistance to Caesar, who was moved by the laudations of Cato which Cicero, Brutus and Fabius Gallus wrote to disseminate his own *AntiCato*.[211]

Caesar returned to Rome during the summer of 46 and soon signalled that one phase of the civil war had come to an end by celebrating a quadruple triumph, over Gaul, Egypt, Pontus and Africa. Anecdotes attest to the magnificence of the celebrations, and its scale, recording *four* campaigns, firmly transcended Pompeius' triple triumph of 61. Cicero responded to the possibility of a new start in his senatorial speech *Pro Marcello*, an impromptu response to Caesar's unexpected agreement that the Pompeian Marcus Marcellus, consul in 51, could return to Rome. In the version that Cicero disseminated, which may well closely resemble his remarks in the Senate, he urges Caesar to turn his attention now to pressing domestic issues: the legal situation, financial credit, conspicuous consumption and the birth rate.[212] Nonetheless, there is an element of illusion in Cicero's presentation of the situation; Caesarian forces were losing control of Further Spain, under pressure from those Pompeians who had survived Thapsus, and Sex. Julius Caesar, whom Caesar had left in charge of Syria, was killed after his troops defected to the command of Caecilius Bassus, a Pompeian supporter.[213] Bassus captured Apamea and successfully resisted the next Caesarian commander (helped by the arrival of the Parthians)

---

209. Cass. Dio 43.4.
210. *Imperator se bene habet* ('The commander is well'): Livy, *Per.* 114, Val. Max. 3.2.13, Sen. *Suas.* 6.2, *Ep.* 24.9–11.
211. R. Fehrle, *Cato Uticensis*, Darmstadt : Wissenschaftliche Buchgesellschaft 1983; R. Goar, *The Legend of Cato Uticensis from the First Century B.C. to the Fifth Century A.D.*, Brussels: Latomus 1987.
212. Cic. *Marc.* 23.
213. Livy, *Per.* 114; Joseph *AJ* 14.160–80; A. Coşkun, '"Amicitiae" und politische Ambitionen im Kontext der "causa Deiotariana" (45 v. Chr.)', in A. Coşkun, ed., *Roms auswärtige Freunde in der späten Republik und frühen Prinzipat*, Göttingen: Duehrkohp & Radicke 2005, 127–54.

Figure 6 Caesar: a portrait in the Castello d'Aglie in Turin

until well after Caesar's assassination. The Roman world had not yet universally acknowledged Caesar's victory.

To a certain extent, Caesar did begin to address the question of what a post-civil war *res publica* might look like in the second half of 46 and again after his return from Spain in the autumn of 45.[214] But his measures are surprisingly poorly documented in contemporary sources: and since Cicero's correspondence from the period is fairly extensive, the argument from silence, despite his semi-retirement, has some validity. Caesar's measures were not such as to provoke much comment from Cicero.

There were increases in the number of magistracies, an essential change given the number of discrete overseas commands and Caesar's ruling that praetorian governors should hold office for one year only.[215] It shows that Caesar regarded his ad hoc employment of whoever happened to be at hand during the civil war as a temporary expedient, and that he was intending to re-establish the basic framework of administration; his intentions, however, for the Senate are less clear. Its size would now gradually double with the influx of ex-quaestors, and in the meantime it had been greatly increased by adscription. Augustus would decide to impose a radical cull on its membership, as well as returning to an annual total of 20 quaestors.

214. J. Gardner, 'The dictator' in Griffin, *Companion to Julius Caesar*, 57–71.
215. There were to be 40 quaestors, 6 aediles and 16 praetors; Cic. *Phil.* 1.19; Cass. Dio 43.25.

Moreover, the aspirations towards orderly government via elected magistrates which these changes indicate were not quite fulfilled in practice. The consuls of 47 were elected only late in that year. Elections were held in due time for 46, but Caesar's tenure of the consulship – his third – was irregular, as was his choice of another patrician, Lepidus, for the other position. In 45, Caesar was sole consul, and elections for other curule magistracies were not held until after his return from Spain in September; in October 45, Caesar resigned his consulship, and suffects were elected. His second term as dictator appears to have come to an end in the latter months of 47, and for the rest of that year the nature of Caesar's *imperium* is unclear. His third dictatorship, bestowed in 46 after the campaign in Africa, was for ten years; and he became perpetual dictator (*dictator perpetuus*) early in 44. His masters of horse had similarly extended tenures, and there was innovation, too, in the government of the city of Rome, with the use of city prefects.[216] The decline in the status of the consulship, and the collapse in the mechanisms of government more generally, are summed up for Cicero by the case of C. Caninius Rebilus, elected on the last day of December 45 to replace the suffect consul Fabius Maximus, who had died suddenly that day: he was the consul who never slept.[217] Constitutional propriety remained firmly secondary to Caesar's assessment of what needed to be done.

Other changes had more lasting effects. Caesar faced the same problem as other commanders after long campaigns had done since Marius, to find land with which to reward his veterans; he eschewed widespread confiscation and, since there was little public land left unallocated in Italy, many of his colonial foundations were overseas. Suetonius gives a figure of 80,000 settled outside Italy: not all were veterans.[218] The colonies at Carthage and Corinth are most promi-nent in the ancient sources, because of the historical resonance of the sites; but there were also settlements in Spain, after the campaign in 46-45, and in Gaul. Caesar also extended the citizenship to Cisalpine Gaul, and granted Latin status to the inhabitants of Sicily, as well as a number of grants of citizenship to individuals, and the wholesale enfranchisement of Gades in Spain. These developments took the implications of the enfranchisement of Italy and the earlier estab-lishment of colonies overseas to their logical conclusion: partici-

---

216. Gardner, 'Dictator', 57–60.
217. Cic. *Fam.* 7.30.1.
218. P. A. Brunt, *Italian Manpower, 225 B.C.–A.D. 14*, Oxford: Oxford University Press 1971, 234–65 and 589–601.

pation in the civic life of Rome itself was no longer an essential component of being a Roman citizen, and hence citizen communities could be found anywhere that was a part of the Roman *imperium*. Conversely, senators need not come from Italian communities; even if we reject the stories of trousered Gauls asking for directions to the Senate house as satirical comment, we can find, among Caesar's new recruits to the Senate, men with provincial origins.

Some of the urban poor of Rome may have been among the beneficiaries of colonial settlement. Caesar maintained the corn dole, and created two new aediles to administer it, but attempted to reform its administration by limiting the number of recipients to 150,000. He had ambitious building projects for the city, though few were started during his lifetime and none completed; but his intentions, real or alleged, in this area, gave authority to Augustus' later efforts. And he sorted out the calendar, which had, until 46, not been aligned with the sun: correspondence between the calendar and the seasons had depended upon the insertion, by the college of *pontifices*, of an extra month every other year between February and March. Since the extra time had political implications, and was not automatic, intercalation was potentially contestable; and by 46 the calendar was three months ahead of the sun. Caesar's response was two-fold: he inserted three intercalary months into 46, to ensure its end fell ten days after the winter solstice; and in 45 a new calendar started, with 365 days rather than 354 and provision for a leap year.[219]

Domestic reform was interrupted by further campaigning in Spain, where the resurgence of the Pompeians under the command of the younger Gnaeus Pompeius and Labienus demanded Caesar's presence. The campaigning which followed after Caesar's arrival towards the end of 46 was hard and culminated in the battle of Munda, where Caesar was successful, though he came very close to defeat. He celebrated his fifth triumph, after his return to Rome, in October 45; he also resigned his consulship and held elections.

The Senate honoured Caesar to an unprecedented degree in the period after his return from Spain.[220] He was marked out as distinct

---

219. The year 46 BC thus contained 445 days. A. Michels, *The Calendar of the Roman Republic*, Princeton: Princeton University Press 1967, 16–22; D. Feeney, *Caesar's Calendar: Ancient Time and the Beginnings of History*, Berkeley: University of California Press 2007, 196–211.

220. Cass. Dio 43.42–5, 44.1–11; Suet. *Iul.* 76; App. *B Civ.* 2.106; Plut. *Caes.* 57.1; Livy, *Per.* 116; J-L. Ferrary, 'À propos des pouvoirs et des honneurs décernés à César

through his appearance, which made permanent the transitory phenomenon of the triumph: he wore the clothes of a *triumphator* at all times, and his 24 lictors carried laurel wreaths.[221] In addition, special seating marked his distinctiveness at public gatherings, and statues commemorated his presence. He was uniquely inscribed into Roman religious practice, with membership of the college of augurs alongside his position as *pontifex maximus*, the renaming of the month of July in his honour, a four-yearly festival, and cult along with a dedicated *flamen*.[222] This last honour opened up the possibility of Caesar's deification, without giving that possibility clear shape. At the same time, his power came ever closer to the regal, culminating in the confirmation by the Senate of his dictatorship as a position for life in the opening weeks of 44 and followed by the events at the festival of the Lupercalia on 15 February, at which Caesar rejected the offer of a diadem.[223]

These honours are recorded in the sources as lists, overwhelming in their accumulated detail. As Lintott notes, they contribute to the picture 'of an arrogant claim to supremacy, leading to the tragic fall of an otherwise good man'.[224] Alongside their honorific potential is the suggestion that Caesar's opponents used them in an attempt to discredit him.[225] That view may represent hindsight after 15 March; but we can at least see these measures as the unstructured exploration of what Caesar's rule could and should be, in which individual opportunism combined with more serious reflection about power, stability and the future. How far Caesar himself attempted to direct these developments is unclear, and his planned departure for the eastern Mediterranean meant that the resolution of his position, in Rome, could be deferred. Continuity of government during his absence was ensured through the advance identification of magistrates for subsequent years.

entre 48 et 44', in G. Urso, ed., *Cesare: precursore o visionario? Atti del convegno internationale, Cividale del Friuli, 17–19 Settembre 2009*, Pisa: ETS 2010, 9–30.
221. Cass. Dio 44.4; Beard, *Triumph*, 275–7.
222. D. Wardle, 'Caesar and religion', in Griffin, *Companion to Julius Caesar*, 100–11.
223. Cass. Dio 44.11; Suet. *Iul.* 79; App. *B Civ.* 2. 109; Nic. Dam. 71–5; J. North, 'Caesar at the Lupercalia', *JRS* 98, 2008, 144–60; Wiseman, *Remembering*, 170–5.
224. A.Lintott,'The assassination', in Griffin, *Companion to Julius Caesar*, 72–82, at 72.
225. Cass. Dio 44.3.1.

Caesar's assassination

Caesar's imminent departure was the trigger for his assassination, by a loose but effective coalition of senators, at a meeting of the Senate on 15 March 44.[226] The conspiracy was based at the heart of Caesar's regime: its leaders were the praetors Marcus Brutus and Gaius Cassius (both pardoned Pompeians), and those involved included Decimus Brutus and Gaius Trebonius, who had fought with Caesar in Gaul in the 50s and during the civil war. Trebonius had been suffect consul in 45 and was due to depart for his province of Asia; Decimus Brutus was consul designate for 42. The close links between Caesar and the men who killed him support the tragic colouring evident in the ancient accounts of his death, and are also discernible in some modern analyses.[227]

The motives of the conspirators are, in general terms, straight-forward to grasp: they wished to eliminate Caesar because he was a tyrant. (Strikingly, personal motives do not enter the narrative: the conspirators were not Caesar's enemies.) Over the previous six months, it had become clear that Caesar intended to consolidate his position as sole ruler: the more-or-less complete end of civil war had not marked a point at which Caesar began to reduce his exceptional position. Instead, he had become *dictator perpetuus*. He had also demonstrated that he would not tolerate criticism or opposition, most strikingly in his support for the measure which deprived two of the tribunes of 44 of their powers, in response to the latter's public resistance to Caesar's explorations of the possibility of regal power.[228] And he had made it entirely obvious, through the desig-nation of magistrates for the coming years, that his departure from Rome would not lead to any diminution in his control of affairs. These moves, and his imminent departure from Rome, were enough to galvanise his opponents to seize what could reasonably be assumed as the last chance to eliminate Caesar and thus restore the

226. Listed in W. Drumann and P. Groebe, *Geschichte Roms*, vol. 3, 2nd edn, Leipzig: Borntraeger 1906, 627–42, with Lintott, 'Assassination', 77, noting Rubrius Ruga.
227. Wiseman, *Remembering*, 174–5; J. Tatum, *Always I Am Caesar*, Oxford: Black-well 2008, 145–66, emphasises the obligations of friendship; see also G. Woolf, *Et Tu Brute? The Murder of Caesar and Political Assassination*, London: Profile 2006.
228. L. Caesetius Flavus and C. Epidius Marullus: they prosecuted those who had hailed Caesar as a king, and removed a diadem from a statue of him (*MRR* 2.323). The tribunate posed an interesting challenge to Caesar; though it was inaccessible to him as an office (because of his patrician status), he had assumed its defining characteristic of *sacrosanctitas*, and sat with the tribunes at the games. Defence of tribunician rights had of course been his rallying cry at the start of the civil war in 49.

res publica. The assassination itself was carried out with great efficiency; unfortunately, the forward planning did not extend to what might happen next.[229]

229. J. S. Richardson, *Augustan Rome, 44 BC to AD 14: The Restoration of the Republic and the Establishment of Empire*, Edinburgh: Edinburgh University Press 2012, 10–19.

CHAPTER 7

Imperial expansion: novelty and success

At some point in 55 or 54, Catullus addressed a poetic message to his mistress, sending it via his *comites* (companions) Furius and Aurelius, who were to follow her

> whether she penetrates the furthest Indies, where the shore is pounded by the far-resounding dawn wave, or the Hyrcanians or soft Arabs, or the Sacae or arrow-bearing Parthians, or the sea which the seven-mouthed Nile darkens, or if she crosses the high Alps, visiting the monuments of great Caesar, the terrifying water of the Gallic Rhine and the distant Britons.[1]

This is a geography, above all, of recent Roman conquest. Catullus' *puella* (girl) has available to her the results of Pompeius' campaigns, with their astonishing opening-up of the east; Egypt and Parthia were both, at the time of writing, the focus of activity; and the detailed notice of Caesar's tremendous activity in the north provides firm chronological evidence.[2] The poem testifies to the excitement as the Roman world expanded in the last decades of the Republic, with the conquest of and imposition of direct rule on large areas and the extension of Rome's influence and indirect authority even further. At the same time, the nature of Roman *imperium* was changing: these changes, too, were linked to domestic political decisions, even though their full implications did not emerge until after the death of Caesar and well into the imperial period.

1. Catull. *Carmen* 11.2–12.
2. C. Krebs, '*Magni viri*: Caesar, Alexander and Pompey in Cat. 11', *Philologus* 152, 2008, 223–9 (noting also the invocation of Alexander); on the interpretation of *Carmen* 11 more widely, D. Konstan, 'Self, sex and empire in Catullus: the construction of a decentered identity', in V. Bécares, F. Pordomingo, R. Cortés Tovar and J. Fernández Corte, eds, *Intertextualidad en las literaturas griega y latina*, Madrid: Ediciones Clásicas 2000, 213–31; J. Dugan, '(*Non*) *bona dicta*: intertextuality between Catullus 11.16 and Cicero *De oratore* 2.222', in E. Tylawsky and C. Weiss, eds, *Essays in Honor of Gordon Williams: Twenty-Five Years at Yale*, New Haven: Henry R. Schwab 2001, 85–99.

Patterns of expansion

During the senatorial debate in 65 on the position of the king of Egypt, Cicero spoke; and fragments of his speech *De rege Alexandrino* survive.[3] It is of considerable interest for Cicero's own career: in it, the first senatorial speech which he disseminated, Cicero attempted, through his opposition to Crassus' plan for annexation, to position himself more closely with Catulus and Hortensius (whom he had opposed, the previous year, with his support for the *lex Manilia*) whilst maintaining his support for Pompeius, who would presumably not have been displeased to see Crassus' ambitions curbed. How much even the entire speech might have told us about the context of Roman foreign policy around Egypt is less clear, since this was not an area in which Cicero took much interest; what survives suggests that Cicero concentrated on attacking Crassus and arguing that his motive was personal greed. But there is also a striking use of prosopopoeia (fr. 8) where he makes Rome's *imperium* speak: 'If you don't give me something, I shall judge you an enemy; if you do, I shall judge you a friend and ally.'[4] *Imperium* here appears to refer to unified and continuous ideal of 'imperial power', though not necessarily one with a territorial basis; as such, it can speak for and on behalf of Rome and give utterance to the acquisitive tendencies of its rulers. Cicero's aim was to influence the Senate's decision-making by appealing to the moral instincts of its members and, by extension, those of the Roman state.[5] The link between personal ambition and imperial power contributed both to the extraordinary expansion of Rome in the post-Sullan period and to the disquiet with which at least some observers witnessed the phenomenon.

The final phase of Republican government involved the most significant expansion of Roman power since the end of Polybius' 53 years in 167. The excitement of the 60s and 50s needs to be understood in the context of the eight decades since 146, in which – despite many triumphs – military campaigns were often greatly extended, punctuated by frequent reverses, and productive of only relatively modest shifts in territorial power. Pompeius' conquests,

---

3. J. Crawford, *M. Tullius Cicero: The Fragmentary Speeches*, Atlanta: Scholars Press 1994, 43–56.
4. *Ego te, nisi das aliquid, hostem, si quid dederis, socium et amicum iudicabo.*
5. Crawford, *Fragmentary*, 55; on the meaning of *imperium*, J. S. Richardson, *The Language of Empire: Rome and the Idea of Empire from the Third Century BC to the Second Century AD*, Cambridge: Cambridge University Press 2008, 66–79.

building on those of Lucullus, had greatly extended Roman power to the east and south of its previous limits: Pompeius himself is said to have boasted that 'he found Asia as the furthest province and placed it at the centre of the fatherland'.[6] As a result of his campaigns, Bithynia and Cilicia, which had indeed previously been allocated as provinces, were both extended in area, and Bithynia was reorganised around 12 cities; the Seleucid dynasty's control of Syria came to an end, and it now received a Roman governor; and Pompeius secured Crete, and may have instituted regular Roman rule in Cyrene, too. The revenues of Cyprus were seized soon after, and the island governed from Cilicia. These areas of direct control under Roman governors were supplemented by new, or renegotiated, relationships with local rulers in the interior of Asia Minor and in Judaea. Caesar's campaigns during the 50s transformed the nature of Roman power in the north and west and changed it decisively from being purely Mediterranean: his conquests were fragilely rooted, but their glamorous impact at Rome through the 50s redefined its geographical scope.

Pompeius' decision to bring the Seleucid kingdom to an end and establish direct Roman rule over it brought Rome directly into contact with Parthia: there was no longer a buffer zone between the two powers. Moreover, this was surely conscious policy on Pompeius' part, supported by the allocation of two legions to the new province. Whether he had serious ambitions himself to turn his attention towards the Parthian kingdom is difficult to untangle from subsequent historiographical concern with the topic which turns Pompeius' attention covetously east.[7] But the possibility of direct conflict was now very obvious. Gabinius was exploring the possibilities when he was called away from Syria by Egyptian matters; for Crassus, his successor, war with Parthia was the whole purpose of his Syrian command. But whilst his campaign had its origins in the domestic political environment, its failure cannot be traced directly back to the conditions under which it was set up. The Parthians turned out to be too strong a power for the forces which Rome devoted to fighting them; and as a result expansion in the eastern part of the Roman empire came to an abrupt halt.[8] But their victory

6. Plin. *HN* 7.99.
7. Plut. *Pomp.* 38.4; Cass. Dio 37.7; C. Lerouge, *L'image des Parthes dans le monde gréco-romain*, Stuttgart: Steiner, 58–63.
8. On the strategic and tactical reasons for Crassus' failure, R. Sheldon, *Rome's Wars in Parthia*, Edgware: Vallentine Mitchell 2010. Marcus Antonius would try again, and

did not lead to any reduction in Rome's existing power: despite considerable fear, which we can see in Cicero's letters from Cilicia, that Syria would be attacked, nothing in fact happened.[9]

Elsewhere in the eastern Mediterranean, territorial expansion was closely linked to internal political activity. Egypt remained nominally independent, but Roman hegemony over Ptolemaic possessions was undisputed, and the acceptance, implicit or explicit at various points, that Egypt was a monarchy went alongside the extension of direct rule over Cyrene and Cyprus, both previously under Ptolemaic control. In these cases, too, annexation was only one outcome among a number of possibilities, though one adopted sooner than in the case of Egypt. Twenty years intervened between the Senate's accepting Apion's bequest of Cyrene and its sending Lentulus Marcellinus to the area in the mid-70s: there is little sign of Roman interest in the area during the years of putative freedom (despite some lurid tyrannical excesses) beyond one occasion where it appeared as a potential source of military reinforcements. Moreover, we cannot be sure that Marcellinus' job extended beyond securing revenue from the land which had belonged directly to Apion: the next attested Roman presence is only in 67, when one of Pompeius' legates, another Lentulus Marcellinus (perhaps the brother of the quaestor of the mid-70s), appears. We cannot, therefore, be sure that there was any attempt at this point to exert direct Roman control.[10] In Cyprus, similarly, Cato's task in 58 appears to have been concerned primarily with revenue rather than with territory: Clodius needed money to fund his measures, and implicating the upright Cato in his activities was a pleasing side-effect. Cyprus was then attached to Cilicia, until Caesar returned the island to Ptolemaic control in 47 BC. In the case of Cyprus, institutional inertia was overcome by a single, determined individual who had temporarily established, through his control of legislative assemblies, a method of ensuring action; moreover, the military weakness of Cyprus meant

fail, in the 30s, and the kingdom remained a perpetual stumbling block throughout the imperial period; J. S. Richardson, *Augustan Rome, 44 BC to AD 14: The Restoration of the Republic and the Establishment of Empire*, Edinburgh: Edinburgh University Press 2012, 59–63.

9. A. N. Sherwin-White, *Roman Foreign Policy in the East, 168 B.C. to A.D. 1*, London: Duckworth 1984, 290–7.

10. R. M. Kallet-Marx, *Hegemony to Empire: The Development of the Roman Imperium in the East from 148 to 62 B.C.*, Berkeley: University of California Press 1995, 364–7.

that its annexation did not require large forces or the involvement of a senior figure.

Roman dealings with Egypt were also concerned with revenue rather than rule.[11] Money featured as an alleged motive in Cicero's account of Crassus' proposal concerning Egypt in 65. Egypt's potential wealth also underpinned Cicero's argument in a passage in his second speech on the agrarian law, delivered in 63 BC.[12] The speech as a whole is tendentious in the extreme, and we should not place much trust in Cicero's argument in this passage, that Rullus and his commissioners plan to extend their reach to include Rome's eastern conquests. But the passage does show that it was plausible, in 63, to discuss Egypt, and Alexandria in particular, as though they could be considered the possession of the Roman people as a result of the will of Ptolemy Alexander: 'So – Alexandria, and the whole of Egypt: it is lurking there, it has been tucked in, it is all being secretly handed over to the commissioners; since who among you does not know that it is said that that kingdom became the property of the Roman people through the will of the Alexandrian king?'[13]

The threat of dispossession inherent in such discussion underpinned Ptolemy's increasingly lavish attempts to have himself recognised as a friend and ally of the Roman people.[14] In turn, his bribes, and the profitable opportunities generated by the loans he took out in order to offer them, made even an unannexed Egypt financially attractive to Rome. The 'Egyptian question' of 57–56 concerned the restoration of Auletes to his kingdom, not the imposition of direct Roman control; and the alternative under at least informal discussion was support for a different monarch. Ptolemaic rule was perfectly compatible with Roman profit, as the actions of Rabirius Postumus clearly demonstrate. This man – the nephew of the Rabirius prosecuted for *perduellio* in 63 – acted as intermediary with members of the Senate in both 59 and 57 when Ptolemy was borrowing money, as well as lending from his own resources; he was rewarded after Ptolemy's restoration with the position of διοικητής, state treasurer, and held the post for a year until he was driven out of Egypt because of the ferocity of his exactions. He was

---

11. Cic. *Att.* 2.16.1, noting the lack of internal sources of revenue in 59; see further W. V. Harris, *Rome's Imperial Economy: Twelve Essays*, Oxford: Oxford University Press 2011, 257–87.
12. Cic. *Leg. agr.* 38–44.
13. Cic. *Leg. agr.* 2.41.
14. See above, pp. 178–81.

subsequently tried, and acquitted, on *repetundae* charges related to
Gabinius' trial.[15] Wealthy Romans were lending money to the king
of Egypt at high rates of interest; and some of the lenders received
their loans back immediately in the form of bribes. This was a
profitable status quo, and the Roman treasury would have had no
cause to repay a deposed king's debts. When the complexity of the
financial links between Rome and Egypt are put next to Egypt's
distinctive bureaucratic organisation and the absence of a *casus belli*,
failure to impose direct rule ceases to be surprising, particularly in
the context of an understanding of power which was only slowly
acquiring a territorial flavour.[16] The evolving relationship between
Rome and Egypt demonstrates, once again, that annexation was not
an essential part of Rome's imperial activity in either conception or
execution; as well as, in the details of the 'Egyptian affair' itself
in 58–57, demonstrating how strategic thinking, let alone 'foreign
policy', could be and was subverted by chance and individual
ambition.

The situation in north-western Europe was rather different.
Caesar's conquests were in areas whose prior involvement with
Rome, and vice versa, was relatively limited, militarily, economically
and socially, and where the mechanisms of civic government, as
Rome understood them, simply did not exist. The *prouincia* of
Gallia Transalpina remained in 60 BC fundamentally what it had
been after Domitius Ahenobarbus' conquests sixty years earlier,
despite the subsequent extensive campaigns against the Cimbri and
Teutones: the land route to Spain along the Domitian road, and a
claim to obedience from the Allobroges further up the Rhone
valley.[17] It regularly received a praetorian governor, but there had
been no attempt to extend Roman power beyond this area since the
second century. But there was increasing economic involvement in
the area by Roman traders and investors. Cicero's first disseminated
speech, *Pro Quinctio*, concerns a dispute over agricultural land

15. M. Siani-Davies, *Cicero's Speech Pro Rabirio Postumo*, Oxford: Oxford University
Press 2001.
16. Richardson, *Language*, 89–91.
17. C. Goudineau, 'La Gaule Transalpine', in C. Nicolet, ed., *Rome et la conquête de la
monde mediterranéen*, Paris: Presses Universitaires de France 1978, 679–99; J. Drinkwater, *Roman Gaul: The Three Provinces 58 B.C.–260 A.D.*, London: Croom Helm 1983,
5–8; U. Hackl, 'Die Gründung der Provinz Gallia Narbonensis im Spiegel von Ciceros
Rede für Fonteius', *Historia* 37, 1988, 253–6; G. Woolf, *Becoming Roman: The Origins
of Provincial Civilisation in Gaul*, Cambridge: Cambridge University Press 1998, 24–47.
18. Cic. *Quinct*. 11–22.

owned by a partnership of two citizens in Transalpine Gaul. Its location is not specified in any more detail, but all of those involved in the business – the late C. Quinctius, his brother and heir Publius, who was Cicero's client, and Naevius – had at various points settled in Gaul, and Publius owned property at Narbo, perhaps inherited from his brother.[18] The regular journeys which punctured the acrimonious collapse of the partnership, as described by Cicero, point to the spatial interlinkedness of Rome and Transalpine Gaul (despite the ongoing civil war in Italy at the time). Twelve years later Cicero defended Fonteius on charges arising from his governship of Gaul: *Pro Fonteio* evokes a Gaul 'stuffed full of Roman business-men, full of Roman citizens. No Gaul carries out any business without a Roman citizen, no coin moves in Gaul without passing through the accounts of Roman citizens.'[19] Much was at stake in any military attack from non-Roman Gaul, quite apart from ancestral panic about Celtic invasions. The grievances of the Allobroges, which led to their seeming to Catiline to be potential collaborators in 63, came to open war in 62, and barely had that campaign been concluded by Pomptinus (who then had to wait until 54 to triumph) when attacks by the Helvetii early in 60 caused alarm in Rome, a diplomatic flurry, and the Senate's overturning of the allocations of the *lex Sempronia* to make both Gauls consular.[20] Nonetheless, Caesar's involvement north of the Alps after his consulship was not part of his original plan: that, judging by the inclusion in the *lex Vatinia* of Illyria, was to move eastwards around the head of the Adriatic into the Balkans.[21] The fortuitous death early in 59 of Metellus Celer, who had received one of the Gauls in the previous year's panic, opened the way for a shift of direction, which the Senate had confirmed. But there was no senatorial authorisation for Caesar's campaigns further north, let alone his invasion of Britain; hence Cato's attack, and

19. Cic. *Font.* 11. Cicero's picture seems convincing even though, as always, he is constructing an argument: in this case, that the volume of potential evidence makes it incredible that none can actually be produced which reveals any financial wrong-doing by Fonteius.
20. Cic. *Att.* 1.19.2. Senatorial recognition the following year of Ariovistus as king and friend must nominally have been connected, even if Caesar's receipt of a bribe was the decisive factor.
21. Strabo (7.3.11) records the emergence of the Getae at this point in strong though short-lived unity under their leader Boerebistas; this information made Illyria an attractive province for a militarily inclined proconsul and contributed to the situation which Piso faced in Macedonia.

Caesar's apparent fear of *maiestas* charges. The opposition to the military campaigns of Caesar and Pompeius from members of the Senate doubtless had in many cases an element of envy, but it was also a reaction to the extraordinary autonomy which both men exercised as they rewrote – or indeed arguably created – the map of Roman power.

The inhabitants of Rome experienced the transformative effect of conquest in intense symbolic form at the triumph, and it is surely no coincidence that Pompeius' and Caesar's imperial innovations were accompanied by relentless innovation in the form of the triumph, too.[22] Both, too, took the familiar route of building to record military success, but in ways that were novel and memorable.[23] And both ensured that their exploits were made available to Rome's reading audience. Pompeius was recorded by Theophanes, a relationship which recalled that of Alexander with his historians; Caesar became his own memorialist with his annual report in the books of the *Bellum Gallicum*. His account of his conquest of Gaul juggles the reassurance of Roman military force, order and justice with the appeal of the exotically alien.[24] In practice, Caesar's departure from Transalpine Gaul in 50 had left much unfinished. Unlike most other parts of the Roman empire, his new conquests played no part in the civil war; and substantial steps towards the establishment of Roman rule in the areas outside the old province would happen only after Caesar's death and, in the case of Britain, not for nearly a century.

The impression created by the expansion of Roman power in these decades is that a potential willingness to devote great resources to the issue sat alongside the absence of a consistent overall plan. There was an ongoing shift towards the expression of power with direct rule instead of through relationships that generated obedience; and individual profit, or the profit of particular groups, had created certain kinds of imperial relationship which were in practice hard to

22. M. Beard, *The Roman Triumph*, Cambridge, MA: Harvard University Press 2007.
23. The presentation of Pompeius' theatre as steps to his temple of Venus Victrix is a jest which points to strain over novelty.
24. L. Yarrow, *Historiography at the End of the Republic*, Oxford: Oxford University Press 2006, 54–67; A. Riggsby, *Caesar in Gaul and Rome: War in Words*, Austin: University of Texas Press 2006; on the contrast between the approaches of Pompeius and Caesar, L. Hall, 'Ratio and romanitas in the *Bellum Gallicum*', in A. Powell and K. Welch, eds, *Julius Caesar as Artful Reporter: The War Commentaries as Political Instruments*, Swansea: Classical Press of Wales 1998, 11–43.

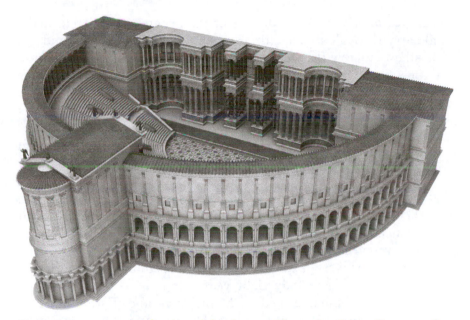

Figure 7 Computer visualisation of the theatre of Pompeius, Rome. Courtesy of Martin Blazeby for the King's Visualization Lab, King's College London

unpick. In addition, increasing use of extended tenures of *imperium* which were granted directly by the Roman people made the processes of planning more complex. Proposals developed by tribunes of the plebs and authorised by the people sat alongside senatorial decisions about the allocation of provinces and resources. The last major campaign in which popularly bestowed *imperium* was not involved was that of Lucullus; in the subsequent two decades its increasing importance contributed to a number of qualitative changes in the expression and adminstration of Roman power outside Italy.

Structures and methods of imperial conquest and government

Direct allocation of *imperium* by the Roman people emerges as an important factor in these developments: both Pompeius and Caesar made their conquests, which form the major part of Roman expansion during this period, whilst holding *imperium* through a popular law. This method of allocating command was not unprecedented; nor was it out of harmony with the people's fundamental position in the *res publica*.[25] But it did affect the Senate's capacity to make and carry through strategic decisions about foreign policy, and the 50s BC are notable for the number of occasions when the allocation of consular provinces by the Senate under the *lex Sempronia* was disrupted by subsequent tribunician legislation: it happened in 59, 58 and 55, and twice during the decade, in 57 and 55, there was also consular legislation which granted or extended *imperium*.[26] The immediate causes of this shift in the allocation of power and resources for foreign policy are closely connected with domestic politics: extended *imperium* became a political currency in which individuals' worth could be evaluated, particularly in comparison with Pompeius, through the direct support of the people. But extended commands themselves were not the product simply of popular intervention: the Senate had also been prepared to prorogue commands for very extended periods. Lucullus is an obvious example, returning to Italy eight years after the consulship which generated his command against Mithridates and Tigranes.[27] This was a response to a variety of factors: individual ambition (promoted through effective lobbying of senators), the unsuitability of annual commands for the administration of empire, and a short-age of commanders. The last seems to be a genuine feature of the post-Sullan period, paradoxically so given that Sulla increased the number of *imperium*-holding magistracies. But – for whatever reason – the increase was accompanied by a much greater readiness, by praetors and consuls, to decline the province which was offered to them.[28] The causes of the shift are not entirely clear. One may be a consequence of the tendency for magistrates to remain in Rome for most of their year of office, which meant that undertaking a province was no longer in practice integral to being an *imperium*-holding magistrate. Provincial government was perhaps becoming less attractive: the chances of a triumph following a 'normally' allocated

25. Compare, for example, Scipio Aemilianus' Carthaginian command, and direct popular intervention in overseas matters in favour of Marius.
26. *Lex Vatinia* (59), *leges Clodiae* (58), *lex Trebonia* (55); the *lex Cornelia Caecilia* (57), giving Pompeius charge of the grain supply, and the *lex Pompeia Licinia* (55), extending Caesar's command in Gaul. In 60 the panic over the Helvetii led to a senatorial revision of consular provinces under the *lex Sempronia*.
27. Though its initial identification involved some irregularity, since it was not the province allocated to him by the *lex Sempronia*. On earlier very extended commands, see above on C. Valerius Flaccus.
28. J. P. V. D. Balsdon, 'Consular provinces under the late Republic, I: general consider-ations', *JRS* 29, 1939, 57–73'; T. C. Brennan, *The Praetorship in the Roman Republic*, New York: Oxford University Press 2000, 400–2.

province were not high, and the task brought with it the danger of prosecution.[29] And some magistrates may have felt that their careers were better promoted in Rome. The result was a shortage of governors: the extension of tenures regularly beyond one year may therefore have been a response not simply to the demands of effective government, but to a constraint on the Senate's decisions, because qualified individuals could not be persuaded to undertake the task.

The potential dislocation between holding office in Rome and exercising *imperium* overseas is reflected in the *lex Pompeia de prouinciis* from 52. This measure had its origins, the previous year, in attempts to control electoral competition for the consulship, but the implications of its separation of domestic from foreign adminstration had significant implications for the latter sphere as well. The Senate was now to choose – it appears – its provincial governors from a pool of men who had held the praetorship and/or consulship, but not within the previous five years.[30] Some effects were immediately apparent: Cicero, and M. Calpurnius Bibulus – both ex-consuls, of more than five years' standing, who had declined their consular province – were dispatched to the east. There are no certain examples, between the passage of the law and the outbreak of civil war, of former praetors governing provinces after 52 before the specified interval. The sample of consuls is tiny (those who held the office in 50 and 49 found whatever plans they might have had for provincial government upset by the civil war): of the four from 52 and 51, one (Pompeius) already held proconsular *imperium*. Metellus Scipio, Sulpicius Rufus and M. Claudius Marcellus did not go to a province, though Scipio, as *priuatus*, was appointed, in the opening weeks of the civil war, as governor of Syria.[31]

29. Cicero's letter to his brother Quintus, when the latter was governor of Asia (*Q Fr.* 1.1), indicates a number of unattractive aspects to the job; we can note also Quintus' desire not to have his command extended. Can we go so far as to suggest a fundamental divergence in approaches to provincial government, between those who sought to stick to the law, and those who ignored it in the pursuit of profit? The consuls' decree in 53 (see below) suggests that this may have been the case, and if so it would be another example of political specialisation.

30. Consuls after 52 could still hope to be allocated a province immediately (so Aemilius Paullus [cos. 50] was apparently talking about a province in the weeks before he took office: Cic. *Fam.* 8.10.3; *Att.* 6.1.7), which suggests that their tenure of *imperium* was formally unaltered; but that remains compatible with a new system to allocate provinces, which did not consider consuls (as opposed to ex-consuls) as candidates.

31. Caes. *B Civ.* 1.6; that Caesar did not describe this appointment as illegal is good

Domestic office-holding did not now lead automatically, or immediately, to overseas power: the law 'furnished the first clear sign that Rome had begun to look upon provincial government as something more than an appendage to an urban magistracy'.[32] Pompeius was in a sense generalising his own career: after all, he had never held *imperium* as a direct result of being elected to a magistracy.[33] How, in practice, this system might have developed, and the consequences for how the Romans ran their empire, are a matter of speculation, because the outbreak of civil war followed so quickly. But the similarities to the system which emerged during the principate are clear.[34] The way in which commands were created underscores the ongoing and unresolved co-existence of two models of how to organise foreign affairs: the Senate continued to allocate provinces to consuls in accordance with the *lex Sempronia*, but these arrangements were liable to be overruled by subsequent legislation. Attempts by tribunes to direct foreign affairs can also be seen during the manoeuvrings over Egypt, though in the end the restoration of Ptolemy was carried out by a proconsul, Gabinius, acting without direct instructions from Rome.

There is a qualitative as well as a quantitative shift in the nature of Roman conquest in this period. The ambition, and success, harked back to the glittering years of the first half of the second century and there were strong continuities in the way such success was displayed at Rome, in terms of stuff displayed to the populace, totals of the enemy killed, and buildings created from the resources so acquired. But the expansion of empire itself in territorial form became – as Catullus indicates – the measure and criterion of military activity. Whereas the record of campaigns of the second century stressed the great opponents whom Rome defeated, that of the first was a story of new areas brought under Roman control.[35] Imperialism now became empire-building, and here too there were two locations of power. The Senate retained its expectation of managing

evidence that such an appointment had not been banned by the *lex Pompeia*, merely rendered unnecessary, in the normal course of events, by new procedures.

32. E. S. Gruen, *The Last Generation of the Roman Republic*, Berkeley: University of California Press 1974, 459.

33. He never held the praetorship, and none of his consulships was followed by a linked proconsulship; see below, pp. 239–41.

34. Richardson, *Augustan Rome*, 81–91.

35. There are surprisingly few great villains of late Republican imperialism apart from Mithridates: the pirates and Parthians are largely anonymous and Vercingetorix comes to prominence only late in Caesar's narrative.

the transition from war to peace and determining the resulting administrative structures. But Pompeius redesigned Rome's eastern empire on his own initiative, and was willing to acquiesce in Caesar's emergence as a genuine rival in order to preserve his arrangements from subsequent scrutiny or modification by the Senate.

Multiple locations of power did not only concern the Senate, its commanders and the will of the people. Decisions were increasingly being made in locations other than Rome. To a certain extent this had always been a feature of Roman *imperium*, given the slowness of communications: *imperium*-holders had discretion to act as they saw fit, with the expectation of answering for their actions on return to Rome. Increasingly, however, alternative structures of government were established, with no necessary connection to Rome. Sulla pointed the way, with his assertion of legitimate authority outside Italy. Sertorius followed suit, with what was, in effect, a Roman Spain independent of the Senate during the 70s. By the time of the civil war which started in 49, Roman power had the capacity to split and regroup across the Mediterranean, with the result that Caesar's victory required four separate campaigns, and it is only the accident of Pompeius' subsequent death which makes the battle of Pharsalus appear decisive: had he not been executed in Egypt, we should assume that he would have continued the fight from a new base. The example of a relatively obscure individual makes the case nicely: Q. Caecilius Bassus, a supporter of Pompeius, managed to secure for himself and his followers a base in Syria in the years after Pharsalus, and outlast Caesar there.

The relationships between Romans and provincials continued to be a source of frequent tension. Cicero's *repetundae* speeches are an extensive resource for this issue during the final decades of the Republic, though one which needs careful handling, since his presentation of the interests of non-Romans depends largely on whether or not he is defending. Provincials provide the opportunity for the deployment of crude but effective stereotyping which demonstrates their unfitness as witnesses and renders them unworthy of the compassion of a Roman jury, when their interests are at odds with those of Roman commanders. But in the prosecution of Verres, his abuse of provincials reinforces the case against him, though that has, as its crowning enormity, the mistreatment of citizens.[36] If these

36. J. Prag, 'The provincial perspective on the politics of *repetundae* trials', in C. Steel and H. van der Blom, eds, *Community and Communication: Oratory and Politics in Republican Rome*, Oxford: Oxford University Press, forthcoming, 265–81.

manoeuvres are too predictable a result of forensic necessity, Cicero's letters attest to his continual anxiety about the effect his actions, or those of his brother Quintus, may have on local communities.[37] Whatever the initial impulses behind the *lex Calpurnia* of 149, it, and its successors, had locked Roman officials into an uneasy dance between the demands of their fellow citizens to make money, the power which abused provincials might – in alliance with rivals at Rome – wield and, according to personal temperament and inclination, their own desires to return to Rome enriched. The weight given to non-Romans in this equation is of incalculable significance in the development of a unified Mediterranean culture during the empire. Light can also be thrown on the development of Roman imperialism by the responses it provoked among those conquered. The integration of individual intellectuals into the circles of Roman aristocrats was a practice with a long history of enthusiasm on both sides of the bargain. A wider perspective is apparent in some of the writing, predominantly in Greek, by authors whose communities had been incorporated into the Roman empire. As Yarrow has argued, Hellenistic historiography of the period shows intense intellectual effort devoted to accepting Roman rule, both through realism about the consequences of resistance and in the hope of the benefits which it might provide.[38] Some of the authors she explores are Augustan in date, and we should be cautious about extrapolating backwards; but Diodorus, writing during Caesar's dictatorship, combines interest in the intersections between Roman domestic politics and provincial experiences, and in the failings of individual Romans, with an acceptance of the reality of Roman power and the absence of alternatives.[39]

Moreover, the numbers of Roman citizens living outside Italy had exploded in the last decades of the Republic.[40] This was in part because there were now, in general, very many more Roman citizens than there had been prior to the Social War. Communities of Roman citizens had been founded across the Mediterranean in the wake of

37. E.g. Cic. *Att.* books 5 and 6 (from Cilicia).
38. Yarrow, *Historiography*.
39. The connection between imperial exploitation and unacceptable personal profit also fuelled a Roman narrative of anti-Romanness, of which Sallust's letter of Mithridates is an example (*Hist.* 4.69 M).
40. M. Crawford, 'States waiting in the wings: population distribution and the end of the Roman Republic', in L. de Ligt and S. Northwood, eds, *People, Land and Politics: Demographic Developments and the Transformation of Roman Italy, 300 BC–AD 14*, Leiden: Brill 2008, 631–43.

long military commands, supplementing the communities of citizens which had long existed in allied towns to pursue economic opportunities.[41] These settlements did not necessarily have a strong identification with Rome or its political structures, and there was little in the Sullan and post-Sullan system to encourage them to develop such beliefs. 'Roman identity' – whatever that might be – was increasingly separable from actions that could only be carried out in Rome. It is perhaps unsurprising that 'the Senate and people of Rome' was a concept which did not find enough adherents to ensure its continuing authority.

Roman imperialism in the last years of the Republic is both like and unlike what had gone before. The ambition of individual generals, the absence of an overall plan and a capacity to understand citizenship as something located far from Rome are important continuities. But there are novelties as well. The idea of Rome's destiny as a territorial world power emerged in these years; Rome was displaced as a physical point of reference; and civilian and military office began to split. It is not a coincidence that Pompeius played a major role in these developments; his transformative effect on domestic politics was similarly great.

41. Cicero's letters of recommendation (book 13 of the *Fam.* collection) offer a brilliant snapshot of the phenomenon, with correspondents and protegés scattered across the empire: H. Cotton, 'The role of Cicero's letters of recommendation: *iustitia* versus *gratia*?', *Hermes* 114, 1986, 443–60; C. Steel, *Reading Cicero: Genre and Performance in Late Republican Rome*, London: Duckworth 2005, 93–7.

CHAPTER 8

*Elite competition, popular discontent and
the failure of collective government*

Roman history in the latter part of the first century BC poses acute problems of periodisation. At one end, we can identify the year 50 as the last one in which two consuls, both eligible to stand according to Republican norms, were elected with due process, and the state's armies were not fighting one another. At the other end, 27 BC marks the point at which Caesar Octavianus assumed the name Augustus and announced the restoration of the *res publica*. Yet it is impossible to identify a single decisive moment of transition between these two radically different models of government, not least because the process of transformation, which ended up with one-man rule as Augustus constructed it, included experimentation with other forms of government, including Julius Caesar's model of one-man rule, so very different from that of his great-nephew, and the temporary division of Rome's empire into a number of competing political entities. Moreover, what a key date looks like depends on one's criteria for assessing political change. If one concentrates on structures, then the passage of the law which appointed Lepidus, Marcus Antonius and Caesar Octavianus as the three-man commission for the reconstruction of the state in November 43 BC is a good candidate for the decisive moment, when the Roman people voted to change their form of government. If, on the other hand, one tries to pinpoint the moments at which events went one way and could have gone another, then the closing weeks of 50, the battles of the civil wars, Caesar's assassination in March 44 and its immediate aftermath clearly demand attention. And, of course, choosing to set a historical break somewhere between 50 and 27 BC itself assumes that political systems are what is really important and interesting about Roman history.

This preamble is in part a warning of the number of loose ends that will remain at the end of this volume. But it also serves to introduce one of the major problems that arises in approaching these decades: what exactly is it that we are trying to explain? The issue arises too in trying to determine what is a natural starting point for the final years of Republican government. The year 70 is a candidate because the restoration of the powers of the tribunate that year can be seen as the moment when decisive elements of Sulla's model of the *res publica* are reversed – and the last major set of changes to the constitution before the end of the Republic. But that assessment of Sulla's reforms is not unchallenged; moreover, the form of government that was in place by the end of 70 was still very different from that in existence just before the Social War. Indeed, a major argument of this book is that Sulla's dictatorship marks a profound and unhealed break in Roman political life; and on this reading, the curiosity of this period of history is not the end of Republican government in 49, or 43, or 27, but its continuation, in any form, after the battle of the Colline Gate. Sulla's attempt to reshape the Roman *res publica* created a system which lasted for thirty years and even achieved its greatest degree of practical stability in its final years: but in the end it did not command sufficient assent from either people or the political elite to continue.

Even if we confine our attention to the inner circle among the elite, the years 70 to 49 look very different depending upon whose perspective we assume; contrast, for example, the experiences of Pompeius Magnus or Julius Caesar, on the one hand, absent from Rome for years at a stretch whilst engaged, successfully, in extending Rome's power, with those of Cicero, an exile in northern Greece in 58–57 and a reluctant commander in Cilicia in 51–50, but otherwise based in Rome, or of Pomponius Atticus – a friend of all three men – who, at the beginning of the period, was a voluntary expatriate in Athens, and returned to Rome during it for shorter or longer stretches of time to resume a role of confidant and money-lender which, though he eschewed the formal practice of politics entirely, nonetheless put him at the heart of elite relations.

Political culture at the end of the Republic

During his gloomily moralising account of the collapse of Republican government, the historian Velleius Paterculus paused at the moment of Augustus' birth to note the period's flourishing literary culture (2.36):

> It may seem almost unnecessary to indicate the periods of outstanding talents. Who does not know, after all, that Cicero and Hortensius flourished at this point, separated by their ages, and previously

Crassus, Cotta, Sulpicius and later Brutus, Calidius, Caelius and Calvus and, closest to Cicero, Caesar, and their pupils, Corvinus and Asinius Pollio and Thucydides' imitator Sallust and Varro and Lucretius, writers of poetry, and Catullus, second to none in the genres he undertook.

The paradox of this juxtaposition of outstanding creativity with political uproar is often noted. A detailed account of the literary developments of the period is beyond the scope of this study, but the depth of elite participation and the range of subject matter are both worth emphasising because of the part they played in creating a distinctive political culture in which texts took on a new importance.[1] One consequence is the unprecedented level of detail available for the post-Sullan period, despite huge textual losses: our ability to 'do' late Republican history in a qualitatively different fashion from the period before 82 is directly dependent on the exploration of written communication which took place then. Cicero inevitably takes a leading role in such discussions, since his works survive, unlike those of most of his contemporaries, and he seems to have pushed the potential of texts further than others.[2] But enough is known of what his contemporaries were doing to identify the ways in which Cicero's accomplishment was characteristic of the period as well as made extraordinary by the quality of his own talents.

The preservation of speeches, both forensic and deliberative, by their authors for a wider reading public went back over a century. The elder Cato seems to have been the first to exploit writing systematically and extensively to record his activities, and thus supplement the memorialising capacity of public record with an autobiographical perspective.[3] Some orators followed his example: Gaius Gracchus is a particularly prolific example. But disseminating a version of a speech after its delivery remained very distinctly a

1. D. Levene, 'The late Republican/triumviral period, 90–40 B.C.', in S. J. Harrison, ed., *A Companion to Latin Literature*, Oxford: Blackwell 2005, 31–43, is an excellent introduction; E. Rawson, *Intellectual Life in the Late Roman Republic*, London: Duckworth 1985, remains fundamental.
2. S. Butler, *The Hand of Cicero*, London: Routledge 2002; S. Kurczyk, *Cicero und die Inszenierung der eigenen Vergangenheit: Autobiograpisches Schreiben in der späten römischen Republik*, Cologne: Böhlau 2006.
3. E. Sciarrino, *Cato the Censor and the Beginnings of Latin Prose: From Poetic Translation to Elite Transcription*, Columbus: Ohio State University Press 2011; G. Marasco, ed., *Political Autobiographies and Memoirs in Antiquity: A Brill Companion*, Leiden: Brill 2011.

choice.[4] M. Antonius (cos. 99) did not publish his speeches, despite his oratorical eminence, claiming 'that he had never written down a single speech, so that he could deny having said something, if it turned out to be inconvenient to have said it'.[5] L. Crassus created few texts, none forensic.[6] When Cicero disseminated a written version of his speech on behalf of Quinctius, he was not simply announcing a new forensic talent in the relatively empty forum of 81 but also making a confident and novel claim that an audience existed for an inexperienced orator in an obscure case.[7] He proceeded to create a systematic presentation of his career, which self-consciously narrates his rise from being an outsider, bravely challenging vested interests (in *Pro Roscio Amerino* and the *Verrines*), through contional oratory (*De imperio Cn. Pompeii*) to the judicious moderator of the popular will (*De lege agraria*, *Pro Rabirio perduellionis*), as well as recording the network of obligations which his forensic defences created. It is a heavily edited account in its choice of which speeches to record.[8] Cicero wrote down only a proportion of the speeches he gave: failure or political discomfiture explain some of the silences, the tedium or triviality of the case itself, others.[9] In

4. The implication of Cic. *Brut.* 122 is that *haec turba nouorum uoluminum*, 'this flood of new books', is a new phenomenon in 46, which has led to the neglect of second-century oratory. *ORF*[4] presents the surviving fragments of Republican oratory; Cicero's *Brutus* offers a partial but illuminating history of oratory and its written record.

5. Cic. *Clu.* 140.

6. Cic. *Orat.* 132; E. Fantham, *The Roman World of Cicero's De Oratore*, Oxford: Oxford University Press 2004, 26–48.

7. How far Cicero expected an audience, since he was offering the practical counterpart to his theoretical treatment in *De inuentione*, is an intriguing though unanswered question. Curio (cos. 76) put his attack on the young Caesar into writing (Suet. *Iul.* 49, 52) and fragments seem to survive; Cicero's damning of Hortensius (*Orat.* 132) as someone 'who spoke better than they wrote' implies that at least some texts could be consulted. Cotta did not write down his speeches, according to the same passage of *Orator*, which makes the fragment preserved in Charisius (*ORF*[4] 80 fr. 17) a puzzle.

8. The extent of editing at the level of an individual speech remains highly debated: J. Powell and J. Paterson, eds, *Cicero the Advocate*, Oxford: Oxford University Press 2004, 52–7. Cicero may have introduced changes to the *Catilinarian* speeches, particularly to defend himself against the charges which arose from the conspirators' execution: *Att.* 2.1.3 attests to a collected edition of consular speeches, produced in 60, though this does not necessarily indicate substantial rewriting (A. Dyck, *Cicero: Catilinarians*, Cambridge: Cambridge University Press 2008, 10–12). The ancient reception of *Pro Milone* seems to indicate that the speech we have is a subsequent rewriting, with its section *extra causam* being entirely new: D. Berry, 'Pompey's legal knowledge – or lack of it: Cic. *Mil.* 70 and the date of *Pro Milone*', *Historia* 42, 1993, 502–4; L. Fotheringham, 'Cicero's fear: multiple readings of *Pro Milone* 1–4', MD 57, 2006, 63–83.

9. For the unpublished orations, see J. Crawford, *M. Tullius Cicero: The Lost and Unpublished Orations*, Göttingen: Vandenhoeck & Ruprecht 1984. Failure is the most

addition, the development of texts as a parallel to performances opened up the possibility of rewriting events through fictitious speeches. The second hearing of the *Verrines* was probably never delivered; the *Second Philippic* existed only as a pamphlet. With texts separable from performances, forgery was a possibility: we can note Cicero's suggestion, to Atticus, that one of his speeches, rendered embarrassing by changing political circumstances, could be dismissed as such.[10] One reason Cicero gave for publishing his speeches was the demand of learners.[11] Pedagogy is compatible with other motives, such as popularity and memorialisation, and in Cicero's case was probably subordinate to them. But attracting the emulation of the younger generation was in itself a marker of distinction. And writing was part of the apparatus of orators after Cicero.[12]

The link between oratory and a public career is obvious: opportunities for the former derived from the latter. Other elements in Cicero's literary output demonstrate less conventional connections. His poetry offers a revealing contrast between private and public.[13] The *Aratea*, the only one of his poems to survive more or less complete, seems to sit firmly within the private sphere: a translation of a popular Hellenistic didactic poem, it is an intellectual diversion.

easily traceable motive for silence: apart from *Pro Milone*, a very special case, only the (now lost) *Pro Vareno* records a speech from a case where Cicero's client is known to have been convicted. But the avoidance of triviality and the shape of Cicero's career are also factors: C. Steel, 'Cicero's autobiography: narratives of success in the pre-consular orations', *Cahiers Glotz*, forthcoming.

10. Cic. *Att.* 3.12.2. In this case, Cicero claims that the speech was disseminated without his knowledge.

11. W. Stroh, *Taxis und Taktik: Die advokatischen Dispositionskunst in Ciceros Gerichtsreden*, Stuttgart: Teubner 1975, 7–30.

12. This emerges most clearly from Tacitus' *Dialogus*, esp. 25.3: 'in the same way, with us Cicero is rightly ahead of the other eloquent men of his time, but Calvus, Asinius, Caesar, Caelius and Brutus are placed ahead of their predecessors *and* those subsequent to them. Nor does it matter that their styles differ ... take all their *books* [my emphasis] in your hands and you realise that there is a similarity and link in judgement and attitude between them, despite their varying approaches.' Brutus also explored the possibilities of fictional speeches, with a *Pro Milone* following Clodius' murder (Quint. *Inst.* 3.6.93). On Brutus' oratory, A. Balbo, 'Marcus Junius Brutus the orator: between philosophy and rhetoric', in C. Steel and H. van der Blom, eds, *Community and Communication: Oratory and Politics in the Roman Republic*, Oxford: Oxford University Press 2013, 315–28; for the fragments of these and other speakers, *ORF*[4].

13. On Cicero's poetry, C. Steel, *Reading Cicero: Genre and Performance in Late Republican Rome*, London: Duckworth 2005, 28–33; P. Knox, 'Cicero as a Hellenistic poet', *CQ* 61, 2011, 192–204; E. Gee, 'Cicero's poetry', in C. Steel, ed., *The Cambridge Companion to Cicero*, Cambridge: Cambridge University Press, forthcoming.

It is comparable to, albeit more ambitious than, Catulus' experiments in Hellenistic epigram; indeed, some of the titles of Cicero's lost poems suggest that he too experimented with epigram.[14] The survival of the *Aratea* perhaps indicates that Cicero disseminated the poem among his friends; similarly, though rather later, his brother Quintus occupied a quiet moment in Gaul by the composition of a number of tragedies (though the consensus is that these were original works rather than translations) and sent copies to Cicero in Rome.[15]

In contrast with this dilettantish engagement with Hellenistic poetry, other parts of Cicero's poetic oeuvre were overtly public. In the contentious aftermath of his consulship in 63 BC, he sought to promote a favourable account of his actions. He attempted to commission a poem on his consulship; when that failed, he wrote one himself, an epic in three books, *De consulatu suo*. It survives only in fragments (the longest of which is a self-quotation by Cicero in *De diuinatione*), but there is enough to indicate that it meshed the apparatus of epic, including a council of the gods, with the actions of Roman politicians; the passage preserved in *De diuinatione* is a speech of the muse Urania.[16] Gildenhard has emphasised the strangeness of the work when read against Rome's civic religion and the ambition of the claims Cicero makes on his own behalf; and Cicero's contemporaries responded with hostility, seizing upon two lines in particular to construct their attack, *o fortunatam natam me consule Romam* ('O fortunate Rome, born during my consulship') and *cedant arma togae, concedat laurea laudi* ('let arms give way to the toga, let the bay wreath yield to praise').[17] These attacks set up Cicero's alleged vanity as their target, but they suggest that his poetry was threatening, in its presentation of Cicero's power and achievements, as well as potentially ridiculous.[18]

14. E. Courtney, *The Fragmentary Latin Poets*, Oxford: Oxford University Press 1993, 149–56.

15. Cic. *Q Fr.* 3.5.7. Hortensius, Memmius (pr. 58) and a Metellus wrote erotic verse (Ov. *Tr.* 2.433–42). We can note also Licinius Calvus, greatly admired for his poetic experimentation in his *Io*; Cornificius, who reached the praetorship during Caesar's dictatorship and wrote a *Glaucus*; Pollio (pr. 45); Caesar himself (Suet. *Iul.* 56.5–7); and Brutus (Tac. *Dial.* 21.6): 'they [sc. Brutus and Caesar] also wrote poetry, and put them in libraries – no better than Cicero, but more fortunately, since fewer people know that they did'.

16. Fragments in Courtney, *Fragmentary*, 156–73.

17. I. Gildenhard, *Creative Eloquence: The Construction of Reality in Cicero's Speeches*, Oxford: Oxford University Press 2011, 292–8.

18. The grounds for attack are laid out in Cic. *Pis.* 72–4 and [Sall.] Cic. 3.

Cicero attempted to repeat the impact of *De consulatu suo* with a poem on his exile and return, *De temporibus suis*, which also framed his actions with divine comment.[19] He circulated the work in draft stage to his brother Quintus, then in Gaul, and directly or indirectly to Caesar, and was keen to hear the reaction:

> What, dear brother, does Caesar think about my poem? He wrote earlier to me to say that he'd read the first book and that he hadn't read anything better than the first part, even in Greek; but that the rest, to a certain point, were a bit 'slack' (that's his word). Tell me the truth: is it the subject or the handling that he doesn't like?[20]

Cicero's desire for Caesar's feedback – and approval – is notable, given the role which Caesar had played in Cicero's exile; we must assume that the poem took the same line as the speeches he delivered after his return, and ascribed responsibility to Piso and Gabinius alone.[21] But it also points to Cicero's anxiety about the work's reception, perhaps heightened by the attack from Piso on *De consulatu suo*. In a letter to Lentulus Spinther from late 54 Cicero expresses uncertainty over this poem's publication, apparently because of the difficulty in ensuring that everyone who helped him would be adequately mentioned.[22] It was probably not disseminated in a complete form; no quotations from it are preserved, and if it was not, it may suggest that Cicero was unsure about the effectiveness of and response to his second experiment in politicised high epic.[23]

A rather different form of 'political' poetry is offered by Catullus, ephemeral, personal and not evidently for wider circulation, alongside his experiments in translation from the Greek and in self-conscious adaptation of Hellenistic models. His polymetric poetry records dialogue with Cicero (49) and Licinius Calvus (14, 50, 53, 96) as well as abuse of Vatinius (52), of Mamurra (Caesar's chief of engineers [*praefectus fabrum*], 29, 57) and of Caesar himself (57, 93) and a relationship with a woman usually identified with a member of the patrician Claudii. This poetry also sketches the first stages in

---

19. Courtney, *Fragmentary*, 173–4.
20. Cic. *Q Fr.* 2.16.5.
21. As Cicero (*Q Fr.* 3.1.24) suggests ('I am thinking about including a wonderful interlude in book two of *My Vicissitudes*, with Apollo predicting in a council of the gods the manner of return of the two commanders, one having destroyed his army and the other sold it').
22. Cic. *Fam.* 1.9.23, though there is a lacuna in the text.
23. How Cicero handled the career of Marius in his poem of that title is, unfortunately, completely unclear, as is its date (Courtney, *Fragmentary*, 174–8).

what might have been intended as a public career, with his presence in Bithynia in the governor's *cohors* (28, 31) as well as a geographical exuberance, in poem 11, linked to the great Roman expansion of the 60s and 50s (see above, Chapter 7). And insofar as we might wish to place any autobiographical weight on Catullus' poetry, it casts oblique light on wealthy equestrians from outside Rome who migrated there, entertained the possibility of entering public life, and were socially integrated with the governing class.[24] The third surviving poet of the late Republic, Lucretius, is entirely elusive in biographical terms; but his *De rerum natura* can also be read against the political practices of the elite, not simply in its dedicatory relationship to Memmius, the unsuccessful consular candidate for 53, but in its critique of contemporary political and social practices and its articulation of the need for political *dis*engagement.[25] Epicureanism had, paradoxically, its adherents among the politically active;[26] it may even have affected their behaviour.[27] Verse played a part in Varro's vast output, integral, it seems, to his *Menippean Satires*; and the genre of mime, with its ready engagement with contemporary themes, was developing a new profile as it made the transition to written form.[28]

Nonetheless, the end of the Republic was above all a period of prose writing.[29] In addition to speeches, politics generated a complex and vibrant epistolary culture. Indeed, by far the most varied surviving collection of non-Ciceronian prose from the Republic is from his correspondents. Elite Romans were mobile, and Cicero's correspondence demonstrates the centrality of epistolary contact to maintaining complex political and business interests

24. S. Stroup, *Cicero, Catullus and a Society of Patrons: The Generation of the Text*, Cambridge: Cambridge University Press 2010.

25. On the political significance of *De rerum natura*, D. P. Fowler, 'Lucretius and politics', in M. Griffin and J. Barnes, eds, *Philosophia Togata I*, Oxford: Oxford University Press 1989, 120–50; A. Schiesaro, 'Lucretius and Roman politics and history', in S. Gillespie and P. Hardie, eds, *The Cambridge Companion to Lucretius*, Cambridge: Cambridge University Press 2007, 41–58.

26. C. J. Castner, *A Prosopography of Roman Epicureans from the 2nd century BC to the 2nd century AD*, Frankfurt: Lang 1988.

27. For Piso's Epicurean adherence, see M. Griffin, 'Cicero, Piso and their audiences', in C. Auvray-Assayas and D. Delattre, eds, *Cicéron et Philodème: la polemique en philosophie*, Paris: Rue d'Ulm 2001, 85–99.

28. On the links between mime and political life at the end of the Republic, C. Panayotakis, *Decimus Laberius: The Fragments*, Cambridge: Cambridge University Press 2010, 13–16.

29. Rawson, *Intellectual Life*, 215–316.

across the Mediterranean.[30] Letters also provided the formal structure for reports from *imperium*-holders to the Senate and people.
Caesar's *Bellum Gallicum* too arose directly from his official activity,
even though the *commentarius*, its notional genre, remains difficult
to define precisely.[31] This offered a year-by-year account of his campaigns in Gaul, which used simplicity of style and third-person
narrative to resolve the difficulty of yoking credibility to self-descrip-
tion and was surely intended to provide an ongoing account of
Caesar's successes for those in Rome; it also 'corrected' Pompeius'
self-presentation through its simplicity, Latin and voice.[32]

There were other treatises on a wide range of topics: religion,
philosophy, history, language, agriculture, law, and oratory and
rhetoric.[33] Many of the authors were members of the Roman Senate;
others were linked to senators, through friendship or dependence. It
is difficult, indeed, to find prose writing from this period that is not,
in some sense, about public life and engagement with the *res publica*,
however much the relationship is complicated by questions of
authorship, authenticity and privacy. Historiography was primarily
a record of public events; and although Cicero may have regarded it
as a genre yet to reach an adequate standard in Latin, that was not
for want of practitioners. Attested writers included both senators
and non-senators, using a variety of formats to present the recent
and more distant past; how far political stances and activities were
reflected is difficult to ascertain from what survives.[34] The direct

30. P. White, *Cicero in Letters: Epistolary Relations of the Late Republic*, New York:
Oxford University Press 2010, for a superb introduction to the workings of the
collections; see also J. Hall, *Politeness and Politics in Cicero's Letters*, Oxford: Oxford
University Press 2009. Cicero's correspondence reached its apogee just after the end of
the period covered in this volume, as he struggled to hold the anti-Antonian coalition
together.
31. A. Riggsby, *Caesar in Gaul and Rome: War in Words*, Austin: University of Texas
Press 2006, 133–55.
32. T. P. Wiseman, 'The publication of *De Bello Gallico*', in A. Powell and K. Welch,
eds, *Julius Caesar as Artful Reporter: The War Commentaries as Political Instruments*,
Swansea: Classical Press of Wales 1998, 1–9; Riggsby, *Caesar*, 9–15. The contrast
between Caesar's approach to his *res gestae* and Pompeius' is discussed above,
Chapter 7.
33. Caesar and Varro wrote on the Latin language (see A. Garcea, *Caesar's De Analogia:
Edition, Translation, and Commentary*, Oxford: Oxford University Press 2012) and
Varro on agriculture; writers on religious matters, in addition to Cicero and Varro,
included App. Claudius (cos. 54) and Nigidius Figulus (pr. 58).
34. Senatorial historians in the post-Sullan period include Sisenna, Licinius Macer,
Hortensius and Lucceius; the dating of many non-senatorial writers is more difficult.
On the historical culture of the late Republic, U. Walter, *Memoria und res publica: Zur*

creation of a textual record thus becomes a common, though not universal, element in a public career. But material demonstrations of wealth also remained a currency in which the elite sought to acquire and to display power, and patterns of behaviour show strong continuities with earlier periods. Private excess opened the way to moralising critiques, whereas public consumption was balanced between acceptable largesse and unacceptable aspirations towards tyrannical individual power. There was renewed activity after the restoration of tribunician power in 70 to police the ways in which imperial wealth was translated into the domestic sphere. This involved legislation not only on extortion (which culminated in Caesar's comprehensive law in 59) but also on other financial dealings between non-Romans and Romans. Catullus articulated expectations about the potential profitability of official activity overseas from the perspective of a member of a governor's entourage, with his complaint (28) about the unprofitablity of his time with Memmius.[35] Public spectacles provided their organisers with opportunities for novel display, ranging from fads for coloured awnings and big cats to the development of a long-lasting fascination with armed human combat.[36] And the triumph remained not simply the pinnacle of individual achievement, but an unparalleled opportunity to combine the augmentation of the *res publica* with personal glory.[37]

Geschichtskultur im repulikanischen Rom, Frankfurt: Verlag Antike 2004; D. Levene, 'Roman historiography in the late Republic', in J. Marincola, ed, *A Companion to Greek and Roman Historiography*, Oxford: Blackwell 2007, 275–89, at 278–80, usefully questions the coincidence of senatorial historians with thematic treatments of events. T. P. Wiseman, *Remembering the Roman People*, Oxford: Oxford University Press 2009, 18–24, 59–80, discusses the links between Macer's history of early Rome and his own political activity.

35. D. Braund, 'The politics of Catullus 10', *Hermathena* 160, 1996, 45–57.

36. Coloured awnings: Lucr. 4.75–83. Big cats: Plin. *HN* 8.64; Cic. *Fam.* 8.9.3. Pliny's reference is to the aedilician games held by Aemilius Scaurus in 58, which were notorious for their expense and novelty: Plin. *HN* 8.96, the first display of crocodiles and hippopotamus, the latter bleeding together mid-display after an accidental encounter with a sharpened reed; *HN* 34.36, 3,000 statues and (*HN* 36.50) marble walls displayed in his temporary theatre; summed up, *HN* 36.113–15, 'I rather think that his aedileship did the most damage to morals and that such power of a stepson was a greater evil from Sulla than the proscription of so many thousands of people.' Cic. *Off.* 2.57 gives a brief history of aedilician display which emphasises the process of transcending what has happened before.

37. See above, pp. 161–3, 204.

The career of Pompeius

The emergence of Pompeius as de facto leader of the Senate in its opposition to Caesar can seem inevitable, given the increasing tension between the two men after Pompeius' third consulship, but unexpected in relation to what had happened over the previous three decades: Pompeius' entire career up until 52 had been in opposition to the *nobiles*. The reconfiguration is not difficult in itself to explain, as the result of Caesar's increasingly threatening articulation of his demands, and tensions within the Pompeian side can easily be traced in quarrels over status and organisation. But the causes of Pompeius' earlier troubled relationship with established power are important in explaining why the *res publica* could not function with lasting stability after Sulla.

One of the benefits of the exceptional level of documentation we possess for political activity in the 50s is its demonstration of the complexity of groupings. The simple binary model of *optimates* (best men) and *populares* is clearly inadequate to explain the position of Pompeius, Crassus and Caesar in 59 and again in 55, or the motives of those who attacked them.[38] C. Cato is a good example of the problem. He is first attested towards the end of Caesar's consulship when he tried to prosecute the consul-elect Gabinius for electoral bribery: the praetors refused to meet him, thus blocking progress. Cato addressed a *contio* to complain, called Pompeius a *priuatus dictator*, 'unofficial dictator', and was almost killed in the ensuing uproar.[39] His next appearance showed similar hostility to Pompeius, as he orchestrated popular feeling against Ptolemy at the start of his tribunate late in 57, manoeuvred the Senate into accepting the *Quindecimviri*'s opinion, and launched a full-scale attack on Pompeius in the Senate.[40] He was also working in Clodius' interests at the start of his tribunate by preventing Clodius' prosecution before the elections. These are most obviously interpreted as the actions of someone seeking popularity by acting as the voice of public opinion. But that position also involved Cato in offering high

38. For a sceptical reading of *optimates* and *populares*, M. Robb, *Beyond Populares and Optimates: Political Language in the Late Republic*, Stuttgart: Steiner 2010.
39. Cato was a *priuatus* in 59 (F. Pina Polo, *Contra arma verbis: Der Redner vor dem in der späten römischen Republik*, Stuttgart: Steiner 1996, 36); one of the three tribunes hostile to Pompeius and Caesar is the most likely candidate to have called the *contio*. For Cicero (*Q Fr.* 1.2.15) his treatment – 'a silly young man, but still a Cato and a Roman citizen' – was proof of the collapse of the *res publica*.
40. See above, pp. 179–80.

praise to Cicero, and made plausible the rumour – whether or not true – that he was being bankrolled by Bibulus, among others.[41] Moreover, Cato was among those mollified by the conference of Luca and he contributed the delays to the elections which ensured the election of Pompeius and Crassus to second consulships. He is last heard of being acquitted, in 54, on charges which arose from those delaying tactics; the subsequent silence suggests that he died soon afterwards.[42] It is reasonable to assume that one aspect of Cato's shift in position was the promise of support in subsequent elections. Cato can fairly be described as *popularis* in his methods, but for the most part they were employed against a man who himself claimed a special relationship with the Roman people.

Popularis politics undoubtedly existed, but competition between men who used a common set of issues and methods sat alongside the articulation of class interests against those of the ruling elite. The concept of *optimates*, as articulated by Cicero, deceives in a slightly different way. Not only was his very broad coalition of *boni* an illusion, and its component parts inclined to differ on a range of issues, but his picture took genuine support for the economic and legal stability of post-Sullan Italy and misinterpreted it as a commitment to the political status quo.[43] One thing which became apparent in 49 was that the wealthy across Italy were not wedded to any group at Rome. But, despite such justifiable scepticism about the unity and reality of a very broad group of *boni*, 'optimates' is nonetheless a useful shorthand for a core of senior and potentially senior magistrates and ex-magistrates who formed a distinct, cohesive and continuing group within the Senate. Such a nexus is a feature of the Senate throughout the Republic, but its post-Sullan form displays some new features.[44] Its core was Sulla's loyal supporters and the younger generation whom they promoted: despite the sharp break in the nature of the Senate, itself discussed in Chapter 5, and the relatively small number of individuals prominent

41. Cic. *Q Fr.* 2.3.3–4; *Q Fr.* 2.5.3 attests to Cato's financial difficulties (unable to support his troupe of gladiators, he unwittingly sold them, through an agent, to Milo, whom he had been attacking that spring). Robb, *Beyond*, 149 n. 8, observes that he is never described as *popularis*.
42. Cass. Dio 39.27–31; Cic. *Att.* 4.15.4, 4.16.5–6.
43. Cic. *Sest.* 96–8 with R. A. Kaster, *Cicero: Speech on Behalf of Publius Sestius*, Oxford: Oxford University Press 2006, ad loc.; divisions between equestrians and senators were pronounced in the late 60s.
44. R. Syme, *The Roman Revolution*, Oxford: Oxford University Press 1939, 10–27, remains the classic discussion.

before and after the break, the post-Sullan inner circle was largely composed of *nobiles* who could offer extensive histories of family prominence within the *res publica*.[45] Indeed, it is tempting to make a paradoxical link between the expansion of the Senate and electorate, and the striking success of the *nobiles* in retaining control of the consulship in the post-Sullan period: the threat of chaos made even the modest welcoming of new families into the consular circle characteristic of the pre-Sullan period unwelcome after his changes, a trend surely enhanced by Pompeius', and to a lesser extent Crassus' and Caesar's, successful attempts to influence elections.[46] But the capacity of these men to control senatorial business effectively was undermined by the heterogenous quality of the Senate's members, and the absence of a *princeps senatus*.[47] In the decade after Sulla, this group was committed to maintaining his constitution with its near-total exclusion of the people from the political process; as a result, it lost the initiative to those who could harness popular support, and continued to be vulnerable to effective *popularis* leadership. In addition, it faced challenge from within, above all from Marcus Cato, who combined rigid opposition to Pompeius and Caesar early in the 50s with a willingness to make *popularis* moves which did not necessarily command its support.[48] The experiences of Clodius and Cicero demonstrate some of the cross-currents which worked against anything we might describe as effective 'government' by this group. Clodius' radical *popularis* programme and his violent methods were antithetical to their interests: but he was also, on

45. In addition to Philippus, unattested after the mid-70s, and Perperna (apparently in retirement), prominent embodiments of individual continuity among the *nobiles* were Metellus Pius, Servilius Vatia (pr. during the Social War, cos. 79, and censor 55; died in 44), Licinius Lucullus, Lutatius Catulus and Hortensius (whose public career, it should not be forgotten, began in 95).

46. Cicero and Afranius were the only complete outsiders to reach the consulship between 80 and 49 (Gabinius had senatorial ancestry, and Aufidius and Murena praetorian fathers) and 18 of the 64 consuls were patrician. An even more striking indication of the adminstrative embeddedness of the *nobiles* is their continuing dominance of the priestly colleges.

47. The Senate's proneness to bureaucratic standstill after 70 is noticeable: over Clodius' problems in 61, Pompeius' settlement throughout 60, the Egyptian command early in 56, let alone the unprecedented impotence of 59. On the procedural effects of the disappearance of the *princeps senatus* after Sulla, including increased competion among the elite, M. Bonnefond-Coudry, *Le Sénat de la République romaine: de la guerre d'Hannibal à Auguste: pratiques délibératives et prises de décisions*, Rome: École Française de Rome 1989, 706–9.

48. This was of course in addition to endemic competitiveness and personal enmities (*inimicitiae*), particularly as manifested in the law courts.

occasion, an effective opponent of Pompeius, and he could rely on family support from his two brothers, Appius (cos. 54) and Gaius (pr. 56; a consular campaign precluded by conviction on extortion charges in 51). Cicero's relationship, meanwhile, with them was fraught. From his perspective, they were the *piscinarii*, the fish-pond-fanciers, whose jealousy made his strategic planning so difficult in early 60 and justified his return to Pompeius' warm embrace in 56.[49] Conversely, Cicero was ready to use *popularis* methods during his political climb and, as consul and consular, demonstrated a fondness for radically authoritarian solutions to problems as well as an unfortunate personal tendency to jocular insult.

Central, however, to the *nobiles*' failure to fulfil Sulla's role for them were Pompeius and the manifold ways in which he challenged the status quo and redefined the nature of political success. A crucial point in his career was in 79, when he refused to disband his army and demanded a triumph. Up until that point his actions, despite the initial illegality of his *imperium*, could have been rehabilitated into the consensus of Sullan government, as Sulla clearly intended (not least through his interference in Pompeius' matrimonial affairs). Even the deaths of his opponents, so vividly recalled a quarter-century later by Helvius Mancia, could be consigned, as so many other acts of violence were, to an unexplored past.[50] But from that point on, and with Sulla's reluctant approval, Pompeius' public actions avoided the normality which the rest of Sulla's activities were attempting to reimpose after the experiments of the Cinnan period.

Throughout his career Pompeius eschewed the *cursus honorum*. He would have been eligible to stand for the quaestorship and enter the Senate in 75, but by that time he was some years into the tenure of *imperium* which the Senate had bestowed on him in 77. He eventually entered the Senate when he was elected to the consulship, without having held any other magistracy, and after his second triumph: signalling his status as an outsider with his commissioning of a handbook on procedure.[51] In total he held *imperium*, and

49. *Piscinarii, Att.* 1.19.6, 1.20.3; in 56, *Att.* 4.5.1–2; *Fam.* 1.7.7.
50. Val. Max. 6.2.8, the source of the description 'teenage butcher', *adulescentulus carnifex*. Helvius Mancia gave this speech during the censorial hearings on Senate membership in 55.
51. See Chapter 4, above, for a more detailed discussion. The fact that these anomalous aspects of Pompeius' career occurred before or during 70 is another argument against 70 as a periodising date.

commanded Roman legions, for nearly thirty years. Not only is this a length of time entirely out of keeping with Republican practice; only one of Pompeius' five tenures of *imperium* was related to holding a magistracy. The first period began in murky circumstances, with Sulla 'creating' Pompeius' *imperium* during the civil war of the 80s by hailing him as *imperator* (commander). Pompeius returned to private life in 79 after extorting his first triumph. His second period of *imperium* began in 77 by senatorial decree and lasted until his second triumph on 29 December 71, which he celebrated as consul-elect. This command included the transition from fighting Lepidus to fighting Sertorius via an unspoken threat of violence when Pompeius refused to disband his army when instructed to do so by the consul Catulus. In 71, a few hours as a *priuatus* intervened after his second triumph until he resumed consular *imperium* on 1 January 70. He returned to private life after his consulship until 67 and the passage of the *lex Gabinia*. The command against the pirates segued into that against Mithridates and Tigranes created by the *lex Manilia*, and came to an end with Pompeius' third triumph in September 61. The fifth and final period began in September 57 with a consular law giving him the command to organise the corn supply. This *imperium* continued unbroken until his death in 48, though with changing rationales: he continued to hold proconsular *imperium* over the corn supply during his second consulship in 55, until it was superseded by the five-year proconsular command in Spain under the *lex Trebonia* (combined during 52 with his third consulship) and the extension of his *imperium* during the civil war which started in 49.

This progress stretched Republican understandings of *imperium* almost to incomprehension. Precedents could be found for the bestowal of *imperium* upon a private individual, and for extended periods of *imperium* granted directly by the people: Pompeius' position depended on the cumulative effect of many such exceptions combined with the novelty of holding separate grants of *imperium* at the same time, as happened during his second and third consulships. Pompeius' use of *imperium* ignored the way that it normally fitted into a public career – that is, as the result of electoral success for the praetorship and consulship. Pompeius never held the praetorship, and his first consulship was followed (at precisely the point at which a 'normal' politician should have been embarking on command) by one of only four periods in his adult life that he spent as a private individual (the others being after his triumphs, though the gap was slim in the case of the second). The logic of Pompeius' behaviour was that there were two different frameworks for *imperium*. One was in the city of Rome and attached to the tenure of a senior magistracy; the other was generated by the geopolitical demands of imperial power. In the latter case, the *res publica* needed to be able to bestow *imperium* as dictated by military or other considerations, free from the restrictions of duration and personnel which were inherent in the connection between Rome-based *imperium* and elected office. The implications of this logic underpins the *lex Pompeia de prouinciis*, and arguably influenced Augustus' policies in this area.[52] It is also clear that Pompeius had no sustained conviction about the formal source of *imperium*: he was happy to work with and for either the people or the Senate.

Pompeius' constitutional exceptionalism was fuelled by and made dangerously destabilising through the sheer scale of his military achievements. Each stage of his career was built on and made possible by previous successes, and cumulatively these, together with the wealth and networks of patronage that he thereby acquired, shifted Pompeius from the competitive framework described above onto a new level of achievement, which in turn provoked the emulation of the most ambitious of his contemporaries. The consequences for Roman imperialism are discussed in the previous chapter; the consequence for domestic politics was the creation of the 'extraordinary command' – extended tenure of *imperium* authorised by law – itself subject to an escalation of distinction. Pompeius was authorised as a *priuatus* in 77 and again in 67 to fight the *res publica*'s enemies, with mission drift from Sertorius to Spartacus and from pirates to Mithridates and Tigranes; Caesar's command was protected from later interference by specifying its duration; Pompeius was allowed to exercise his proconsular *imperium*, from 55 onwards, through legates, and was not himself ever present in his Spanish provinces; and in 55 and 52, in an apparent constitutional absurdity, he held both consular and proconsular *imperium*. The development of such commands turned them into political currency, which could be spent in the pursuit of other ends. Military success, insulated from senatorial control, for Piso and Gabinius was unlikely, in itself, to have been of interest to Clodius, or to Pompeius and Caesar; nor was the relevant legislation innately popular. But, in 58, the possibility of such a reward now existed, and it turned out to be the price of

---

52. See above, pp. 221–2. The *lex Pompeia de prouinciis* was a flawed solution, because it constrained the pool of potential commanders.

consular acquiescence. Piso's and Gabinius' standing dictated that they be released from mundane senatorial authority.[53] One result was the position of Caesar in 49, able to draw on the support of experienced legions whom he had commanded for nine campaigning seasons.

A corollary to the increasing importance of 'extraordinary' commands was that the opportunities to achieve *gloria* were increasingly detached from the normal *cursus honorum*. The vast majority of praetorian proconsulships were now held in peaceful areas, as the pattern of praetorian triumphs shows: Afranius triumphed in 70 and Pupius Piso in 69; thereafter, the next praetorian triumph was that of Pomptinus in 54. But after 70, even consuls found it difficult to triumph: if we set Pompeius himself aside, the only consular triumphs were those of Lucullus, in 63, Metellus Creticus, in 62, and Spinther, in 51. Lucullus, Creticus and Pomptinus all faced considerable opposition to their claims to a triumph (as Marcius Rex and Julius Caesar also did in the late 60s, and in their cases they did not succeed in obtaining one). The opportunity to excel militarily was ceasing to be available to men who followed a normal route through the available offices. This development may be linked the phenomenon of consuls who chose not to go to a province.[54] Proconsular *imperium* increasingly meant peaceful administration, with a limited prospect of military distinction and the very real danger of extortion charges on return to Rome.

The sidelining of the role of promagistrates in military activity was taking place at the same time as a different organisational model based on legates was being implemented. The use of legates was not a post-Sullan innovation, of course, but Pompeius and his collaborators created a distinctive model of how to use the position. In Spain in the 70s his use of legates was entirely conventional; that is, a small number of men, who acted on the instructions of the *imperium*-holder and whose appointments were confirmed by the

---

53. The operation of the *lex Sempronia* was under sustained challenge in the 50s: its provisions for the years 59, 58 and 55 were overturned and the consuls of 54 appear to have been unhappy with it (it is otherwise difficult to explain what Ahenobarbus and Appius Claudius stood to gain from the electoral compact with Memmius and Calvinus). These challenges were not generated by military crises (which the Senate had the capacity to deal with, for example in the attaching of Egypt to Lentulus' Sempronian province of Cilicia) – there was no response to Carrhae, for example – but by consular ambition.
54. J. P. V. D. Balsdon, 'Consular provinces under the late Republic, I: general considerations', *JRS* 29, 1939, 57–73.

Senate.[55] The moment of change was the *lex Gabinia*, which included, among the resources it gave Pompeius, the right to appoint 15 legates without need for senatorial approval.[56] Four of these 15 went on to hold the consulship, as did Gabinius himself, who became a legate after the passage of the *lex Manilia*, Afranius and Metellus Celer.[57] That is, 7 out of the 22 men elected to the consulship in the ten years 65–56 – almost one-third – had been Pompeius' legates.[58] At the very least, this indicates the interconnectedness between Pompeius' campaigns in the 60s and Roman domestic politics. The nature of the link between service as a legate and subsequent electoral success varied from individual to individual. Afranius and Gabinius seem to have relied very heavily on their connection with Pompeius to reach the consulship.[59] But what was the nature of the exchange in the case of the other five, all of them *nobiles*? How important was the association with Pompeius in helping them to the top? Part of the challenge here is to include the 'also-rans' of Roman politics, the men who failed to be elected, in order to gauge the stiffness of the competition.[60] And, even more broadly, there are those who considered standing – but, from whatever calculation of their chances, did not.[61] The association with Pompeius probably brought a competitive advantage, but it would be misleading to assume that it was all that these five could offer voters, or that they gave Pompeius back nothing in return.

55. Attested legates were D. Laelius, who was killed at the battle of the Lauro in 76, M. Terentius Varro and L. Afranius.

56. Plut. *Pomp.* 25.3; Dio 36.37. *MRR* 2.148–9 lists the 15. On the use of legates more generally, M-M. Salomonsson, 'Roman legates in the Republic', *Opuscula Romana* 25–6, 2000, 79–88.

57. L. Manlius Torquatus (cos. 65), M. Pupius Piso (cos. 61), Q. Caecilius Metellus Nepos (cos. 57) and Cn. Cornelius Lentulus Marcellinus (cos. 56). A.Plotius was praetor in 51; the praetorships of Ti. Claudius Nero and M. Terentius Varro may follow their service as legates. The group also contained two ex-consuls (Gellius and Lentulus Clodianus) and an ex-praetor (the historian Sisenna). M. Lollius Palicanus, tr. pl. 71 and consular candidate in 66, is a counter-example: his Picene origins and collaboration with Pompeius over the restoration of the tribunate suggest a close adherent, but his ambitions for the highest office could be crushed, in Pompeius' absence and despite his popularity, by the consul Piso (Val. Max. 3.8.3).

58. Four consuls were elected in 65 (the first pair were disqualified by subsequent convictions for bribery).

59. However, Afranius did contribute the glamour of a praetorian triumph.

60. See above, Introduction n. 12.

61. An example is L. Valerius Flaccus, praetor in 63. Why, once acquitted on *repetundae* charges, did he not stand for the consulship of 57? But there is no evidence that he did so.

Pompeius' inclusion of the consuls of 72 among his legates – neither of whom had had a promising military career – surely shows a wish to embed his exceptional power in existing structures of authority. The presence of young *nobiles* may have served a similar purpose. In addition, the Metelli were, until his return to Italy, his half-brothers-in-law.

In practice, Pompeius' legates were a disappointment to him as consuls. Piso was largely distracted throughout 61 by the Bona Dea affair. Metellus Celer was, in fact, a vigorous and effective opponent of Pompeius, against whom Afranius was helpless.[62] Lentulus Marcellinus tried to prevent Pompeius from holding the consulship in 55. The value of Pompeius turned out to be too low to translate a cadre of military assistants into personal political dominance: it was not enough to make loyal figures, such as Afranius, into effective operators, or sufficient to ensure the ongoing support of *nobiles*, whatever benefit they had acquired from it earlier in their careers. In the end, Pompeius had to turn to Caesar and Crassus to find an effective way of working in Rome. And Caesar – despite having a generous allocation of legates in Gaul – did not follow Pompeius' example in giving the positions to the politically ambitious, or in supporting such ambitions if they emerged.[63] Pompeius' relationship with his legates offered an alternative *cursus honorum*, in which he, rather than the Roman people, provided the means to success. The careers of Afranius and Gabinius demonstrated that he could deliver such success: but he was unable completely to replace the existing pattern of political life, and the conflict between the two was a major source of instability.[64]

---

62. Anger over Mucia's divorce may have been a factor in Celer's behaviour, but we should not overschematise: Pompeius' radical measures provoked disquiet on their own terms.

63. K. Welch, 'Caesar and his officers in the Gallic War Commentaries', in Welch and Powell, *Julius Caesar as Artful Reporter*, 85–110. Labienus had demonstrated political ambitions during his tribunate in 63, but these did not turn into Caesarian support for further offices (G. Wylie 'Why did Labienus defect from Caesar in 49 B.C.?', *Ancient History Bulletin* 3, 1989, 123–7). We can also note Q. Cicero, who did not achieve his likely consular ambitions (T. P. Wiseman, 'The ambitions of Q. Cicero', *JRS* 56, 1966, 108–15).

64. R. Morstein-Marx ('"Cultural hegemony" and the communicative power of the Roman elite', in Steel and van der Blom, *Community and Communication*, 29–47, at 37) observes 'a discernible trough of quietude during Pompeius' absence (66–61 BC)' in terms of contested legislation. This is surely not a coincidence: Pompeius was always ready to appeal directly to the people, and thereby raised the political temperature by alarming his opponents.

The challenge which Pompeius posed to existing practice is traceable not simply in the often violent action and reaction of those who wished to be his peers, but also in the writing of the period. Varro's handbook was an early example. Historiographically, Pompeius was a traditionalist, using a non-Roman intellectual – Theophanes – to record his achievements and exploiting his appropriation of Alexander to build a self-image as a Hellenistic monarch. When Cicero turned to writing political theory in the mid-50s with his treatises *De oratore* and *De republica*, the nature of leadership was a central concern.[65] He found himself with the *otium* to begin *De oratore* because of the reconfiguration of power that produced Pompeius' and Crassus' second consulships, which is highlighted in the work's opening paragraphs. These contrast the happiness of those who were able, 'in an excellent commonwealth', to choose between political activity pursued in safety and an honourable retirement and his position, constrained both by 'the serious challenges of our shared situation' and by 'my various problems'. Instead of historiography or memoir, Cicero chose philosophical dialogue as his medium; and despite conscious invocations of Plato, these works are placed unequivocally in a Roman context, exploring what is required for and of the *res publica* and the men who devote themselves to it.

Neither work can be reduced to a simple interpretation: Cicero revels in the accumulation of detail, ramifying threads of argument and idea, and the multiplication of competing voices.[66] But some principles do emerge. Both works are committed to a participatory *res publica* in which citizens have a role. In *De republica* this emerges explicitly from the discussion of the role of the people and the office of the tribunate; it is implicit in *De oratore*'s concern with the capacity of the speaker to affect high questions of public policy, and his duties in so doing.[67] It is because the people has some

65. M. Schofield, 'Cicero's definition of *res publica*' in J. Powell, ed., *Cicero the Philosopher*, Oxford: Oxford University Press 1995, 63–83; Fantham, *Roman World*, 305–28; J. Zetzel, 'Political philosophy', in Steel, *Cambridge Companion to Cicero*, offers an incisive analysis of all three treatises of the 50s. *De legibus* was begun but apparently not finished before the civil war: see further A. Dyck, *A Commentary on Cicero, De Legibus*, Ann Arbor: University of Michigan Press 2004.

66. See more generally M. Fox, *Cicero's Philosophy of History*, Oxford: Oxford University Press 2007.

67. Cic. *Rep.* 1.69 (the value of the mixed constitution, which preserves *libertas*); *Rep.* 2.57–9 (origins of tribunate of the plebs); *Rep.* 3.43–8 (a legitimate *res publica* is the property of the people).

decision-making capacity that oratory is such a vital skill, which must be exercised by the morally virtuous. None of this is to argue that Cicero was expressing support for democratic or *popularis* views in these works; the people best employs its capacity when it receives wise guidance. But he was setting himself against the Sullan attempt to remove the people from most political activity.[68] And in the context of the 50s, these works offer a critique of the policy of Pompeius, Crassus and Caesar, whose actions have eliminated legitimate popular involvement and left room for illegitimate political violence of the kind employed by Clodius.

Political leadership in *De oratore* is concerned with the public speaker: indeed, when the orator is defined (1.209–12) one of the parallel examples of how to proceed is that of the statesman. Oratory is essential to the *res publica*, but does not provide all necessary skills. *De republica* shifts the focus to the figure of the *rector rei publicae*: not a disguised monarch, but a reflection on the characteristics of the outstanding statesman within a *res publica* such as Rome.[69] Cicero is arguing for men who work within the framework of the laws and use debate to establish a course of action. These reflections must be set against the background of a Rome dominated by Pompeius' actions and reputation. Cicero had long been concerned to find a way to work with Pompeius. His hopes of playing Laelius to Pompeius' Scipio, of co-operation that would be a happy union of civilian and military competences, had failed not so much through Pompeius' dissimulation, or even in the betrayal of exile, but rather through Cicero's inability to accept Pompeius' other allies, or, we might say, because of his commitment to a *res publica* incompatible with the force that Pompeius and Caesar wielded to buttress their power. We cannot read *De republica*, in particular, without seeing an appeal to Pompeius to confine his ambitions to the bounds of the legally constituted *res publica* and to seek glory through the admiring memory of his community.[70]

Both *De oratore* and *De republica* presented dialogues in the past, in September 91 and January 129 respectively. Cicero devoted considerable care to the verisimilitude of the settings and to the

---

68. Cf. Cic. *Leg.* 3.17, where Quintus Cicero argues against the existence of the tribunate.
69. J. Powell, 'The *rector rei publicae* of Cicero's *De re publica*', *SCI* 13, 1994, 19–29.
70. On the 'dream of Scipio', a myth-making account of the reward of immortality due to 'all those who have saved, aided or increased the fatherland' (6.13), J. Zetzel, *Cicero: De Re Publica, Selections*, Cambridge: Cambridge University Press 1995, 223–53.

method by which he had become privy to the content of discussions in which he had not participated.[71] Historical settings saved him from the potential embarrassment of choosing among his contemporaries and inserting them into his fictions; they also offered him, a new man, the opportunity to give himself an intellectual genealogy.[72] But the device also suggested that healing the state demanded a historically informed approach and that the tools for that task might be found before the changes of recent decades. Inherent in the settings, too, is a pessimism about the prospects of success: both dialogues are set just before the deaths of their protagonists. Skill, talent and dedication alone are not sufficient, since accidental death waits. Moreover, the implication of foul play in Aemilianus' death, and the identity of the rest of the cast of De oratore apart from Crassus, illustrate the catastrophic effects of internal conflict.[73]

Thus during the 50s Cicero was exploring in his treatises ways of incorporating monarchic aspirations and the talents of exceptional men within a mixed system of government. But the outcome of political upheaval was one-man rule. Indeed, for Tacitus, the whole period from Sulla onwards is, fundamentally, a tyranny: Marius and Sulla overcame freedom and turned it into a despotism (dominatio), and the one object of desire thereafter was pre-eminence (principatus).[74] In Tacitean mode, we could construct a narrative of the end of the Republic which is all about aspirations towards tyrannical power, starting with Lepidus and ending – for the chronology of this volume – with Caesar. But personal ambition, and the new targets at which individuals could aim, have only limited explanatory force. It is difficult to determine how different this supremacy was, in terms of its perception and effects at Rome, from the reputation of earlier military heroes, despite the obvious differences in the formal conditions of Pompeius' acquisition of power. In that respect,

71. Steel, Reading Cicero, 106–14; P. Burton, 'Genre and fact in the preface to Cicero's De amicitia', Antichthon 41, 2007, 13–32; M. Schofield, 'Ciceronian dialogue', in S. Goldhill, ed., The End of Dialogue in Antiquity, Cambridge: Cambridge University Press 2009, 63–84.
72. See e.g. Cic. Q Fr.3.5.1–2, discussing the composition of De republica; M. Fox, 'Heraclides of Pontus and the philosophical dialogue', in W. Fortenbaugh and E. Pender, eds, Heraclides of Pontus, New Brunswick: Transaction 2009, 41–67; H. van der Blom, Cicero's Role Models: The Political Strategy of a Newcomer, Oxford: Oxford University Press 2010, 151–74.
73. Of the seven interlocutors in De oratore, only Gaius Cotta survived the 80s; four of the others died violently.
74. Tac. Hist. 2.38.

constitutional exceptionalism may be less important than sheer scale of achievement; and, although innovations which surrounded Pompeius were attractive to his emulators, their attraction arguably lay in their capacity to create achievements (*res gestae*) than in their novelty per se. Thus extended commands authorised by the people and extensive retinues of legates were desirable because they made great conquest easier. Indeed, one of the most significant innovations in the handling of power turned out to be the introduction of fixed terms, and that was Caesar's doing. In other words, although the nature of personal power at the end of the Republic was a crucial enabling factor for the civil wars which followed, it must be supplemented by the circumstances under which it was created. To claim that personal ambition was vital to the events of 50–49 is uncontroversial, and not uninteresting; the motives and judgements of Pompeius and Caesar contributed directly to the sequence of events which turned suspicion into conflict.

But they found themselves in positions to give bloody shape to their desire for domination because of the way that Roman politics worked or failed to work after Sulla: and that topic must centre on the role of the Roman people.

Popular arbitration

The year 70 acts as a periodising date in large part because tribunes of the people then regained their capacity to propose legislation; at that point, the Sullan experiment in purely senatorial government was over.[75] We have already seen the importance of tribunician legislation in setting up the extended commands which, in turn, were an enabling factor for civil war in 49; it is thus possible to construct a narrative of the end of the Republic in which the Roman people removed their assent from existing methods of government and turned to individual leaders instead. It is possible, moreover, to identify a number of factors which led to this decision. Popular leaders promised more effective relief from material deprivation; the people had a collective sense of its identity and rights which was consistently outraged by the behaviour of magistrates and the Senate in the post-Sullan period; and – though potentially in contradiction to the previous point – the extension of citizenship through Italy and

75. *Contra*, E. S. Gruen, *The Last Generation of the Roman Republic*, Berkeley: University of California Press 1974, 6–46.

beyond weakened the attachment to existing forms of government which depended on participation in Rome. Antagonism and indifference combined to turn the people from oligarchy to monarchy.[76]

The general validity of this framework is difficult to question: the end of the Republic was unthinkable without these economic and social factors, in combination with an ideology of popular rights. But it was also a political crisis, and a focus on the details of domestic politics is necessary because what happened in Rome determined not only the process of transformation but also the extent to and ways in which the decades of upheaval brought about change. The role of the people was to exercise choice within defined limits: in order to understand how its choices came to have such extensive effects we need to consider the sources of instability after 70 which affected the ability of Senate and magistrates to define those limits.

First, senatorial government was, in general, unpopular. In part this was because of incompetence, or perceived incompetence: the Senate's failure to deal with piracy, and consequent rapid inflation in the price of food, generated overwhelming support for the *lex Gabinia* in 67; similar problems in 57 led to the demonstrations which forced the Senate's hand. Corruption was another potent trigger. The *lex Manilia* transferring the Mithridatic command to Pompeius did not offer direct immediate benefit, but it was still a response to senatorial failure, and to what could be presented as the corruption of one specific senator, Lucullus.[77] C. Cato could stir up popular feeling rapidly at the end of 57 with the suggestion that senators were complicit in the illegal activities of Ptolemy. As importantly, the year 70 did not resolve the dispute about the extent of popular rights: it was simply a moment in an ongoing battle. The consul Piso in 67 consistently resisted the popular will, not only in his opposition to the tribunes Gabinius and Cornelius, but also at elections, when he refused to allow Lollius Palicanus' candidacy for consul.[78] In 64 citizens were prevented from meeting in their *collegia*

76. The relationship between politics and (the lack of) prosperity is emphatically articulated by P. A. Brunt, 'The army and the land in the Roman revolution', *JRS* 52, 1962, 69–86.
77. Cf. M. Jehne, 'Feeding the *plebs* with words: the significance of senatorial public oratory in the small world of Roman politics', in Steel and van der Blom, *Community and Communication*, 49–62, who emphasises in his discussion of Cicero's speech the importance of popular authority within the debate.
78. In the following year, the consul Volcatius refused to accept Catiline's candidacy (Asc. 89C); it is unclear whether Catiline was yet a 'popular' figure in the way that Palicanus appears to have been.

and celebrating the Compitalician Games; in 61 the consul-designate Celer insisted on the ban. Cicero had citizens executed in 63 without trial, in defiance of appeal (*prouocatio*), and faced swift challenge from the incoming tribunes of 62; his colleague Antonius superintended the slaughter of citizens in the defeat of Catiline's forces, and his subsequent departure into exile after conviction on *repetundae* charges was celebrated in Rome. In 52 Clodius was murdered by Milo, whose public career had been built around violent intimidation in the interests of Cicero and the Senate.[79]

Conflict between the people and the governing elite was not, of course, a new phenomenon. But practical changes in the period after Sulla contributed to raising the temperature. One point is that there simply was more politics in Rome after Sulla than before, because the consuls were present, whereas earlier they had tended not to be.[80] This created a space for consuls to fill by taking action; and it added to the likelihood of conflict, by creating a chance for consular *imperium* to clash against tribunician *sacrosanctitas* in a confrontation for which there was no clear method of resolution. C. Calpurnius Piso, who consistently opposed tribunician legislation as consul in 67, was able to do so because he was present in Rome: hence an impulse towards the violent clashes which are so notable a feature of both Gabinius' and Cornelius' legislation.[81] Flavius' imprisonment of the consul Celer – he who had so vigorously shut down the Compitalician Games – was not simply an improvisatory move in a dispute about agrarian legislation: it demonstrated to Rome that some political disputes were unfixable. One element in the story was the Senate's own weakness: far more heterogenous than before the Social War, it seems not to have developed internal structures of organisation which facilitated decision-making. The absence of a *princeps senatus* contributed: the Senate no longer had a leader, who could act as a instigator of continuity and stability.

There was a vacuum into which those claiming to be popular leaders rushed to be welcomed by a citizen body willing to express its views loudly. It is difficult to see how these very public conflicts

79. Wiseman, *Remembering*, 177–210; J. Vanderbroeck, *Popular Leadership and Collective Behaviour in the Late Roman Republic, 80-50 B.C.*, Amsterdam: Gieben 1987.
80. F. Pina Polo, *The Consul at Rome*, Cambridge: Cambridge University Press 2011, 149; on Piso, 308–9.
81. Piso's colleague Glabrio received the provinces of Bithynia and Pontus under a law of Gabinius and presumably left Rome during the spring of 67 (though after he had co-operated with Piso in the latter's compromise bribery law).

would not have increased levels of tension at Rome, or made attractive the solutions which Caesar and Clodius appeared to offer. Caesar's consulship can seem to resemble, in its techniques as well as its policy, the tribunate which he never held: it contained land legislation; attempts to regulate senatorial behaviour, through his law on extortion, and publication of Senate proceedings; and the performance of respect to the *res publica* in his being followed, rather than preceded, by his lictors in the months when he did not hold the *fasces*.[82] It also involved violent demonstrations, directed particularly against his colleague Bibulus. And Caesar enabled Clodius, a fellow patrician, to hold the tribunate, presumably well aware of the measures Clodius intended and the means he would employ to ensure their passage. On this interpretation, Caesar and Clodius tapped into widespread support among inhabitants of Rome, whose aspirations had been frustrated over the previous decades by the restraints placed on the tribunes and, even after the restoration of the tribunes, by opposition to popular measures from the consuls and the rest of the Senate. That is not to deny that Clodius systematically and successfully organised the use of violence; and by so doing made possible the developments later in the 50s, when organised violence became a technique which could be used in support of any end.

The process by which Cicero was brought back from exile is an excellent example of this technique employed for ends not obviously *popularis*: Cicero's own narrative, in *pro Sestio* (71–92), presents the tribunes Sestius and Milo responding with violence of their own to the violence of Clodius' followers, which began at an assembly convened on 23 January to vote on a measure recalling Cicero. Milo's use of violence is justified:

> He alone seems to me to have taught, through his deeds, not words … that men should resist the criminality of those reckless individuals who would destroy the *res publica* with laws and the law courts; but that if the laws are not in force, and the law courts do not exist, if the *res publica* is under military occupation through the organised violence of the reckless, then it is necessary that life and liberty be defended through armed protection.[83]

---

82. Pina Polo, *Consul*, 299–300; lictors (a revival of earlier custom), Suet. *Iul.* 20.1.
83. *Sest.* 86; J. Harries, *Cicero and the Jurists: From Citizens' Law to Lawful State*, London: Duckworth 2006, 193–7; Gildenhard, *Creative Eloquence*, 152–6; on Cicero's 'standard version' of his return from exile, Kaster, *Sestius*, 10–14.

Cicero's supporters were able, over a period of months, to orchestrate sufficient support for him to pass a law of recall (though it had to be done via the centuriate assembly, not the tribal). There were prosecutions for *uis* arising from these events, but none led to a conviction.[84] Violence emerged as a tool which was not only potentially effective but also, if one's opponents were going to use it, essential; and safe to use. Unsurprisingly, it began to be used to support intra-elite competition. Milo's violence reached its height in January 52, when his followers murdered Clodius, sparking a violent response from the people and thus opening the way to a brief autocratic interlude which allowed Pompeius to impose martial law. He appears to have succeeded in ending violence at Rome; but if Morstein-Marx's recent argument is accepted, this did not mean that popular discontent had no role to play in the outbreak of civil war, or that the exclusion from the political process during the 50s of anyone not prepared to risk encountering lethal violence did not contribute to the system's decisive loss of support.[85]

The Roman *res publica* was based on managing two sets of tensions: between the separate interests of individual members of the political elite and those of the citizen body in relation to the wealthy as a whole. Its success in so doing broke down utterly in the 80s BC; and Sulla could not recreate it, since in the post-Sullan state the identity of both the Roman people and the elite had changed too radically. The domestic history of the three decades from 80 to 50 is of a series of failed attempts to find a sustainable consensus.

The implications of Caesar's dictatorship

From that perspective, Caesar's dictatorship is merely a footnote, which demonstrated the extent of the problem without indicating any solution. He did not introduce any major structural changes in

---

84. Clodius was prosecuted twice by Milo for *uis* during 57 (M. Alexander, *Trials in the Late Roman Republic 149 BC to 50 BC*, Toronto: University of Toronto Press 1990, 128); on the first occasion, he was protected by his brother Appius (pr. 57), the consul Nepos and one of the tribunes of 57, and the second trial was abandoned because he took up office as aedile; Clodius then prosecuted Milo (Alexander *Trials*, 129–30), but the prosecution was abandoned; Sestius was prosecuted, also in 56 by a team led by P. Albinovanus, defended by Hortensius, Crassus and Cicero, and acquitted unanimously.

85. R. Morstein-Marx, '*Dignitas* and *res publica*. Caesar and Republican legitimacy', in K-J. Hölkeskamp, ed., *Eine politische Kultur (in) der Krise?*, Munich: Oldenbourg 2009, 115–40.

administration: he used the same offices to run the *res publica* as before the civil war, multiplying their numbers as he saw fit. But by taking away free elections he ended the Republic, because access to power, and hence to armed force, was now restricted to his circle. Popularity, always and essentially during the Republic a transient and changeable phenomenon, now became fixed in the person of the autocrat. In so far as we can trace a policy and a prospect of any solution, it is in the articulation of the idea of an autocrat. Caesar had followed Sulla in identifying the dictatorship – when combined with overwhelming military force – as the mechanism which allowed autocratic power to be expressed. But he enhanced that position, through a concern with presence and display that evoked Hellenistic monarchs combined with his personal centrality to Rome's super-natural existence in the position of *pontifex maximus*.[86] This was a potent mix, but one still inextricably tied to Caesar. As became overwhelmingly clear as soon as he was dead, no one else could yet control the mixture: the struggle to do so would be long and destructive.

86. E. Rawson, 'Caesar's heritage: Hellenistic kings and their Roman equals', *JRS* 65, 1975, 148–59; on the *pontifex maximus*, I am grateful to John Bollan for illuminating conversations.

Chronology

Political/Military	Religious/Cultural	Events elsewhere
146 Destruction of Corinth; destruction of Carthage		
134 Destruction of Numantia		
133 Tribunate and death of Ti. Gracchus		133 Death of Attalus III; bequest of Pergamum
		132 Slave revolt in Sicily
129 Death of Scipio Aemilianus		
125 Revolt of Fregellae		
123 First tribunate of C. Gracchus		
122 Second tribunate of C. Gracchus		
121 Death of C. Gracchus and followers		
	120 Dedication of temple of *Concordia*	120 Death of Mithridates V; accession of Mithridates VI
118 Foundation of Narbo Martius		118 Death of Micipsa
	114 Trial of Vestal Virgins	114 Migration by Cimbri and Teutones
109 *Quaestio Mamilia*		
107 Marius' first consulship		

Political/Military	Religious/Cultural	Events elsewhere
105 Romans defeated at Arausio		
100 Saturninus' second tribunate; death of Saturninus, Glaucia and followers		
	92 Censors' edict against Latin rhetors	
91 Tribunate of Livius Drusus		91 Rome's Italian allies revolt
88 Sulla's first consulship		89 or 88 Mithridates invades Asia
86 Cinna and Marius consuls; death of Marius		
84 Sulla returns to Italy		
	83 Temple of Capitoline Jupiter burns	
82 Battle of the Colline Gate; Sulla dictator; proscriptions		
	80 Cicero's speech *pro Roscio Amerino*	
		73 Spartacus' slave revolt
70 First consulship of Pompeius and Crassus		
67 *Lex Gabinia*; Pompeius' campaign against piracy		
66 *Lex Manilia*; Pompeius begins his eastern campaigns		
63 Cicero's consulship; Catilina's revolt	63 Julius Caesar elected *pontifex maximus*	
59 Consulship of Julius Caesar		59 Migration of Helvetii

Political/Military	Religious/Cultural	Events elsewhere
58 Tribunate of Clodius	58 Caesar's *Bellum Gallicum*; Catullus and Lucretius writing	58 Ptolemy Auletes deposed
55 Second consulship of Pompeius and Crassus	55 Cicero's *De oratore*; dedication of Pompeius' temple/theatre complex	
53 Battle of Carrhae		
52 Death of Clodius; Pompeius' third consulship	52 Cicero's *Pro Milone*	
		51 Accession of Cleopatra
49 Caesar invades Italy; Caesar's first dictatorship		
48 Battle of Pharsalus; death of Pompeius		
46 Battle of Thapsus	46 Cicero's *Brutus*	
45 Battle of Munda	45 Cicero begins series of philosophical works; Sallust retires from public life	
44 Caesar becomes dictator for life; assassination of Caesar		

Guide to further reading

The bibliography on the last century of the Roman Republic is uncontrollably vast: the following is merely a brief guide to some helpful starting points.

Volume 9 of the second edition of the *Cambridge Ancient History* (*The Last Age of the Roman Republic, 146–43 B.C.*, Cambridge: Cambridge University Press 1994) remains a thorough and reliable survey of the events and themes of the period. More recently, the boom in *Companions* has served the late Republic well: both *The Cambridge Companion to the Roman Republic* (ed. H. Flower, Cambridge: Cambridge University Press 2004) and Blackwell's *A Companion to the Roman Republic* (eds N. Rosenstein and R. Morstein-Marx, Oxford: Blackwell 2006) provide an excellent range of accessible and contrasting introductory essays. Two short, excellent books on the practice of politics at Rome in this period are Beard and Crawford's *Rome in the Late Republic: Problems and Interpretations* (2nd edn, London: Duckworth 1999) and Patterson's *Political Life in the City of Rome* (Bristol: Bristol Classical Press 2000).

K-J. Hölkeskamp's *Reconstructing the Roman Republic: An Ancient Political Culture and Modern Research* (Princeton: Princeton University Press 2010), which translates and updates his 2004 *Rekonstruktionen einer Republik: Die politische Kultur des antiken Roms und die Forschung der letzten Jahrzehnte* (Munich: Oldenbourg), is a stimulating, and relatively brief, discussion of the current state of scholarship on the period. (The long review by Crawford in *BICS* 54.2, 2011, 105–14 is a provocative counter.) It also provides helpful orientation for anglophone readers in contemporary debates conducted largely in German, French or Italian.

One of the major debates concerns the role of the people. Fergus Millar's *The Crowd in Rome in the Late Republic* (Ann Arbor: University of Michigan Press 1998) puts forward the argument for democracy at Rome. Among the many responses, in English, to it are Mouritsen's *Plebs and Politics in the Late Roman Republic* (Cambridge: Cambridge University Press 2001); Morstein-Marx's *Mass Oratory and Political Power in the*

Late Roman Republic (Cambridge: Cambridge University Press 2004); and Wiseman's *Remembering the Roman People* (Oxford: Oxford University Press 2009). There are important recent studies of the praetorship by Brennan (New York: Oxford University Press 2000) and the consulship by Pina Polo (Cambridge: Cambridge University Press 2011), and the institution of the triumph has received sustained and sceptical scrutiny from Beard (*The Roman Triumph*, Cambridge, MA: Harvard University Press 2007). A. Wallace-Hadrill, *Rome's Cultural Revolution* (Cambridge: Cambridge University Press 2008) is a wide-ranging survey of Roman culture which extends well into the Augustan period.

Important reference works for the period are T. R. S. Broughton's *Magistrates of the Roman Republic* (3 vols, New York/Atlanta: Scholars Press 1951–86); J. Rüpke's *Fasti Sacerdotum* (Oxford: Oxford University Press 2008, a revision and translation of the three-volume German original [Wiesbaden: Steiner 2005]); and M. Crawford's *Roman Statutes* (2 vols, London: Institute of Classical Studies 1996).

Bibliography

Adams, J. N. (2003), *Bilingualism and the Latin Language*, Cambridge: Cambridge University Press.

Adshead, K. (1981), 'Further inspiration for Tiberius Gracchus?', *Antichthon* 15, 119–28.

Alexander, M. (1990), *Trials in the Late Roman Republic 149 BC to 50 BC*, Toronto: University of Toronto Press.

Alexander, M. (2002), *The Case for the Prosecution in the Ciceronian Era*, Ann Arbor: University of Michigan Press.

Andreau, J., and Bruhns, H., eds (1990), *Parenté et stratégies familiales dans l'antiquité romaine*, Rome: École Française de Rome.

Astin, A. E. (1967), *Scipio Aemilianus*, Oxford: Oxford University Press.

Astin, A. E. (1985), 'Censorships in the late Republic', *Historia* 34, 175–90.

Badian, E. (1955), 'The date of Pompeius' first triumph', *Hermes* 83, 107–18.

Badian, E. (1962), 'Waiting for Sulla', *JRS* 52, 47–61.

Badian, E. (1964), 'Notes on provincial governors from the Social War down to Sulla's victory', in Badian, E., *Studies in Greek and Roman History*, Oxford: Blackwell, 71–104.

Badian, E. (1965), 'M. Porcius Cato and the annexation and early administration of Cyprus', *JRS* 55, 110–21.

Badian, E. (1967), 'The testament of Ptolemy Alexander', *RhM* 110, 178–92.

Badian, E. (1969), '*Quaestiones Variae*', *Historia* 18, 447–91.

Badian, E. (1984), 'The death of Saturninus: studies in chronology and prosopography', *Chiron* 14, 130–40.

Baehrends, O. (2002), 'La "lex Licinia Mucia de ciuibus redigundis" de 95 a. C.' in Ratti, S., ed., *Antiquité et citoyenneté*, Besançon: Presses Universitaires Franc-Comtoises, 15–33.

Bailey, D. R. S. (1960), 'The Roman nobility in the second civil war', *CQ* 10, 253–67.

Bailey, D. R. S. (1986), '*Nobiles* and *novi* reconsidered', *AJPh* 107, 255–60.

Balbo, A. (2013), 'Marcus Junius Brutus the orator: between philosophy and rhetoric', in Steel, C., and van der Blom, H., eds, *Community and*

Communication: Oratory and Politics in the Roman Republic, Oxford: Oxford University Press, 315–28.

Balsdon, J. P. V. D. (1939), 'Consular provinces under the late Republic, I: general considerations', *JRS* 29, 57–73.

Barker, G., ed. (1995), *A Mediterranean Valley: Landscape Archaeology and Annales History in the Biferno Valley*, Leicester: Leicester University Press.

Bastien, J-L. (2007), *Le triumph romain et son utilisation politique à Rome aux trois derniers siècles de la République*, Rome: École Française de Rome.

Bauman, R. (1967), *The Crimen Maiestatis in the Roman Republic and Augustan Principate*, Johannesburg: Witwatersrand University Press.

Bauman, R. (1992), *Women and Politics in Ancient Rome*, London: Routledge.

Beard, M. (2007), *The Roman Triumph*, Cambridge, MA: Harvard University Press.

Beard, M. and Crawford, M. (1999), *Rome in the Late Republic: Problems and Interpretations*, 2nd edn, London: Duckworth.

Beard, M., North, J. and Price, S. (1998), *Religions of Rome*, 2 vols, Cambridge: Cambridge University Press.

Bellemore, J. (2005), 'Cato's opposition to Caesar in 59 B.C.', in Welch, K. and Hillard, T., eds, *Roman Crossings: Theory and Practice in the Roman Republic*, Swansea: Classical Press of Wales, 225–57.

Bendlin, A. (2000), 'Looking beyond the civic compromise: religious pluralism in late Republican Rome', in Bispham, E., and Smith, C., eds, *Religion in Archaic and Republican Rome: Evidence and Experience*, Edinburgh: Edinburgh University Press, 115–35.

Benferhat, Y. (2002), 'Plaidoyer pour une victime de Cicéron: Pison', *REL* 80, 55–77.

Beness, L. (2005), 'Scipio Aemilianus and the crisis of 129 B.C.', *Historia* 54, 37–48.

Bernstein, F. (1998), *Ludi Publici: Untersuchungen zur Entstehung und Entwicklung der öffentlichen Spiele im republikanischen Rom*, Stuttgart: Steiner.

Berry, D. (1993), 'Pompey's legal knowledge – or lack of it: Cic. *Mil.* 70 and the date of *pro Milone*', *Historia* 42, 502–4.

Berry, D. (1996), *Cicero Pro Sulla Oratio*, Cambridge: Cambridge University Press.

Bispham, E. (2007), *From Asculum to Actium: The Municipalization of Italy from the Social War to Augustus*, Oxford: Oxford University Press.

Bonnefond-Coudry, M. (1989), *Le Sénat de la République romaine: de la guerre d'Hannibale à Auguste: pratiques délibératives et prises de décisions*, Rome: École Française de Rome.

Bonnefond-Coudry, M. (1993), 'Le *princeps senatus*', *MEFRA* 105, 103–34.

Bradley, G. (2006), 'Colonization and identity in Republican Italy', in Bradley, G. and Wilson, J-P., eds, *Greek and Roman Colonization: Origins, Ideologies and Interactions*, Swansea: Classical Press of Wales, 161–87.

Bradley, G. (2007), 'Romanization: the end of the peoples of Italy?', in Bradley, G., Isayev, E., and Riva, C., eds, *Ancient Italy: Regions without Boundaries*, Exeter: University of Exeter Press, 295–322.

Bradley, K. (1989), *Slavery and Rebellion in the Roman World, 140 B.C.–70 B.C.*, London: Batsford.

Braund, D. (1983), 'Royal wills and Rome', *PBSR* 51, 16–57.

Braund, D. (1996), 'The politics of Catullus 10', *Hermathena* 160, 45–57.

Brennan, T. C. (2000), *The Praetorship in the Roman Republic*, New York: Oxford University Press.

Brodersen, K. (1993), 'Appian und sein Werk', *ANRW* 2.34.1, 339–63.

Broughton, T. (1991), *Candidates Defeated in Roman Elections: Some Ancient Roman 'Also-Rans'*, Philadelphia: American Philological Association.

Brunt, P. A. (1962), 'The army and the land in the Roman revolution', *JRS* 52, 69–86.

Brunt, P. A. (1971), *Italian Manpower, 225 B.C.–A.D. 14*, Oxford: Oxford University Press.

Brunt, P. A. (1982), '*Nobilitas* and *novitas*', *JRS* 72, 1–17.

Brunt, P. A. (1988), *The Fall of the Roman Republic and Related Essays*, Oxford: Oxford University Press.

Burnett, A. (1998), 'The coinage of the Social War', in Burnett, A., Wartenburg, U. and Witschonke, R., eds, *Coins of Macedonia and Rome: Essays in Honour of Charles Hersh*, London: Spink, 165–72.

Burton, P. (2007), 'Genre and fact in the preface to Cicero's *De amicitia*', *Antichthon* 41, 13–32.

Butler, S. (2002), *The Hand of Cicero*, London: Routledge.

Carlsen, J. (2006), *The Rise and Fall of a Roman Noble Family: The Domitii Ahenobarbi 196 BC–AD 68*, Odense: University Press of Southern Denmark.

Carlsen, J. (2008), 'Cn. Domitius Calvinus: a noble Caesarian', *Latomus* 67, 72–81.

Castner, C. J. (1988), *A Prosopography of Roman Epicureans from the 2nd Century BC to the 2nd Century AD*, Frankfurt: Lang.

Christ, K. (2002), *Sulla: Eine römische Karriere*, Munich: Beck.

Churchill, J. B. (1999), '*Ex qua quod vellent facerent*: Roman magistrates' authority over *praeda* and *manubiae*', *TAPhA* 129, 85–115.

Clark, A. (2007), *Divine Qualities: Cult and Community in Republican Rome*, Oxford: Oxford University Press.

Cloud, D. (1994), 'The constitution and public criminal law', *CAH* 9^2, 491–530.

Cluett, R. (2009), 'The continuators: soldiering on', in Griffin, M., ed., *A Companion to Julius Caesar*, Chichester: Wiley-Blackwell, 192–205.

Conole, P. (1981), 'Allied disaffection and the revolt of Fregellae', *Antichthon* 15, 129–40.

Corbeill, A. (2010), 'A text in Cicero's *De haruspicum responsis*', in Berry, D. and Erksine, A., eds, *Form and Function in Roman Oratory*, Cambridge: Cambridge University Press, 139–54.

Coşkun, A. (2004), '"Civitas Romana" und die Inklusion von Fremden in die römische Republik am Beispiel des Bundesgenossenkrieges', in Gestrich, A. and Lutz, R., eds, *Inklusion/Exklusion: Studien zu Fremdheit und Armut von der Antike bis zur Gegenwart*, Frankfurt: Lang, 85–111.

Coşkun, A. (2005), '"Amicitiae" und politische Ambitionen im Kontext der "causa Deiotariana" (45 v. Chr.)', in Coşkun, A., ed., *Roms auswärtige Freunde in der späten Republik und frühen Prinzipat*, Göttingen: Duehrkohp & Radicke, 127–54.

Cotton, H. (1986), 'The role of Cicero's letters of recommendation: *iustitia* versus *gratia*?', *Hermes* 114, 443–60.

Courtney, E. (1993), *The Fragmentary Latin Poets*, Oxford: Oxford University Press.

Crawford, J. (1984), *M. Tullius Cicero: The Lost and Unpublished Orations*, Göttingen: Vandenhoeck & Ruprecht.

Crawford, J. (1994), *M. Tullius Cicero: The Fragmentary Speeches*, Atlanta: Scholars Press.

Crawford, M. (1968), 'The edict of M. Marius Gratidianus', *PCPhS* n.s. 14, 1–4.

Crawford, M. (1973), '*Foedus* and *sponsio*', *PBSR* 41, 1–7.

Crawford, M. (1996), *Roman Statutes*, 2 vols, London: Institute of Classical Studies.

Crawford, M. (1996), 'Italy and Rome from Sulla to Augustus', *CAH* 10^2, 414–33.

Crawford, M. (1998), 'How to create a *municipium*: Rome and Italy after the Social War', in Austin, M., Harries, J. and Smith, C., eds, *Modus Operandi: Essays in Honour of Geoffrey Rickman*, London: Institute of Classical Studies, 31–46.

Crawford, M. (2008), 'States waiting in the wings: population distribution and the end of the Roman Republic', in de Ligt, L. and Northwood, S., eds, *People, Land and Politics: Demographic Developments and the Transformation of Roman Italy, 300 BC–AD 14*, Leiden: Brill, 631–43.

Crawford, M. (2011), *Imagines Italicae*, London: Institute of Classical Studies.

Crawford, M. (2011), 'Reconstructing what Roman Republic?', *BICS* 54, 105–14.

David, J-M. (2009), 'L'exercice du patronat à la fin de la République', in Hölkeskamp, K–J., ed., *Eine politische Kultur (in) der Krise?*, Munich: Oldenbourg, 73–86.

De Cazanove, O. (2000), 'Some thoughts on the "religious Romanization" of Italy before the Social War', in Bispham, E. and Smith, C., eds, *Religion in Archaic and Republican Rome: Evidence and Experience*, Edinburgh: Edinburgh University Press, 71–6.

De Ligt, L. (2004), 'Poverty and demography: the case of the Gracchan land reforms', *Mnemosyne* 57, 725–57.

De Ligt, L. (2007), 'Roman manpower resources and the proletarianization of the Roman army in the second century B.C.', in de Blois, L. and Lo Cascio, E., eds, *The Impact of the Roman Army (200 B.C.–A.D. 476)*, Leiden: Brill, 3–20.

De Souza, P. (1999), *Piracy in the Graeco-Roman World*, Cambridge: Cambridge University Press.

Dobson, M. (2008), *The Army of the Roman Republic: The Second Century B.C., Polybius and the Camps at Numantia, Spain*, Oxford: Oxbow.

Drinkwater, J. (1983), *Roman Gaul: The Three Provinces 58 B.C.–260 A.D.*, London: Croom Helm.

Drumann, W. and Groebe, P. (1906), *Geschichte Roms*, vol. 3, 2nd edn, Leipzig: Borntraeger.

Drummond, A. (1995), *Law, Politics and Power: The Execution of the Catilinarian Conspirators*, Stuttgart: Steiner.

Drummond, A. (1999), 'Tribunes and tribunician programmes in 63 B.C.', *Athenaeum* 87, 121–67.

Drummond, A. (2000), 'Rullus and the Sullan *possessores*', *Klio* 82, 126–53.

Dugan, J. (2001), '(*Non*) *bona dicta*: intertextuality between Catullus 11.16 and Cicero *De oratore* 2.222', in Tylawsky, E. and Weiss, C., eds, *Essays in Honor of Gordon Williams: Twenty-Five Years at Yale*, New Haven: Henry R. Schwab, 85–99.

Dumont, J-C. (1987), *Servus: Rome et l'esclavage sous la République*, Rome: École Française de Rome.

Dyck, A. (1996), *A Commentary on Cicero, De Officiis*, Ann Arbor: University of Michigan Press.

Dyck, A. (2004), *A Commentary on Cicero, De Legibus*, Ann Arbor: University of Michigan Press.

Dyck, A. (2008), *Cicero: Catilinarians*, Cambridge: Cambridge University Press.

Dyck, A. (2010), *Cicero: Pro Sexto Roscio*, Cambridge: Cambridge University Press.

Dzino, D. (2002), '*Annus mirabilis*: 70 B.C. re-examined', *Ancient History* 32, 99–117.

Eckstein, A. (1982), 'Human sacrifice and fear of military disaster in Republican Rome', *AJAH* 7, 69–95.

Eckstein, A. (2006), *Mediterranean Anarchy, Interstate War, and the Rise of Rome*, Berkeley: University of California Press.

Eilers, C., ed. (2009), *Diplomats and Diplomacy in the Roman World*, Leiden: Brill.

Erskine, A. (1990), *The Hellenistic Stoa: Political Thought and Action*, London: Duckworth.

Evans, R. (1983), 'The *consulares* and *praetorii* in the Roman Senate at the beginning of Sulla's dictatorship', *Athenaeum* 61, 521–8.

Evans, R. (2008), *Utopia Antiqua: Readings of the Golden Age and Decline at Rome*, London: Routledge.

Fantham, E. (2004), *The Roman World of Cicero's De Oratore*, Oxford: Oxford University Press.

Farney, G. (2004), 'Some more Roman Republican "also-rans"', *Historia* 53, 246–50.

Farney, G. (2007), *Ethnic Identity and Aristocratic Competition in Republican Rome*, Cambridge: Cambridge University Press.

Feeney, D. (2007), *Caesar's Calendar: Ancient Time and the Beginnings of History*, Berkeley: University of California Press.

Fehrle, R. (1983), *Cato Uticensis*, Darmstadt: Wissenschaftliche Buchgesellschaft.

Ferrary, J-L. (1975), 'Cicéron et la loi judiciaire de Cotta (70 av. J.-C.)', *MEFRA* 87, 321–48.

Ferrary, J-L. (1979), 'Recherches sur la législation de Saturninus et de Glaucia, II', *MEFRA* 91, 85–134.

Ferrary, J-L. (1988), '*Rogatio Servilia Agraria*', *Athenaeum* 66, 141–64.

Ferrary, J-L. (1997), 'The Hellenistic world and Roman political patronage', in Cartledge, P., Garnsey, P. and Gruen, E., eds, *Hellenistic Constructs: Essays in Culture, History and Historiography*, Berkeley: University of California Press, 105–19.

Ferrary, J-L. (2002), 'La création de la province d'Asie et la présence italienne en Asie Mineure', in Müller, C. and Hasenohr, C., eds, *Les italiens dans le monde grec: IIe siècle av. J.-C.–Ier siècle ap. J.-C. Circulation, activités, intégration*, Paris: École Française d'Athènes, 133–46.

Ferrary, J-L. (2010), 'À propos des pouvoirs et des honneurs décernés à César entre 48 et 44', in Urso, G., ed., *Cesare: precursore o visionario? Atti del convegno internationale, Cividale del Friuli, 17-19 Settembre 2009*, Pisa: ETS, 9–30.

Flaig, E. (2004), *Ritualisierte Politik: Zeichen, Gesten und Herrschaft im Alten Rom*, 2nd edn, Göttingen: Vandenhoeck & Ruprecht.

Flower, H. (1996), *Ancestor Masks and Aristocratic Power in Roman*

Culture, Oxford: Oxford University Press.

Flower, H. (2004), 'Spectacle and political culture in the Roman Republic', in Flower, H., ed., *The Cambridge Companion to the Roman Republic*, Cambridge: Cambridge University Press, 322–43.

Flower, H. (2006), *The Art of Forgetting: Disgrace and Oblivion in Roman Political Culture*, Chapel Hill: University of North Carolina Press.

Flower, H. (2010), *Roman Republics*, Princeton: Princeton University Press.

Flower, H. (2013), 'Beyond the *contio*: political communication in the tribunate of Tiberius Gracchus', in Steel, C. and van der Blom, H., eds, *Community and Communication: Oratory and Politics in Republican Rome*, Oxford: Oxford University Press, 85–100.

Fotheringham, L. (2006), 'Cicero's fear: multiple readings of *Pro Milone* 1–4', *MD* 57, 63–83.

Fowler, D. P. (1989), 'Lucretius and politics', in Griffin, M. and Barnes, J., eds, *Philosophia Togata I*, Oxford: Oxford University Press, 120–50.

Fox, M. (2007), *Cicero's Philosophy of History*, Oxford: Oxford University Press.

Fox, M. (2009), 'Heraclides of Pontus and the philosophical dialogue', in Fortenbaugh, W. and Pender, E., eds, *Heraclides of Pontus*, New Brunswick: Transaction, 41–67.

Frederiksen, M. (1984), *Campania*, Rome: British School at Rome.

Frier, B. W. (1971), 'Sulla's propaganda and the collapse of the Cinnan Republic', *AJPh* 92, 585–604.

Gabba, E. (1976), *Republican Rome, the Army and the Allies*, trans. Cuff, P., Oxford: Blackwell.

Gabba, E. (1994), 'Rome and Italy: the Social War', *CAH* 9^2, 104–28.

Garcea, A. (2012), *Caesar's De Analogia: Edition, Translation, and Commentary*, Oxford: Oxford University Press.

Gardner, J. (2009), 'The dictator', in Griffin, M., ed., *A Companion to Julius Caesar*, Chichester: Wiley-Blackwell, 57–71.

Garnsey, P. (1988), *Famine and Food Supply in the Graeco-Roman World: Responses to Risk and Crisis*, Cambridge: Cambridge University Press.

Gee, E. (forthcoming), 'Cicero's poetry', in Steel, C., ed., *The Cambridge Companion to Cicero*, Cambridge: Cambridge University Press.

Gelzer, M. (1968), *Caesar: Politician and Statesman*, trans. Needham, P., Oxford: Blackwell.

Gelzer, M. (1969), *The Roman Nobility*, trans. Seager, R. J., Oxford: Blackwell.

Gildenhard, I. (2011), *Creative Eloquence: The Construction of Reality in Cicero's Speeches*, Oxford: Oxford University Press.

Giovannini, A. (1983), *Consulare imperium*, Basle: Reinhardt.

Goar, R. (1987), *The Legend of Cato Uticensis from the First Century B.C. to the Fifth Century A.D.*, Brussels: Latomus.

Goldmann, F. (2002), '*Nobilitas* als Status und Gruppe: Überlegungen zum

Nobilitätsbefriff der römischen Republik', in Spielvogel, J., ed., *Res publica reperta: Zur Verfassung und Gesellschaft der römischen Republik und des frühen Prinzipats*, Stuttgart: Steiner, 45–66.

Goudineau, C. (1978), 'La Gaule Transalpine', in Nicolet, C., ed., *Rome et la conquête de la monde mediterranéen*, Paris: Presses Universitaires de France, 679–99.

Greenidge, A., and Clay, A. (1960), *Sources for Roman History 133–70 B.C.*, 2nd edn, rev. Gray, E., Oxford: Oxford University Press.

Griffin, M. (1973), 'The tribune Cornelius', *JRS* 63, 196–213.

Griffin, M. (2001), 'Cicero, Piso and their audiences', in Auvray-Assayas, C. and Delattre, D., eds, *Cicéron et Philodème: la polemique en philosophie*, Paris: Rue d'Ulm, 85-99.

Gruber, J. (1988), 'Cicero und das hellenistische Herrscherideal: Überlegungen zur Rede *De imperio Cn. Pompeii*', *WS* 101, 243–58.

Gruen, E. S. (1965), 'The *lex Varia*', *JRS* 55, 59–73.

Gruen, E. S. (1966), 'The Dolabellae and Sulla', *AJPh* 87, 385–99.

Gruen, E. S. (1968), *Roman Politics and the Criminal Courts, 149–78 B.C.*, Cambridge, MA: Harvard University Press.

Gruen, E. S. (1969), 'The consular elections for 53 B.C.', in Bibauw, J., ed., *Hommages à Marcel Renard*, vol. 2, Brussels: Latomus, 311–21.

Gruen, E. S. (1974), *The Last Generation of the Roman Republic*, Berkeley: University of California Press.

Gruen, E. S. (1984), *The Hellenistic World and the Coming of Rome*, Berkeley: University of California Press.

Gruen, E. S. (1991), 'The exercise of power in the Roman Republic', in Molho, A., Raaflaub, K. and Emlen, J., eds, *City States in Classical Antiquity and Medieval Italy*, Ann Arbor: University of Michigan Press, 251–67.

Hackl, U. (1988), 'Die Gründung der Provinz Gallia Narbonensis im Spiegel von Ciceros Rede für Fonteius', *Historia* 37, 253–6.

Hall, J. (2009), *Politeness and Politics in Cicero's Letters*, Oxford: Oxford University Press.

Hall, L. (1998), '*Ratio* and *romanitas* in the *Bellum Gallicum*', in Powell, A. and Welch, K., eds, *Julius Caesar as Artful Reporter: The War Commentaries as Political Instruments*, Swansea: Classical Press of Wales, 11–43.

Harries, J. (2006), *Cicero and the Jurists: From Citizens' Law to Lawful State*, London: Duckworth.

Harries, J. (2007), *Law and Crime in the Roman World*, Cambridge: Cambridge University Press.

Harris, W. V. (1971), *Rome in Etruria and Umbria*, Oxford: Oxford University Press.

Harris, W. V. (1979), *War and Imperialism in Republican Rome*, Oxford: Oxford University Press.

Harris, W. V. (2011), *Rome's Imperial Economy: Twelve Essays*, Oxford: Oxford University Press.

Hassall, M., Crawford, M. and Reynolds, J. (1974), 'Rome and the eastern provinces at the end of the second century B.C.', *JRS* 64, 195–220.

Hawthorn, J. (1962), 'The Senate after Sulla', *G&R* 9, 53–60.

Hiebel, D. (2009), *Rôles institutionel et politique de la contio sous la république romaine*, Paris: de Boccard.

Hillard, T. W. (1996), 'Death by lightning, Pompeius Strabo and the people', *RhM* 139, 135–45.

Hillard, T. W. (2005), '"Res publica" in theory and practice', in Welch, K. and Hillard, T., eds, *Roman Crossings: Theory and Practice in the Roman Republic*, Swansea: Classical Press of Wales, 1–48.

Hinard, F. (1985), *Les proscriptions de la Rome républicaine*, Rome: École Française de Rome.

Hinard, F. (2006), 'La terreur comme mode de gouvernement', in Urso, G., ed., *Terror et pavor: violenza, intimidazione, clandestinità nel mondo antico*, Pisa: ETS, 247–64.

Hind, J. (1994), 'Mithridates', *CAH* 9^2, 129–64.

Hölkeskamp, K-J. (2004), *Senatus populusque Romanus: Die politische Kultur der Republik*, Stuttgart: Steiner.

Hölkeskamp, K-J. (2010), *Reconstructing the Roman Republic: An Ancient Political Culture and Modern Research*, Princeton: Princeton University Press.

Hollander, D. (2007), *Money in the Late Roman Republic*, Leiden: Brill.

Hopkins, K. and Burton, G. (1983), 'Political succession in the late Republic (249–50 BC)', in Hopkins, K., *Death and Renewal: Sociological Studies in Roman History 2*, Cambridge: Cambridge University Press, 31–119.

Horden, P. and Purcell, N. (2000), *The Corrupting Sea*, Oxford: Blackwell.

Horsfall, N. (2003), *The Culture of the Roman Plebs*, London: Duckworth.

Hurlet, F. (1993), *La dictature de Sylla: monarchie ou magistrature republicaine?*, Brussels: Institut Historique Belge de Rome.

Itgenshorst, T. (2005), *Tota illa pompa: Der Triumph in der römischen Republik*, Göttingen: Vandenhoeck & Ruprecht.

Jehne, M., ed. (1995), *Demokratie in Rom? Die Rolle des Volkes in der Politik der römischen Republik*, Stuttgart: Steiner.

Jehne, M. (2013), 'Feeding the *plebs* with words: the significance of senatorial public oratory in the small world of Roman politics', in Steel, C. and van der Blom, H., eds, *Community and Communication: Oratory and Politics in Republican Rome*, Oxford: Oxford University Press, 49–62.

Kallet-Marx, R. M. (1990), 'The trial of Rutilius Rufus', *Phoenix* 44, 122–39.

Kallet-Marx, R. M. (1995), *Hegemony to Empire: The Development of the*

Roman Imperium in the East from 148 to 62 B.C., Berkeley: University of California Press.

Kaster, R. A. (1995), *C. Suetonius Tranquillus De Grammaticis et Rhetoribus: Edited with a Translation, Introduction, and Commentary*, Oxford: Oxford University Press.

Kaster, R. A. (2006), *Cicero: Speech on Behalf of Publius Sestius*, Oxford: Oxford University Press.

Katz, B. (1977), 'Caesar Strabo's struggle for the consulship – and more', *RhM* 120, 45–63.

Keaveney, A. (2003), 'The short career of Q. Lucretius Afella', *Eranos* 101, 84–93.

Keaveney, A. (2005), *Sulla: The Last Republican*, 2nd edn, London: Routledge.

Keay, S. (1995), 'Innovation and adaptation: the contribution of Rome to urbanism in Iberia', in Cunliffe, B. and Keay, S., eds, *Social Complexity and the Development of Towns in Iberia: From the Copper Age to the Second Century* AD, Oxford: Oxford University Press, 291–337.

Kelly, G. (2006), *A History of Exile in the Roman Republic*, New York: Cambridge University Press.

Knox, P. (2011), 'Cicero as a Hellenistic poet', *CQ* 61, 192–204.

Konrad, C. (1996), 'Notes on Roman also-rans', in Linderski, J., ed., *Imperium sine Fine: T. Robert S. Broughton and the Roman Republic*, Stuttgart: Steiner, 104–43.

Konstan, D. (2000), 'Self, sex and empire in Catullus: the construction of a decentered identity', in Bécares, V., Pordomingo, F., Cortés Tovar, R. and Fernández Corte, J., eds, *Intertextualidad en las literaturas griega y latina*, Madrid: Ediciones Clásicas, 213-31.

Krebs, C. (2008), '*Magni viri*: Caesar, Alexander and Pompey in Cat. 11', *Philologus* 152, 223–9.

Kurczyk, S. (2006), *Cicero und die Inszenierung der eigenen Vergangenheit: Autobiograpisches Schreiben in der späten römischen Republik*, Cologne: Böhlau.

Lerouge, C. (2007), *L'image des Parthes dans le monde gréco-romain*, Stuttgart: Steiner.

Levene, D. (2005), 'The late Republican/triumviral period, 90–40 B.C.', in Harrison, S. J., ed., *The Blackwell Companion to Latin Literature*, Oxford: Blackwell, 31–43.

Levene, D. (2007), 'Roman historiography in the late Republic', in Marincola, J., ed., *A Companion to Greek and Roman Historiography*, Oxford: Blackwell, 275–89.

Lewis, R. G. (2006), *Asconius: Commentaries on Speeches of Cicero*, Oxford: Oxford University Press.

Linderski, J. (1990), 'The surname of M. Antonius Creticus and the cognomina *ex victis gentibus*', *ZPE* 80, 157–64.

Linderski, J. (2002), 'The pontiff and the tribune: the death of Tiberius Gracchus', *Athenaeum* 90, 339–66.

Lindsay, H. (2009), *Adoption in the Roman World*, Cambridge: Cambridge University Press.

Linke, B. and Stemmler, M., eds (2000), *Mos Maiorum: Untersuchungen zu den Formen der Identitätsstiftung und Stabilisierung in der römischen Republik*, Stuttgart: Steiner.

Lintott, A. (1967), 'P. Clodius Pulcher: *Felix Catilina?*', *G&R* 14, 157–69.

Lintott, A. (1971), 'The tribunate of P. Sulpicius Rufus', *CQ* 21, 442–53.

Lintott, A. (1971), 'The offices of C. Flavius Fimbria in 86–85 B.C.', *Historia* 20, 696–701.

Lintott, A. (1981), 'The *leges de repetundis* and associated measures under the Republic', *ZRG* 98, 162–212.

Lintott, A. (1992), *Judicial Reform and Land Reform in the Roman Republic*, Cambridge: Cambridge University Press.

Lintott, A. (1993), *Imperium Romanum: Politics and Administration*, London: Routledge.

Lintott, A. (1999), *The Constitution of the Roman Republic*, Oxford: Oxford University Press.

Lintott, A. (1999), *Violence in Republican Rome*, 2nd edn, Oxford: Oxford University Press.

Lintott, A. (2008), *Cicero as Evidence*, Oxford: Oxford University Press.

Lintott, A. (2009), 'The assassination', in Griffin, M., ed., *A Companion to Julius Caesar*, Chichester: Wiley-Blackwell, 72–82.

Lo Cascio, E. (1994), 'The size of the Roman population: Beloch and the meaning of the Augustan census figures', *JRS* 84, 23–40.

Lomas, K. (2004), 'A Volscian Mafia? Cicero and his Italian clients', in Powell, J. and Paterson, J., eds, *Cicero the Advocate*, Oxford: Oxford University Press, 97–116.

Lovano, M. (2002), *The Age of Cinna: Crucible of Late Republican Rome*, Stuttgart: Steiner.

Magie, D. (1950), *Roman Rule in Asia Minor to the End of the Third Century after Christ*, Princeton: Princeton University Press.

Marasco, G., ed. (2011), *Political Autobiographies and Memoirs in Antiquity: A Brill Companion*, Leiden: Brill.

Marinone, N. (2004), *Cronologia Ciceroniana*, 2nd edn, Rome: Centro di Studi Ciceroniani.

Marshall, B. (1976), *Crassus: A Political Biography*, Amsterdam: Hakkert.

Marshall, B. (1985), *A Historical Commentary on Asconius*, Columbia: University of Missouri Press.

Marshall, B. (1985), 'Catilina and the execution of M. Marius Gratidianus', *CQ* 35, 124–33.

Marshall, B. and Beness, J. (1987), 'Tribunician agitation and aristocratic reaction 80–71 B.C.', *Athenaeum* 65, 361–78.

Martin, P. (2000), 'Sur quelques thèmes de l'éloquence *popularis*, notamment l'invective contre le passivité du peuple', in Achard, G. and Ledentu, M., eds, *Orateur, auditeurs, lecteurs: à propos de l'éloquence romaine à la fin de la République et au début du Principat: actes de la table ronde de 31 janvier 2000*, Lyon: Centre d'Études et de Recherches sur l'Occident Romain de l' Université Lyon III, 27–41.

McDermott, W. (1972), 'Curio *pater* and Cicero', *AJPh* 93, 381–411.

McGing, B. (1986), *The Foreign Policy of Mithridates VI Eupator King of Pontus*, Leiden: Brill.

McGing, B. (2009), 'Mithridates VI Eupator: victim or aggressor?', in Højte, J., ed., *Mithridates VI and the Pontic Kingdom*, Aarhus: Aarhus University Press, 203–16.

McGing, B. (2010), *Polybius' Histories*, Oxford: Oxford University Press.

McGushin, P. (1992), *Sallust: The Histories*, Oxford: Oxford University Press.

Michels, A. (1967), *The Calendar of the Roman Republic*, Princeton: Princeton University Press.

Migeotte, L. (1984), *L'emprunt public dans les cités grecques*, Paris: Les Belles Lettres.

Millar, F. (1984), 'The political character of the classical Roman Republic, 200–151 B.C.', *JRS* 74, 1–19.

Millar, F. (1986), 'Politics, persuasion and the people before the Social War (150–90 B.C.)', *JRS* 76, 1–11.

Millar, F. (1998), *The Crowd in Rome in the Late Republic*, Ann Arbor: University of Michigan Press.

Mitchell, T. (1975), 'The volte-face of P. Sulpicius Rufus in 88 B.C.', *CPh* 70.3, 197–204.

Moreau, P. (1982), *Clodiana religio: un procès politique en 61 avant J.C.*, Paris: Les Belles Lettres.

Morgan, L. (2000), 'The autopsy of C. Asinius Pollio', *JRS* 90, 51–69.

Morley, N. (2001), 'The transformation of Italy, 225–28 B.C.', *JRS* 91, 50–62.

Morstein-Marx, R. (2004), *Mass Oratory and Political Power in the Late Roman Republic*, Cambridge: Cambridge University Press.

Morstein-Marx, R. (2007), 'Caesar's alleged fear of prosecution and his *ratio absentis*', *Historia* 56, 159–78.

Morstein-Marx, R. (2009), '*Dignitas* and *res publica*: Caesar and Republican legitimacy', in Hölkeskamp, K-J., ed., *Eine politische Kultur (in) der Krise?*, Munich: Oldenbourg, 115–40.

Morstein-Marx, R. (2013), '"Cultural hegemony" and the com-municative power of the Roman elite', in Steel, C. and van der Blom, H., eds, *Community and Communication: Oratory and Politics in Republican Rome*, Oxford: Oxford University Press, 29–47.

Mouritsen, H. (1998), *Italian Unification: A Study in Ancient and Modern*

Historiography, London: Institute of Classical Studies.

Mouritsen, H. (2001), *Plebs and Politics in the Late Roman Republic*, Cambridge: Cambridge University Press.

Mouritsen, H. (2008), 'The Gracchi, the Latins, and the Italian allies', in de Ligt, L. and Northwood, S., eds, *People, Land and Politics: Demographic Developments and the Transformation of Roman Italy, 300 BC–AD 14*, Leiden: Brill, 471–83.

Münzer, F. (1999), *Roman Aristocratic Parties and Families*, trans. Ridley, R. T., Baltimore: Johns Hopkins University Press.

Nicolet, C. (1980), *The World of the Citizen in Republican Rome*, trans. Falla, P., London: Batsford.

Nicolet, C. (2004), 'Dictatorship at Rome', in Baehr, P. and Richter, M., eds, *Dictatorship in History and Theory: Bonapartism, Caesarianism and Totalitarianism*, Cambridge: Cambridge University Press, 263–78.

Nippel, W. (1995), *Public Order in Ancient Rome*, Cambridge: Cambridge University Press.

Nisbet, R. (1992), 'The orator and the reader: manipulation and response in Cicero's Fifth Verrine', in Woodman, A. and Powell, J., eds, *Author and Audience in Latin Literature*, Cambridge: Cambridge University Press, 1–17.

Nisbet, R. and Hubbard, M. (1978), *A Commentary on Horace Odes Book II*, Oxford: Oxford University Press.

North, J. (1990), 'Democratic politics in Republican Rome', *P&P* 126, 3–21.

North, J. (1990), 'Family strategy and priesthood in the late Republic', in Andreau, J. and Bruhns, H., eds, *Parenté et stratégies familiales dans l'antiquité romaine*, Rome: École Française de Rome, 527–43.

North, J. (2008), 'Caesar at the Lupercalia', *JRS* 98, 144–60.

O'Gorman, E. (2004), 'Cato the Elder and the destruction of Carthage', *Helios* 31, 99–125.

Oost, S. I. (1963), 'Cyrene, 96–74 B.C.', *CPh* 58, 11–25.

Ooteghem, J. van (1961), *Lucius Marcius Philippus et sa famille*, Brussels: Palais des Académies.

Östenberg, I. (2009), *Staging the World: Spoils, Captives and Representations in the Roman Triumphal Procession*, Oxford: Oxford University Press.

Panayotakis, C. (2010), *Decimus Laberius: The Fragments*, Cambridge: Cambridge University Press.

Patterson, J. (2000), *Political Life in the City of Rome*, Bristol: Bristol Classical Press.

Piccinin, P. (2004), 'Les Italiens dans le *Bellum Spartacium*', *Historia* 53, 173–99.

Pieri, G. (1968), *L'histoire du cens jusqu'à la fin de la République romaine*, Paris: Sirey.

Pina Polo, F. (1996), *Contra arma verbis: Der Redner vor dem in der späten römischen Republik*, Stuttgart: Steiner.

Pina Polo, F. (2001), 'Über die sogenannte *cohors amicorum* des Scipio Aemilianus', in Peachin, M., ed., *Aspects of Friendship in the Graeco-Roman World*, Portsmouth: Journal of Roman Archaeology, 89–98.

Pina Polo, F. (2011), *The Consul at Rome*, Cambridge: Cambridge University Press.

Pobjoy, M. (2000), 'The first *Italia*', in Herring, E. and Lomas, K., eds, *The Emergence of State Identities in Italy in the First Millennium* BC, London: Accordia Research Institute, 187–211.

Powell, J. (1990), 'The tribune Sulpicius', *Historia* 39, 446–60.

Powell, J. (1994), 'The *rector rei publicae* of Cicero's De re publica', *SCI* 13, 19–29.

Powell, J. and Paterson, J., eds (2004), *Cicero the Advocate*, Oxford: Oxford University Press.

Prag, J. (2013), 'The provincial perspective on the politics of *repetundae* trials', in Steel, C. and van der Blom, H., eds, *Community and Communication: Oratory and Politics in Republican Rome*, Oxford: Oxford University Press, 265–81.

Primmer, A. (1985), *Die Überredungsstrategie in Ciceros Rede Pro Rabirio perduellionis reo*, Vienna: Verlag der Osterreichischen Akademie der Wissenschaften.

Purcell, N. (1994), 'The city of Rome and the *plebs urbana* in the late Republic', *CAH* 9^2, 644–88.

Purcell, N. (1995), 'On the sacking of Carthage and Corinth', in Innes, D., Hine, H. and Pelling, C., eds, *Ethics and Rhetoric: Classical Essays for Donald Russell on his Seventy-Fifth Birthday*, Oxford: Oxford University Press, 133–48.

Raaflaub, K. (1996), 'Born to be wolves? Origins of Roman imperialism', in Wallace, R. and Harris, E., eds, *Transitions to Empire: Essays in Greco-Roman History, 360–146 B.C., in Honor of E. Badian*, Norman: University of Oklahoma Press, 273–314.

Raaflaub, K. (2009), '*Bellum Civile*', in Griffin, M., ed., *A Companion to Julius Caesar*, Chichester: Wiley-Blackwell, 175–91.

Rawson, E. (1973), 'Scipio, Laelius, Furius and the ancestral religion', *JRS* 63, 161–74.

Rawson, E. (1974), 'Religion and politics in the late second century BC at Rome', *Phoenix* 28, 193–212.

Rawson, E. (1975), 'The activities of the Cossutii', *PBSR* 43, 36–47.

Rawson, E. (1975), 'Caesar's heritage: Hellenistic kings and their Roman equals', *JRS* 65, 148–59.

Rawson, E. (1983), *Cicero: A Portrait*, 2nd edn, London: Bristol Classical Press.

Rawson, E. (1985), *Intellectual Life in the Late Roman Republic*, London: Duckworth.

Ribera i Lacomba, A. (2006), 'The Roman foundation of Valencia and the town in the 2nd–1st c. B.C.', in Abad Casal, L., Keay, S. and Ramallo Asensio, S., eds, *Early Roman Towns in Hispania Tarraconensis*, Portsmouth: Journal of Roman Archaeology, 75–89.

Rich, J. (1976), *Declaring War in the Roman Republic in the Period of Transmarine Expansion*, Brussels: Latomus.

Rich, J. (1983), 'The supposed Roman manpower shortage of the later second century A.D.', *Historia* 32, 287–331.

Rich, J. (1993), 'Fear, greed and glory: the causes of Roman war-making in the middle Republic', in Rich, J. and Shipley, G., eds, *War and Society in the Roman World*, London: Routledge, 38–68.

Richardson, J. S. (1986), *Hispaniae: Spain and the Development of Roman Imperialism*, Cambridge: Cambridge University Press.

Richardson, J. S. (1994), 'The administration of the Empire', *CAH* 9², 564–98.

Richardson, J. S. (2008), *The Language of Empire: Rome and the Idea of Empire from the Third Century* BC *to the Second Century* AD, Cambridge: Cambridge University Press.

Richardson, J. S. (2012), *Augustan Rome, 44* BC *to* AD *14: The Restoration of the Republic and the Establishment of Empire*, Edinburgh: Edinburgh University Press.

Rickman, G. (1980), *The Corn Supply of Ancient Rome*, Oxford: Oxford University Press.

Ridley, R. (1986), 'To be taken with a pinch of salt: the destruction of Carthage', *CPh* 80, 140–6.

Riggsby, A. (2006), *Caesar in Gaul and Rome: War in Words*, Austin: University of Texas Press.

Robb, M. (2010), *Beyond Populares and Optimates: Political Language in the Late Republic*, Stuttgart: Steiner.

Rodgers, B. S. (2008), 'Catulus' speech in Cassius Dio 36.31–36', *GRBS* 48, 295–318.

Rose, P. (1995), 'Cicero and the rhetoric of imperialism: putting the politics back into political rhetoric', *Rhetorica* 13, 359–99.

Roselaar, S. (2010), *Public Land in the Roman Republic: A Social and Economic History of Ager Publicus in Italy, 396–89* B.C., Oxford: Oxford University Press.

Rosenstein, N. (1986), '"Imperatores victi": the case of C. Hostilius Mancinus', *Cl Ant* 5, 230–52.

Rosenstein, N. (1990), *Imperatores Victi: Military Defeat and Aristocratic Competition in the Middle and Late Republic*, Berkeley: University of California Press.

Rosenstein, N. (2004), *Rome at War: Farms, Families and Death in the*

Middle Republic, Chapel Hill: University of North Carolina Press.

Rosenstein, N. (2008), 'Revolution and rebellion in the later second and early first centuries BC: Jack Goldstone and the "Roman revolution"', in de Ligt, L. and Northwood, S., eds, *People, Land and Politics: Demographic Developments and the Transformation of Roman Italy, 300 BC–AD 14*, Leiden: Brill, 605–29.

Rosenstein, N. (2012), *Rome and the Mediterranean 290 to 146 BC: The Imperial Republic*, Edinburgh: Edinburgh University Press.

Rosillo Lopez, C. (2010), *La corruption à la fin de la République romaine*, Stutttgart: Steiner.

Roth, U. (2007), *Thinking Tools: Agricultural Slavery between Evidence and Models*, London: Institute of Classical Studies.

Rubinsohn, Z. (1971), 'Was the *Bellum Spartacium* a servile insurrection?', *Rivista di Filologia* 99, 290–9.

Rüpke, J. (2008), *Fasti Sacerdotum*, Oxford: Oxford University Press.

Russell, A. (2013), 'Speech, competition and collaboration: tribunician politics and the development of popular ideology', in Steel, C. and van der Blom, H., eds, *Community and Communication: Oratory and Politics in Republican Rome*, Oxford: Oxford University Press, 101–15.

Ryan, F. X. (1997), 'The praetorship of L. Roscius Otho', *Hermes* 125, 236–40.

Ryan, F. X. (1998), *Rank and Participation in the Republican Senate*, Stuttgart: Steiner.

Salerno, F. (1999), *Tacita libertas: l'introduzione del voto segreto nella Roma repubblicana*, Naples: Edizioni Scientifiche Italiane.

Salmon, E. T. (1967), *Samnium and the Samnites*, Cambridge: Cambridge University Press.

Salmon, E. T. (1969), *Roman Colonization under the Republic*, London: Thames and Hudson.

Salomonsson, M-M. (2000), 'Roman legates in the Republic', *Opuscula Romana* 25–6, 79–88.

Sandberg, K. (2001), *Magistrates and Assemblies: A Study of Legislative Practice in Republican Rome*, Rome: Institutum Romanum Finlandiae.

Santangelo, F. (2006), 'Sulla and the Senate: a reconsideration', *Cahiers du Centre Gustave-Glotz* 17, 7–22 [publ. 2008].

Santangelo, F. (2007), *Sulla, the Elites and the Empire*, Leiden: Brill.

Santangelo, F. (2008), 'The fetials and their *ius*', *BICS* 51, 63–93.

Scheid, J. (2003), *An Introduction to Roman Religion*, Edinburgh: Edinburgh University Press.

Scheidel, W. (2004), 'Human mobility in Roman Italy, I: the free population', *JRS* 94, 1–26.

Scheidel, W. (2005), 'Human mobility in Roman Italy, II: the slave population', *JRS* 95, 64–79.

Scheidel, W. (2008), 'Roman population size: the logic of the debate', in de Ligt, L. and Northwood, S., eds, *People, Land and Politics: Demographic Developments and the Transformation of Roman Italy, 300 BC–AD 14*, Leiden: Brill, 17–70.

Schiesaro, A. (2007), 'Lucretius and Roman politics and history', in Gillespie, S. and Hardie, P., eds, *The Cambridge Companion to Lucretius*, Cambridge: Cambridge University Press, 41–58.

Schneider, W. C. (1998), *Vom Handeln der Römer: Kommunikation und Interaktion der politischen Führungsschicht vor Ausbruch des Bürgerkriegs im Briefwechsel mit Cicero*, Hildesheim: Olms.

Schofield, M. (1995), 'Cicero's definition of *res publica*', in Powell, J., ed., *Cicero the Philosopher*, Oxford: Oxford University Press, 63–83.

Schofield, M. (2009), 'Ciceronian dialogue', in Goldhill, S., ed., *The End of Dialogue in Antiquity*, Cambridge: Cambridge University Press, 63–84.

Sciarrino, E. (2011), *Cato the Censor and the Beginnings of Latin Prose: From Poetic Translation to Elite Transcription*, Columbus: Ohio State University Press.

Scobie, A. (1986), 'Slums, sanitation and mortality in the Roman world', *Klio* 68, 399–433.

Seager, R. (1967), '*Lex Varia de maiestate*', *Historia* 16, 37–43.

Seager, R. (1994), 'Sulla', *CAH* 9², 165–207.

Seager, R. (2002), *Pompey the Great*, 2nd edn, Oxford: Blackwell.

Shayegan, R. (2011), *Arsacids and Sasanians: Political Ideology in Post-Hellenistic and Late Antique Persia*, Cambridge: Cambridge University Press.

Sheldon, R. (2005), *Intelligence Activities in Ancient Rome*, London: Cass.

Sheldon, R. (2010), *Rome's Wars in Parthia*, Edgware: Vallentine Mitchell.

Sherwin-White, A. N. (1973), *The Roman Citizenship*, 2nd edn, Oxford: Oxford University Press.

Sherwin-White, A. N. (1984), *Roman Foreign Policy in the East, 168 B.C. to A.D. 1*, London: Duckworth.

Siani-Davies, M. (2001), *Cicero's Speech Pro Rabirio Postumo*, Oxford: Oxford University Press.

Smith, C. J. (2006), *The Roman Clan: The Gens from Ancient Ideology to Modern Anthropology*, Cambridge: Cambridge University Press.

Smith, C. J. (2008), 'Sulla's memoirs and Roman autobiography', in Smith, C. J. and Powell, A., eds, *The Lost Memoirs of Augustus*, Swansea: Classical Press of Wales, 65–85.

Smith, C. J. and Yarrow, L., eds (2012), *Imperialism, Cultural Politics and Polybius*, Oxford: Oxford University Press.

Spann, P. (1987), *Quintus Sertorius and the Legacy of Sulla*, Fayetteville: University of Arkansas Press.

Spielvogel, J. (1997), 'P. Clodius Pulcher: eine politische Ausnahmeerscheinung in der Späten Republik?', *Hermes* 125, 56–74.

Staples, A. (1998), *From Good Goddess to Vestal Virgins: Sex and Category in Roman Religion*, London: Routledge.

Staveley, E. S. (1972), *Greek and Roman Voting and Elections*, London: Thames and Hudson.

Steel, C. (2001), *Cicero, Rhetoric, and Empire*, Oxford: Oxford University Press.

Steel, C. (2005), *Reading Cicero: Genre and Performance in Late Republican Rome*, London: Duckworth.

Steel, C. (2007), 'Name and shame? Invective against Clodius and others in the post-exile speeches', in Booth, J., ed., *Cicero on the Attack: Invective and Subversion in the Orations and Beyond*, Swansea: Classical Press of Wales, 105–28.

Steel, C. (2009), 'Friends, associates and wives', in Griffin, M., ed., *A Companion to Julius Caesar*, Chichester: Wiley-Blackwell, 112–25.

Steel, C. (2010), 'Tribunician sacrosanctity and oratorial performance in the late Republic', in Berry, D. and Erskine, A., eds, *Form and Function in Roman Oratory*, Cambridge: Cambridge University Press, 37–50.

Steel, C. (2012), 'The *lex Pompeia de prouinciis*: a reconsideration', *Historia* 61, 83–93.

Steel, C. (2013), 'Pompeius, Helvius Mancia and the politics of public debate', in Steel, C. and van der Blom, H., eds, *Community and Communication: Oratory and Politics in Republican Rome*, Oxford: Oxford University Press, 151–9.

Steel, C. (forthcoming), 'Cicero's autobiography: narratives of success in the pre-consular orations', *Cahiers Glotz*.

Stevenson, T., 'Readings of Scipio's dictatorship in Cicero's *De re publica* (6.12)', *CQ* 55, 140–52.

Stockton, D. (1979), *The Gracchi*, Oxford: Oxford University Press.

Stroh, W. (1975), *Taxis und Taktik: Die advokatischen Dispositionskunst in Ciceros Gerichtsreden*, Stuttgart: Teubner.

Stroh, W. (2004), '*De domo sua*: legal problem and structure', in Powell, J. and Paterson, J., eds, *Cicero the Advocate*, Oxford: Oxford University Press, 313–70.

Stroup, S. C. (2010), *Cicero, Catullus and a Society of Patrons: The Generation of the Text*, Cambridge: Cambridge University Press.

Suolahti, J. (1972), '*Princeps senatus*', *Arctos* 7, 207–18.

Syme, R. (1939), *The Roman Revolution*, Oxford: Oxford University Press.

Syme, R. (1986), *The Augustan Aristocracy*, Oxford: Oxford University Press.

Szemler, G. (1972), *The Priests of the Roman Republic: A Study of Interactions between Priesthoods and Magistracies*, Brussels: Latomus.

Tan, J. (2013), 'Publius Clodius and the boundaries of the *contio*', in Steel, C. and van der Blom, H., eds, *Community and Communication: Oratory and Politics in Republican Rome*, Oxford: Oxford University Press, 117–32.

Tansey, P. (2003), 'The death of M. Aemilius Scaurus (cos. 115 B.C.)', *Historia* 52, 378–83.

Tatum, W. J. (1999), *Publius Clodius Pulcher: The Patrician Tribune*, Chapel Hill: University of North Carolina Press.

Tatum, W. J. (2008), *Always I Am Caesar*, Oxford: Blackwell.

Tatum, W. J. (2013), 'Campaign rhetoric', in Steel, C. and van der Blom, H., eds, *Community and Communication: Oratory and Politics in Republican Rome*, Oxford: Oxford University Press, 133–50.

Taylor, L. R. (1950), 'The date and meaning of the Vettius affair', *Historia* 1, 45–51.

Taylor, L. R. (1951), 'On the chronology of Caesar's first consulship', *AJPh* 72, 254–68.

Taylor, L. R. (1960), *The Voting Districts of the Roman Republic: The Thirty-Five Urban and Rural Tribes*, Rome: American Academy in Rome.

Taylor, L. R. (1962), 'Forerunners of the Gracchi', *JRS* 52, 19–27.

Thommen, L. (1989), *Das Volktribunat der späten römischen Republik*, Stuttgart: Steiner.

Thonemann, P. (2004), 'The date of Lucullus' quaestorship', *ZPE* 149, 80–2.

Toner, J. (2009), *Popular Culture in Ancient Rome*, Cambridge: Polity.

Torelli, M. (1999), *Tota Italia: Essays in the Cultural Formation of Roman Italy*, Oxford: Oxford University Press.

Tröster, M. (2009), 'Roman hegemony and non-state violence: a fresh look at Pompey's campaign against the pirates', *G&R* 56, 14–33.

Tyrell, W. B. (1978), *A Legal and Historical Commentary on Cicero's Oratio pro C. Rabirio Perduellionis*, Amsterdam: Hakkert.

Urbainczyk, T. (2008), *Slave Revolts in Antiquity*, Stocksfield: Acumen.

van der Blom, H. (2010), *Cicero's Role Models: The Political Strategy of a Newcomer*, Oxford: Oxford University Press.

van der Blom, H. (2013), 'Fragmentary speeches: the oratory and political career of Piso Caesoninus', in Steel, C. and van der Blom, H., eds, *Community and Communication: Oratory and Politics in Republican Rome*, Oxford: Oxford University Press, 299–314.

Vanderbroeck, J. (1987), *Popular Leadership and Collective Behaviour in the Late Roman Republic, 80–50 B.C.*, Amsterdam: Gieben.

Várhelyi, Z. (2007), 'The specters of Roman imperialism: the live burials of Gauls and Greeks at Rome', *ClAnt* 26, 277–304.

Vasaly, A. (1993), *Representations: Images of the World in Ciceronian Oratory*, Berkeley: University of California Press.

Vasaly, A. (2009), 'Cicero, domestic politics, and the first action of the *Verrines*', *Classical Antiquity* 28, 101–37.

Wallace-Hadrill, A. (1998), 'To be Roman, go Greek: thoughts on Hellenization at Rome', in Austin, M., Harries, J. and Smith, C., eds, *Modus Operandi: Essays in Honour of Geoffrey Rickman*, London: Institute of Classical Studies, 79–91.

Wallace-Hadrill, A. (2008), *Rome's Cultural Revolution*, Cambridge: Cambridge University Press.

Walter, U. (2004), *Memoria und res publica: Zur Geschichtskultur im repulikanischen Rom*, Frankfurt: Verlag Antike.

Wardle, D. (2009), 'Caesar and religion', in Griffin, M., ed., *A Companion to Julius Caesar*, Chichester: Wiley-Blackwell, 100–11.

Weggen, K. (2011), *Der Lange Schatten von Carrhae: Studien zu M. Licinius Crassus*, Hamburg: Kovac.

Weinrib, E. (1968), 'The prosecution of Roman magistrates', *Phoenix* 22, 32–56.

Welch, K. (1998), 'Caesar and his officers in the Gallic War Commentaries', in Welch, K. and Powell, A. eds, *Julius Caesar as Artful Reporter: The War Commentaries as Political Instruments*, Swansea: Classical Press of Wales, 85–110.

White, P. (2010), *Cicero in Letters: Epistolary Relations of the Late Republic*, New York: Oxford University Press.

Wikander, Ö. (1976), 'Caius Hostilius Mancinus and the *Foedus Numantinum*', *ORom* 11, 85–104.

Williams, R. S. (1984), 'The appointment of Glabrio (cos 67) to the Eastern Command', *Phoenix* 38, 221–34.

Williamson, C. (2005), *The Laws of the Roman People: Public Law in the Expansion and Decline of the Roman Republic*, Ann Arbor: University of Michigan Press.

Wiseman, T. P. (1966), 'The ambitions of Q. Cicero', *JRS* 56, 108–15.

Wiseman, T. P. (1967), 'Lucius Memmius and his family', *CQ* 17, 164–7.

Wiseman, T. P. (1969), 'The census in the first century B.C.', *JRS* 59, 59–75.

Wiseman, T. P. (1971), *New Men in the Roman Senate 139 B.C.–A.D. 14*, Oxford: Oxford University Press.

Wiseman, T. P. (1993), 'Rome and the resplendent Aemilii', in Jocelyn, H., ed., *Tria Lustra: Essays and Notes Presented to John Pinsent*, Liverpool: Liverpool Classical Monthly, 181–92.

Wiseman, T. P. (1994), 'The Senate and the *populares*, 69–60 B.C.', *CAH* 9^2, 327–67.

Wiseman, T. P. (1994), 'Caesar, Pompey and Rome, 59–50 B.C.', *CAH* 9^2, 368–423.

Wiseman, T. P. (1998), *Roman Drama and Roman History*, Exeter: University of Exeter Press.

Wiseman, T. P. (1998), 'The publication of *De Bello Gallico*', in Powell, A. and Welch, K., eds, *Julius Caesar as Artful Reporter: The War Commentaries as Political Instruments*, Swansea: Classical Press of Wales, 1–9.

Wiseman, T. P. (2009), *Remembering the Roman People*, Oxford: Oxford University Press.

Woolf, G. (1998), *Becoming Roman: The Origins of Provincial Civilisation in Gaul*, Cambridge: Cambridge University Press.

Woolf, G. (2006), *Et Tu Brute? The Murder of Caesar and Political Assassination*, London: Profile.

Wylie, G. (1989), 'Why did Labienus defect from Caesar in 49 B.C.?', *Ancient History Bulletin* 3, 123–7.

Yakobson, A. (1995), 'The secret ballot and its effects in the Late Roman Republic', *Hermes* 123, 426–42.

Yakobson, A. (1999), *Elections and Electioneering in Rome: A Study in the Political System of the Late Republic*, Stuttgart: Steiner.

Yarrow, L. (2006), *Historiography at the End of the Republic*, Oxford: Oxford University Press.

Yarrow, L. (2006), 'Lucius Mummius and the spoils of Corinth', *SCI* 25, 57–70.

Zetzel, J. (1995), *Cicero: De Re Publica, Selections*, Cambridge: Cambridge University Press.

Zetzel, J. (forthcoming), 'Political philosophy', in Steel, C., ed., *The Cambridge Companion to Cicero*, Cambridge: Cambridge University Press.

Ziolkowski, A. (1993), '*Urbs direpta*, or how the Romans sacked cities', in Rich, J. and Shipley, G., eds, *War and Society in the Roman World*, London: Routledge, 69–91.

Zollschan, L. (2012), 'The longevity of the fetial college', in Tellegen-Couperus, O., ed., *Law and Religion in the Roman Republic*, Leiden: Brill, 119–44.

Index

Individual Romans are listed under their *gens*, except for writers, who are listed under the form normally used in English. Dates of offices are given only where necessary to distinguish homonyms.

CPSIA information can be obtained
at www.ICGtesting.com
Printed in the USA
LVHW052331200122
708832LV00005B/255